73

237

CORNELL PUBLICATIONS IN COMPARATIVE PLANNING

of the Division of Urban Studies of the
Center for Housing and Environmental Studies

CITY AND REGIONAL PLANNING IN POLAND

COMMITTEE ON COMPARATIVE PLANNING

M. GARDNER CLARK
ALLAN R. HOLMBERG
ROGER HOWLEY
BARCLAY G. JONES
STEVEN MULLER
J. MAYONE STYCOS

City and Regional Planning in Poland

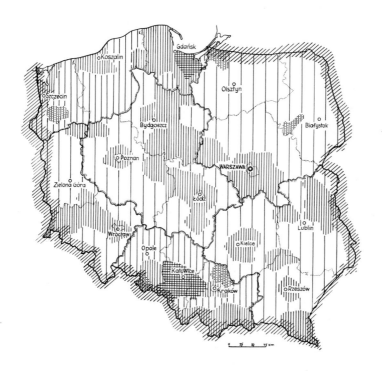

Edited by JACK C. FISHER

Department of City and Regional Planning
College of Architecture
Cornell University

CORNELL UNIVERSITY PRESS

Ithaca, New York

CORNELL UNIVERSITY PRESS

First published 1966

Second printing 1967

Library of Congress Catalog Card Number: 65-23997

PRINTED IN THE UNITED STATES OF AMERICA
BY THE MAPLE PRESS COMPANY

Foreword

CITY and Regional Planning in Poland is the first volume of a series administered by the Committee on Comparative Planning of the Division of Urban Studies in Cornell University's Center for Housing and Environmental Studies. The purpose of the series, which was initiated at the suggestion of Jack C. Fisher, Assistant Professor of City and Regional Planning, is to provide firsthand documentation of the methods of practice and administration of city and regional planning in various countries throughout the world.

In accordance with this policy, *City and Regional Planning in Poland* has been written by Polish authorities and is, therefore, a Polish interpretation of that country's postwar planning process. It is neither an American interpretation of Polish planning nor a critical review of Polish accomplishments. It is a compilation of unusually detailed presentations, by prominent Polish planners, of the inner workings of their organizations. Assembled and edited by Professor Fisher, the volume represents over two years of preparation by the Polish authors and translators and the American editor. It is the product of close international cooperation.

Because the Poles have been willing to present their material for our open review, the basic philosophic differences in approach that distinguish their planners from those in the United States are revealed in this book. It is hoped that American readers will find the material informative as a statement of the objectives and methodology of planning processes in another country by those persons engaged in formulating and applying them.

GLENN H. BEYER
Director, Center for Housing
and Environmental Studies

Ithaca, New York
January, 1965

Preface

SPATIAL planning, at every administrative level, has begun increasingly to concern all nations regardless of their political orientation. In the United States the traditional stress on city planning is now being reinforced by a renewed interest in regional development, expressed in metropolitan-wide planning, in dealing with the problems of depressed areas, and in the search for improved means of developing and safeguarding natural resources. The nature of the American system, with its emphasis on individual responsibility, dictates that private initiative directed toward desirable public goals should play a larger part in planning activities than should governmental action. The administrative nature of the socialist system and nationalization of the means of production, however, made centrally directed planning in eastern Europe inevitable.

Up to now American scholars have concentrated on the economy and the nature of economic planning in Communist countries, and have devoted little attention to city and regional planning. Three reasons help to account for this relative neglect: lack of adequate data on administrative coordination among national, provincial, and local agencies; insufficient interest on the part of American planners and architects; the traditional sensitivity of the eastern European nations on the subject, as reflected in their reluctance to release maps and disclose certain statistics.

This book represents, it is hoped, a departure in area studies. Traditional area programs have made and will continue to make important contributions to our understanding of economic and political processes in Communist countries. Yet such specialists as architects, city planners, and engineers are primarily interested in the professional practices and actual products of their foreign counterparts. We hope this publication, which focuses on these areas, will encourage American practitioners to cooperate with those in other social systems on joint projects dedicated to professional goals. We should appreciate the planning achievements of other countries and learn from them. On the other hand, candid criticism should not be withheld when the product falls short of stated objectives.

American readers, to whom this argument will sound plausible, may nevertheless ask what useful or even novel contributions the countries of eastern Europe have made to planning since the war. If the results of physical planning in eastern Europe during the last fifteen years do not meet the cultural and esthetic expectations of Western professionals, we must keep in mind that our Eastern counterparts usually have had to work under severe limitations. Because of limited resources and insufficient building materials, as well as because of political considerations, the end product has almost invariably turned out to be less original and creative than the preliminary plan or blueprint. American planners are not entirely free from similar handicaps. Lack of coordination among federal programs instituted by various federal departments is a major stumbling block to effective comprehensive planning in local areas of the United States. The discussion in this volume of the nature of planning coordination in Poland at various administrative levels should thus be of interest to American planners faced with tasks for which financial support comes from a combination of local, state, and especially federal sources.

This book provides what no other study has attempted, a documentary record of city and regional planning as conceived and practiced in the People's Republic of Poland. The postwar Polish efforts in city and regional planning are placed in perspective, and an attempt is made to explain what happened within a national social-decision model of the socialist type; to examine what is happening now; and to project probable courses of future action.

The examination naturally takes place within a socialist framework and under the influence of goals and values derived from the sociopolitical environment. This orientation should make the book valuable not only to historians of planning but to all those who are interested in the development process within socialist countries. The last few years in eastern Europe have witnessed increasing investment in building and planning programs, a trend that can be expected to accelerate. The nations of eastern Europe are changing rapidly and radically. Now is the time, therefore, to increase understanding of the professional techniques applied in implementing planned action in Poland.

The three major divisions of the book correspond to the three administrative levels of planning in Poland: city planning, regional planning, and national economic planning. At the beginning of each section Wojciech Morawski, the Polish coordinator for the book, and I have collaborated on a short introduction which describes the nature of that particular level of planning in the country, its relationship to other planning levels, and a review of the topics covered by the articles.

National economic planning may be called active planning, that is, it represents an active projection of economic activities as opposed to a passive forecasting of the most probable developments. In the final section of the book the reader will find a brief overview of selected elements of national economic planning, including Józef Pajestka's article, which is a significant summary of the economic planning function within a socialist state. This section tries to enhance the American reader's understanding of the subject but is not intended to be either comprehensive or definitive. That it may, in fact, from the Western viewpoint raise more political questions than economically viable solutions is perhaps due to the sharp division of our two societies on the basic assumptions of economic planning.

Part Two provides the most inclusive discussion of the operational aspects of Polish regional planning available to date. In Poland regional planning is viewed as the spatial dimension of economic planning and, therefore, as within the scope of the Planning Commission of the Council of Ministers. It is not considered a separate, distinct discipline. Such a view places regional planning in a unique institutional framework and gives it over-all functions different from those in some other socialist countries. Most socialist nations, for example, have placed little emphasis on planning rural and agricultural activities, so that Minister Marian Benko's discussion of Polish long-range policies designed to alter the country's rural settlement pattern is unusually significant.

It was in the preparation of Part Two that various constraints of the Polish system became evident. The authors had trouble explaining the evolution of certain courses of developmental action. Discussion tended to remain general and limited in scope. Possibly maps proved to be the most troublesome problem. Although they are the best obtainable and an important addition to those publicly available, they are still inferior, in precision and quality, to those prepared for regional planning activities in Poland.

The assumptions underlying Parts Two and Three, which may be alien to American social thought, are much less evident in Part One, which provides a thorough and comprehensive view of the theory and practice of postwar Polish city planning. There are few scholarly articles on urban history as comprehensive as that of Professor Wacław Ostrowski. Following a presentation of urban planning theory and methods, three case studies provide concrete examples of postwar city planning achievement in Poland. The appendices to Part One make available translations of the pertinent laws under which Polish city planning evolved and on which it is currently based.

City and Regional Planning in Poland could never have been produced through the efforts of American scholars alone and is the result of many years of individual effort and administrative coordination on both sides of the Atlantic. The subject matter, the distance between Cornell University and Warsaw, and the initial skepticism toward the project which was felt by some on both sides added to the complexity of the task. Once the project was agreed upon, I was able, working through the Polish Editorial Committee created for the book, to recruit potential writers suggested by the Committee and others whom I considered appropriate. The final list of authors includes names from both sources. The contributors were dedicated to the project and eager to cooperate. They include many of the most important Polish planners, scholars, and administrators in the field.

The concept and character of the book evolved during 1961 and 1962. Discussions with Professor Stanisław Leszczycki and subsequently Dr. Marian Dobrosielski of the Polish Embassy in Washington made up the first stage of the process. Trips to Poland laid the groundwork for the project, to which Polish authorities gave their approval in 1962. A Polish committee was appointed under the auspices of the Committee for Space Economy and Regional Planning. This committee, in turn, appointed Wojciech Morawski, Chief of Division, Department of Transportation of the Planning Commission, as the coordinator for the volume.

The bulk of the manuscript was received at Cornell during 1962 and editorial work began. The articles, which had been written in Polish and translated into English in Warsaw, were revised, then mimeographed and distributed to members of the Cornell faculty who had special competence in the various professional fields represented. I prepared a review of each manuscript from the comments and changes suggested by the outside readers. Clear areas of disagreement were indicated, along with points that we felt should be expanded. The entire manuscript was then returned to Poland.

In 1963 I was able to visit Poland to discuss the suggested changes with each author, the section leaders, Professor Malisz and Dr. Zaremba,

and the Polish Committee. Many of our recommendations were accepted, and in some cases articles were totally rewritten. The section on
city planning was completely revised under the able guidance of Bolesław
Malisz. During this visit I reviewed the maps and illustrations and
recommended changes and additions. Late in 1964 the entire manuscript,
with more than 200 maps and illustrations, arrived in Ithaca. In ready-
ing it for publication, we tried, as new ideas and concerns developed, to
adjust the scope of the volume to them. The result is a book—to my
knowledge the first since the war—in which eastern European experts
have written professional manuscripts which were subjected to American
professional review and criticism and subsequently revised by the authors.
Recognizing the differing assumptions upon which our two societies are
based, we present this volume as a substantial contribution to the literature of planning and as a unique strand in the web of cultural exchange.

It is difficult to give adequate acknowledgment to the many people
and institutions that contributed to the project. Approval of the undertaking by the Polish Academy of Sciences, with the concurrence of the
Ministry of Foreign Affairs, provided the foundation for the work in
Poland. I owe a deep debt of gratitude to the Institute of Geography of
the Polish Academy of Sciences for the help and encouragement offered
by its staff. The Polish Committee for the book, composed of Professors
Leszczycki, Secomski, Dziewoński, and Kukliński, provided the expert
advice and friendly cooperation that were so essential throughout the
project. The support extended by the Committee cannot be too warmly
praised, nor can the contribution of Wojciech Morawski. The day-to-
day work, problems, and frustrations, my demands and prejudices, were
borne by Morawski for more than two years, while he held a full-time
staff position on the Planning Commission. His intelligence, devotion to the
project, and friendship contributed immeasurably to the production of
this volume. As so often before, my friend Antoni Kukliński was, from
the very beginning of the undertaking, a source of good advice and
counsel.

The project would, of course, never have proceeded but for the will-
ingness of the Polish authors to give so freely of their time and effort. My
thanks to them for a task well done. The existence of a climate of good
will made it possible for all these people and many others unnamed to
work toward the completion of the book.

In the United States the project was carried on in the Division of
Urban Studies, Center for Housing and Environmental Studies, of
Cornell University. Guidance was provided by the Division's Committee

on Comparative Planning, consisting of M. Gardner Clark, Professor of Economics and Chairman of the Committee on Soviet Studies; Allan R. Holmberg, Professor of Anthropology; Roger Howley, University Publisher; Barclay G. Jones, Professor of City and Regional Planning and Director of the Division of Urban Studies of the Center for Housing and Environmental Studies; Steven Muller, Associate Professor of Government and Director of the Center for International Studies; and J. Mayone Stycos, Professor of Sociology and Director of the International Population Program. The College of Architecture supplied the first financial support. The Center for International Studies, an initial supporter, provided major financial resources and incentive. I am indebted to Dean Burnham Kelly of the College of Architecture and my colleagues in the Department of City and Regional Planning for their encouragement.

Professors George Staller and Chandler Morse, Department of Economics; John Reps and Thomas Mackesey, Department of City and Regional Planning; George Myers and Allan Feldt, Department of Sociology; and Stephen Jacobs and Frederick M. Wells, Department of Architecture, with the members of the Committee on Comparative Planning, generously contributed their time to review selected Polish articles.

Alison Bishop and Anne Clavel provided editorial aid during the preparation of the manuscript.

Without the support and assistance of my Cornell colleagues the book would never have been completed. Yet my function as editor must be clearly indicated. Final responsibility for the essential character of the project and for the contents of the finished book must fall to me alone.

Jack C. Fisher

Ithaca, New York
January, 1965

Contents

Part Three: NATIONAL ECONOMIC PLANNING

List of Illustrations

MAPS

FIGURES

List of Tables

City Planning

Commentary and Orientation

JACK C. FISHER

WOJCIECH MORAWSKI

CITY planning is a component of spatial planning,[1] which also embraces regional planning. Although city planning is a broad field, we feel that its basic themes and representative examples have been successfully selected for this book. We hope that the reader will come to understand the specific problems of Polish urban planning, its organization and methodology, theoretical trends, and results. The book does not attempt to present the engineering aspects of city planning and building. Nor are architectural issues discussed at length; the article on architecture should be regarded as a statement of contemporary Polish theory.

In Part One the historical and theoretical aspects of Polish city planning are presented; and contemporary work is described in specific

[1] The term *spatial planning* is used to replace *physical planning,* which is current in professional literature. The difference between *physical* and *spatial* is not merely one of terminology. Perfection of the cognitive instruments used in city and regional planning, especially economic analysis, and the very close link between national economic planning and city and regional planning in Poland have so changed in quality the scope of the term "physical planning" that its continued use might be misleading. Generally one could say that the two terms have in common research and studies dealing with economic and social phenomena arranged according to area—the spatial units. The following excerpt from an article entitled "Regional Economic Planning for the Development of Satellite and New Towns," prepared for a United Nations conference by Antoni R. Kukliński, a Polish geographer and planner, discusses the conceptual differences between the two terms:

We should try . . . to establish a proper attitude in relation to so-called physical planning. In my opinion, this is perhaps an obsolete term reflecting the historical conditions when the methods of economic analyses were not applied to the solutions of urban and regional problems. The historical tradition associated with the term "physical" planning implies the contradiction between economic and physical planning. This contradiction does not exist nor should it exist, because it sometimes has harmful implications in attempting to arrive at modern solutions of regional problems.

A new situation is coming into being in which a clear distinction could be introduced between the *topical* types of planning: economic, social, political, and the *areal* scale of planning: international, national, regional, metropolitan and urban

case studies of operational planning in Warsaw's large metropolitan district, in expanded industrial zones, and in small units that have been integrated into districts. The problem of housing is discussed in an analysis of the urbanization process, and the sociological implications of Polish planning are investigated. These studies are supplemented by abstracts of relevant laws—the 1961 Spatial Planning Act of the People's Republic of Poland, the 1951 Provisional Town Planning Standards, and the 1961 Main Standards for Programing Housing Estates.

Figure 1 is designed as a preliminary introduction to the organization and interrelations of city planning bodies in Poland.

What is the character of the dependence of spatial planning, and hence of city planning, on national economic planning? The connections and their causes and effects particularly characteristic of Poland are discussed in some detail by Bolesław Malisz in Part One and Józef Zaremba in Part Two. We wish, however, to cite here the opinion current in Poland that this dependence contributes greatly to the formulation of realistic programs for regional and local development and ensures an executive authority over the programs. In other words, the dependence establishes closer links between studies and conclusions both for particular spatial units and for the macroeconomic pattern. (In Poland, the macroeconomic pattern subsumes the economic and social relations that prevail throughout the nation. The possibilities and requirements of this pattern are not necessarily spatially determined.) At the roots of the dependence on national economic planning is an attempt to limit the postulative tendencies of city and regional planning, to turn the efforts of city or regional planners to spatial implementation of the national economic plans, and, finally, to reveal the resources and possibilities of the particular spatial units. Through the channel of national economic plans, spatial planners receive directives which provide infor-

---

or local planning. Looking for a common denominator for all planning activities which stress the areal dimensions, we may use the term "spatial" planning.

This was the word chosen for the Polish Spatial Planning Act of January 31, 1961, which introduced spatial planning. . . . The Act defines the basic aim of spatial planning in the following way. Spatial planning should a) assure the proper development of all areas of the country, taking into account their mutual interrelations and the efficiency of the national economy; b) establish the proper spatial proportions of productive and service facilities in those areas, creating in this way the proper conditions for the universal satisfaction of the needs of the population, for the development of production and the conservation of the natural resources of the country.

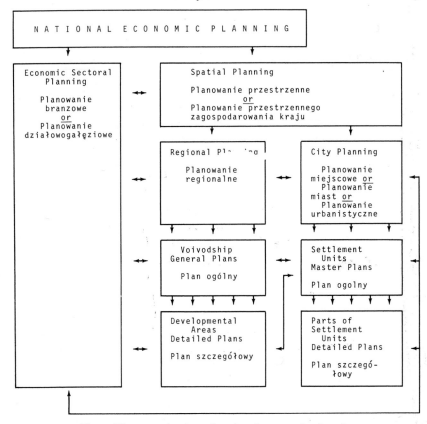

Fig. 1. The organization of national economic planning

mation on the general framework of economic strategy for the duration of the plan. Both city and regional planners strive to emphasize the requirements and possibilities of particular spatial units in terms of natural environment, demographic dynamics, infrastructure, suitability of terrain, and so on. They must then match the potential and the specifics of the area studies with national requirements, trends, and economic and social possibilities within the framework of national economic planning and its sectoral indications.

The dependence of city and regional planning on national economic planning is not all one-sided; there is a feedback. Work on plans for particular spatial units discloses needs and possibilities in demography, land economy, housing substance, infrastructure, and the over-all scope of investment. Such requirements and possibilities are studied and taken into account when the national economic plans are worked out. They become important premises for reaching economic decisions. In this context, therefore, spatial planning is a tool for establishing or verifying the proportions of general economic growth incorporated into the national economic plans.

Readers to whom problems of national economic planning are not familiar will find more information on the subject in Part Three; here we discuss only the most important elements of national economic plans on which city planners rely. These are, first of all, general directives concerning the economic and social development of the country,[2] which facilitate the adaptation of master plans for settlement units to the general rate of national growth. National economic plans also include a number of detailed directives—having the character of skeleton economic directives—which refer to the planned development of specific voivodships (or provinces)[3] and selected areas that are expected to be sites of particularly intensive investment programs. It has to be stressed, however, that the skeleton economic directives for particular areas need not be absolutely observed by the city planners. On the contrary, the directives represent a set of approximate and flexible data which should make it possible for the spatial planner to view the general trends and structure of the country's economic and social growth at a given time and in the spatial unit concerned. It is worth noting that physical planning in the past was largely visionary and not related to any concrete executive authority. This characteristic, although still an aspect of spatial planning, is no longer primary. Polish spatial planning seeks the strongest possible linking of the vision, or design solution, with the actual conditions, possibilities, and socioeconomic requirements of the country.

Spatial planning is an applied discipline with institutional forms. In the organization of state management and authority, execution of

[2] Without fully discussing the matter we shall attempt to point out the key issues of the national economic plans which provide the basis for the work of city planners: the creation and division of the national income, demographic forecasts, the growth and structure of employment, increase of industrial and agricultural output, expansion of services, prevailing trends and extent of building and investment processes.

[3] Among the major studies planned at the voivodship cross-section are: number and structure of population and employment, size and trends of investment, extent of housing construction and construction of public welfare facilities (for example, hospitals, schools, city-transport system, water-supply and sewerage systems), major expanded and newly erected industrial establishments, major investment programs for the transportation network, output of the local industry, agricultural production. These studies refer to the voivodship cross-section within the framework of the economic plan which embraces the whole country. More detailed data are worked out in their plans by the particular voivodships.

regional planning is closely tied to national economic planning; it is carried out under the supervision of the Planning Commission of the Council of Ministers. City planning, its conditions governed by local problems connected with the municipal economy, is implemented through voivodship and local authorities.[4] Within the organizational pattern of voivodship and local authorities, city planning is the responsibility of the Board for Building, City Planning, and Architecture Supervision. If necessary, additional specialized agencies are set up, as, for instance, the office of Head Architect of Warsaw. The relevant units of local administration usually carry out the following functions: initiating plans for the settlement units for which they are responsible; formulating general figures in the form of directives for those plans; passing their opinion on plans and parts of plans prepared by specialized bureaus and workshops; applying to appropriate authorities for approval of master and detailed plans; and coordinating the work of the various investing bodies in the course of realizing the plans.

Research and methodology in city and regional planning are initiated and coordinated by the Committee for Space Economy and Regional Planning attached to the Polish Academy of Sciences. These activities, in Poland as in other countries, benefit from the research techniques and scientific facilities of various disciplines. Theoretical development and teaching of regional planning are mainly the concern of the Institute of Geography of the Polish Academy of Sciences and the Higher School for Planning and Statistics, both in Warsaw; city planning is taught mainly at the Institute for Town Planning and Architecture in Warsaw and the departments of architecture at some technical universities.

---

[4] Until the end of 1963 city planning was represented in the system of the central agencies by the Committee for Building, City Planning, and Architecture; and is now the responsibility of the Ministry of Building.

CHAPTER 1

History of Urban Development and Planning

WACŁAW OSTROWSKI

Medieval Beginnings

THE POLISH STATE came into being a thousand years ago in the territory stretching from the Odra River to the Bug River and from the Baltic Sea to the Carpathian Range. Mieszko I united under his rule the various Slav tribes living there. The conversion of the population to Christianity according to the Latin rites in 966 facilitated the penetration of cultural influences from western and southern Europe.

At that time the Polish territories were inhabited by several hundred thousand people, who lived mostly where the soil was fertile. When they sought new areas to settle in, they moved cautiously along the river valleys and avoided the forests, which they could not easily turn into fields for cultivation with their primitive implements. From the seventh century of our era numerous burghs (equivalent to the Polish *gród*) began to spring up in the areas where the tribes had settled. The earliest of them were most probably built as places of refuge from enemy attacks. Later, other burghs were built; these were the fortified seats of the nobles. For security reasons they were most frequently located in the bends and forks of rivers and on peninsulas jutting out into lakes or marshes, and they were made even less accessible by moats. Near these centers handicraft and trading settlements sprang up—suburbs, as it were, supplying both the inhabitants of the burgh and the agricultural population of the surrounding country. These suburbs were also surrounded with fortifications to ensure security.

The majority of the settlements grew into towns as time went on. It is not easy to establish exactly when this change was accomplished in a given instance; even the determination of features which distinguish the town from a settlement that had only certain features of a town is open

to discussion. In the light of the most recent archaeological research there
can be no doubt that burghs with suburbs, meriting the name of "towns,"
existed in Poland as early as the tenth century. They were centers
of secular and church administration and of handicrafts and trade; they
were larger than other settlements and differed from them in that they
were more compact and were fortified. The most important towns of the
tenth century were Gniezno, Poznań, and Kruszwica (the first administrative and military centers of the Polish state); Wolin, Szczecin,
Kołobrzeg, and Gdańsk in Pomerania; and Kraków and Czerwień
in the south (Map 1).

In the eleventh and twelfth centuries the area in which settlements
had been established increased, and trading between the villages and
towns expanded. The number of towns was growing, some of them developing from rural settlements where markets were held regularly. The
population of the towns also increased and the standard of building im-

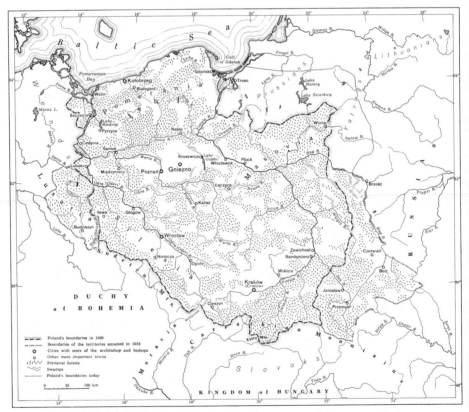

Map 1. Poland about the year 1000 (prepared by W. Szczawiński and W.
Trzebiński)

proved. This period marked the beginnings of separate municipal law, and some progress was made in the field of town planning.

The thirteenth century was a period of flourishing development in the history of European towns. The Polish rulers, wishing to take advantage of increasing economic activity and the development of trade relations with neighboring countries, encouraged the founding of towns, giving them a legal status based on western and central European examples. As a result there was an influx of artisans and merchants of various nationalities, mostly German. These people settled in the existing towns and developed them considerably. As the number of foreign immigrants as well as native Polish artisans grew, new settlements were founded in previously uninhabited areas. In the creation of these new settlements advantage was taken of the experience gained in building towns in the preceding period both in Poland and in western Europe, where enormous progress was then being made in town planning.

The duties and rights of the inhabitants of such towns were set out in special charters. These charters established relations between the feudal lords and the colonists, following the example of the German towns, whose citizens (like those of other western European towns) had regulated their legal status earlier so as to create favorable conditions for economic development. The most important changes introduced by the "German law" were the replacement of the payment of dues in kind to the feudal lord by payment in money, and the granting to the burghers of quite extensive judicial and administrative self-government. In most cases, the charters referred to the Magdeburg law or the Środa or Chełmno laws, which were modeled on the Magdeburg system.

Because of this reference, some German historians are inclined to regard Polish medieval towns as the fruit of "east German municipal colonization," or even as "east German towns." But towns—in the economic, social, and architectural sense of the word—existed in Poland before the Germans began to settle there; many of the settlements where "German law" was later introduced already had the character of towns. Their population was not exclusively German, but included artisans and merchants of other nationalities and also Poles, who became ever more numerous as time went on. The appearance of regular towns, characteristic of the later Middle Ages, was preceded in both Poland and western Europe by transitory forms which gradually gave way to layouts better suited to the new social needs. Polish medieval towns were the result of a long process of social and economic evolution. The influx of German settlers undoubtedly accelerated this process: indeed this was the aim of the colonization campaign of the Polish dukes and feudal lords.

The greatest wave of urban colonization in Poland occurred from the thirteenth to the fifteenth centuries. It took a long time for the towns to develop the character they had at the end of the Middle Ages. The wooden houses, for example, which were very modest at first, were replaced by larger and finer buildings of brick, whose depth and number of stories were increased.

At the same time progressively more public buildings were erected to meet the needs of the growing population. As the towns developed, as the social division of labor and the prosperity of the burghers increased, and as municipal self-government was strengthened and consolidated, churches and town halls, buildings to house artisans' guilds and merchants' associations, shops and warehouses, grain and fulling mills, monasteries and hospitals were reconstructed or built. The walls of the towns were strengthened. Complicated work was undertaken to redirect the flow of small rivers and streams to the towns so that they could be used to supply power, and also water in the event of a siege or fire. The largest towns built the first water mains, sewerage systems, and hard-surfaced roads—these were, however, still very primitive.

During the Middle Ages enormous progress was made in town development. The first towns usually developed spontaneously along the

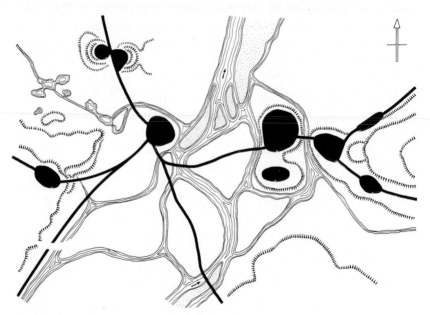

Fig. 2. Poznań in the first half of the thirteenth century (from T. Ruszczyńska and A. Sławska, *Poznań*, Warsaw, 1953)

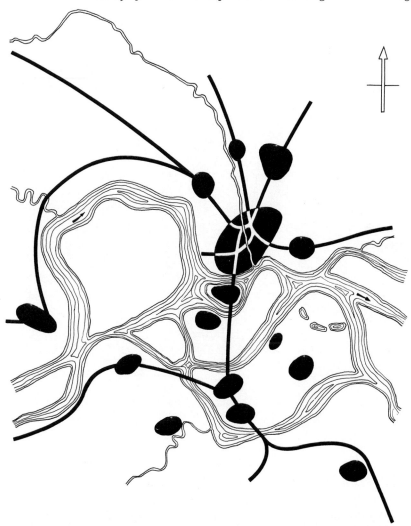

Fig. 3. Kraków in the first half of the thirteenth century (by J. Mitkowski in J. Dąbrowski, ed., *Kraków—studia nad rozwojem miasta,* Kraków, 1957)

existing roads. Separate settlements built by various nobles and clergy often grew up around the largest burghs, for the feudal lords liked to settle near the seats of their dukes. As a result of this process, the large early medieval towns, such as Poznań and Kraków (Figures 2, 3), were each more a growing group of settlements than a compact municipal organism; to use the modern term, they were primitive "conurbations."

The building of regularly planned large towns (Figure 4) in the

Fig. 4. Opole. The late medieval town (after F. Idzikowski)
1. Castle. 2. Town Hall.

place of small primitive settlements (Figure 5)—the replacement of
a rather chaotic growth by a layout based on a rational plan (Figures 6,
7)—was the great achievement of late medieval town planning. In most
cases the central point of the planned medieval town was a square
market place, relatively large in Polish towns, where most of the buildings connected with trade and municipal self-government were erected.
From the market place, which was surrounded by the dwellings of the
richest burghers, streets led out at right angles, along which were blocks
of buildings of more or less equal size. Town plans were logically and
skillfully adapted to the local conditions. In towns which were situated
on navigable rivers, for example, the network of main streets ran down
to the river quays where the loading and unloading of goods took place.
Despite the fact that standard principles of town planning were applied,
each medieval town had its own individuality.

The Middle Ages were an important period in the history of Polish towns. The majority of our present-day cities had their origin in this period and it is usually not difficult to see the characteristic medieval layout of streets in their plans. In many cases, buildings or groups of buildings dating back to this era (or reconstructed later in line with the original character and scale) have survived. Through their rational layout the medieval towns were able to meet the needs of the population for many centuries with only very slight modification. It was only in the

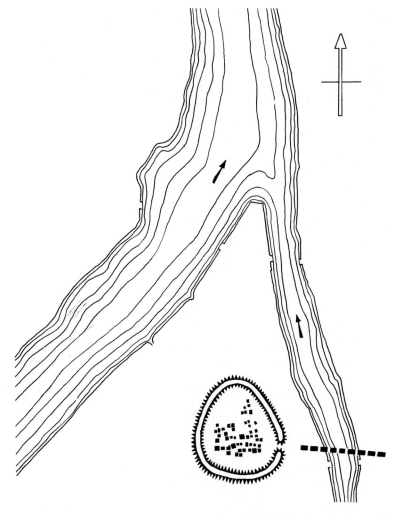

Fig. 5. Opole. The first medieval settlement (from W. Hołubowicz, *Opole w wiekach X-XII,* Katowice, 1956)

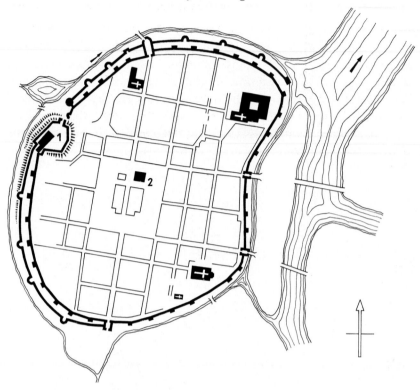

Fig. 6. Poznań. Central part of the town in the sixteenth century (from T. Ruszczyńska and A. Sławska, *Poznań*, Warsaw, 1953)

nineteenth century that the need for more serious changes began to make itself felt.

Physical planning in the Middle Ages was evident not only in the towns. The Polish kings and dukes and the big landowners (both clerical and lay) often took steps which can be regarded as the beginning of national or regional planning. They supported rural colonization, inviting people to settle in the forest areas which were systematically being cleared. Next, they founded new towns in these areas and granted various privileges to the towns. They established and developed towns situated on main communication routes or in places of greatest strategic importance. They built castles and helped to build walls round the towns. King Kazimierz the Great (1333–1370) was particularly active in this respect; he joined Ruthenian territories to the Polish lands previously united by his father. King Kazimierz fortified about thirty towns and built more than fifty castles (Map 2). Similar action was taken

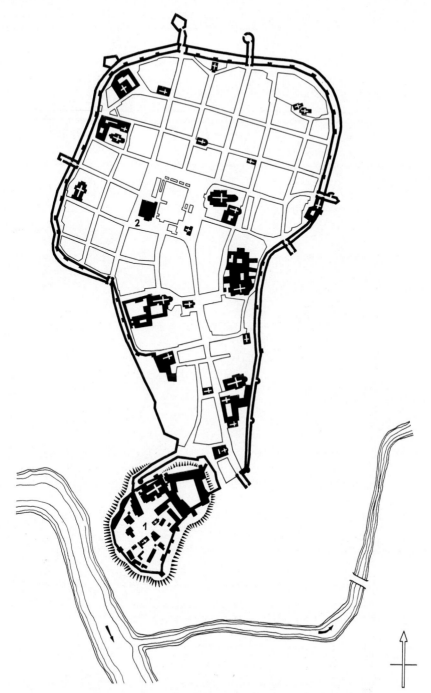

Fig. 7. Kraków. Central part of the town in the late Middle Ages (from T. Tołwiński, *Urbanistyka,* I, Warsaw, 1947)

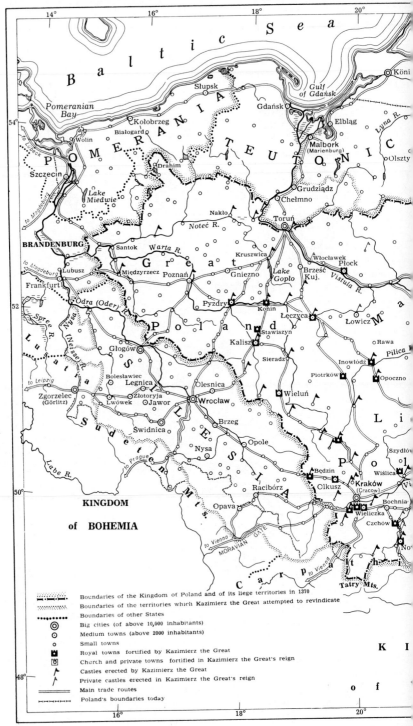

Map 2. Kingdom of Poland under Kazimierz the

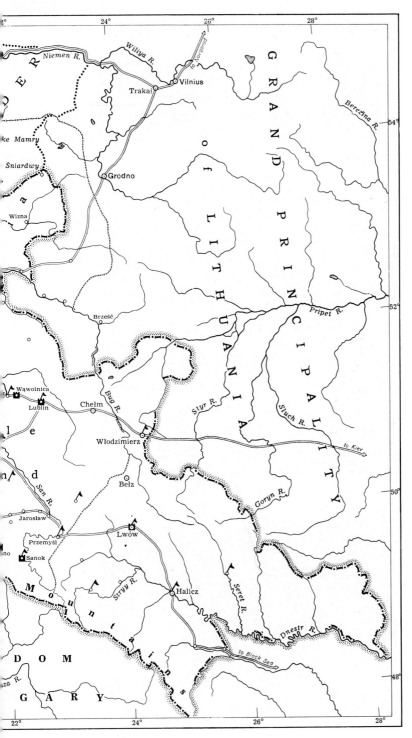

Labels on map:

24° 26° 28°

Niemen R.
Wiliya R.
ER
Vilnius
Trakai
GRAND PRINCIPALITY of LITHUANIA
Bereżna R.
54°
ke Mamry
Sniardwy
Grodno
a
Wizna
l
Brześć
52°
Pripet R.
Wąwolnica
Lublin
Chełm
Bug R.
Styr R.
Słuch R.
Włodzimierz
to Kiev
l e
Bełz
50°
n d
San R.
Goryn R.
Jarosław
Lwów
Przemyśl
no
Sanok
Stryy R.
Seret R.
Halicz
Dnestr R.
Mountains
to Black Sea
48°
D O M
G A R Y
za R.

22° 24° 26° 28°

1370 (prepared by W. Szczawiński and W. Trzebiński)

Fig. 8. Poznań. By Braun and Hogenberg, 1618 (photo: Instytut Sztuki, PAN, Warsaw)

20

by the Order of the Teutonic Knights in the northern Polish lands between the twelfth and fifteenth centuries.

As a result of this activity the area under rural settlement increased, being covered gradually by a network of towns usually at a distance of not more than twenty to forty kilometers from one another. Among them were both small market towns and also large centers of handicraft and trade, which were well-populated, prosperous, and proud of their numerous churches, powerful fortifications, magnificent town halls, and impressive residential buildings, a testimony to the wealth of the burghers (Figures 8, 9, 10).

During the late Middle Ages the Polish landscape gradually changed. The towns assumed a different appearance as, to a certain extent, did the villages. The wave of monumental Romanesque building from the West broke at the Vistula River; the present location of the relatively few buildings erected from the tenth to thirteenth centuries indicates where the main centers of settlement were at that time. Gothic architecture, which is found much more frequently, is more evenly distributed over the territories which comprised the Polish state at the end of the fourteenth century. The Ruthenian lands joined to Poland by Kazimierz the Great, which had until then been dominated by Eastern culture and architecture, now began to assimilate elements of Western culture. One result of this change was the building of towns according to the legislative and architectural patterns developed in western Europe.

Sixteenth, Seventeenth, and Eighteenth Centuries

Poland's expansion to the east, into territories that were ethnically alien, continued from the fourteenth century until the first half of the seventeenth century. During this period some lands which were originally Polish and were inhabited to a greater or lesser extent by Polish people, remained outside the western frontiers of the state. It was through the union with Lithuania, which began when King Władysław Jagiełło, the Great Prince of Lithuania, came to the throne in 1386, that Poland became a European power. After the victorious wars against the Order of the Teutonic Knights (1410, 1454–1466) part of the Teutonic state, including Gdańsk, was joined to Poland, and part of it became her vassal. Poland thus gained access to the Baltic. In 1569 large areas of the Ukraine that had formerly belonged to Lithuania were joined to the lands of the Polish Crown. At the beginning of the seventeenth century the multinational Polish state, second only to Russia in land area among European nations, covered over 800,000 square kilometers and

Fig. 9. Kraków. By A. Cellarius, 1659 (photo: Instytut Sztuki, PAN, Warsaw)

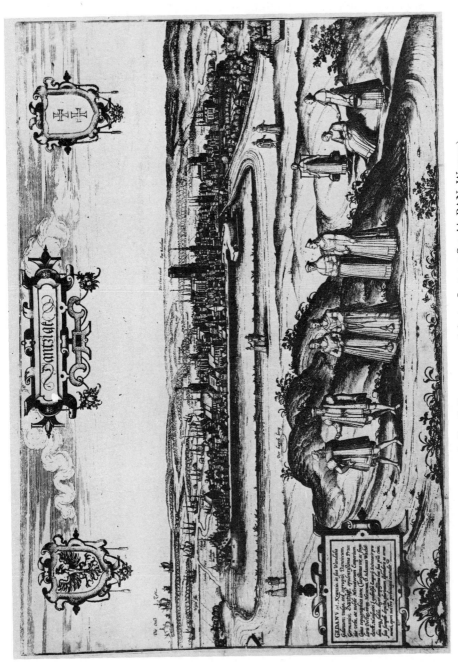

Fig. 10. Gdańsk. By G. Braun, 1575 (photo: Instytut Sztuki, PAN, Warsaw)

23

had about eight million inhabitants, of whom four million were Polish (Map 3).

But the first half of the seventeenth century marked the beginning of a decline, first economic and then political. This was brought about by various factors. First, in the sixteenth century, while in western Europe the land-leasing system was being developed in agriculture, trade was expanding, and towns were becoming wealthier, in Poland the feudal system was being consolidated. After a short period of economic activation, this system led to a growing oppression of the peasants and to restrictions in trade between the rural areas and the towns, which, in turn, weakened the towns both economically and politically. The towns had no representatives in the parliament, where the nobles, guided by their own narrow interests, introduced laws that were unfavorable to the townsmen. In the Ukrainian territories which had been joined to Poland

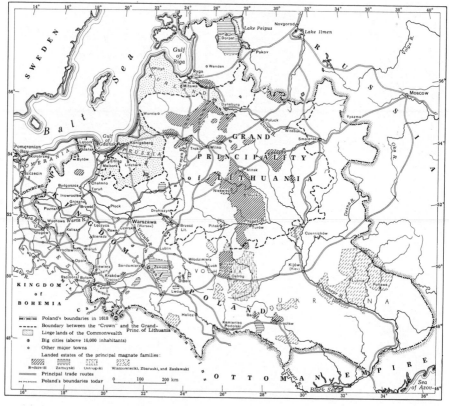

Map 3. Commonwealth of Poland at the close of the sixteenth century (prepared by W. Szczawiński and W. Trzebiński)

in the east, the huge *latifundia* owned by the magnates tended to become autonomous political and military entities, weakening central and local authority, and leading to anarchy and helplessness in the face of external attacks. The numerous wars of the seventeenth and eighteenth centuries brought heavy losses and accelerated the process of decline. The reforms undertaken in the second half of the eighteenth century only partially arrested this process. The three partitions of Poland, made by Russia, Prussia, and Austria, who took advantage of the difficulties of the country (1772–1795), initiated a period of more than one hundred years of political oppression.

Meanwhile economic, social, and political change was reflected clearly in the history of urban building. In the sixteenth century the Renaissance spirit triumphed in Poland in the fields of science, literature, and art. The growing prosperity of the towns permitted their reconstruction in accordance with new social needs. The rich merchants erected fine, spacious houses, reconstructed their town halls, cloth halls, and other public buildings, adding rich ornamentation to them. The growing preponderance of secular buildings over sacred ones in the towns was the consequence both of the secularization of culture under the influence of humanism and of the vitality and prosperity of the burghers.

The country was already covered with a fairly dense network of towns and the new settlements did not cover any large areas, with the exception of the eastern territories. A number of new towns were founded (Map 4), but they usually did not develop to any great extent. An exception to this rule were the towns set up by the magnates owning the huge *latifundia*—for example Zamość (Figures 11, 12, 13), which was a fortified town and the residence of Chancellor Jan Zamoyski, who had been educated in Italy. It was not long before numerous merchants engaged in trade with the East settled in Zamość. Built according to the town planning principles then advocated by Italian theoreticians, Zamość is one of the most beautiful and best integrated European examples of the application of these theories.

In the seventeenth and even at the beginning of the eighteenth century, a number of towns with similar layout were built; the majority of these did not develop much and the houses erected in them were rather modest. But the plans of these towns are worthy of attention. Apart from Italian influences, native traditions are evident. The regular layout was extended beyond the town itself to include the suburban gardens and farmlands allotted to the burghers. The dominant feature of these plans was the rectangular blocks, which made rational building

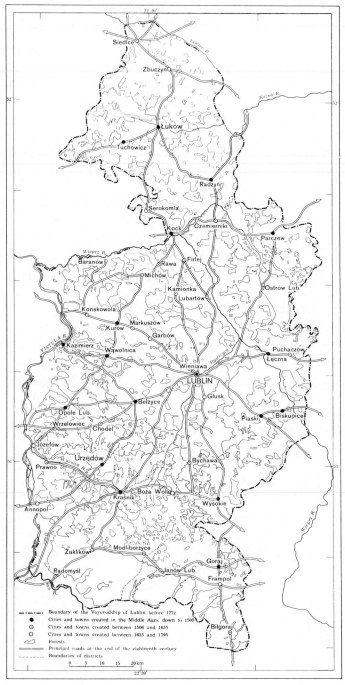

Map 4. Voivodship of Lublin in the second half of the eighteenth century (prepared by W. Szczawiński and W. Trzebiński)

26

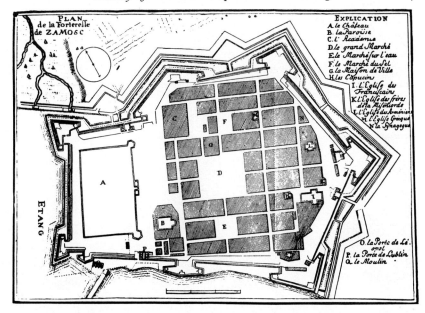

Fig. 11. Zamość. By Jonsac, 1774 (photo: Instytut Sztuki, PAN, Warsaw)

easier. The size and shape of the building plots were differentiated according to the requirements of the various social groups. Questions of fortification did not usually play as important a role as in Italy (Figure 14).

The relatively prosperous situation of the towns deteriorated in the second half of the seventeenth century. The numerous wars, particularly the Swedish invasions, destroyed many towns, some of which never recovered. And as the purchasing power of the peasants diminished, all the towns, especially the smaller ones, began to decline.

Warsaw (Figure 15) was rebuilt rather quickly after the wars with Sweden. The frontiers of the state had been extended by the union with Lithuania, and Warsaw became the capital of Poland at the end of the sixteenth century, because it was more centrally situated than the previous capital, Kraków. Magnates and nobles, merchants and artisans came to settle near the royal court. In layout the city was made up of two separate formations. First, there was the medieval town with its rather regular network of streets and compactly built houses inhabited by the merchants and artisans, centering around two market places. Around this was the area where the nobles and magnates had built their residences, developed rather chaotically on farmlands that had previously belonged to the burghers or to the king (Figure 16). Here

Fig. 12. Zamość. Town Hall (photo: Czarnogórski, Central Photographic Archives)

magnificent palaces stood side by side with the poor homes of the artisans who had settled in the suburbs because they were free from the restrictions imposed by the guilds. The magnates' town—or rather a
number of small towns, developing independently of one another and
very often occupying larger areas than medieval Warsaw—broke away
from the burghers' jurisdiction. There was no social force that could give
any consistent order to this agglomeration.

Certain new elements began to make their appearance as a result of the activity of King August II (1697–1733). August, whose aim was not to improve urban structure but to strengthen the royal power in Poland, began to build a palace modeled on those erected by the absolutist rulers of western Europe. This palace was built in a royal courtyard flanked by stables, and had an extensive park. Six barracks were built on the avenue leading out of the park along the same axis as the whole group of palace buildings, at right angles to the Vistula. The entire palace complex was a kilometer and a half long.

Another of August's development projects that had some similar features was the Calvary Way, with numerous shrines. It ran parallel to the Vistula toward the southern outskirts of the city. Finally, August initiated a third big building scheme in Warsaw: the construction of a decorative canal from the front of the royal summer palace toward the river.

Stanisław August (1764–1795), the last Polish king, built an exten-

Fig. 13. Zamość. Houses in the market square (photo: Targoński, Central Photographic Archives)

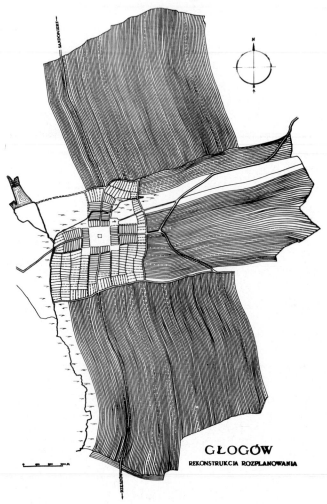

Fig. 14. Głogów. Reconstruction of the original plan (after T. Zarębska)

sion onto the west side of this palace, developing a regular network of avenues. The whole composition was modeled on the layout of park avenues and sylvan vistas of eighteenth-century France. An original feature of this scheme was the construction of several dozen kilometers of tree-lined roads among fields and gardens.

The building done under August II and Stanisław August played a very important, probably quite unintentional, part in the development of Warsaw. It introduced layouts of an extensiveness and geometrical

Fig. 15. Warsaw. By Probst, eighteenth century (photo: Instytut Sztuki, PAN, Warsaw)

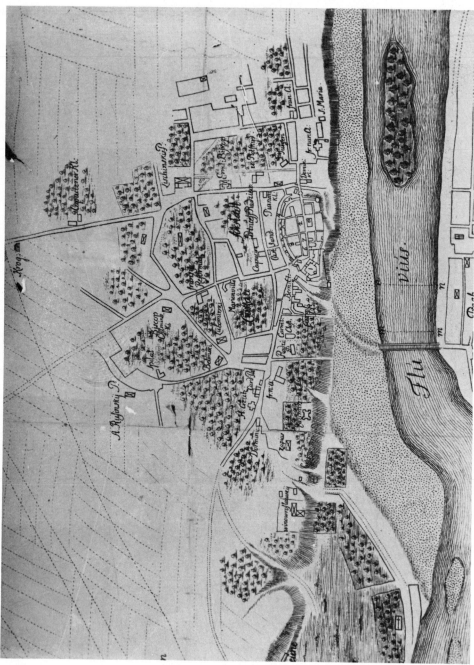

Fig. 16. Warsaw. The medieval town surrounded by scattered settlements. Plan by Albrecht, 1705 (photo: Instytut Sztuki, PAN, Warsaw)

regularity previously unknown in the city. The example set by these kings had a certain influence on the further expansion of Warsaw. In the middle of the eighteenth century more concern to develop the capital properly was shown by the central administration, particular care being taken in planning the network of streets in the new districts that were then springing up. Marshal Bieliński, who was then responsible for the development of the capital, accomplished much in this field. Efforts were made at the same time to improve the provincial towns.

In Warsaw, as time went on, Calvary Way and most of the other avenues that once led through fields were built up and became city streets. Looking at an eighteenth-century plan of Warsaw (Figure 17), one sees two great axes at right angles to the Vistula linked by Calvary Way and its extension in the direction of the royal castle and by the network of side streets that grew up behind it. In time, the magnates' settlements began to merge into one whole, linked by streets crossing each other at right angles. This considerable regularity and uniformity, however, was not so much the result of the building activity of the Polish kings, who were more concerned with the development of their own residences, or of the efforts of the magnates, who usually cared little about what was happening in the neighboring settlements. Nor was it due mainly to the influence of the rather weak royal administration. It was to the credit of the medieval surveyors who once marked out the boundaries of the agricultural lands belonging to the city. These former agricultural boundaries, which were either parallel or at right angles to the river, now became the streets of the city.

The economic growth of the country, evident from about 1740, induced the magnates to look for ways of improving the situation of their big estates. In order to promote the development of industry, handicrafts, and trade, they began to build new towns and expand existing ones on their estates in a way characteristic of the architectural trends of the epoch. In the medieval Polish town the market place was usually surrounded by residential buildings, and various buildings were erected in the market place itself for municipal government and trade purposes. The parish church was usually located apart from the hustle and bustle of the market place. Now, however, the market place was usually left open, and the monumental public buildings—the church, town hall, and others—were erected facing onto it. The architectural composition of these frequently very charming little towns was very symmetrical. The character of the buildings faithfully reflects the decline taking place in the economic and social position of the burghers. The new houses were

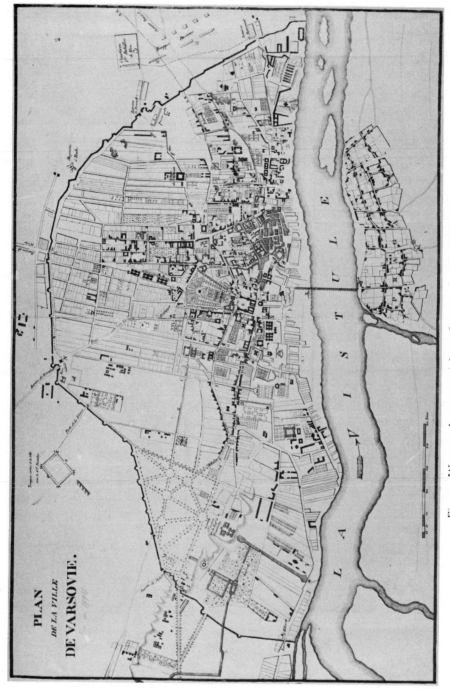

PLAN
DE LA VILLE
DE VARSOVIE.

Fig. 17. Warsaw about 1794 (photo: Instytut Sztuki, PAN, Warsaw)

very unpretentious, one-story buildings, mostly of wood; even those that had a brick-built front wall facing the street were usually wooden at the back. Sometimes there was a magnificent town hall; but its function was very different from those of the Middle Ages or of the Renaissance. Now it largely housed shops and inns, the main source of income of the owners of the township, while the town government offices were reduced to the very minimum.

In the second half of the seventeenth century there was a rising wave of religious devotion and fanaticism. At this time the building of churches and monasteries was relatively the most prosperous activity in the towns, which were then going through a period of serious decadence. The building of *Góra Kalwaria* (Calvary Hill), founded in 1670 by Bishop Wierzbowski, was characteristic of the alignment of social forces at that time (Figure 18). Góra Kalwaria included a Way of the Cross with shrines and a settlement providing services for pilgrims, where various kinds of handicraft and trade developed, particularly the production and retail sale of spirits and beer; fairs were held in the town directly after

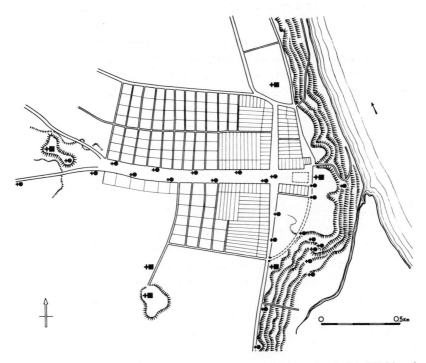

Fig. 18. Góra Kalwaria. Reconstruction of the original plan (by A. Liczbiński and T. Zarębska in *Kwartalnik Architektury i Urbanistyki*, II, 3-4, Warsaw, 1957)

all the big church holidays. At Góra Kalwaria six churches, thirty-five chapels, and five monasteries were constructed, while building plots were marked out for only one hundred houses. The township, situated on a high point protruding into the Vistula valley, was planned in the form of a cross, the ends of which were marked by the massive church and monastery buildings, while the longer arm was flanked on both sides by the shrines; there was a chapel at the point where the two arms crossed. Góra Kalwaria is an interesting example of a baroque town, the function and planning of which were completely subordinated to religious rites and the symbolism of the cult connected with them.

Early Industrial Centers

After the Napoleonic wars a new partition of Polish lands, which was to last until World War I, was decided on at the Congress of Vienna in 1815. At this time Poland's ethnic territories were divided between the three neighboring powers. The largest part was joined to Russia as the Polish Kingdom; the Russian Tsar was to be the Polish king. The Kingdom received a certain measure of political independence, which was limited after the uprising of 1830 and completely withdrawn after the uprising of 1863. Kraków, with its immediate surroundings, was given the status of a free city in 1815; in 1846 it was annexed to Austria.

The Polish lands were now joined to alien states. Most of the towns were in a very difficult economic situation. The markets for their products were cut off by the new frontiers. In Prussia and Austria, Polish handicrafts had to cope with keen competition from existing industry. The Polish population was politically oppressed and economically exploited.

There were relatively favorable conditions for economic development in the Polish Kingdom, which included most of the ethnic area of Poland together with the capital. Russian industry was not so highly developed and the Russian market opened new selling possibilities for Polish artisans and industry. The government organized supervision of architecture and town development all over the country. Bold reconstruction plans were drawn up for a number of provincial towns which were centers of state administration. Some of these plans were realized. (Map 5).

Warsaw, which had undergone a period of stagnation after the abdication of Stanisław August, began to develop rapidly again. It now came to life as a center of consolidated and expanded state administration, banking, trade, and industry. The new municipal authorities

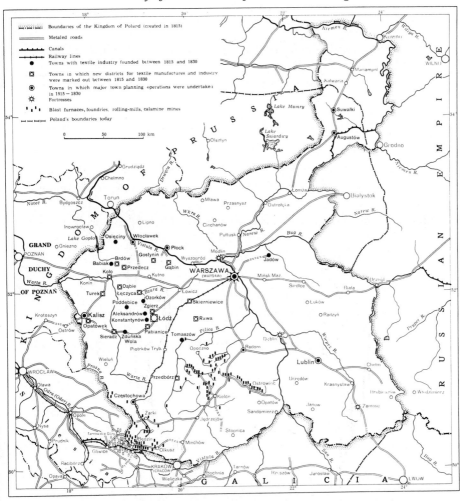

Map 5. Kingdom of Poland in the middle of the nineteenth century (prepared by
W. Szczawiński and W. Trzebiński)

began energetically to integrate and introduce order into the random
conglomeration of buildings which made up the city. The existing
streets and squares were reconstructed and new ones were laid out.
Various kinds of impressive public buildings were erected.

Special attention should be drawn to that side of government activity which was connected with setting up small towns and industrial
settlements in the Polish Kingdom. Here we find an intermingling of
anachronistic and progressive elements characteristic of Polish conditions of that time. As in the eighteenth century, wealthy landowners

tried to increase their incomes by encouraging artisans to settle on their land. The artisans engaged in the production of handmade textiles in the Poznań region and Silesia were placed in a difficult situation by the loss of the Polish markets for their goods and the competition from the factory production then developing in western Europe. As a result, several rapidly developing artisans' settlements were founded in the central Polish territories in the first and second decades of the nineteenth century.

The initiative of the wealthy landowners was taken up by the government of the Polish Kingdom, which started a large-scale campaign to encourage home industry. Attention was concentrated mainly on two branches of production: the textile industry and the iron and steel industry. The former was located in carefully selected areas where streams and rivers could easily be utilized to meet production needs. The government encouraged artisans and factory-owners with considerable capital to settle there, allotting them large plots of ground in suitably planned townships, granting them various privileges and tax reductions, making loans, and authorizing them to take timber from state forests. And this was not all: the government built town halls, churches, and houses for settlers, both to ensure that the new arrivals would have a place to live and to create a pattern that was to be followed in further residential development. An interesting example of this type of town is Łódź (Figure 19). The town, first founded in the Middle Ages, was in a state of decadence at the beginning of the nineteenth century. Within the framework of the government development scheme, a settlement was founded next to Łódź for artisans specializing in the production of handmade woolen cloth. Later, in the years 1824–1828, over 500 plots of land for artisans producing cotton cloth and flax linen were marked out, and a number of large sites were allotted for building big factories. The functional arrangement of the plan for the whole town is striking. Weavers of linen and cotton cloth were to live along the main street, along which the merchants drove when coming to the town; behind their houses and allotments were plots double the size for the linen spinners, who could cultivate flax on their land. The large factories were located on an axis perpendicular to the main street, along a river which powered the water wheels and supplied water for production. The town hall and a church were erected on the octagonal square of the clothiers' settlement.

Łódź is an example of the rational planning of an industrial town, quite unique in the history of European town planning; not only did it

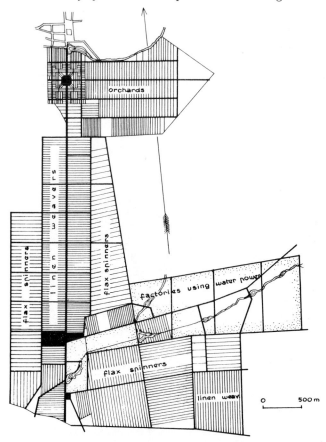

Fig. 19. Łódź. The medieval town extended to locate textile
industry, 1824–1828 (from W. Ostrowski, *Świetna karta z
dziejów planowania w Polsce,* Warsaw, 1949)

provide for the needs of the artisans, but also for large factories. It was
not long before mills employing several hundred workers and equipped
with steam-driven machines were built on the allotted sites. It may
seem paradoxical that the modern planning of Łódź was in some measure due to the economic backwardness of the country. In England,
more or less at the same time, the Manchester economists were developing theories violently opposing the interference of the state in the
economic life of the country; meanwhile the new "Polish Manchester"
was calling for the assistance of the state, without which it could
not have grown. The government gave this assistance, guaranteeing
customs protection and placing land and buildings at the disposal

of both small and large producers to meet the new needs of the town.

The government of the Polish Kingdom also gave its support to the development of mining and iron and steel production in areas rich in ore and forests. As the main driving power in such industry was water, large industrial concentrations were not usually built; instead, groups of cooperating factories were erected along fast-flowing rivers, sufficiently distant from one another to allow for raising the water level. The rivers were regulated, dams and canals were built, roads were constructed, and industrial buildings and workers' settlements were put up. The whole of this work was so diverse and far-reaching that it can be regarded as the first sign of true national and regional planning.

But this favorable period in the history of physical planning in Poland was short-lived. Łódź and other small towns like it were not to be model industrial towns for long. When a shortage of building sites was felt, the large plots originally intended as gardens for the artisans were used for building factories and flats; and the large influx of new population settled on chaotically divided plots in the suburbs. The doctrines of mercantile planning gave way to laissez faire. What were once model towns shared the sad fate of other towns in Europe in the throes of quick industrialization.

In the eighteen-sixties the capitalist system was consolidated in the Polish Kingdom. Urbanization was accelerated and accompanied by disorderly expansion of the towns, intensification of building, and the appearance of slums. It could not have been otherwise in the economic conditions prevailing at that time, particularly since the country was deprived of political and economic independence, the towns having at best only small powers of municipal self-government.

About 1900 the building restrictions connected with the obsolete fortifications of some large cities were removed. This made it possible to plan new districts on almost virgin sites. To obtain a plan for Greater Kraków, a competition was organized which fostered a discussion of the basic problems of contemporary town planning (1910).

The Interwar Period

After World War I Poland regained her independence (Map 6). The territories that had been under the rule of the three partitioning powers now had to be integrated again into one nation. The great difference in the level of development of the various districts had to be removed; and rail and road networks had to be linked up, which involved building completely new lines. It was necessary to reconstruct the towns damaged

Map 6. Poland between the two world wars

by war and to redevelop other towns. Town planning and the building legislation of the formerly partitioned areas had to be modernized and made uniform.

One of the important problems to be coped with in the field of physical planning was that of making the best use of the seacoast. The small coastal area granted to Poland by the Versailles Treaty did not have a large port. To avoid dependence on Gdańsk, which had been excluded from the Polish territories and given the status of a free city, a new town was founded on the site of the little fishing village of Gdynia on the Baltic Coast (Figure 20). The town developed quickly, and in 1939 it had a population of about 125,000. Gdynia is one of the few new

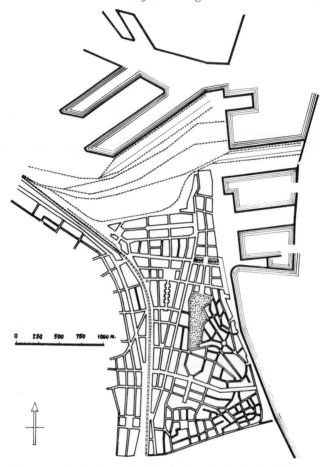

Fig. 20. Gdynia (from T. Tołwiński, *Urbanistyka*, II, Warsaw, 1948)

towns built in central and western Europe during the interwar period. The record speed with which the town was built, facilitated by the big investments made by the state and the tax reductions granted to local construction, is undoubtedly an achievement in town building, although from the point of view of current theoretical postulates of town planning, many mistakes were made in the building of Gdynia. They can be explained to a certain extent by lack of experience in realizing such a big scheme. The main shortcomings of the town, however, resulted from the social and economic conditions under which it was built.

First, the future size of Gdynia had to be established without any clear economic premises. The decision taken in 1922 to build a town with space for a population of 60,000 in the place of a fishing village of about 1,000 inhabitants seemed to be very bold, but it was soon found that in fact it was not bold enough. The first change made in the plan was to take over part of the housing area for port building. Efforts were then made to find new sites to meet housing needs; but this, in view of the existing topographical conditions, was difficult. The building of Gdynia was rather like the founding of a medieval town. The site of the town was divided into small plots on which various kinds of buildings, mostly residential ones, were erected by the many investors—building speculators and people spending their modest savings, all of them attracted by the prospect of easy profits in a speedily developing port town and tempted by the tax reductions. The basic component of the town was the tenement house, filling the whole front of the small plots. The buildings grew upward, to the height permitted by the zoning plan, and they were built without much concern for the neighboring buildings. Large groups of residential buildings were erected without essential services; typical corridor streets, monotonous and dull, began to appear. The main trading center came into being spontaneously in the busiest street, where the ground floors were occupied by shops and the upper stories by dwellings. Residential building, both from public funds and on a cooperative basis, which was not aimed at gaining the maximum profits but at ensuring the best possible living conditions, played only a very insignificant role in the development of the town. The few examples of this kind of building, carried out according to a uniform plan on larger areas, give some idea of what housing could be in a twentieth-century town. But it was impossible to carry out this type of building on a larger scale under the social and economic conditions that existed at that time. Gdynia also experienced a phenomenon which was to occur later in many countries where there was a great difference in the standard of living of various social classes: the erection on the outskirts of town of shanty-towns, overcrowded with people who could not afford better accommodations.

Social conditions also very seriously restricted the possibilities for planned development of the country in other ways. The master plans for towns were drawn up under the pressure of the property owners, who opposed any radical restriction on their freedom of action. In the areas zoned for building, houses and blocks of flats sprang up here and there without any fixed time schedule, which made it impossible to develop a town properly and guarantee the most essential services. The plans that were drawn up bore the character of what might be called "wishful planning," whittled down under the pressure of the property owners and giving no guarantee that the work would be carried out in a fixed period of time. This was also true of the regional plans, which began to be drawn up earlier in Poland than in many European countries. In the preparation of these plans, some very interesting studies and apt suggestions were made, which were not, however, usually realized. One of the most important plans of this kind was the project for the Central Industrial Region, which for strategic reasons was to be set up as far as possible from the frontiers of the country, in an area that had been agricultural until that time and where there was abundant available manpower. Large state investments were made in the realization of this plan, which started in 1936, and the project progressed quite favorably until work was stopped by the outbreak of World War II.

Residental building was supported by the government not so much to supply dwellings to meet the most urgent social needs as to reduce unemployment. This resulted in great differences in the housing standards of population groups with varying incomes and also in a relatively slow development of nonspeculative building.

Although the achievements of Polish town planners in the interwar years were limited, mainly by difficulties connected with the social system, some of their achievements should not be underestimated. During this period important progress was made in discovering the needs of a modern town and the methods of satisfying them. More interest was taken in the complicated problems of physical planning; the first research work in this field was carried out and a theory of town planning began to take shape. Valuable projects were elaborated on national, regional, and local scales. The first socially and architecturally progressive housing estates were built. A cadre of qualified town planners emerged, and conclusions were drawn from both the successes and the failures in earlier town planning. It was only after the war that these men were able to utilize their experience to the full.

Recent Developments

Poland suffered particularly heavy losses in World War II: loss of population—about six million Poles were killed; loss of national property, of which 40 per cent was destroyed; and loss of invaluable and irreplaceable works of art. The Polish people, ruined by the war and deprived of even the simplest technical means, were faced with the tremendous task of reconstructing innumerable towns and villages. It was not a question of faithfully rebuilding the towns as they had been, but of a reconstruction corresponding to the new needs and possibilities of a socialist nation. The nationalization of the basic means of production and the introduction of a planned economy meant an immense growth in the possibilities of physical planning in comparison with the interwar period. The physical plans of regions, towns, and villages lost their former "wishful" character and became plans of action, to be consistently carried out in fixed periods of time.

But this change did not in the least mean that it was now possible to plan according to theoretical needs. The rebuilding and expansion of towns and villages after the war were taking place under difficult conditions with which the town planner had to reckon. These conditions seriously limited the boldness of the proposals put forward, influencing the character of plans and the time necessary to carry them out.

When World War II broke out, Poland was an economically backward nation, the index of the national income per capita being lower than in most European countries. The losses brought by the war made the situation even worse. The speedy industrialization of the country, begun after 1945, brought in its wake a sudden increase in the migration of the rural population to the towns. The growth in urbanization indices in Poland during the fifteen years following the conclusion of the war was equal to that of fifty years in France. The rapid increase in the urban population meant that a relatively modest standard of housing and of social and cultural facilities had to be accepted.

Before the war the best housing was built for the wealthy; the level of income was the decisive factor in determining the size of apartments and their equipment. The great majority of the people had very poor dwellings, without sanitary installations, situated in districts which did not have the most elementary facilities. The chief principle applied in postwar building is the leveling of the standard for all residential buildings. This standard is much higher now than that of the majority of prewar dwellings, but lower than in countries with a high standard of living, particularly in housing destined for the rich.

One of the most serious difficulties of town planning results from the necessity of taking into account current needs and economic possibilities without creating difficulties in the realization of later investments when the possibilities will be greater. As long as the disproportion between current needs and the means at our disposal is wide, it may be necessary to limit theoretically correct plans motivated by concern for the future rather than for the present.

Directly after the war proposals were put forward to activate economically backward regions of the country by building new factories in them. Economic reasons, which in many cases dictated the expansion of existing factories or industrial regions, prevented rapid effectuation of this undoubtedly correct principle. In the socialist economy the distribution of new industrial investments is not the consequence of spontaneous development, but of planned action; the location of new factories is not decided solely by considerations of obtaining the maximum profit, but by considerations of the maximum social effects. The possibility of coordinating the location of various investments—the mining of raw material, the building of processing and auxiliary plants, communication facilities, power supplies, housing estates, and so on— facilitates the development of industry on virgin territory. Although this gives the planner much more of a free hand, it does not free him from the duty of reckoning with the economic consequences of the decisions he takes.

Finally, the town planner must take into account not only the theoretical principles of physical planning, but also the wishes of those concerned. This applies, among other things, to the choice of a location for new factories. In making such decisions, he must consider whether it will be possible to find the necessary personnel in a given place.

For these reasons the expansion and reconstruction of Polish towns in the postwar years did not progress fully in accordance with theoretical needs and ambitious town planning schemes. To some extent, this was the result not only of objective difficulties, resulting from economic conditions, but also of errors made. These errors were not easy to avoid for those who, seeking new solutions corresponding to the social and political changes taking place and wishing to reconcile harmoniously the various material and spiritual needs of the people, were faced with immense and complicated tasks, the magnitude of which had no precedent.

In spite of all this, if what has been done in town building in the postwar years is summed up, the general picture is undoubtedly a favorable one. Many successes in physical planning have been achieved.

First of all, the migration of the population to the towns has been directed in accordance with accepted principles. The alteration of frontiers after the war meant that several million persons who previously lived in the east had to be resettled in the western territories, where most of the towns were in ruins. This process has in the main been completed. The towns in the territories joined to Poland after the war have risen from the ruins. New residential and industrial districts have been built; and some of the towns now have a larger population than before the war. The extent of their expansion has depended on the function they have been allotted in the new settlement structure of the country.

Warsaw, which was badly destroyed, has been reconstructed and considerably expanded. Its population is already nearing the prewar figure, and the people are living and working under much better conditions.

The reconstruction of valuable architectural monuments, undertaken in spite of the difficult economic situation in the country, is of great importance for Polish towns, or rather for Polish culture. In the efforts to reconstruct the cultural relics destroyed during the war, not only single monumental buildings, but also whole historical districts were restored. Thus whole quarters of great architectural and historical value have been reconstructed in Warsaw, Gdańsk, Wrocław, and other towns. Where the devastated districts were not of any particular value, reconstruction work was confined to restoring the most interesting buildings, while the rest of the district was built up with new houses to harmonize with the historical monuments; one of the towns where this principle was adopted is Szczecin. Within the framework of the reconstruction of these towns sanitary conditions have been improved and distortions of architecture removed (Figures 21–35).

Fig. 21. Warsaw. The medieval market square after wartime destruction (photo: L. Jabrzemski)

Fig. 22. Warsaw. The medieval market square after reconstruction (photo: L. Jabrzemski)

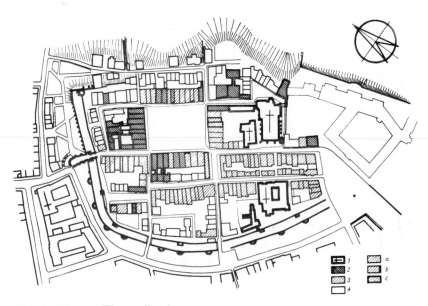

Fig. 23. Warsaw. The medieval town
    Present functions of the buildings: 1. Churches. 2. Museum and clubs. 3. Shops and restaurants. 4. Residential dwellings. 5. Nonresidential functions occupy: *a.* the ground floor, *b.* two floors, *c.* three or more floors.

48

Fig. 24. Warsaw. The medieval town after reconstruction (photo: E. Kupiecki)

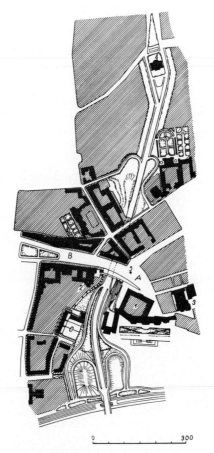

Fig. 25. Warsaw. The "East–West Road"
running across the Old Town in a
tunnel

Fig. 26. Warsaw. Part of the Old Town after wartime destruction (photo: L. Jabrzemski)

In the efforts to activate economically neglected regions, many large industrial plants have been located in virgin territories or in small towns, which consequently had to be radically expanded and reconstructed. A large number of Polish towns, owing to the great increase in population and the high percentage of postwar building, can today be regarded as new towns. The residential buildings, erected in large

Fig. 27. Warsaw. Same part of the Old Town with the entrance to the tunnel under the "East–West Road" (photo: L. Jabrzemski)

Fig. 28. Gdańsk. The medieval town after wartime destruction (photo: K. Komorowski)

Fig. 29. Gdańsk. The medieval town after reconstruction (photo: Kosycarz, Central Photographic Archives)

Fig. 30. Gdańsk. Part of the rebuilt medieval town (photo: Kosycarz, Central
Photographic Archives)

neighborhood units, stand out distinctly from the old ones. The structure of other towns is changing too.

Another exceptionally difficult task of tremendous social importance
has also been tackled: the renewal of badly built existing districts. This
work, involving huge outlays of capital and the demolition of houses in
spite of the acute shortage of dwellings, cannot be carried out on a very
large scale as yet. But a start has already been made in this field,

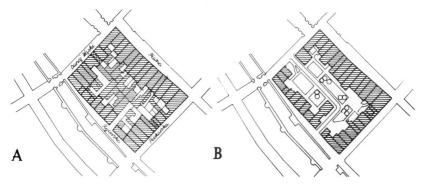

Fig. 31. Gdańsk. A typical block of the medieval town (A) before the war and (B)
after rebuilding

Fig. 32. Wrocław. The medieval town hall rebuilt (photo: Wołoszczuk, Central Photographic Archives)

Fig. 33. Wrocław. Houses in the medieval market square after reconstruction (photo: Wołoszczuk, Central Photographic Archives)

54

Fig. 34. Szczecin after wartime destruction (photo: Komorowski, Central Photographic Archives)

Fig. 35. Szczecin. The area of the medieval town under reconstruction, with rebuilt churches and new buildings erected to replace old ones without artistic value (photo: Kazberuk, Central Photographic Archives)

in Łódź, for instance, where so much bad building was done at the end of the nineteenth century and the beginning of the twentieth century.

Today, there are 31 million people living in the territories stretching from the Odra River to the Bug River and from the Baltic Sea to the Carpathians. They are making great efforts to erase the last traces of the war and to reconstruct their country in a way that corresponds to the ideals and the needs of a socialist community.

CHAPTER 2

Urban Planning Theory: Methods and Results*

BOLESŁAW MALISZ

Introduction

CITY planning is influenced by many factors, one of which is the socio-economic system of the country concerned. In the socialist planned economy, urban planning differs from that in Western countries. Thus it seems advisable to begin with a short explanation of the organization for planning in Poland. This chapter presents trends of modern city planning in the People's Republic of Poland through a description of city planning methods and some of their results.

In Poland *physical planning*, including urban planning, means the *spatial* aspect of planning; it is administered separately from economic and social planning, which are carried on by the State Planning Commission of the Council of Ministers. This central body has its branch offices on *voivodship*[1] and county levels. The offices for the five largest cities (Warsaw, Łódź, Kraków, Poznań, and Wrocław) are at the voivodship level; those for the other large cities are on the county level; and the smaller towns are included within the jurisdiction of the county planning offices.

The organization for physical planning is less direct. According to the Spatial Planning Act of January, 1961,[2] it has been carried on at three levels: the national, the voivodship, and the county or local.

---

* This article is based on a paper prepared by the author for the United Nations Seminar in Warsaw, Poland, September 19–29, 1962.

[1] Voivodship: province. There are now seventeen voivodships in Poland, and the five largest cities are also treated as voivodships. Voivodships are divided into counties. There are about 320 counties. Large cities are also administered as counties; smaller ones are within county boundaries.

[2] This Act is set forth in Appendix I of this section.

The economic planning authorities are responsible for the physical planning of the country as a whole and of voivodships. Local planning until 1964 was under the Committee for Building, City Planning, and Architecture. This Committee, set up in 1953 and enlarged in 1960, co-ordinated all building activity until October, 1963. In January, 1964, a central reorganization of building and local planning activities placed local planning under the Ministry of Building. On the voivodship and county levels these functions are performed by voivodship and county (or city) architects, whose offices include city and rural planning work-shops.

The organization for planning has changed as planning methods have developed. The first part of this chapter presents Polish city planning methods in the prewar period, the early postwar period, and the present period, which encompasses a transition to advanced proc-esses for reaching rational decisions in planning programs. In the second part of the chapter a brief account of the results of these later methods is given. This topic is too broad to be treated in a short article; the main effort here is concentrated in describing types of major changes in urban spatial structure, especially those visible in land-use patterns, in the "green spaces" policy, in the transportation network, and in the renewal of city centers. Examples of planning in several cities are detailed in following chapters.

Development of City Planning Methods

To give a clear understanding of the evolution of contemporary city planning, one must show how it—as a part of physical planning—operates within the whole system of the Polish planned economy. The underlying conviction of the school of city planning now emerging is that the more the methods of action conform to the economic system in which they are used, the more successful they will be.

PREWAR DEVELOPMENT OF CITY PLANNING

The beginnings of contemporary city planning in Poland date back to the first decades of this century. As early as the nineteen-twenties the first concepts of regional planning were put forward as city planners be-gan to look beyond the boundaries of the town. In the thirties these concepts evolved into a method of regional research. By the outbreak of World War II nearly half of Poland had been covered by regional plan-ning studies, although only a few had resulted in actual programs. The majority of Polish planners at that time were convinced that town development could not be successful unless attention was given to all the social and economic processes taking place in the immediately contiguous areas and the surrounding region. This led to an extension of the scale of new development proposals from the town proper to the settlement pattern of the region as a whole.

The proposal of this kind which appears to have had the greatest influence on future city planning theory was outlined by J. Chmielewski and S. Syrkus in *Warszawa Funkcjonalna* (Functional Warsaw), published in 1936. The authors, having pointed out the fundamental faults in the development of Warsaw—above all excessive concentration of functions in a limited area—proposed a decentralized layout (Figure 36). Basing their proposal on a principle of dynamic belts, the authors conceived of a metropolitan pattern of development arranged according to the main traffic flows separated into specific routes according to the kind of traffic (passenger, consumer goods, industrial, and so on). Each route created a zone of influence which determined the location of the related human activity. Within the Warsaw region there were two main directions of traffic: east-west and parallel to the Vistula River. These two directions were divided into subdirections, the intersections of which determined the proper location of industrial and residential areas and service centers.

This idea led to a conception for the regional development of Warsaw known as the Warsaw Metropolitan Area. The ideas and methods developed by Chmielewski and Syrkus were adopted by contemporary planners in many regional development schemes. They were also favorably received in other countries, indicated by the fact that the Warsaw Metropolitan Area was a subject of discussion at one of the C.I.A.M.[3] congresses.

This broadened interpretation of the concept of city planning and the related development of physical planning in Poland resulted, in the years preceding World War II, in attempts to work out a physical plan on a national scale. National planning, however, was not favored by the existing authorities, afraid of the influence of a socialist system of planning. Regional planners had to conform to the existing legislative possibilities, as far as official planning[4] was concerned. Thus the new concepts in city planning theory and methods could not be tested through implementation. Nor did the economic policy of the time provide any means by which private landowners and entrepreneurs could be induced to co-

---

[3] Congrès International de l'Architecture Moderne.

[4] The regional studies were prepared in regional state offices.

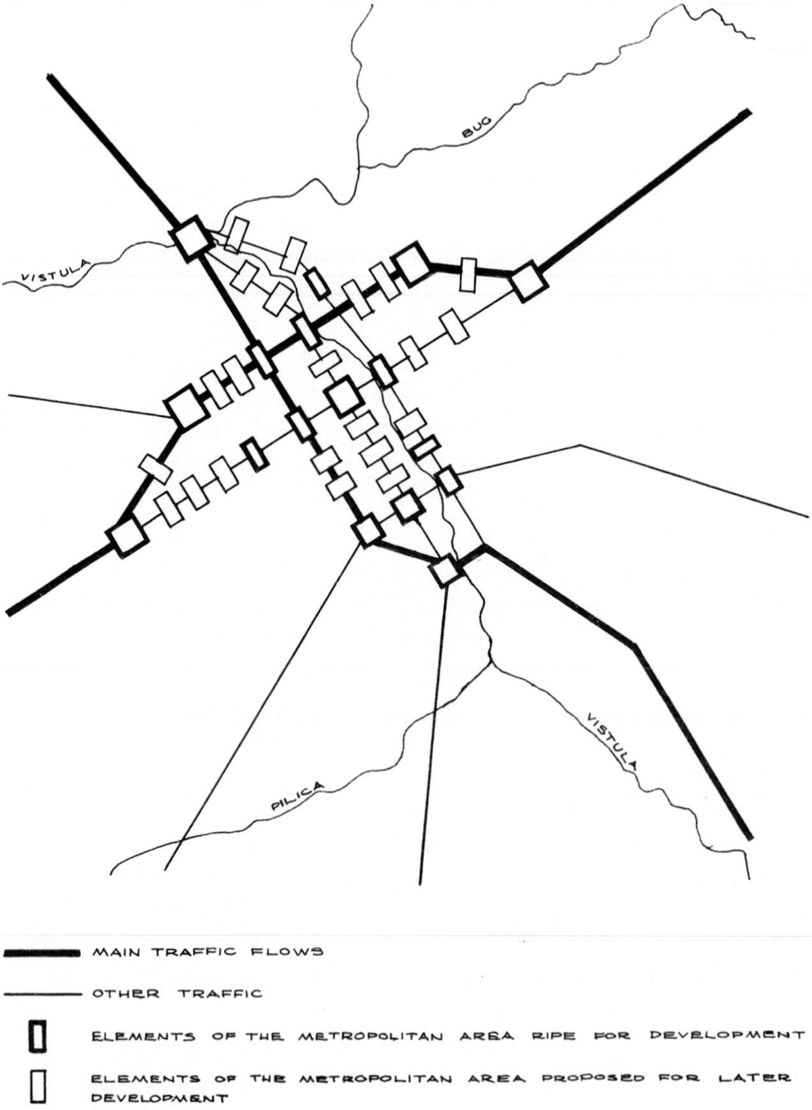

MAIN TRAFFIC FLOWS

OTHER TRAFFIC

ELEMENTS OF THE METROPOLITAN AREA RIPE FOR DEVELOPMENT

ELEMENTS OF THE METROPOLITAN AREA PROPOSED FOR LATER DEVELOPMENT

Fig. 36. Sketch of the proposal for Warsaw Metropolitan area by J. Chmielewski and S. Syrkus

operate with the proposed plans. The master plan for a city could become reality only through enforcement of a restrictive zoning law. Even with such a plan, there was no way to supplement its negative control with a positive investment program. Without this, nearly all the town and regional development plans had to remain on paper.

THE POSTWAR PERIOD: DIVERGENCES BETWEEN PHYSICAL AND
ECONOMIC PLANNING

With the emergence of the People's Republic of Poland, the new system of government created conditions suitable for a planned socialist economy by nationalizing the means of production and by rendering land accessible for social purposes. These conditions were fully appreciated by the physical planners. The decree concerning the planned physical development of the country, issued in 1946, allowed for extensive development of physical planning. It provided for three levels of planning: national, regional (within the areas of particular voivodships), and local (urban and rural). All physical planning work for these three levels was done in state planning offices directed by the Central Physical Planning Office. It was also in this central office that the schemes for the national plan were prepared. In the capital of each voivodship there was a Regional Planning Office, responsible for the regional plan. On the local planning level, within the larger cities, local planning offices were formed. City planning schemes for the smaller cities were prepared in the Regional Planning Office, because of the shortage of staff.

This extensive organization for physical planning, however, was set up without providing for adequate relations with economic planning, for which a separate Central Economic Planning Office was responsible.

The goals envisaged by an economic plan must be achieved during the designated planning period. Based on calculations imposed by the nation's difficult postwar situation, such plans could hardly take into account the long-range proposals of physical planning, which at that time represented something like "dreams of the future." At this time, when physical planning as described above had a rather decentralized organization, economic planning was highly centralized. Also, while physical planners looked far ahead when working out their schemes, economic planners drafted their first national plan for only three years (1947–1949). This difference in planning periods made it impossible to build a workable program for the long-range period for which city plans were prepared.

The centralized national economic plan had been set up in terms of over-all indices and the specific characteristics for different areas were not detailed. Thus city planners could not be given sufficient data for a single city's program. Further, the authorities in charge of particular sectors of the national economy could not discuss the detailed proposals of physical planning, let alone agree on these proposals. The consequences of the differences between these two kinds of planning soon became apparent. Physical planning, with no basis of economic programing, was restricted to the formal shaping of purely functional schemes. Its land-use proposals contained latent assumptions about social and economic conditions and their development which were often too optimistic or not paralleled in the current economic plans. As a result, physical planning was forced to return to its prewar traditions of graphic representation of possible spatial solutions, with no knowledge of the real economic possibilities.

It was assumed that the establishment of some general principles for the country's physical plan would lead to establishing a basis for the rational planning of voivodships; and that by working from these, planners would be able to map out the proper development of towns and rural areas. Therefore, attention was concentrated above all on the national plan, and on selected metropolitan areas which were deemed essential to the country's settlement network.

These plans were based on the method devised by Chmielewski and Syrkus.[5] The planners in a given area first sought the pattern of traffic flows and drafted a schematic transportation network based on it. This network was the basis for locating the active zones (zones influenced by traffic) proposed for intensive land use. These schemes were then revised on the basis of studies of existing physical features. The land-use pattern proposed was determined by two main factors: natural and man-made physical features, and technical possibilities created by various kinds of transportation. The results of these studies were finally examined in the light of a model settlement network based to a large degree on Christaller's principles.

Under these circumstances, what was the method of working out the master plan of a city? Describing this method helps characterize the beginnings of modern city planning in Poland and shows the progress that has been made during the last fifteen years or so.

The work on the master plan of a city was begun by a survey which included an examination of the existing natural and man-made features. The plan was drafted first in the form of a town development program and then as the proper master plan. The program was mainly a preliminary stage in drafting the spatial concept rather than a set of

---

[5] See pp. 59, 60.

figures defining the scale of development and proposals for land use. The program was drafted for a conventional period, usually twenty-five years. The future population of the town was estimated, using extrapolation curves of past and present development (excepting the war period) and the general directives of the regional plan. But, as was said earlier, the regional plans of this period lacked the support of economic planning and could not be treated as actual programs. The physical planners tried to anticipate the size of the future population by an imperfect hypothesis of population growth and by rough estimates of urban population development in towns of various sizes.

To calculate the areas required for different types of land use, the planners generally accepted the primitive indices of density then in use. These indices related only to residential zones and were based on the number of stories in a built-up area. The program for service areas was usually sketchy, consisting of those elements which the planners alone thought proper to include. In locating the various elements of a program in a given city area, the planner followed the scheme drafted by planners on the next higher level. The layout was based on the pattern of flows and the main traffic routes. The city planner had to alter this theoretical pattern according to the physical features of the area and existing conditions of land use.

The transportation network was the main skeleton of the city plan. Particular routes were classified by function, and the various land-use zones were located in the areas between them. The tendency was to group the industrial areas near the main transportation routes. Residential districts were arranged in a belt pattern according to Milutin's formula,[6] that is, in terms of walking distance from the place of work. The functions and intersections of the main roads determined the role and range of particular service centers. The principle of functionalism was followed rather strictly with a tendency to form pure land-use zones separated from one another by green belts.

The proposed scheme was usually seen as a final state of city development. The static nature of such plans was revealed by the lack of any attempt to bridge the gap between existing and future states of development. Any stage plans drafted were of a very general and formal character with little relation to actual investment possibilities.

[6] See discussion of the belt pattern of Stalingrad given by Ludwig Hilbersiemer, *The New City* (Chicago: P. Theobald, 1944), p. 70.

CRITIQUE AND FIRST IMPROVEMENTS OF THE METHOD

The divergences between economic and physical planning and the criticism of the latter by the economic planners finally led (in 1950) to a division of the whole organization for physical planning into two parts: city and rural planning were granted separate status, while regional planning was subordinated to economic planning. Regional planning at the voivodship level was almost replaced by the territorial section of economic plans. Regional plans were made only for those areas where the rate and scope of investment required the spatial coordination of physical planning.

Separating regional and local planning created a gap which was to be filled by directives of economic authorities given to local planners. These directives were necessarily limited to the five-year period of the economic plans. Uncertainty about proper methods for preparing the territorial section during successive phases of drafting the economic plans made the scope of the directives rather narrow. They concerned mostly the rate of industrial development and of other basic functions of the town, the size of which was measured by the expected rate of growth of employment during the period of the next five-year plan.[7]

Although the field of operation was limited, the planners did improve the method of programing for the cities. From given data one could determine the size of a city-forming population, that is, the basic labor force, and then by analyzing needs for a service labor force, calculate the future population of the town. This method essentially resembles economic base theory[8] used in Western countries. The specific feature of this method in a planned economy lies in the fact that data concerning the growth of the basic activity of the town are drawn from the economic plans of a higher level. Thus the local plans could be related to the total national economy and included in the national long-term plan, their realization thus ensured.

Another essential improvement of city planning methods resulted from the criticism of decentralized development schemes. The tendency to separate various districts by function usually led to extensive use of land and to overextension of the utility network. It was known, however, that the cost of accommodating a given number of inhabitants could be

[7] While it is not the aim of this chapter to go into details of economic planning, one of the features of a five-year plan is the balance between the increase of estimated productive population and the number of working places which should be created.

[8] As described by F. Stuart Chapin, Jr., in *Urban Land-Use Planning* (New York: Harper, 1957), pp. 104–117.

divided into two parts: the relatively fixed cost of erecting the buildings and developing areas adjacent to them, and the variable costs that depended on the length and kind of basic utilities networks. This led to the principle of town compactness: of two given plans the less expensive was that for which the cost of the basic utilities network was lower. Of course, the cost was lower only when the developed area was located closer to the existing utility lines. This principle, which for a long time became the main criterion in assessing urban plans, had unfavorable as well as favorable results. It was, of course, good to try to lower the costs of the basic utilities networks. On the other hand, excessively high densities of population were created in order to decrease the size of the area served by the utility network.

Nevertheless, these economic criteria brought about some progress. The principle of town compactness called for standards for rational use of a developed area. In 1951 the Institute for Town Planning and Architecture developed the Town Planning Standards,[9] after an analysis of standards in use in Poland and a comparison with those used in other countries, especially in the Soviet Union. Such standards determined the space needed for particular uses, and combined indices for certain areas of the town, chiefly for the settlement area which embraced the housing, services, park areas and the network of streets connected with them. The Standards were, in many respects, imperfect. They covered only certain kinds of land use and assumed development of vacant land only. Complicated redevelopment schemes for existing substandard areas could not be based on them. Moreover, the combined indices were based on the notion of a street block instead of a neighborhood unit. This was not consistent: new land for development need not be divided into traditional street blocks, and existing areas could not be embraced by these Standards. This retarded development of rational planning for the functional structure of housing areas. The deficiencies of the Standards, plus a widespread tendency to interpret them too narrowly, resulted in many planning errors. Still, the Standards were an important tool in improving the method of drafting master plans. Issued as temporary rules, they were gradually improved as zoning methods were developed.

The 1951 Standards are still in use, although new ones will soon appear, their revision based on past experience. They will be published in the form of a filing-card system, so that standards on particular cards

---

[9] *Tymczasowe Normatywy Urbanistyczne,* published by the Ministry of Building in 1951. These are reproduced in Appendix II.

can be changed according to the development of various branches of the national economy. The Standards have been uniformly systematized and the over-all indices refer to sequentially, hierarchically arranged structural units of the urban area. Besides establishing standards for areas developed from vacant land, they set up the procedures necessary for the gradual planned redevelopment of built-up areas.

THE STAGE-PLAN TECHNIQUE

These improvements introduced some essential changes in city planning technique. But real progress in physical planning methods dates from the introduction of the short-term or stage plan,[10] conceived as an integral part of city planning.

The methods used in this kind of plan had taken shape in the early fifties in plans for Warsaw. Intensified investment processes in connection with the reconstruction and complete redevelopment of the capital city called for more effective methods of coordinating work in time and space. These methods were later applied in a number of the larger cities; since 1956 stage plans have been drafted for all the more intensively developed cities.

The stage-plan method links the process of city planning with the rhythm of economic planning. The realization of the long-term master plan, or, as it is called in Poland, the perspective plan, of a city is expected to take place by stages, each stage determined by the national economic five-year plans. The main difficulty of staging the plan lay in tying development projects in a given city with over-all national development indices and investment limits. This difficulty was hard to overcome with no intermediate link between the national economic plan and local city plans. Although the territorial sections of the economic plans and the regional plans should have served as links, the former were prepared only for whole voivodships (not for individual cities), and the latter only for some selected areas of extensive development. To overcome this difficulty, stage plans for a city were drafted in two phases: (1) *provisional plan*, based on a comprehensive analysis of the needs and development possibilities of the city in a given period, is a basis for discussion with the economic planning authorities; it helps to show the real needs which should be accounted for in the economic plan; and (2) *final, or verified, plan*, based on the economic plans for related periods.

Here it should be noted that decentralization of the administration

---

[10] The stage plan is prepared "for a period conforming to the current period and the next period of the short-term national economic plan." *Spatial Planning Act of 1961,* Art. 3.1.3.

of the national economy began in 1956. Since then, the praesidia of peoples' councils at the levels of voivodships, counties, and individual cities have gradually been given more power in economic matters within their areas. The stage plan has become a fundamental tool to coordinate investments according to the needs of each area. Together with economic planning, the stage plan gives the local peoples' council guidelines for better allotment of centralized investment limits and for their own development policy.

There were several major problems in relating the stage plan to the territorial section of the economic plan. The first was to program the development of urban facilities realistically in a given stage. Such programing should be based on the indices of the needs of city-dwellers for the period; use of long-range indices of city planning standards offered no solution because of limited realization possibilities. Therefore, planners first sought to establish stage-standards for apartments, social and economic services, and community facilities. This method proved inflexible and unreliable because the disproportions in urban land development and in the demographic structure of the population between various parts of the country make great differences in existing standards of living in particular cities. The technique now used consists in interpolating indices between the existing level of investment in a given area and the national level that could be obtained or deduced from the next five-year economic plan.

Another problem for stage planning was to provide a comprehensive analysis of alternative locations for all elements of the program (or plan). The traditional way of drafting master plans did not take into account alternative layouts of the utilities network of the city, nor did it use adequate techniques to select the economical variant. To cope with this problem, it became necessary to draw on the knowledge and experience of such specialists as engineers, architects, economists, geographers, and sociologists.

Initially, the method was carried on so that several location proposals were prepared separately by various groups of specialists. Each of these proposals was based on different criteria (according to a given aspect), such as: physiographical features, communication requirements, water-supply and sewerage possibilities. The final plan was that synthesis which accounted for the largest number of these criteria. This original method has been improved by the use of economic calculations. The choice of an area for further city development is now based on three different investigations: the cost of preparing the terrain for development (land or site adjustment), the cost of changing the existing land use, and the cost of servicing the land with the various kinds of utility networks (roads, sewers, water systems, central heating). With the appropriate technological assumptions, these three types of costs are calculated for each part of the city area (based on homogeneous spatial units).[11]

The first two types of costs are more or less stable; the third type of costs, calculated for each area, depends on the length of specific utility lines. For the purpose of cost calculation, all utility networks are considered to have three main elements: the central installation or source, the main line, such as the main sewer or the main water-supply pipe, and the service network. Thus, the location of the central installations determines the costs for each part of the city area. In an attempt to account for intensity of land use, which of course also has its effect, costs are calculated *per capita* according to the proposed population density of built-up areas.

After the preliminary studies in the first phase of planning, all sensible alternatives for the location of the central installations are compared and the least expensive is chosen. In the second phase, based on the assumed location of these installations, selection of the most convenient development area is made; and in the third phase different city planning schemes are prepared for this area. In the last phase the least expensive scheme is chosen. Statistical techniques were originally used for this procedure, but recently the technique of electronic machines has been introduced to simplify the task. The results of this technique, involving purely economic calculations, must be confronted with other criteria, such as biological, social, and esthetic, which often cannot be measured quantitatively.

In present-day planning choices which formerly were based *only* on intuition and logical consideration of mutually dependent factors are now being made by both intuitive and mathematical means. The first experimental work along these lines was carried out in the preparation of the last master plan of Warsaw.[12] In some other cities controversies concerning the location of industrial or communication facilities have been settled by econometrics. In Kraków,[13] for instance, discussion of two possible alternative plans for enlarging the downtown area continued for ten years. The first plan assumed that the railway lines would remain fixed, cutting through the enlarged city center. The second plan

---

[11] The area of the city of Warsaw consists, for example, of 3,800 such units.

[12] See Chapter 3.

[13] See Chapter 5.

proposed the relocation of the railway lines in the attempt to enlarge the central area. Three years ago this conflict was resolved by means of economic calculation based on the principle of the economic efficiency of investments. The rough mathematical formula for this kind of calculation is:

$$E = \frac{I + K}{P}$$

where E = efficiency of the variant
    I = total cost of investments
    K = *operational costs*
    P = the *economic effect of investment*[14]

In a comparison of city planning schemes it is difficult to estimate the total effects of each, because they often involve values which cannot be measured. The two variants had to be designed so as to have about the same effect from the city planners' point of view. Then it could be shown that the second plan for central Kraków was 50 per cent more expensive. This was due to the freezing of capital, for the final effect would be obtained only when the relocation of the railway lines was completed; whereas with the first plan the work could be divided into phases, each having a partial effect. The results of such calculations so far have been encouraging. It is hoped that these methods will be used as a basis for the widespread application of scientific processes in making decisions for the creation of city plans.

Finally comes the problem of checking the soundness of the stage plan. The main advantage of the method in use is that it balances all factors influencing the plan's implementation. This method stresses the analysis of three main groups of factors: cost of investments in a given stage, productive potential of the building enterprises concerned, and acquisition of the necessary land. The analysis of these factors is made with the cooperation of surveyors, construction engineers, and specialists on land-use policy, thus ensuring the soundness of city planning schemes. The system of successive approximations of various solutions and their economic control in actual practice have made the stage plan an important tool of land-use policy.

The city plan, once it has been worked out and supported by documents, influences the shaping of economic plans. The long-term economic

[14] In the case of industrial location, the effect is measured by annual production (in money value); for housing the effect is the number of flats. This quantitative measurement, however, cannot be used without additional criteria.

plan, in its final version, becomes the basis for the next phase of the stage plan. In this phase of development the plan assumes the form of a directive. It gives a number of guidelines for drafting detailed plans of areas of the city as implementation projects. It also coordinates physical development within the town.

INTRODUCTION OF PERSPECTIVE ECONOMIC PLANNING AND ITS EFFECT ON CITY PLANNING

From the foregoing discussion of evolving planning methods in Poland, it can be seen that most steps toward uniting physical planning with economic planning were taken by the city planners. But an important change in economic planning took place in the late fifties with the introduction of perspective planning of the national economy, which supplements the existing system with economic plans drafted for a period of fifteen to twenty years (actually to 1980).

As long as economic plans were drafted for periods of five years at the longest, there was no satisfactory connection between long-range city development plans and relatively short-range economic plans. Despite the correlation of stage plans with economic five-year plans, the city plans remained, as it were, hanging in the air. The schemes they proposed had no counterparts in the economic plans nor in the investment policies of particular branches of the national economy.

Perspective planning of the national economy was not introduced with the sole purpose of linking economic and physical planning. The need for a long-term approach arose within economic planning itself from its search for new methods. There was particularly a need to consider the long-range reshaping and development of the national economy in terms of adapting to the planned division of labor within the international framework of socialism. Still, perspective planning is a fundamental link between physical planning and the entire system of the planned economy; extending the time period for which economic plans are drafted has automatically strengthened the spatial aspect of planning.

One of the chief goals of the planned economy, for example, is to eliminate irrational extremes in the development of different parts of the country. This aim can be achieved only by consistently applied and farsighted economic planning policy, goals of which must include consideration of the probable future development of the different economic regions of the country. To ensure consistent implementation of the plan in a specific region, the cooperation of the proper local authorities is needed. Therefore the voivodships should have the status of economic regions and be embraced by regional planning. The regional plans[15] of voivodships would then become an integral part of perspective economic planning, permitting an optimal balance of the processes of production and consumption of the national income.

The immediate effect of perspective planning of the national economy was to hasten the decentralization of economic planning authority. The national economic plan, first set up only for the entire country, is now being prepared for all voivodships and even at the level of counties and larger cities. Thus the most important divergence between economic and physical planning has been overcome. The introduction of perspective planning is also important for physical planning methods. The period of fifteen to twenty years for which economic plans are now being drafted is nearly as long as that for which city planners have traditionally drafted their long-term plans. Such a change in the time-span of economic planning has caused city planning to follow these exact time periods. Thus not only does the stage plan of a town correspond in terms of time to the five-year economic plans, but also the long-term physical plan[16] is firmly supported in the appropriate long-term economic plan. The consequences of this for city planning are important. The physical plan of the next higher level (in this case the regional plan) imposes on the particular towns production tasks which serve as a basis for determining the elements of the town's economic and physical planning program. At the same time a detailed analysis of actual conditions, carried out locally, permits correction of the higher-level plan.

Thus the whole process of planning is coordinated up and down the hierarchy. The plans of different levels are confronted with one another, which establishes more adequate estimates of the entire national economy.

The evolution of uniting economic and physical planning described so far may be clarified by the diagram in Figure 37. This diagram shows that now five-year economic and physical plans are prepared every five years. At the same time the long-term plans are being revised and extended.

---

[15] See Appendix I, *Spatial Planning Act,* and Chapter 10, for definition and discussion of the scope of regional plans.

[16] Long-term physical plans are prepared "for a period conforming to the period of the long-term national economic plan with particular consideration for the period of the short-term national economic plan." *Spatial Planning Act of 1961,* Art. 3.1.2.

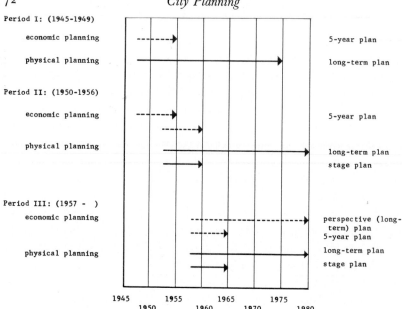

Period I: (1945-1949)

    economic planning   5-year plan

    physical planning   long-term plan

Period II: (1950-1956)

    economic planning   5-year plan

    physical planning   long-term plan
                                                      stage plan

Period III: (1957 -)

    economic planning   perspective (long-
                                                      term) plan
                                                      5-year plan

    physical planning   long-term plan
                                                      stage plan

1945   1955   1965   1975
    1950   1960   1970   1980

Fig. 37. Interrelation of economic and physical planning

LONG-RANGE STUDIES

From this discussion, it might seem that all the original serious divergences between economic and physical planning have been removed. But the problem is not so simple. The main difficulty now lies in the fact that spatial patterns created by man are long-lasting. This is especially true of the planning of settlement systems (urban agglomerations), with long periods of building amortization and even longer periods of amortization of the basic utility network. Even a twenty-year span, long as it is for economic prognosis, cannot be regarded as sufficient when long-lasting basic investments have to be considered. Thus there proved to be a need for studies covering periods of time greater even than that considered by economic perspective planning. It became necessary to introduce another concept into physical planning, namely that of the long-range study.[17]

It was at first suggested that the long-range studies for settlement systems should be prepared for a specified period, for example, for the period of two economic perspective plans. The year 2000 was mentioned

[17] Long-range studies are prepared "for a period overrunning the period set for the long-term national economic plan, with particular attention to the period set for this plan and distinguished from the period of the short-term national economic plan." *Spatial Planning Act of 1961,* Art. 3.1.1.

as the most suitable for that purpose. This method, however, would not give good results, for it would force the planner to establish a city program for the year 2000. The premises on which such a program would be based could never be checked since neither the demographic prognosis nor the over-all balanced economic plan could confirm them.

The method of working out the long-range studies now used in Poland depends not on designing a doubtful and subjective vision of the city of the future, but on an analysis of the consequences of various development possibilities.

The starting point of what in Poland is now called the "threshold theory"[18] was the question: for how long a period should the long-range study be prepared? It should be longer than the period of economic perspective plans; but it is impossible to construct a program for an unlimited time. An answer seems on hand in the territorial limitations which check the spatial development of the city when the number of inhabitants is growing. It is evident that such limitations exist; they can be traced in geographical situations (for example, an island or a valley). Still other limitations result from technological interdependence, especially where various kinds of utility networks are concerned; there are, for instance, definite limits for a sewerage system. When the territorial expansion of the city exceeds these limits, a whole new system has to be introduced. Similarly, there are concrete limits to a water-supply system; even in communications systems such limits can be observed (for instance, in the form of a radius within which the area can be served by a single transportation system).

These limits, or "thresholds," are not absolute. When the city's population is growing, they can be overcome, but only at the relatively high cost of building a new utility network. The "threshold" character of the curve of costs is clearly visible when we take the cost per capita into account.

Figure 38 shows that the cost per capita of each new inhabitant increases disproportionally in comparison with average costs during the period when the threshold is being overcome. This increase is of course compensated later, when new inhabitants can be accommodated without additional costs. But the expected high threshold costs will hold the territorial expansion of the city in the threshold boundaries as long as possible. Therefore, instead of trying to set the period for which the

---

[18] See B. Malisz, *Ekonomika kształtowania miast* [Economics of City Planning], published by the Polish Academy of Sciences, Committee for Space Economy and Regional Planning [Komitet Przestrzennego Zagospodarowania Kraju], Studies, 1964.

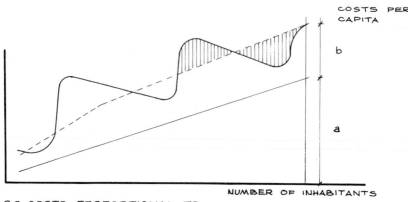

a = COSTS PROPORTIONAL TO
    NUMBER OF INHABITANTS

b = "THRESHOLD" COSTS

Fig. 38. Cost per capita of new inhabitants

long-range study should be prepared, we should concentrate on the years from the next threshold period to the end of the perspective period (at present, the year 1980).

It is possible to define the next threshold for the actual environment of a given city. Using density standards, we can also find the number of inhabitants who can be accommodated within the boundaries of this threshold. Thus we have only to compare this population figure with that of the urban population expected for the year 1980. When the former is much higher than the latter, we need not bother about the long-range study. But when it is lower, it seems advisable to prepare the perspective plan (for the years through 1980) with the coming threshold in view.

When we come to the long-range study itself there are two possibilities: to hold city development within the threshold boundaries or to overcome these boundaries. Choosing the latter opens two more alternatives: to permit the city to develop in a compact form or to propose a decentralized system. A spatial solution must be prepared for each possibility. These alternatives then have to be compared, the criterion being maximum efficiency, that is, relatively minimal costs for a given effect.

It is essential that the chosen variant of the long-range spatial solution be taken into account when preparing the long-range economic plan. Otherwise we may hinder rational city development in the future. But in some cases it is not possible to choose only *one* variant. In these situations the perspective plan has to be more flexible and provide for further development along the lines of either of two possible alternatives of the long-range study. Thus the long-range study should be seen as a method of study which allows us to evaluate the perspective plan in terms of its consequences for further city development. Such studies permit us to determine the spatial conditions which should be observed when preparing the perspective plan.

This briefly outlined method of working out long-range studies has been the subject of experimentation for two years. The results so far show that this method is useful in many ways; in fact it has influenced the whole of the Polish city planning method. Previously a new stage plan was prepared every five years and the long-term physical plan for each city was revised—a tremendous undertaking. The process has now been simplified, thanks to the threshold method. A comprehensive study is prepared for each city and its surrounding environment. This study consists of three main parts: a survey of the physiographical features, and their possible adjustment; a survey of existing land use, from the point of view of changing it; and a threshold study for all kinds of utility networks. Based on these three kinds of research, a map is prepared, showing clearly the city's development priorities. By introducing the established factors which determine the location of the main land-use zones (industry, settlement, and service centers), we obtain a matrix for city development. Now we have only to construct a definite program, for five or twenty years, which can easily be done if we have the directives of the economic plan, and to locate the elements of this program on the matrix. The variant method just described[19] has to be used. This procedure is relatively easy in the majority of cities, but in the largest ones, mathematical techniques are necessary.[20]

Another use of the threshold method appears when urbanization policy is planned. A major problem of the regional plan is to distribute the population increase over the settlement network. As the agricultural population of the countryside is more or less stable, this increase is centered in the towns. The size of population growth in each city is determined by the regional plan, and is based mainly on the distribution of industrial growth and employment within the tertiary sector.[21] Industry may be divided into two types, one dependent on and one not dependent on local raw materials. The latter type may be located

[19] See p. 74.
[20] See p. 69.
[21] Tertiary sector is a notion introduced by Fourastier, covering all nonproductive employment (service, administration, banking and finance, etc.).

in any of a number of cities in accordance with the principle of uniform development of the country. Previous urbanization policy lacked satisfactory criteria for city development. Now, analyses made within the framework of local long-range studies permit us to determine the *development threshold* of a city, that is, the limits beyond which the city should not grow in a given period lest the cost of proper investments be disproportionately high. Regional planning can now make use of the growth limits so calculated for all towns in a given region.

If the anticipated increase in urban population (as a result of natural growth and migration) in a given region is greater than the total threshold capacity of its cities, the threshold must be exceeded in certain cities. The choice is made by selecting those cities where exceeding the threshold will be least expensive. The additional investments in these selected cities should be used as much as possible to accommodate new inhabitants. This procedure seems to fill the gap which has existed so far in studies on the optimal distribution of population. But even in cases where population increase does not exceed the sum of threshold capacity in a given region, it is advisable to transcend the thresholds in certain selected cities. Otherwise, at some future time, *all* the cities within the region will be confronted with a threshold.

We are just beginning to develop these methods for the use of urbanization policy. But in all city planning offices on the voivodship level a process has been introduced which correlates the results of studies made for all cities within the voivodship territory. The city planning offices are now better prepared to be partners of the regional planning authorities. In the dialogue of these two kinds of planning offices seems to lie the essence of a comprehensive planning method.

This brief description of the evolution of city planning methods appears to confirm the thesis proposed at the beginning of this chapter: that the closer planning methods conform to the conditions of the economic system the more successful they will be. As a result of the gradual improvement of its methods, physical planning has become an integral part of the planned economy. This result has found expression in the Spatial Planning Act of 1961.[22]

The Act provides for the integration of physical planning at local, regional, and national levels, while separating the administration of

[22] See Appendix 1.

local planning from the higher levels. The physical planning of the whole country and its regions is treated as an integral part of economic planning, and city and rural planning, for which the Ministry of Building is now responsible, is strictly integrated with economic planning. The law provides for the correlation of physical plans at various levels—the city and rural plans, which are worked out in much greater detail than other plans, however, are to be used as a basis for all decisions concerning land use. They are particularly to determine the conditions which should be met by the implementation plans prepared in all branches of the national economy.

THE BACKGROUND OF SCIENTIFIC RESEARCH

A discussion of the theoretical foundations of city planning will give a better grasp of the planning methods outlined above. The progress made in developing such planning methods resulted chiefly from practical experience. For a long time theory did not catch up with the dynamic tempo of the industrialization and urbanization of the country. Practical city planning was supported in its work by the Institute for Town Planning and Architecture, though this support was chiefly confined to direct help in improvement of city planning workshops. Fundamental studies which might have aided the development of physical planning theory received only little attention. Further development of theory in physical planning clearly depends on scientific studies and generalizations from many branches of knowledge; and the importance of such studies was commonly acknowledged only in the late fifties. At the instigation of various professional groups the Committee for Space Economy and Regional Planning was formed at that time and attached to the praesidium of the Polish Academy of Sciences. From then on, physical planning was considered a separate, complex branch of science.

The Committee includes physical planning theoreticians and representatives of other related branches of social science (mainly geography, economy, and sociology); it initiates and coordinates scientific studies in all these fields. There are four Commissions, each dealing with specific areas: the study of the geographical environment, particularly of physiography, the study of the allocation of productive forces, the study of population and settlement problems, and the study of the problems of the various economic regions of the country.[23]

---

[23] In 1964 these Commissions were reorganized, but the responsibility of the Committee as a whole remained the same.

The Committee's work is confined chiefly to building up scientific foundations for national and regional planning.[24] This provides a background of knowledge and techniques on which to base development of city planning theory and methodology.

Various basic studies are being made under the auspices of the Committee. Those aimed at creating physiographical foundations for physical planning are concerned with finding both existing conditions in the entire country and the changes taking place in natural resources as a result of man's economic activity. The primary purpose of these studies is to build up a scientific foundation for the rational management of natural resources. Other studies relate to the location of productive forces, including the present distribution of industry, the direction of industrial growth, and methods of optimal distribution of the productive forces through proper economic policy. Econometric methods are widely used in these studies. Extensive demographic studies are also in progress. A long monograph on the population of Poland is in preparation. This work will deal with all aspects of the population structure. The great population movements just after World War II and the growing urbanization gave rise to many questions upon which research was necessary. For this research the Committee's task consists mainly of introducing spatial factors into demographic studies.

Research on the settlement network has two branches. One deals with the country's urbanization processes, and the other—because of special problems of our agriculture—with the changing settlement network in rural areas. The studies in this field, like those discussed above, not only concern the actual settlement network and its rate of development, but also aim at the construction of optimal models of this network —adapted, of course, to the specific conditions of a given region. Other problems, such as the economic aspect of the settlement systems, closely connected with the problem of city planning, are also studied. These studies stress the application of techniques for rational decision-making to city planning methods. Much of this development has been discussed in the preceding pages of this chapter. The work on the theory of economic regions aims at a synthesis of these studies. Special consideration is given to techniques for rational delimitation of economic regions based on the activity in them. In this connection, extensive research is being carried out on the regional distribution of the production and

[24] The Institute for Town Planning and Architecture carries out research particularly related to problems of urban planning.

consumption of the national income. The analysis of personal income appears to be an important key to the rational distribution of investment in the planning of economic development.

Last are equally important and progressively more extensive investigations of the sociological consequences of industrialization and the expansion of the urban style of life. These phenomena are of considerable importance in Poland where the dynamic processes of growth call for particular attention to the biological and cultural development of man.

All the studies mentioned here seem to open new prospects for the development of physical planning. This expansion of the field, both in breadth and in depth, will surely lead to still further developments and new conceptions of city planning.

The Changing Shape of Polish Cities

The creation of a model for a town of the future has been the main problem to occupy the minds and engage the efforts of people concerned with the development of contemporary city planning. That is why, when the results of city planning are considered, we are chiefly interested in the new shape which the towns in a given country are taking. In this respect there is no doubt that Polish towns are undergoing extensive transformations. It is sufficient to recall that from 1945 to 1960 the urban population almost doubled. During the next fifteen years it will become three times the size it was at the end of the war. Concentration, of course, results in an even greater rate of growth in the larger cities.

The economic function and social character of our towns have become fundamentally different since the end of the war. The change has come about as a result of the application of principles of the socioeconomic system and as a result of the trend and rate of development of the national economy. The former division into rich and poor districts has entirely disappeared from the cities. The policy of industrializing the nation has caused a remarkable transformation in the role and functions of many towns. Small neglected towns, once based only on small private businesses, have often become industrial centers, spreading their influence over a considerable area. Towns with a one-sided profile based on a single industry or administrative service are today becoming centers of differentiated economic and social functions. In consequence, important changes can be seen in the spatial structure of towns. Against the background of rapid urbanization the shape of the *new* town is becoming increasingly clear.

SPATIAL AND STRUCTURAL CHANGES THROUGH IMPROVED
CONTROL OF LAND USE

One of the decisive features of town structure is the way in which the
town grows and the use it makes of adjoining land. Before the war, towns
in Poland grew without the control of adequate plans because the preparation and implementation of a city plan depended on the good will of
local authorities. Even with a plan, subdivision and development of land
adjoining the area embraced by the plan could be halted or restricted
only if appropriate extensions of the plan were prepared and approved
within two years. This subjected the hinterland of the towns to land
speculation on an enormous scale. Even with an approved master plan
there was no control of building activities within the city limits. The land
was developed in a haphazard pattern which did not allow appropriate
and economically concentrated investment.

In contrast, present legislation requires all towns and rural communities to have a master plan. By 1964 plans had been drawn up for all
towns and rural districts. Every five years new stage plans will be prepared and the long-term plans revised. The city plan constitutes the basis
for every kind of spatial decision and, first of all, for the location of land
use. In this way the cities of modern Poland can be enlarged and
extended according to economic programs and to the intention of the
physical plan. The threshold analysis mentioned above,[25] and the preparation of joint plans for conurbations, will aid decisions as to the time
at which a growing urban agglomeration should be decentralized.

Changes in the size of towns and settlement systems are accompanied
by important transformations in the internal structure of particular
land-use zones. The new shape of Polish towns can be seen above all in
the location of industrial sites. A heritage from the past was the high
degree of mixed use to which urban land had been put. In particular,
industrial plants often intruded into residential districts and even into
the central part of the town.

At present, master plans generally provide for the zoning of industrial
areas according to the degree to which the industries are either a nuisance to or harmful to the surroundings. New industry in the towns falls
in one of four general categories:

(1) The biggest industrial works (large iron and steel mills, chemical works, oil refineries) are complexes of related activities built under

[25] See pp. 73–76.

the direction of one general plan. The location of such a complex is the subject of comprehensive economic and city planning studies. The area of an actual industrial complex is, of course, isolated from the residential districts by sufficiently wide green belts. The construction of a new complex always involves significant enlargement and transformation of a city, as in the case of the Nowa Huta foundry complex, the chemical combine at Oświęcim, the big iron and steel works at Częstochowa, and the large refinery combine now being constructed at Płock. These changes consist mainly in the development of the transportation system, the creation of new residential districts, and the improvement of municipal service standards and other facilities.

(2) The second category of industry-grouping is the city-industrial district. These districts include many different types of enterprises only loosely tied together as far as their production cycle and use of common equipment are concerned. In such cases a joint power, water-supply, and sewerage-disposal system is usually organized, while the employees of the various plants benefit from a common social service center. A large number of districts have been built on this basis in Warsaw, Kraków, Olsztyn, Wrocław, and many other cities—not to mention the harbor and industrial districts in Szczecin, Gdańsk, and Gdynia.

(3) The third type of industrial group—the industrial set—differs from the city industrial districts only in being of a smaller size.

(4) The final category consists of small-scale industrial and handicraft enterprises located in residential districts. This locating is hardly a nuisance to the inhabitants; it provides nearby employment (especially important for women) and relieves the municipal transportation system.

The relocation of existing obsolete and noxious plants has, of course, been more difficult. Nevertheless, some efforts have been made in this field in Upper Silesia, Łódź, and other old industrial districts.

Residential zoning has progressed greatly in recent years. The prewar method of zoning residential areas depended on the market price of real estate: hence the formerly typical picture of a town tightly built up in the center and gradually becoming more open toward the outskirts. The interrelationship of residential zones was poor and not functional; common services were rather scarce and located haphazardly.

In the present system the difference in monetary land values and rents has ceased to be a factor in land use. Intensity of development, however, is still controlled by economic premises. Sites conveniently located from the viewpoint of communication and easy to equip with technical and sanitation facilities must be as fully utilized as possible. The level of development is set by housing standards based on per capita requirements for green space and standards of service facilities.

An important and beneficial feature of postwar building has been the ability to plan a residential area as a unit, rather than in terms of single plots. This method allows for the maintenance of proper housing conditions as well as for consistency of architectural design. Although architecture from the period 1945–1956 often seems stiff, monotonous, and old-fashioned, living conditions in the new districts are incomparably better than they were in the cities of the past. Better housing design is evident in newer developments all over the country.

The planned development of green spaces is also important in changing internal city structure. In the city of the first half of the twentieth century greenery was barely tolerated. It was subject to encroachment from all types of urban activities. In prewar Warsaw the index was half a square meter of park per inhabitant. The present standard for green spaces in towns varies from 10 to 15 square meters per inhabitant, not counting the natural open spaces. In many cities parks, green belts, and other forms of planting are being introduced: in Warsaw, which has radically changed in this respect, in Poznań, famous for its recently completed green-belt system, and in the Upper Silesian conurbation, where three large park systems have been built (one of them, the Central Park in Katowice, covering an area of 600 hectares).

CHANGES IN THE TRANSPORTATION NETWORK

The municipal transportation system is becoming the main element of the redevelopment of towns throughout the world. In most Western countries, however, the emphasis seems to be on ensuring freedom of movement for cars. In this, Poland cannot boast of especially striking novelties, as the rate of automobile ownership is only beginning to rise. Nevertheless, there is a remarkable improvement in the network of roads throughout the entire country, and modern arterial systems have been introduced in many towns. In larger cities limited access routes are being built. Most city planning schemes provide for the gradual reconstruction of major thoroughfares and for the reservation of land to reconstruct the traffic system.

In view of rapidly growing transport needs, much greater emphasis is being put on the problem of urban public transportation. For all larger cities and especially for conurbations comprehensive transportation studies are being prepared as an integral element of the master plan.

One of the first large-scale undertakings of this type carried out in Poland was a competition for a new municipal transportation system for the Warsaw agglomeration.

An important problem in this connection is how much the state railway system should be used in municipal transportation facilities. In Warsaw, where the entire area has been converted to electricity over a radius of dozens of miles, the railway system will provide most of the regional transportation needs, while municipal transport will be provided by streetcars and buses. The master plan provides for the construction before 1975 of a metropolitan rail line which will constitute the beginning of a new rapid transit system. Outside Warsaw, in the Upper Silesian Industrial District, and in the harbor conurbation of Gdańsk-Gdynia, the electric railway lines carry a significant portion of local transportation. The electrification of railroad networks now going on all over the country will allow for the gradual decentralization of the large cities of Wrocław, Poznań, Kraków, and Łódź.

REDEVELOPMENT OF CENTRAL CITIES

The renewal of midtown areas completes the transformation of town structure. Even the greatest expansion of the outskirts of a town does not make as strong an impression as radical redevelopment of its central area —one of the most difficult tasks of city renewal.

The devastation of Polish cities during World War II in many instances aided the reconstruction of obsolete central areas. The principal example of this situation is provided by Warsaw. The possibility of radical redevelopment fascinated Polish architects in the immediate postwar period. Studies started in 1945 by the late Maciej Nowicki were continued until very recently. Many competitions for a solution to the problem posed by the center of Warsaw were held. The emphasis on current rather than long-term needs, however, led to many functional mistakes and errors in design. Despite these, central Warsaw is not only completely new but also of incomparably higher quality in terms of function and composition. Far from completion, the core of the city is still under construction; and new studies are being made to improve the midtown area during the period of the long-range study.

The list of cities where war devastation gave rise to complete reconstruction of the central area is long. In Gdańsk, Wrocław, Szczecin, and many medium-sized and smaller towns, the historical nucleus of the city has been rebuilt and the structures of the central area improved.

There is another group of cities where total redevelopment has been carried out. This group consists of towns which had not acquired central districts in the architectural sense, even though they had a population of some tens of thousands. The low, unattractive groups of buildings in towns such as Białystok and Częstochowa could scarcely claim the right to be called midtown districts. The processes of industrialization in such towns offered an opportunity not only for town extension but also for the creation of new service centers and comprehensive reconstruction.

A third group of cities is experiencing genuine difficulties in the redevelopment of their central areas. They are the big towns in which densely constructed obsolete buildings must be demolished to make room for new constructions. Limited economic possibilities and particularly the problems of meeting the growing need for housing have not yet permitted any extensive redevelopment of these areas. Projects carried out in the Upper Silesian Industrial District, in Łódź, Bydgoszcz, and other towns are fragmentary. The difficulty in redeveloping such areas lies in the fact that decongestion and the creation of decent housing conditions and appropriate service facilities will require rehousing the population of the affected areas. The social and even the economic needs for such renewal make the problem important. A few research studies aimed at the solution of this problem are under way to find the balance between economic possibilities and social needs.

CHAPTER 3

Development of the General Plan of Warsaw

STANISLAW DZIEWULSKI

History of Warsaw's Development through 1945

IN THE fourteenth century Warsaw was a small town on the left-bank escarpment of the Vistula. At the end of the sixteenth century it became the capital of Poland. A period of rapid development followed, most significantly seen in the extension of the residences of church dignitaries, magnates, and gentry beyond the congested area within the town walls. The new growth spread southeasterly along the escarpment.

Building activity reached its height in Warsaw in the latter half of the eighteenth century when Poland experienced its first period of major economic development. The Second Partition of Poland in 1793 halted the development of the town. After the formation of a semi-independent Polish state in 1815, a period of intensive economic development opened up considerable possibilities of expansion for Warsaw. This propitious period came abruptly to an end with the defeat of the November Uprising (1830–1831). The development of Warsaw, which for some time afterward was a provincial town of Tsarist Russia, had once more been impeded.

In the second half of the nineteenth century Warsaw grew in a manner typical of cities undergoing rapid industrialization. The speculative building of tenement houses progressively occupied all vacant land, including the Powisle district of Warsaw along the Vistula. Here, this speculative growth ruined the fine architectural appearance and advantages of the natural site which the district owed to its location on a high escarpment of the river. Between 1864 and 1914 Warsaw's population rose from 223,000 to 885,000. World War I, however, halted the growth of the city and caused a 25 per cent decline in its population.

The twenty-year interwar period of Poland's independence (1919–

1939) was marked by gradually increasing economic prosperity accompanied by further speculation in land and buildings, chaotic growth of residential, commercial, and industrial construction, and further widening of social and economic disparities in living standards. The housing conditions of the majority of the population steadily deteriorated. Population density in certain parts of the city's central district exceeded 2,000 per hectare. In 1939 small one- and two-room flats represented some 70 per cent of the total number of apartments.[1] In August, 1939, Warsaw had 1,307,000 inhabitants, an increase of 370,000 in population during the interwar period, mainly as a result of migration.

The city had grown in a generally concentric manner. Since the second half of the nineteenth century there had been radical development of suburbs along the railway lines. Most of the suburbs were inhabited by people of lower economic status than those who settled in the central city. The suburbs were usually built without plan for basic utilities and community services, and the selection of an area for development was decided by private speculative enterprise. This type of development continued until the outbreak of World War II.

In August, 1944, toward the end of the Nazi occupation of Poland, the Warsaw Uprising took place. After its defeat, the Nazis drove the entire population from that part of the city on the left bank of the Vistula and began systematically to destroy it. Of the total buildings on the left bank of Warsaw, only 13 per cent avoided destruction and only 5 per cent were left completely intact. Of the 595,000 dwelling rooms which existed in 1939 only 165,000 habitable rooms remained. Nine-tenths of the prewar total of 8 million cubic meters of industrial buildings was destroyed. Apart from the few public facilities which continued to operate in the Praga (right bank) district, the social, economic, and technical life of the city was brought to a standstill. The urban traffic system was paralyzed. All bridges were destroyed. The water-supply, sewerage, electric, and gas systems were damaged in various degrees. None was capable of normal operation at the time the city was liberated by Russian and Polish forces. On the day of its liberation, January 17, 1944, Warsaw had about 160,000 inhabitants. By May 15, 1945, the census recorded a population of 378,000, and one year after the liberation the city had 468,000 inhabitants.

---

[1] In one-room flats the density was 3.8 persons to a room, in three-room flats 1.6 persons to a room, and in six-room flats 0.9 persons to a room. As many as 46 per cent of dwelling houses had no sewerage installations, and 25 per cent neither sewerage, water-supply, electricity, nor gas systems.

CITY CENTER, RESIDENTIAL AREAS

CITY CENTER, RESIDENTIAL
AREA DESTROYED IN 1944

INDUSTRIAL AREAS

GREEN REGULATED AREAS

INDUSTRIAL AREAS
DESTROYED IN 1944

Map 7. Warsaw, destruction during 1939–1944

87

Phases of Development of the General Plan

In the interwar period the activities of Warsaw's Planning Department had been limited to the area confined within the city limits. The area outside the city proper was covered only by the design studies of the Regional Planning Office of Warsaw, an advisory body composed of a few city planners with radical views and no power to act in the field. With the Occupation, secret planning studies of Warsaw which were more comprehensive and more progressive were begun.

EARLY POSTWAR PLANNING

The Uprising put an end to this planning work, but as soon as the city planners found themselves in the Warsaw Reconstruction Office after liberation, they reached for the design studies made during the Occupation. A conflict developed between the theoretical concept of planning and the economic and social reality. The terrifying destruction of the town had given priceless value to every remaining house, every tumble-down shelter, and every dwelling room. It was impossible, despite the planners' profound conviction of the correctness of the redevelopment plan, to demand that accidentally preserved houses be demolished or to prohibit reconstruction of partially destroyed buildings.

At that time the efforts of the planners were twofold: on the one hand, the existing plan was being modified to make it more realistic, while retaining its fundamental premises; on the other hand, a day-by-day struggle was being waged for controlled implementation of the plan, which boiled down, in the initial period at least, to refusing the reconstruction of extensively damaged and wrongly located buildings.

In the initial years after liberation the basic concept of the plan had been influenced by the design studies from the period of the Occupation. Then, the plan was so extensively based on the principle of dispersed development that the city was identified with the Warsaw metropolitan area. The idea of "Greater Warsaw," with an area larger than that confined by the present administrative boundaries, however, had been introduced in late 1945 and early 1946.

The system of planned economy, previously unknown in Poland, was of decisive importance in the reconstruction and replanning of the city. It provided for the concentration of investment on a few projects during definite periods of time rather than dissipating it on thousands of small, relatively ineffective projects with vague time limits. A striking manifestation of the new system was the completion in 1949—that is, in the period still rather primitive technologically—of the so-called "East-

West Thoroughfare." This is an arterial road, 6 kilometers long, with a bridge spanning the Vistula, to serve the greater part of the area of several districts. It radically improved the existing traffic system.

DEVELOPMENT OF STAGE PLANS

According to the accepted practice of prewar town planning, only a long-term plan had been drawn up in the immediate years following liberation. A need for more precise programing of capital improvements finally led to the creation of stage plans covering the five-year periods of economic planning. The general directives of the national Six-Year Plan at the end of 1948 and the beginning of 1949 provided this impetus for a stage plan for Warsaw, the first of its kind in the history of Polish urban planning.

In 1958–1959 work began on a five-year stage plan covering the period from 1961 to 1965. This led to the development of a practical method of drafting stage plans, the primary feature of which was direct cooperation with the Municipal Economic Planning Committee, which resulted in erasing the distinction between the physical stage plan and the economic stage plan. A single plan was prepared to represent a reasonable compromise between existing needs and possibilities.

After preparation of an over-all stage plan in a series of maps scaled at 1 : 20,000, more detailed plans of individual districts were mapped at a scale of 1 : 5000. The outstanding advantage of these district plans was the linking of elements of the stage and long-term plans, by providing for suitable land reserves in each district for development projects unattainable in the 1961–1965 period, but possible and essential in later periods. In January, 1961, the district stage plans scaled at 1 : 5000, supplemented by a number of over-all sketch plans at a scale of 1 : 20,000, were passed by the Committee for Building, City planning, and Architecture and approved by the Municipal People's Council with a recommendation that the long-term plan for the entire Warsaw metropolitan area be reworked in accordance with them.

LONG-RANGE STUDY

This decision coincided with a basic change in city planning methodology: apart from the long-term physical plan (based on the perspective national economic plan, 1960–1980) new laws on physical planning now provided for the preparation of a "long-range study" for still longer periods.[2] Since it was not possible to set up a program for

[2] See Appendix I, Art. 3.1.1.

CITY CENTERS
RESIDENTIAL AREAS   INDUSTRIAL AREAS   GREEN OPEN SPACES

Map 8. Warsaw, long-term plan

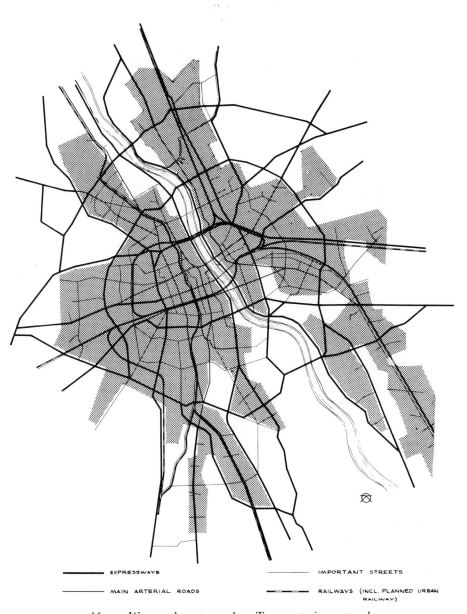

EXPRESSWAYS

IMPORTANT STREETS

MAIN ARTERIAL ROADS

RAILWAYS (INCL. PLANNED URBAN RAILWAY)

Map 9. Warsaw, long-term plan: Transportation network

a period longer than twenty years, such a study sets no dates; instead it constitutes a summary of analyses on the development possibilities of a city (or urban agglomeration) beyond 1980. The following section of this article describes the preliminary results of the work on the "long-range study" for the Warsaw Conurbation.

Long-range Study for the Warsaw Conurbation

The following discussion is divided into four main parts. The first deals with determining the development possibilities of the Conurbation's area from a technoeconomic point of view; the second with premises concerning the inhabitants' living conditions after 1980; the third is devoted to the directives for Warsaw's urban structure; and the fourth discusses the preparation, on the basis of the above-mentioned elements, of several alternatives for the long-range plan.

DEVELOPMENT POTENTIAL

The development potential of every urban body depends to a large degree on the city's physical environment. When speaking about that environment, we understand it as the total of the natural features of the terrain and those resulting from the many-sided activity of man.

Analysis of the physical environment gives several indications about the desirability of designating land for various urban uses. The following are considered the most important indications for development of the Warsaw Conurbation:

(1) It is desirable that urban construction reach first the areas on the high terrace of the left bank of the Vistula, then those on the low terrace of the right bank, and finally, those in certain higher parts of the Vistula valley.

(2) It is also desirable to start urban development on areas situated close to the great rivers—the Vistula and the Bug—in view of the favorable climate and landscape of such lands adjacent to river terraces and valleys.

(3) It is undesirable to build on forest-covered areas or those physiographically suitable for afforestation. It is also undesirable to build on permanently soaked ground and on land particularly appropriate for agricultural purposes.

The general indications, based on the natural properties of the environment, are followed by technical indications. In this group, those pertaining to water economy are most closely linked with the natural environment.

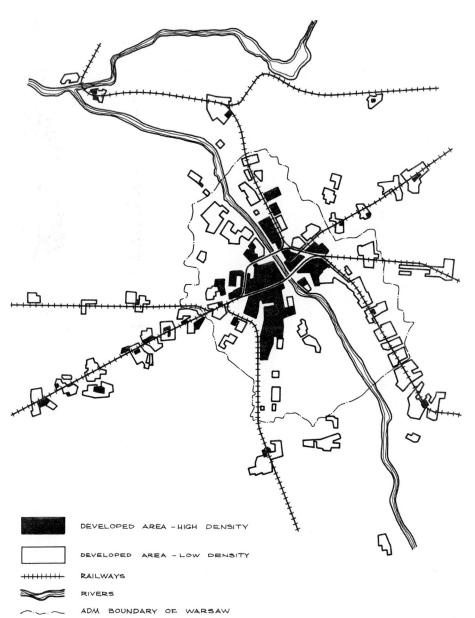

DEVELOPED AREA – HIGH DENSITY

DEVELOPED AREA – LOW DENSITY

RAILWAYS

RIVERS

ADM BOUNDARY OF WARSAW

Map 10. Warsaw Conurbation Development Area, 1960

The subsoil water resources of the Warsaw Conurbation area are rather modest if compared with the demand by today's population of over one million. The surface water resources are quite large, and 90 per cent comes from the Vistula and Bug rivers. Preliminary estimates, calculated in terms of mean future consumption, give grounds to assume the possibility of water supply for 3,200,000 to 3,800,000 inhabitants. This shows that the water resources are nevertheless limited; in several decades the limitation may become a crucial problem to the further development of the Warsaw Conurbation.

Advanced technological studies into the possibilities of constructing new water-intakes on the Bug and Vistula rivers permit us to determine the probable routes of the mains supplying the city with water from those intakes. The area concerned may be divided, in a preliminary layout, into the part situated near the planned mains and, hence, easier to supply with water, and that farther away, liable to present difficulties in respect to supply. These technical thresholds, though determined in a quite general way, clearly indicate the sound development possibilities —as far as water supply is concerned—of the areas situated south of Warsaw, on the left bank of the Vistula, and of those on the right bank, north of the capital.

The problem of the possibilities for the development of sewerage systems is more involved. The extensively developed systems on the left and right banks of the Vistula provide strong development possibilities for the large areas adjacent to those now covered by the sewerage network. The separate sewerage systems of the numerous suburbs already under construction or planned for the near future determine nearby development possibilities. Thus the influence on development of existing utilities and those to be constructed in the years to come is a greater factor than water supply.

Beyond the range of those existing or planned facilities, two factors determine the possibility of providing a sewerage system for a given area. One is the location of waste water receivers of adequate capacity. This directs attention to the possibilities for development offered by the Vistula and Bug valleys. Obviously, location of the future sewage outfall will depend to a large extent on the location of water-intakes. The second factor is the configuration of the terrain. It may be generally stated that it is difficult to sewer completely flat land, and that land with even a small slope is usually much easier to use.

Another important technical question determining the development possibilities of the Warsaw Conurbation is that of transportation. Al-

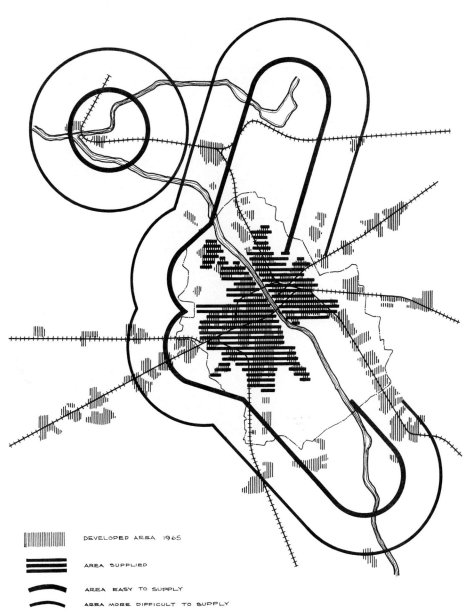

DEVELOPED AREA 1965

AREA SUPPLIED

AREA EASY TO SUPPLY

AREA MORE DIFFICULT TO SUPPLY

Map 11. Warsaw Conurbation water supply

95

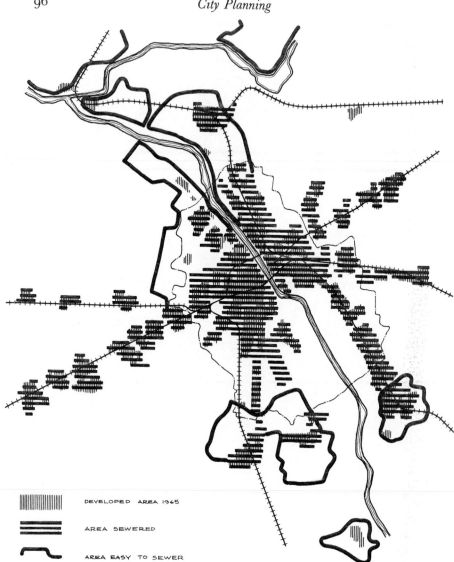

DEVELOPED AREA 1965

AREA SEWERED

AREA EASY TO SEWER

Map 12. Warsaw Conurbation sewerage

though much less closely connected with the natural properties of the environment, it seems to be of even greater importance to urban development. The extensive area of the Conurbation makes passenger transportation, as in other big agglomerations, the key technical problem. Yet the existing patterns of the urban transportation system and the railway network contain large reserves for extending transportation. To estimate those reserves correctly for the long-range study, it is necessary to assume that the two systems will be thoroughly modernized. This modernization will aim at relocating streetcar lines in separate lanes— which is the basic condition for enhancing their efficiency—and at greatly increasing the operational capacity of certain bus lines. Particular difficulties are encountered in determining the scope of the indispensable modernization of the road system in view of the possibility of a

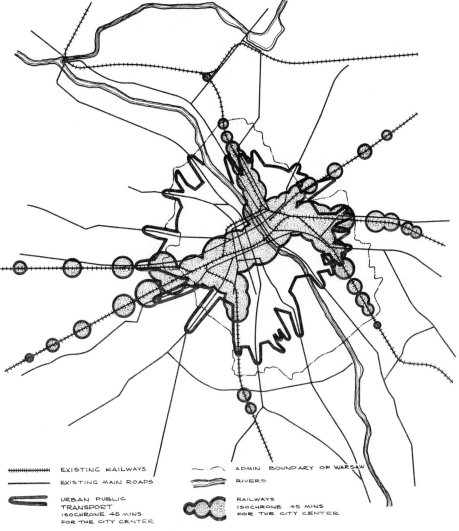

EXISTING RAILWAYS

EXISTING MAIN ROADS

URBAN PUBLIC
TRANSPORT
ISOCHRONE 45 MINS
FOR THE CITY CENTER

ADMIN BOUNDARY OF WARSAW

RIVERS

RAILWAYS
ISOCHRONE 45 MINS
FOR THE CITY CENTER

Map 13. Warsaw Conurbation public transportation

sizable increase in automobile traffic. Whatever the actual scope of this modernization, it must provide for a separate system of expressways with a belt-arterial road around the central districts and a dozen or so outbound regional and national roads of various classes. Construction of a large number of overpasses will also be indispensable.

The possibilities of enhancing the efficiency of the railway system are much broader. The essential difference between the development possibilities of the urban transportation system and those of the railway system is that the former may be modernized by increasing the number of lines, thus making its network denser, while the latter's operation may be expanded mainly along already existing lines and through technological changes to increase its capacity and speed. Construction of a new railway line would always be a typical technical threshold, very expensive, though opening up new development prospects.

Among other technical issues that determine certain possibilities for the growth of the Warsaw Conurbation, we should mention the power industry, although its significance does not equal that of water economy and transportation. For the next twenty years thermoelectric power stations will play the main part. The operational area of such plants already in existence and of the two or three more which will doubtless prove necessary in the perspective period (in the east, west, and, maybe, also in the north) will be highly important in selecting land for urban construction. Yet in view of the assumption that future power supply is to be based on electric current, development trends will not depend on the location of the sources of energy.

These technical deliberations present but one facet of the problem of development possibilities and limitations. The second facet is the feasibility of redeveloping existing built-up areas. In the city planning schemes prepared so far, the problem has not been met decisively. The suggestion of caution in planning demolition of wrongly located buildings or complexes has been all too strong. Such caution, rather justified in the case of stage plans, has often proved erroneous in the long-term ones. The long-range study demands a bold approach to the problem.

A cautiously prepared program for a gradual increase in housing construction would give the year 2000 (hypothetically adopted) almost 50 per cent more flats than assumed for 1980 and would also satisfy the needs for housing any projected future population of the Warsaw Conurbation area. Hypothetically, this means the possibility of eliminating by the year 2000 all the buildings there today; of course, there is no need for such a drastic proposal. Yet for analyses for the long-range study this point of view permits us to reject reservations against the elimination of existing urban development wherever such action is technically and functionally justified.

To grasp the whole of the development possibilities discussed above, we have plotted on a map scaled at 1:50,000 the boundaries of those areas more or less easy to provide with basic utilities. The utilities include the sewage-treatment plants on the left and right banks of the Vistula, water-intakes, and so forth. The first group of developable areas comprises those within the reach of existing utility networks or networks to be constructed by 1965. The second group is on land within the service areas of utility networks planned for construction after 1965, extensions of existing networks, or utilities easily constructed independently of the other systems.

The problem of transportation has been tackled in a different manner. Assuming that travel to work should not exceed 45 minutes and knowing that the city center of Warsaw will remain the center of gravity for the majority of the area's commuters, planners adopted the diagram of the 45-minute isochrone as the limit of the area to be "duly served" by urban transportation. For the urban transportation system this isochrone has been schematically plotted around the center, while for the railway system it has been plotted only along existing lines. The conviction was that the choice of possible new directions for railway lines could be made only after a thorough study of the future structural pattern of the urban system.

A complex picture of future developable areas was derived by plotting on one map all these limit lines, even though they were restricted to a few major kinds of technical equipment. To reach some policy decisions, planners plotted the same lines on another map and color-coded areas according to the ease of providing them with water-supply system, sewerage system, and thermal energy. Areas situated within and beyond the 45-minute isochrone were also differentiated on this map. The "synthesis of development possibilities" thus obtained provides more than a dozen alternative plans. None could be accepted as the exponent of the future reach of developed areas without further investigation. Only with a concept of the structure of the whole conurbation may the practical value of such alternatives be determined.

PREMISES OF THE LONG-RANGE STUDY

The main difficulty in formulating these premises was the need to envision the phenomena that would exist in a future more distant than 1980. Another difficulty lay in the inability to define the extent of the period we were actually concerned with. Since every alternative plan implied a different population size, each obviously referred to a different period in the future. To simplify this problem, we adopted as the starting point for particular questions the development trends indicated in the economic perspective plan. It has generally been assumed that these trends would persist during the decades after 1980.

Warsaw will be, above all, a capital city. In it the functions typical of the center of state administration will be performed. The city will bear responsibility for an increasing number of social, economic, political, scientific, and artistic institutions of both national and international importance. Account will have to be taken of the prospect of organizing various periodical events on a national, European, or even global scale.

Such a broad concept of Warsaw's development as the capital city should not permit the city to monopolize any function of social life to the detriment of other urban centers in this country. Yet such development makes it imperative to ensure frequent visits to Warsaw by people from throughout Poland and from abroad. This, in turn, necessitates a major enhancement of the present program of various social services and increases the desirability of expanding the city's interurban transportation system to equal the most important in central-eastern Europe.

In view of their links and the interest displayed in them by both inhabitants and visitors, the facilities connected with Warsaw's functions as the capital must be concentrated mainly in the city center. Hence, there is a need to reserve much larger areas for expansion of the center and also to provide more efficient transportation than that of a city center serving mainly its own inhabitants.

The basic structural elements of the plan are the delimitation of three huge plots of land intended to meet the inhabitants' needs for *housing, work,* and *recreation.* The fourth, strictly connected with the preceding ones, will be the areas satisfying needs for *social life* and *services.* A prerequisite to linking all these groups is an efficient *transportation system.* It is precisely for this reason that transportation comes to the fore of all the technical problems.

The interrelationship of the main areas of land, which is the essence of the plan, is dictated by the following basic directives: (1) ensuring optimum conditions for the psychological and biological life of the inhabitants; (2) providing the most economical solutions; and (3) conforming to the basic properties of the natural environment.

The basic assumption about future conditions of life should provide for a curtailment of working time and of that used for journeys to work, or lost as a result of other difficulties involved in the life of a major city.

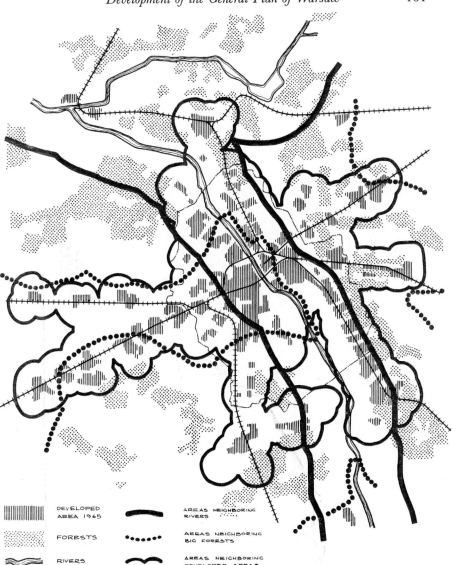

DEVELOPED AREA 1965		AREAS NEIGHBORING RIVERS	
FORESTS		AREAS NEIGHBORING BIG FORESTS	
RIVERS		AREAS NEIGHBORING DEVELOPED AREAS	

Map 14. Warsaw Conurbation recreation potential

It is to be assumed that working time will be reduced to six hours a day, with two days off per week. The most important consequence of this assumption of increased leisure time will be a wide expansion of recreation grounds and an increase in institutions fostering cultural life and scientific interests and providing entertainment. One of the primary problems to be tackled by the plan should be that of the convenient location of, and easy access to, various types of recreation grounds with regard to the location of the main housing districts.

An equally important postulate concerning the inhabitants' conditions of life is assurance of the possibility to utilize fully their vocational qualifications and to satisfy their personal interests. This calls for ease in changing one's place of employment, as well as of residence, and to obtain the most convenient distance between the two.

The economic merits of solutions proposed by the long-range study should be tested for their full utilization of existing basic technical equipment (or that to be constructed by 1965) and, also, for the thorough replacement of existing equipment wherever obviously advantageous for future development.

Yet even such a general principle of economic advantage must not lead to solutions opposed to the basic premises of correct functional structure, which will provide for the optimum living conditions. An accurate determination of the economic advantages of the proposed solutions will be possible only in light of the long-term plan, based on the previously prepared long-range study.

Consonance with the principal properties of the natural environment is significant in that it allows in the plan for the permanent climatic and technical effects of that environment, and ensures harmony between the cityscape and the natural features of the landscape. Here the basic postulate would be incorporation of the Vistula valley into the design of the whole urban area.

STRUCTURE OF THE WARSAW CONURBATION

Deliberations on the correct structural pattern began with the fact that Warsaw had long been the center of a vast conurbation with a radius of some 30 to 40 kilometers. The links between the town and its suburban zone are exceptionally strong. The inhabitants of this zone supply over one-fifth of the labor force in Warsaw. Both regional and national plans hypothesize that by 1980 the Warsaw Conurbation will accommodate some 2,500,000 inhabitants. At the same time, according to the City Planning Office, no more than 1,500,000 can be housed within Warsaw's present administrative boundaries in compliance with the premises of the long-range study. The comparison of these two views leads to the fundamental conclusion that not only the city of Warsaw but the whole Conurbation will be undergoing a process of extremely intensive urbanization.

The pattern of nineteenth-century Warsaw already revealed quite distinct strips of built-up areas, converging toward the center. This phenomenon resulted partly from spontaneous development along radial roads and partly from the distribution of tracts of soaked and sandy land, unsuitable for building purposes. The second half of the nineteenth century saw the origins of a process, highly characteristic of big European cities, of rapid growth of suburbs and shanty-towns on the outskirts. As they spread along the railway lines, these settlements became extensions of the strips of urban development. Finally, the third stage of the process was the development of semi-independent towns and villages along the same railway lines still farther from Warsaw.

These settlement processes in the rise of the Warsaw Conurbation gave it a characteristic radial pattern, which constitutes the major basic structure of both the city of Warsaw and the whole Conurbation. The radial pattern predetermines the fundamental arrangement of the urban body, its basic economic structure. It ensures consonance with postulates for public health and well-being by providing for the penetration of green belts toward the center of the city, giving necessary ventilation to the intensively built-up areas. Another advantage of the pattern consists in the safeguarding of vast stretches of agricultural and forest-covered land between the strips of suburban districts and settlements. Thus, for the traditional town as well as for a large agglomeration, the radial pattern guarantees maintenance of the biologically indispensable balance between built-up and open areas.

The first premise for the spatial structure envisaged by the Warsaw Conurbation plan is maintenance and consistent development of the radial pattern. What is the extent to which this radial pattern may be further developed? Analysis of the geographical environment and several design studies have led to the conclusion that, besides the fully developed strips on the left bank of the Vistula, there are two other strips not yet developed as far as the city limits, though development could extend much farther. These are the strips situated along the escarpment of the Vistula valley, northwest and southeast of the city center. Lack of a railway line running in this direction has so far been the main factor curbing development of these areas, which are most attractive in regard to health, technical conditions, and landscape.

Besides these two strips, the areas on the left bank offer the possibility of shaping—in the radial pattern—only three other new belts: to the west (at the southern edge of a large tract of woods called the Kampinos Forest), to the southwest, and to the south (along the Warsaw—Krakow railway line). On the right bank of the Vistula this structural principle permits only extension of the existing strips of development, with no room for new ones except a small strip on the river, just south of the city. Several design studies have led to the conclusion that attempts to form other strips of development would lead to their amalgamation into vast built-up complexes and, ultimately, in the disappearance of the radial pattern.

Two kinds of development are occurring simultaneously in the Warsaw Conurbation. One is the expansion of the city outward from its center by consecutive development of the strips, one district directly followed by another. In some cases the new districts fill undeveloped stretches of land between the older areas and nearby suburban settlements. The second type of development consists in the expansion of suburban settlements farther out from the city. While the first type of development leads to further accretion of the condensed city, the second aims at consolidating the scattered pattern characteristic of the entire outer zone of the Warsaw Conurbation. Establishing a balance between these two trends is a crucial problem of the plan. To solve it, the following mode of reasoning has been adopted.

In the life of every big city, journeys to work assume particular importance. The loss of time involved is a major irritant to the inhabitants but it is extremely difficult to eliminate. The greater the concentration of employment within the town, the more acute the problem. Warsaw is a city with an extremely strong concentration of employment. The number of establishments in the central districts is expected to amount to some 340,000 by 1965, while those in surrounding industrial districts will number about 120,000. In a few years' time the central conglomeration of the places of employment will have exceeded 450,000.

No particularly large new work district is programed for the Warsaw Conurbation. The long-range study assumes that the central concentration will continue to be dominant in the metropolitan structure. The plan for development should not perpetuate the existing wide dispersal of residences of people working in the central area. A correctly devised plan should enable those people to find dwellings not too far from the central conglomeration of workplaces. Yet it is not easy to determine what distance from the place of residence becomes too great. Actually, it is not the distance as such that matters, but the time consumed by daily travel to and from work. From our own experience and observation of the pattern of journeys to work in large towns, we found that a travel time of less than half an hour is acceptable, whereas travel times of over 45 minutes are burdensome. Journeys exceeding 45 minutes, however, are a frequent phenomenon in many cities the world over.

In a well-designed district, only a part of the working population should travel to distant workplaces. The remaining part should have at their disposal various types of on-the-spot employment, within walking distance of their residences. Thus, persons employed in the central conglomeration of workplaces should constitute but part of the total number of vocationally active people in the neighboring districts.

If we were able to put into the long-range study, the number of workplaces in the central conglomeration, then, following the above-mentioned principle, we would also be able to determine the minimum population within the Warsaw Conurbation's central area, or "condensed city." Taking into account various changes which will have taken place within the central conglomeration of workplaces, we may set the minimum population at some two million people.

On the principle of reducing journeys to work to 45 minutes, the isochrone of those 45-minute trips to the city center has been recognized as covering the "central area" of the Warsaw Conurbation. Similar isochrones for the industrial districts have been treated as controls. The distribution of those districts around the core district, more or less the same distance from it, makes the core of the urban pattern most cohesive, not only for the city center, but also for the industrial districts. Under the urban scheme thus suggested and comprised within the 45-minute isochrone, an overwhelming majority of vocationally active inhabitants would be able to reach their workplaces within much less than 45 minutes.

This view leads to the basic difference of the two main component parts of the Conurbation. Whereas in the case of the "central area" the mass character of travel toward the center (even on its border) imposes the postulate to shape the strips of districts continuously, for the peripheral area such a postulate has no justification. Since on the Conurbation's periphery there are several small towns—situated more or less equidistant from Warsaw, and either already undergoing a process of rapid growth or having sound prospects for the future—there is no need to construct new towns or settlements in that zone. The towns situated beyond the 45-minute isochrone should be so developed as to have the greatest possible independence in relation to the number of employment places and services. This would reduce travel, especially journeys to work in the central districts, although it would not be possible to eliminate such journeys entirely.

ALTERNATIVE PLANS

The analysis of development possibilities has led us to propose extending new growth sequentially onto areas which are now rural or have a scattered, low-density development. Should we, however, attempt

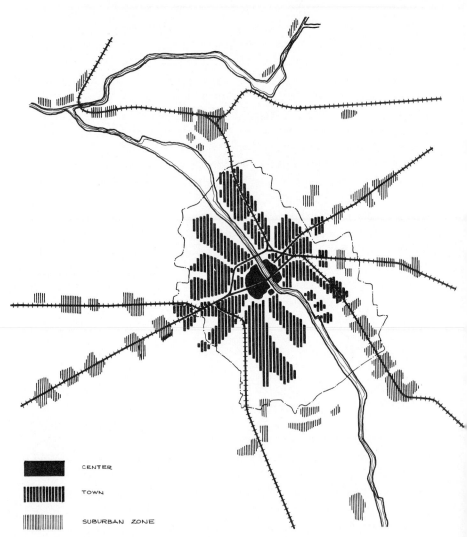

CENTER

TOWN

SUBURBAN ZONE

Map 15. Warsaw Conurbation long-range study: Alternative I

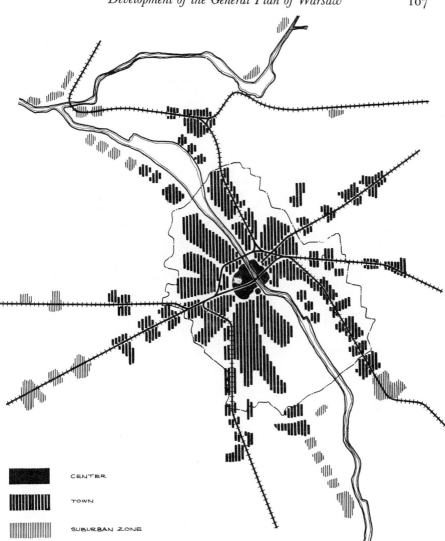

CENTER

TOWN

SUBURBAN ZONE

Map 16. Warsaw Conurbation long-range study: Alternative 2

to fill these areas with urban construction while retaining their present boundaries, the result would be an amorphous creation having little in common with our ideas of a contemporary or, rather, a future city.

The theoretical deliberations behind the premises of the plan and knowledge of the existing and proposed structure of the urban body have enabled us to compose, within the areas concerned, proper plans for future districts. These detailed studies elucidate many aspects of the

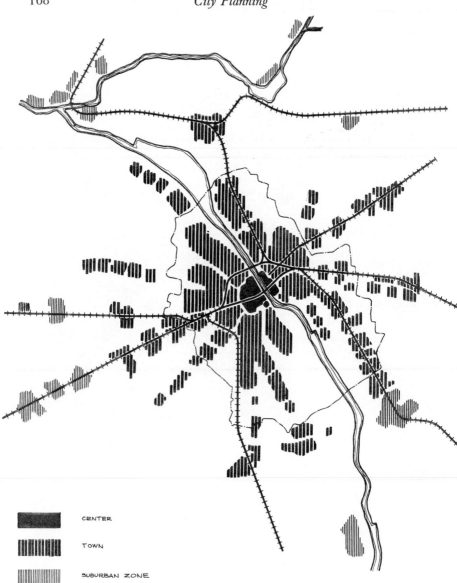

CENTER

TOWN

SUBURBAN ZONE

Map 17. Warsaw Conurbation long-range study: Alternative 3

problems involved and make it possible to prepare several alternative plans. The difference between the plans consists either in the degree to which they utilize the areas considered "easy" to develop from the technical point of view or in the degree to which they initiate development of the "difficult" areas.

From among a larger number of these alternatives, three may be considered most characteristic. The first of them might be called the minimum variant. It is based exclusively on the existing transportation system and utilizes land already provided with a water-supply system and to a large extent already sewered. The population capacity of the Conurbation assumed under this variant amounts to some 2,500,000 inhabitants, about the same figure as that envisaged for 1980. This means that the variant does not adequately allow for development possibilities of the Conurbation after the "perspective" period.

The second variant differs from the first in one essential respect: it adds to the existing transportation system the urban northwest-south-east railway. This makes possible the incorporation into the urban area of the excellent lands on the left-bank escarpment, which would be most advantageous to the future inhabitants' conditions of life and most convenient in regard to the water economy.

The third variant may certainly be defined as the maximum one. It provides for construction, wherever possible, of new strips of districts with due observation of the principle of multistrip pattern. This variant would make it imperative to construct at least six radial lines of urban railway. It also provides for large residential districts reaching far into areas where construction of water-supply and sewerage systems would be extremely difficult. The Conurbation's population capacity assumed by this variant is about 4,000,000 inhabitants, hence the view that this is not the best form of development for the Warsaw Conurbation. None-theless, the threshold method allows a rational analysis of the divergent alternatives of the long-range plan, in order to examine and perfect the "perspective" plan as the basic instrument of town planning activity.

CHAPTER 4

Main Urban Planning Problems in the Silesian-Kraków Industrial Region

CZESŁAW KOTELA

Specific Features of the Silesian-Kraków Industrial Region

THE territory in the south of Poland marked off by Kraków in the east, Kędzierzyn in the west, Tarnowskie Góry in the north, and Oświęcim in the south is an area of significant industrial and residential development. Rich deposits of high-caloric and coke-yielding coal, deposits of zinc ore, nearby deposits of iron ore, and favorable transportation potentialities stimulated the development of this heterogeneous agglomeration.

In the center of the region the Upper Silesian Industrial District—which may be treated as a single urban complex—has developed most rapidly. The urban complex of Kraków has developed independently. Separate from the steady growth of Kraków and of the Upper Silesian Industrial District is the recent stormy growth of the Rybnik Coal-mining District (in the southwest of the agglomeration), the Kędzierzyn District (in the west), and the Kraków Industrial District (in the southeast).

After World War II efforts were made to relieve the excessive congestion of the Upper Silesian Industrial District by locating new industrial units and developing existing units outside the GOP Zone,[1] but at a distance convenient for the transportation of raw materials from the coal-mining region. Accordingly, a large smelting works has been situated in Kraków; another group of mining works is scheduled to be

---

[1] GOP is the Polish abbreviation for the Upper Silesian Industrial District (Górnośląski Okręg Przemysłowy).

situated in Częstochowa, and chemical works in Kędzierzyn and Oświęcim. Many similar projects have been developed in the region.

Although the region is divided into three distinct administrative units—the districts of Kraków, Katowice, and Opole—the functional and spatial interdependence of the sections, as well as technical-economic factors (transportation, water, power, sand deposits), enforce a common solution of regional problems. Tables 1 and 2 provide a few figures illustrating the degree of urbanization of the region.

Table 1. POPULATION AT THE END OF 1960

Sections	Population			Total per sq. km.
	Total in thousands	Urban in thousands	Percentage of urban	
Urban complex of Kraków	871	549	63.0	480
West Kraków Industrial District	553	226	40.0	189
Upper Silesian Industrial District	2,272	1,882	83.0	708
Rybnik Coal-mining District	306	163	54.0	301
Kędzierzyn group	351	135	37.4	117
Total for the Region	4,353	2,955	70.0	581
Poland (1959)	29,480	13,958	47.3	95
Percentage of regional population in relation to total for Poland	14.8	21.2		

Table 2. DEVELOPMENT OF URBAN POPULATION IN THE REGION, 1950–1960

Sections	Urban population (in thousands)		Increase	
	1950	1960	Total	% $\frac{1960}{1950}$
Urban complex of Kraków	382	549	167	144
West Kraków Industrial District	99	226	127	228
Upper Silesian Industrial District	1,324	1,882	558	142
Rybnik Coal-mining District	61	163	102	267
Kędzierzyn group	73	135	62	185
Total for the Region	1,939	2,955	1,016	153
Poland	9,605	13,958	4,353	145
Percentage of regional population in relation to total for Poland	20.2	21.2	23.3	

The tables illustrate the high degree of urbanization in the region, which is considerably above Poland's average; they also show the great divergences inside the region. The increase in urbanization, also higher than the national increase, contributed to an increase in the comparatively high ratio of urban population in the region. The new urban population primarily stimulated the growth of all existing towns in the region. Another part of this population found space in new towns and settlements.

The development of population in towns which are expected to exceed the 100,000 limit by 1980, as well as development in the new towns, appears in the following tables.

Table 3. POPULATION GROWTH IN TOWNS EXPECTED TO EXCEED 100,000 BY 1980

Towns	Population (in thousands)					Scheduled population (in thousands)	
	1939	1946	1950	1955	1960	1965	1980
Bielsko	–	–	–	66	76	82	100
Bytom	101	93	174	181	185	185	185
Chorzów	110	111	129	141	149	160	160
Gliwice	114	96	120	135	135	140	160
Katowice*	134	128	175	200	273	280	300
Kraków	259	299	344	428	479	560	750
Ruda Śląska	–	–	110	117	133	138	155
Sosnowiec	130	78	96	124	133	139	150
Zabrze	126	104	172	183	191	193	205

* Disproportionate growth of Katowice, as compared with other towns, is due to the incorporation of neighboring towns and settlements.

Table 4 includes new towns which have been incorporated into bigger towns, as well as existing towns whose scheduled development is several times higher than their present state. One can view the development of the industrial and residential agglomeration with the eyes of a regional planner, intent on the simultaneous development of all economic and spatial elements of the whole region; or with the eyes of an urban planner, looking at the development of the spatial units of the region with particular consideration of residential problems.

I should like to limit the scope of this study by illustrating the urban problems of only a few spatial units: the urban complex of Kraków, the urban complex of the Upper Silesian Industrial District, and the growing Rybnik Coal-mining District.

Table 4. POPULATION GROWTH IN EXISTING AND NEW TOWNS

Towns	Population (in thousands)					Scheduled population (in thousands)	
	1939	1946	1950	1955	1960	1965	1980
Gołonóg (as a suburb of Dąbrowa Górnicza)	5	6	7	7	14	20	40
Jastrzębie	5	4	5	5	6	21	60
Kędzierzyn					21	31	62
Leszczyny			4	4	7	14	28
Nowa Huta (as a suburb of the city of Kraków)			16	82	100	130	200
Pawłowice	2	2	2	2	2	3	15*
Pyskowice	6	6	7	15	22	26	40
Tychy	10	12	13	27	51	65	120
Wodzisław			6	7	9	20	40
Żory	6	3	5	6	7	14	50

* Subject to further development.

The City of Kraków

Kraków is situated 80 km. from the Upper Silesian Industrial District and 100 km. from Zakopane (the mountain health resort and tourist center); it is 300 km. from Warsaw. These distances indicate the importance of interrelation with the principal traffic centers in the west (Silesia) and in the south (Zakopane-Tatra Mountains). Between Kraków and the Upper Silesian Industrial District, the Kraków West Industrial District is developing rather rapidly. Situated to the north, east, and south are territories with a predominantly agricultural economy.

Kraków's location in the Vistula valley, abundantly fed by waters from the north, west, and south, has always provided naturally favorable conditions for the birth and growth of a prosperous settlement. The first information about Kraków dates from the tenth century. Even at that time the settlement functioned commercially. But only the "location plan" of 1257 supplied a real foundation for the regular development of the town. This sufficed for the needs of the rapidly developing town for many centuries, almost until the middle of the nineteenth century. The chessboard plan of the Gothic town efficiently created a broad basis for rational development which enabled the town to grow and to discharge the complicated functions of the Polish state capital,[2] as well as the functions of center of commerce, production, and culture.

Kraków was encompassed by a belt of fortress walls, and on the Wawel hill dominating the town a castle, the seat of Polish kings, was built. The development of urban life found a splendid architectural setting which, despite conflagrations and the havoc of war was renewed and improved again and again. Even to this day many relics of the past have survived, masterpieces of Romanesque, Gothic, Renaissance, and

[2] Until the sixteenth century.

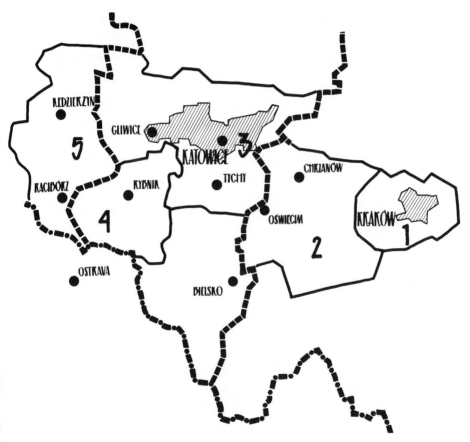

Map 18. Scheme of Silesian-Kraków Industrial Region

1. Kraków city ensemble. 2. Kraków West Industrial Zone. 3. Upper Silesian Industrial District (GOP). 4. Rybnik Coal-mining Zone (ROW). 5. The Kędzierzyn Group.

later architecture, attracting numerous tourists and connoisseurs of art.

The nineteenth century brought turbulent development to the town. The construction of a railway and the rise of industry, which was located chaotically, without plan, eventually produced a typical capitalist town—disorderly, overcrowded, and unsanitary. After World War II the city entered a new period of development. The great complex of smelting works (the largest in Poland) situated east of Kraków caused a rapid extension of the town in this direction, as well as reconstruction and rearrangement of other town districts.

Formerly, the town grew along a north-south axis; the old town extended from Stradom to Podgórze. The construction of the smelting-works ensemble and the development of other industries determined a new axis of development perpendicular to the former. The new axis ran from east to west along the Vistula valley with development areas located mainly on the left bank of the Vistula. In the new pattern the old town center still functions as the center of the whole complex, yet its character will become more adapted to mass tourist traffic. Auxiliary functions will be discharged by the new service cluster located in the neighborhood of the main railway station east of the old town. Around the city center are residential neighborhoods with their own service

Table 5a. LAND AREA AND POPULATION OF KRAKÓW

Year	Area (in sq. km.)	Inhabitants
1945	165	300,000
1955	223	428,000
1960	223	479,000
In perspective	242	750,000

Table 5b. LAND AREA BY USE

Use (% of total)	Present	Perspective
Residential	11.5	19
Industrial	5.8	7
Circulation	3.9	5
Verdure	1.2	4
Agriculture	63.0	55
Other areas	14.6	10
Total	100.0	100

Table 6. LABOR FORCE BY INDUSTRIAL GROUP

Group	Percentage of Total Population		
	1955	1965	Perspective
Total Labor force	55.4	50	44
Manufacturing and power	23.8	22	20
Building	24	25	23
Transportation	7.4	8	10
Services	42.2	43	45
Administration	2.6	2	2
Total of groups	100.0	100	100
Commuters from suburban zones to work places in town (in thousands)	38	38	40

centers and industrial estates. Industry is mainly located in the eastern part of the town. All the areas—residential, service, verdure, industrial —are linked by a radial-belt road system. Of the three circumferential routes, the outer one is designated for through and freight traffic. Future development of the city (after 1980) is possible, but it would have to take place on the right bank of the Vistula, and would require more substantial capital investments for basic utilities.

Nowa Huta

I should like to call special attention to one of the communties in the Kraków area—Nowa Huta, which embraces the originally scheduled town of Nowa Huta as well as Krzesławice Hills and Bieńczyce. The construction of Nowa Huta began in 1949 on the location of a suburban village, Mogiła.

According to the original premises Nowa Huta was to be an independent town, associated with the new smelting-works complex. Soon, however, it was evident that the development of the new town would outstrip the planned limits, and it was incorporated into rapidly growing Kraków in 1950. The original radial design of Nowa Huta was supplemented by including the settlement on Krzesławice Hills to the northeast and the Bieńczyce area to the west. The town of Nowa Huta was at first planned for 100,000 inhabitants. The incorporation of Bieńczyce and Krzesławice expands this to 200,000 inhabitants.

During the short period of construction Nowa Huta was an experi-

Fig. 39. Nowa Huta—Bieńczyce—Settlement "G." Photograph of a plan model (photo: A. Kociołowski, Kraków)

mental laboratory for house-building, from which new methods radiated over the whole country. Nowa Huta is still the largest construction site in Poland. By the end of 1961 dwellings for 100,000 people had been erected. The growth of this neighborhood is scheduled to approach 130,000 by 1965. The neighborhood is comprehensively equipped with social, municipal, educational, and transportation facilities.

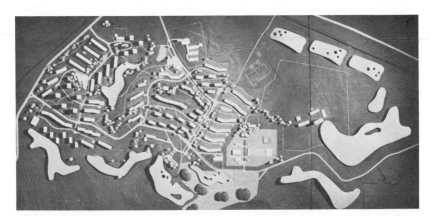

Fig. 40. Nowa Huta—Krzesławice Hills. Photograph of a plan model. Architect: Władysław Leonowicz. Plan prepared in 1958 (photo: W. Łoziński, Miastoprojekt, Kraków)

Upper Silesian Industrial District

The entire District lies in the district of Katowice. It embraces a rather extensive territory, comprising 14 detached towns and 4 sub-regions with a total area of 1,700 sq. km. In the center of the District there is a compact group of 13 detached towns and 19 nondetached towns,[3] as well as settlements[4] covering the area of 700 sq. km. Only 150 years ago there were rustling cornfields, forests, small towns, and widely dispersed rural settlements in this now densely populated territory. I will deal only with this compact urban group.

The earliest exploitation of the region was for nonferrous metals. Unsuitable for agriculture, the area had been noted since the beginning of the Polish state (tenth century A.D.) primarily for its output of silver and lead ore, and subsequently for iron ore. Next to the mines arose the primitive prototypes of the present smelting works. The fourteenth and fifteenth centuries brought the development of mining, particularly in the northern part of the District. In the sixteenth century there were several foundries and thousands of diminutive mines. At a later period development was hindered by wars as well as by technical difficulties in exploiting the ore. Silesia was classified as a thinly populated region. Its largest towns had existed since the early Middle Ages. These towns, such as Bytom, Czeladź, Będzin, Gliwice, Mysłowice, numbered at best several hundred inhabitants each.

On the eve of the twentieth century the situation changed. The use of coal for smelting ore caused the existing foundries to be moved to the direct vicinity of coal pits, while the growing demand for steel accelerated the industrialization of the District. Residential and industrial development during this period was rapid and haphazard in the whole territory of the District and lacked any kind of coordination. This unfavorable situation was accentuated by the partition of Poland among three foreign states, each of which treated its areas of economic expansion as a kind of colonial territory. This can be definitely ascertained by comparing the spatial development of a simultaneously expanding industrial region in Westphalia, Germany.

The residential sections of the territory of GOP were built up without plans, for expedience and convenience. The usual housing was fac-

[3] In Poland towns are divided into "detached" towns, which have the statutory rights of provinces, and "nondetached" towns, which are subordinated to the province in whose territory they are situated.

[4] "Settlement" is in this case an administrative term denoting a housing complex devoid of rural features but not yet developed into a town.

tory owned, located not too far from the mines and plants. Different
mining conditions and local needs led to either a dispersed, erratic
building pattern or a condensed, barrack-type plan. The colonies very
often had no sewerage system. The usual erection of hutches and
latrines characterized the early period of the urbanization of the coal
district. The gradual fusion of a number of settlements and the appearance of bigger urban units necessitated basic utilities, particularly roads,
sewerage, and water supplies. These were installed without reference to
the urban ensemble of GOP. The main development feature of that
period was extensive mixing of residential and industrial areas and
other types of land-use areas. This brought about intolerable living conditions in the towns and settlements of the coal-mining region.

The characteristic growth of certain towns in GOP is shown in
Table 7.

At the outset of the twentieth century the disquieting economic,
social, and spatial effects of this spontaneous development—particularly
criticized by architects, scientists, and economists—compelled the state
and municipal authorities to initiate regional planning. This only
reached the preliminary phase of fragmentary studies and research—
especially since the effects of the long-lasting political partition of the
territory of GOP (which continued in a modified form even during the
period between the two world wars) made it impossible to provide
a uniform plan for the entire District. From 1927 to 1939 two separate
spatial plans were prepared for the eastern and western parts of the region but these plans were never carried out. Only after the war were
conditions favorable for undertaking planning activities on a broad
scale, when the entire region was incorporated within the boundaries of
Poland and when industry was nationalized and a planned economy
introduced. Urban planning activities taken up in 1945 resulted in

Table 7. GROWTH OF POPULATION IN TOWNS IN GOP (IN THOUSANDS)

Town	1860	1880	1900	1910	1921	1931	1939
Bytom	9	23	51	67	53	101	101
Chorzów (Królewska Huta)	13	27	57	73	73	81	110
Gliwice	11	15	52	65	69	111	114
Katowice	8	13	32	43	50	126	134
Sosnowiec	6	8	57	99	86	109	130
Zabrze	11	13	56	63	67	130	126

1952 in a regional plan for GOP, which was approved by state authorities in 1953. This plan produced a series of urban, technical, and economic studies.

The GOP regional plan introduced a subdivision of the District into two areas: the "A" area, of dense industrial and urban investment and extensive mining exploitation, and the "B" area, which at present bears considerably less industrial investment and considerably more verdure, thus constituting to some extent a suburban complement of the "A" area. The "A" area is inhabited by some 1,850,000 people; the density of population is about 2,000 per sq. km. The "B" area, however, is inhabited by only 310,000 inhabitants, and the density of population is 182 per sq. km.

The basic concept of the regional plan was the passive and active deglomeration[5] of housing and industry from the "A" area of GOP into the "B" area. It was assumed that further development of industry and towns in the "A" area would be prevented by the excessive density of buildings. This density of old and new construction impeded or even checked completely the exploitation of coal and zinc ore.[6] Also, the extent of the industry menaced the health of the population with air pollution, water poisoning, and devastation of verdure and of the landscape. To alleviate these evils the plan suggested building within 10 to 15 kilometers from the "A" area satellite towns which would in part become dormitories for industry situated in the "A" area, and would in part discharge their own economic functions. The concept of decongestion was launched around 1950. Subsequently the construction of new towns began: Pyskowice in the west, Tychy in the south, Gołonóg in the east. Simultaneously, the construction of a series of smaller spatial units was started, namely satellite colonies which were almost exclusively used as dormitories (Radzionków, Piekary-Wieczorek, Stolarzowice, Halemba). Only construction of the new town of Grodziec has not yet begun.

The general plan for towns and settlements in GOP was prepared after the approval of the regional plan, and is based strictly on that plan in regard to the scheduled size of towns and their development trends. It must be emphasized that the plans were not prepared for individual

---

[5] The term "passive deglomeration" is used to denote limitation of further development of housing and industry; "active deglomeration" denotes relocating industrial establishments and housing in other areas.

[6] See p. 129.

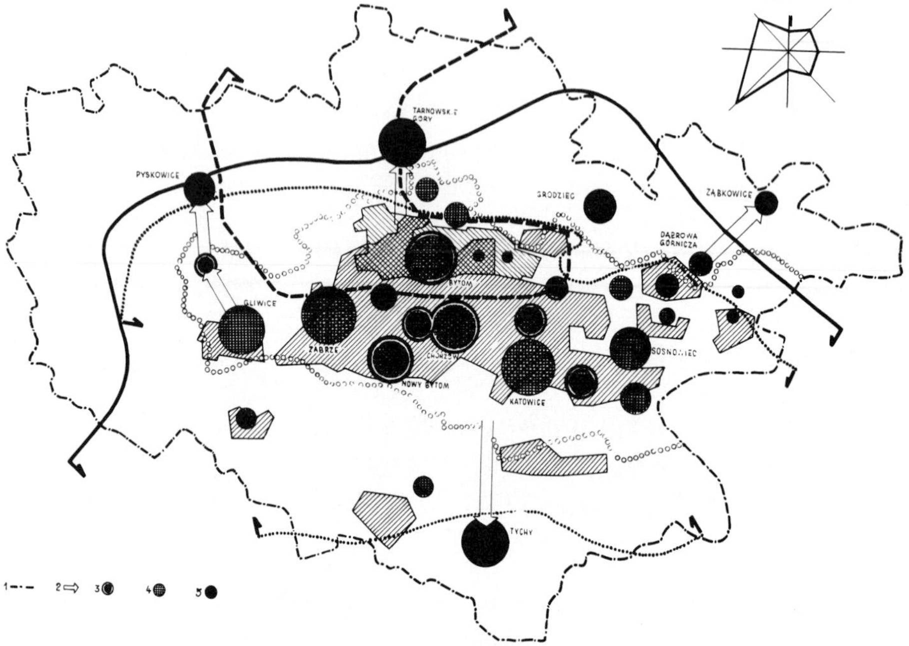

Map 19. GOP plan for deglomeration of the settlements, 1953 regional plan
1. Boundary of zone "A," according to the first phase of the regional plan.
2. Flow of deglomerated population. 3. Existing towns—reconstructed. 4. Existing towns—reconstructed and partially extended. 5. New towns.

towns. They deal with four sectors, each embracing economically inter-related town groups: east, north, west, and center.

Six years later in 1956 the elaboration of the general plan began. New organization of the planning work and expansion of the planning offices permitted deeper studies and analyses. In the actual cycle of preparation of urban plans the work is carried out on two levels. In the District Urban Planning Office general plans for the entire district are prepared, while in the municipal town planning offices development plans for particular towns are prepared. The correlation of planning activities enables the planners to see the same problems from different angles, from the general viewpoint as well as from that of the particular unit.

In the new version of the plan the mechanics of the development of GOP have been studied. The process here differed from that of other big towns, which generally grew from one main body. The minor units which were eventually absorbed in the course of the development did not deform the basic central structure surrounded by neighborhoods. Instead, the urban body of GOP has been amalgamated from scores of units that developed without plans. Accidental interrelations between these units led to their fusion into towns. This process has been termed "integration." The present phase of integration in GOP indicates that the process is not yet finished. On the contrary, it is at a point essential to the whole future development of GOP, verging on the final spatial integration of the entire region.

At the same time studies disclosed further possibilities for situating residential building within GOP (in the "A" area) in comparatively good climatic conditions, and in areas structurally suited to mining. Hence the actual concept of the general plan of GOP schedules further controlled and planned integration of the town group, to be expressed in a functional composition of the separate spatial units with their own

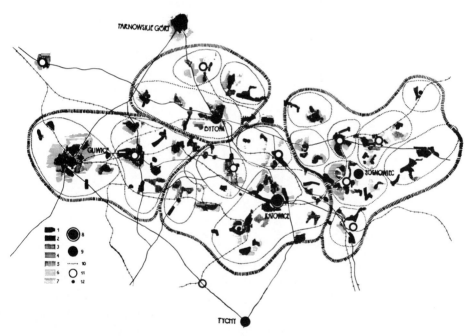

Map 20. Scheme of Settlement Integration in GOP

1. Development before 1780. 2. Development, 1780–1850. 3. Development, 1850–1914. 4. Development, 1914–1945. 5. Development, 1945–1962. 6. Anticipated development after 1962. 7. Division boundaries of 4 spatial units in ultimate development. 8. Central core of GOP. 9. Central core of spatial units. 10. Present division boundaries between spatial units. 11. Main service center. 12. Local service centers.

centers and local services. Four complexes are scheduled as dominant units approximately tallying in their boundaries with the present layout. In relation to this background Katowice is not only the capital of the district, but also the GOP center, with all the responsibilities for communication facilities and program direction. The authors of the plan emphasize that the new satellite towns will eventually become substantial, since building possibilities in GOP are still limited. At the same time it has been indicated that the more intensified development of the new towns will eventually end the integration process in GOP.

Planned integration of settlement units in GOP has been feasible for several reasons. First, decisions of state authorities have been issued to impede the increase of employment in GOP in favor of other regions in this district and in the country. Second, decisions relating to the matter have already been issued. It has been decided, for instance, to purify the air in Silesia of polluting substances. Third, we have a theory conceived by Professors Budryk and Knothe, dealing with stresses in the ground that result from dislocation of geological strata through exploitation of coal fields and ore deposits. This theory applies to construction of buildings and other objects. Fourth, economists as well as urban planners now have experience in the practical realization of the principles of planned economy, and particularly in determining the scope of planned investments and in selecting proper sites. Great new settlements have been developed conforming to these principles, such as the "Millennium" settlement between Chorzów and Katowice, the neighborhood "Syberka" in Będzin, the Katowice center and the Marchlewski neighborhood in Katowice.

The New Town of Tychy

In accordance with the principle of deglomeration in GOP the new town of Tychy has been situated 18 kilometers south of Katowice. The construction of the town began in 1950; in 1961 its population numbered 60,000. The scheduled size was 130,000 people. The master plan of the town has been designed with consideration for the existing topography and is based on two compositional axes. One of these is from east to west, running along a central railway line that bisects the town in a deep open cut. This cut is bridged by a series of viaducts, connecting at street level the northern and southern parts of the town. The other compositional axis is a great green boulevard running from north to south. It links the areas of the north park with the south park and extends still farther to the forest park adjoining the Paprociany

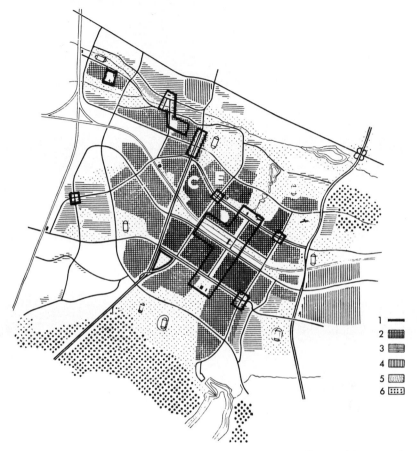

Map 21. New town of Tychy—directive plan (architects: Hanna Adamczewska and Kazimierz Wejchert; plan prepared in 1953)

1. Town center and service centers. 2. Multifamily and multifloor built-up areas. 3. Individual built-up areas (one-family houses). 4. Industrial estates. 5. Town verdure. 6. Forests.

lake. This "green axis" is primarily a pedestrian way. Along it are the most important cultural sites: a philharmonic hall, a music school, two cinemas, a theater, and exhibition halls.

On these main perpendicular axes, a central square of the major internal traffic streets has been designed. The sides of the square are about 1 kilometer long. Within it lies the proper town center with its principal town services. Each corner of the rectangle is the center of a neighborhood. Thus four central neighborhoods are formed, separated from one another by wedges of verdure which in principle are situated

Map 22. New town of Tychy—Neighborhood "B" (architects: Hanna Adamczewska, Kazimierz Wejchert, Z. Łuszczyński, B. Zwoliński. Designed 1952,
constructed 1953–1955). Existing roads and part of the existing development
have been incorporated into the design.

1. Nurseries. 2. Kindergartens. 3. Schools. 4. Boy Scouts' building. 5. Medical centers for outpatients. 6. Post Office. 7. Shops. 8. Community hall. 9. Pan-
oramic cinema.

in areas not fit for buildings. The complex of the old town makes the fifth residential neighborhood, along with the adjoining neighborhoods "A" and "B." The central rectangle of streets is linked to the outer road network, allowing easy access to the town center from all directions. East of the town are industrial estates served by a system of railway sidings and roads.

The master plan called for a complex of buildings of four stories to occupy a major part of the town, interspersed in the central blocks with buildings eight and twelve stories high. This would concentrate dwellings for a great number of people in the vicinity of the central railway station. Close to this station are planned the main commercial center and the grouping of offices and service accommodations.

The development of the town was started in the section adjoining the existing old town of Tychy and thus able to utilize the existing socioeconomic potentialities and the old railway station. Technical

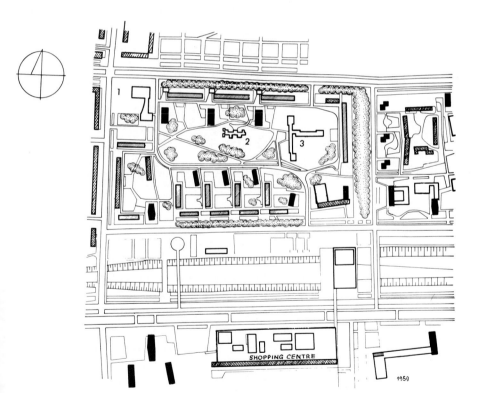

Map 23. New town of Tychy—Neighborhood "D" (architects: Hanna Adamczewska and Kazimierz Wejchert; plan prepared in 1958)
1. Shopping center. 2. Kindergartens. 3. Schools.

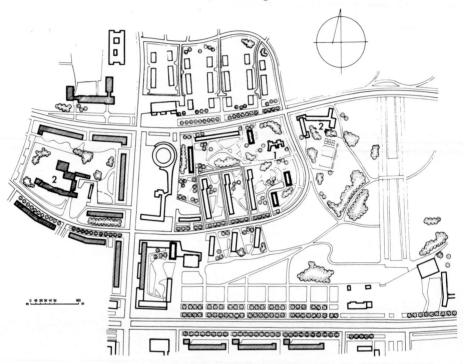

Map 24. New town of Tychy—Neighborhood "E" (architects: Hanna Adam-czewska and Kazimierz Wejchert. Plan prepared in 1959)
1. Kindergartens. 2. Schools.

problems concerning the basic utilities of the area enforced prior con-struction of the part of the town situated north of the central railway line. In this section, development progresses from west to east. The con-struction began with the peripheral neighborhood "A," reaching in 1959 the areas of the central building groups—neighborhood D-1. From 1951 to 1959, 25,000 dwelling rooms were constructed; this area is in-habited by about 40,000 people, which makes the present population of the town 50,000. Thus, by means of government decree and reasoned planning, favorable living conditions have been created for a consider-able part of the population of the industrial zone. The development of the northern part of the town is supposed to be finished by 1965. There-after the construction of the southern part will begin, moving toward the Paprociany forest complex. Termination of construction is antici-pated by 1980.

Limitations of Construction in a Mining Area

Until accurate methods of determining stresses in coal-mining areas were conceived by Professors Budryk and Knothe, the regulations of mining authorities drastically impeded the work of urban planners and constructors.[7] Regulations restricted the scope of construction in regard to the height of buildings (in stories), and regulations designed to protect the new buildings from subsiding were stiff, and limited free architectural planning. By means of the new methods, building conditions in mining zones have been regulated. Each building site is classified as to its security for construction.

At present the urban planner can use a zoned plan of the whole region, and can judge appropriateness of building areas in regard to mining conditions. It must be emphasized that the introduction of these coefficients of deformation into the building regulations (instead of the former rigid regulations as to the height of buildings) has allowed more free use of high buildings in the hitherto proscribed mining areas

[7] In the process of mining the space left by the removal of the coal or ore is filled either with sand (which is washed into the exhausted workings by water) or with waste rock (dry gobbing). This reduces the effects of subsidence to 10 per cent of the thickness of the removed layer.

Table 8. BUILDING REQUIREMENTS BY COEFFICIENTS OF DEFORMATION

Zone	Anticipated Deformation			Scope of building possibilities
	T mm/m	R min. km.	E max. mm/m	
I	2.5	20	1.5	Special means for securing structure not required
II	5	12	3	Partial security not required (insignificant damages)
III	10	6	6	Partial security required
IV	15	4	9	Considerable security required
V	>15	<4	>9	Sites not fit for building

simply by the selection of the proper type of construction. This circumstance is of immense importance for the planned development of GOP because it allows for increasing intensity in building up areas of mining exploitation.

Rehabilitation of the Natural Landscape

The rehabilitation of land devastated by industrial activity is very complicated and requires considerable investment of capital. It calls for recultivation of industrial heaps and cinder piles, open workings of sand, quarries, clay pits, and open coal pits, as well as cleansing running waters and purifying the air. The magnitude of the problem is illustrated in Table 9.

The recultivation of territories laid waste by industry is a large-scale project, theoretically planned for many years. Included in the project are scheduled plantings of verdure, utilization of cinder piles for industrial and mining purposes (for filling the exhausted workings), partial flooding of the open exhausted workings (thus creating natural ponds), as well as other regulating activities. The problem is a subject of research at the Polish Academy of Sciences and is being carefully studied.

Cleansing the running waters is a similar problem. To purify the air, it must first be cleansed of dust and, at a later stage, of gaseous matters. Planting greenery is of great importance for restoration of the natural landscape. At present planned verdure (parks, green areas, workers' vegetable garden lots, and so forth) covers an area of 4,200 hectares, making 25 sq. m. (268 sq. ft.) per inhabitant. This index is probably still inadequate, though it is partially compensated by the great forest masses in the north and south of the region. The great importance of verdure in GOP has been fully recognized. After the war greenery was planted on many hectares of ground; and scores of parks and green

Table 9. WASTELAND TO BE RECULTIVATED

Category	Area (by hectare)
Open workings of sand	2,000
Industrial heaps of cinder-piles	1,250
Other industry-wasted territories	800
Total	4,050

areas have been organized. Particular mention should be made of the
Voivodship Park of Culture and Rest. It has been erected in the center
of GOP between Chorzów and Katowice, with an area of 600 hectares.
The park is divided into several sectors containing the Silesian stadium
for 100,000 spectators, a zoo, or amusement park, a permanent exhibition of technical progress, a planetarium, and entertainment accommodations. (See Map 25.)

ROW—Rybnik Coal-mining District

The Rybnik Coal-mining District is particularly abundant in a
coke-yielding coal whose deposits in other regions of Poland are insufficient. The development of smelting requires increased coke production; consequently there is the demand for increased output of appropriate
kinds of coal and for new investment. New coal mines will be gradually
constructed here over a period of many years. The territory of ROW
bears no resemblance to GOP. Its industrialization is insignificant. The
uneven folds of the territory form a picturesque landscape, which acquires a particular character through the individual appearance of
single coal mines.

The task of the urban planners in this territory was to consolidate
investment (unlike in GOP), to retain functional clarity, and above all
to aim at creating functional settlement units which would secure
a satisfying life for the inhabitants. The size of such a unit was specified
at approximately 60,000 people. For technical reasons (circulation), the
urban planners were forced to decide that some towns would contain
only 30,000 people. These towns, however, are usually located not
farther than 5 to 10 kilometers from bigger towns, which can supply
them with more facilities. In the spatial pattern, ten groups of industrial
settlements have been formed; in each of them at least one town supplies service accommodations to the nearby coal mines and industrial
plants. The central town is Rybnik.

Example of a New Town—Jastrzębie

The selected area for the new town is situated at a point equidistant
from three mines, on an oblong elevation, and bisected by transverse
valleys which impose a natural pattern on the sectional division of the
whole town. In consideration of the natural features of the topography,
the main motive has been to create a functional pattern for the town.
This would include complete separation of sites for industry, housing,
local services, verdure, and communications (excepting local circulation).

In conformity with these principles a master plan has been designed. This shows a town whose backbone is an artery running along the watershed and into the main road from Pawłowice to Wodzisław. The housing units, suspended like grapes upon the central artery, are separated from one another by natural green valleys, running into bigger aggregations of verdure. Along the central artery and connected with the main railroad station, is a community center which has only service buildings and utilities, no housing or industry. A system of microneighborhood and neighborhood shopping centers completes the service facilities of the town center. The estimated service radius of a microneighborhood center is from 200 to 250 meters, that of a neighborhood center about 1,000 meters. The construction of the town has already begun. It must be emphasized that the state economy derives great benefits from the mutual solution of urban and industrial problems. This is particularly relevant to such technical installations as common central heating, water supply, power supply, and transportation equipment. The basic benefit, however, is the concentration of housing, which provides more efficient service for industry.

This brief presentation of the urban planning problems of the Silesian-Kraków Industrial Region illustrates the scale of the problems and the method for their solution. Of foremost importance in this region is the problem of the rapidly growing agglomeration of small units, which will amalgamate into larger units. There is also the problem of shaping the functional pattern and the network of service centers. The unavoidable integration of the whole region can be controlled, however, within the scope of planned economy. To find a purposeful and planned solution to the problem of controlled integration is, in my opinion, the principal task of the urban planner.

CHAPTER 5

City Planning in the Gdańsk-Gdynia Conurbation

WIESŁAW GRUSZKOWSKI

Natural Conditions of the Region

THE region of Gdańsk (known before the war by its German name, Danzig) is situated at the narrowing of the European peninsula between the Baltic Sea and the Black Sea. It lies at the mouth of the Vistula, Poland's longest river, at a junction of sea, river, and land routes. The key importance of the region is also a result of its geographical diversity, for Gdańsk lies at the point where several terrains meet—the Cassubian littoral, the hilly Cassubian Lake district, and the Vistula lowlands (Żuławy Wiślane). There is thus great variety of landscape in the Gdańsk region, for within its confines are to be found coastal cliffs that reach a height of 40 meters, as well as sand dunes, the Hel Peninsula— a product of winds and sea currents that is typical of the Polish Baltic coast—the wooded and markedly eroded edge of the hilly lake district, the gently folded areas of the Cassubian Lake district, the flat country situated between the coastal sand dunes and the edge of the lake district, and, finally, Żuławy, the low-lying district partly situated below sea level.

This diversity of landscape is accompanied by diversity of geotechnical and climatic conditions. Some of the best land for building, as far as solidity is concerned, is in the relatively narrow diluvial terrace (.1 to 3.0 km. broad) extending along the bottom edge of the lake district. Equally good land is to be found in the lake district itself, whereas other areas, especially the artificially drained Żuławy, are very difficult to build on, since the layers of soil capable of carrying buildings often lie at a depth of 10 to 20 meters below the ground surface. These low-lying areas are also less propitious for building from the climatic point of view, because they are subject to cold air and mists.

Historic Development of Gdańsk and the Gdańsk Conurbation

It was no mere chance that Gdańsk was founded here. The geographical position could not have been better than at the confluence of the Motlawa and the Vistula, where sea and river routes converge with the old trade route, the Amber Way, leading from the south of Europe through Moravia, Silesia, and central Poland to the Baltic coast.

Recent excavations by Polish archaeologists have shown that Gdańsk was founded in the second half of the tenth century as a settlement occupying about 2 hectares (approximately 5 acres) of land. It was fortified by a wall made of wood and earth, which was of a construction widely used at that time in Wielkopolska (the present Poznań region).

The inhabitants of Gdańsk in the early Middle Ages engaged in fishing, trade, and numerous crafts such as pottery, forging, boat-building, carpentry, tanning, cobbling, weaving, gold-working, and the making of ornaments from amber. Evidence has been found of trade between Gdańsk and Byzantium, Ruthenia, Bohemia, Hungary, Germany, Friesia, Scandinavia, and England. The population of Gdańsk, which in the tenth century numbered between 1,000 and 1,200 inhabitants, rose to over 2,000 in the twelfth and thirteenth centuries, and to nearly 10,000 at the beginning of the fourteenth century.

The Teutonic Knights, who captured Gdańsk in 1308, destroyed the Slavonic town. While they ruled, the Order contributed to the development of the town by building industrial enterprises, water lines, and other facilities, but it ruthlessly tyrannized the towns it controlled. In

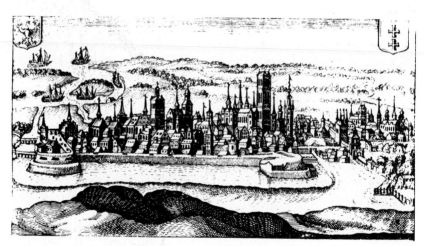

Fig. 41. Gdańsk in the eighteenth century (reproduction of a drawing)

retaliation, the townspeople took advantage of the war between Poland and the Teutonic Order to drive the Knights from Gdańsk and to demolish their castle (1454). In the fourteenth and fifteenth centuries the main outlines of the other parts of medieval Gdańsk—the Old Town, the Old Suburb, the Granary Island[1]—came into being. In general, these outlines remained unchanged to this day.

The "Golden Age" of Gdańsk began after the town was liberated from the predatory rule of the Teutonic Knights in the mid-fifteenth century. The growth of trade and crafts was reflected in the splendid flourishing of Gdańsk architecture. The town's continual commercial contacts with the Baltic countries and with Flanders and Holland also had an important influence on cultural contacts. Thus it is not surprising that in the middle of the sixteenth century many Flemish and Dutch architects settled in Gdańsk and brought to the town a Dutch version of the Renaissance. Similarly the earthwork bastion fortifications with which the town was surrounded at the end of the sixteenth and beginning of the seventeenth century were based on Dutch models. Within the boundaries of its fortifications, Gdańsk covered an area of approximately 540 hectares (approximately 2 square miles), and was one of the biggest towns in Europe at that time. During its "Golden Age" its population also rose, and by the middle of the seventeenth century numbered as many as 77,000 inhabitants.

Gdańsk suffered the fate of the rest of Polish Pomerania and in 1793, after the second Partition of Poland, was attached to Prussia. The isolation of Gdańsk from its natural hinterland (agricultural Poland), as well as the ravages of the Napoleonic Wars, caused the city to decline. It was not until the second half of the nineteenth century, with the general growth of industry in Europe, that Gdańsk began to regain its previous importance as a port. Gdańsk grew so rapidly, both commercially and in population, that the old city was unable to cope with all the new life sprouting within it. The nearby villages became suburbs. In Gdańsk, as in other cities, this process was accompanied by a distinct division of the suburbs into better-class residential districts and meanly built working-class districts. Sopot, a former small estate and village, became a fashionable, though haphazardly built, seaside resort.

After World War I Gdańsk, along with Sopot and the adjacent areas, was recognized as a Free City. The difficulties experienced by Polish shipping in the port of Gdańsk compelled the Polish govern-

[1] Wyspa Spichrzów.

ment to build a new port in the small fishing village of Gdynia, situated only 20 kilometers from Gdańsk. By 1933 the port of Gdynia had outdistanced the port of Gdańsk in amount of cargo handled, and in 1937 was foremost of all the Baltic ports. The town of Gdynia grew rapidly and by 1939 had a population of 120,000. Unfortunately, advantage was not taken of all the opportunities offered by the building of a completely new town. This was due partly to the fact that the target population was initially too small (30,000) and partly to difficulties connected with private ownership of the land. Thus conflicts arose between the extensions of the port facilities and town center and the spontaneous expansion of the suburbs.

World War II began in Gdańsk on September 1, 1939, when salvos from the German warship "Schleswig-Holstein" began to fall on Westerplatte, a Polish stronghold at the entrance to Gdańsk harbor. In the final phase of the war—in March, 1945—Gdańsk suffered heavy damage. Sixty per cent of the city was destroyed, and the city center, for all practical purposes, ceased to exist. The towns of Gdynia and Sopot suffered relatively less damage, although the docks and industrial

Fig. 42. Gdańsk: The medieval town after wartime destruction (photo: Kazimierz Lelewicz)

Fig. 43. Gdańsk: Part of the medieval town (Długa Street) before reconstruction (photo: Kazimierz Lelewicz)

premises presented a picture of ruin and devastation. The destruction of Gdańsk was so great that impassioned arguments took place as to whether or not it was worth while to rebuild the devastated city center. Some expressed the view that the historic part of the town should be deliberately left in ruins, like Herculaneum or Pompeii. The opposing

Fig. 44. Gdańsk: Part of the medieval town (Długa Street) after reconstruction
(photo: Kazimierz Lelewicz)

arguments of those who advocated the rebuilding of Gdańsk, based on economic, political, or sentimental grounds, won the day.

The Main Town, which was to be reconstructed, covered an area of about 40 hectares (as compared with the 20 hectares covered by the Old Town in Warsaw). The following principles were adopted: (1) The medieval network of streets and the old streetfronts were to be maintained (with some slight adjustments). (2) Damaged historical public buildings, such as gateways, bastions, churches, the Town Hall, were to be rebuilt strictly according to historical documents. (3) The facades of burghers' houses where original details were preserved, or for which exact information was available, were to be rebuilt. (4) The remaining buildings were to be designed in such a way that together with the reconstructed houses the street would be characteristic of Gdańsk. (5) The original ground plan of the burghers' houses, stretching back from the street to the full depth of the site (about 20 meters) was to be given up in favor of well-planned modern flats. The courtyards, which would come into being where the kitchen buildings and outhouses had formerly stood, were now to provide space for common gardens, nursery schools, and so forth.

As was only natural, many difficult problems arose in reconstructing for the purpose of contemporary use a district built in an earlier epoch and under a social system long since dead. Compromise was the only way to

Fig. 45. Gdańsk: The medieval town on the river Motława after reconstruction

solve such problems. Nevertheless, the planners succeeded in producing plans that were both artistically satisfying and comparatively functional. Above all, they succeeded in saving historical buildings whose loss would have been a tragedy not only for Polish culture, but for culture generally.

Present State of the Conurbation

Directly after the cessation of hostilities in World War II, it was obvious that the towns of Gdańsk, Sopot, and Gdynia formed a single conurbation. The connections between the ports, shipyards, and various types of industry, the location of housing districts and shopping centers, the partly interlocking drainage and water systems and gas mains, and above all the short distances between the diverse elements of the group were very clearly leading to the integration of the three towns, although each of them still maintained its own administration. The opening of an electric railway line for local traffic along the main axis of the conurbation (trains running every 7 minutes), as well as bus and trolley communication between the towns, were additional elements welding the three towns together.

Thus a large urban organism (numbering 520,000 inhabitants in 1962) grew up at Gdańsk Bay. This organism consisted of the following principal elements: (1) the city center of Gdańsk, occupying the historical part of the town, and acting as the main center not only for Gdańsk, but for the whole region generally; (2) the port and industrial areas on the Vistula; (3) the residential districts of Gdańsk, extending along the railway line from Pruszcz in the direction of Sopot, chiefly on the terrace between the edge of the high-lying ground and the sea and low-lying districts; (4) the small town of Sopot, picturesquely situated in the bay, with wooded hills in the background; (5) the residential districts of Gdynia, occupying nearly all the suitable building land stretching along the seacoast between the sea and the hills, and even extending up some of the fairly steep slopes; (6) the city center of Gdynia, directly adjacent to the port; (7) the industrial areas stretching from the port of Gdynia toward the northwest; (8) the little town of Rumia, which is a suburb of Gdynia.

The length of the entire area is 50 kilometers, and the distance from the center of Gdańsk to the center of Gdynia about 20 kilometers. Thus the shape of the Gdańsk Conurbation, determined by geography and by the historical development of the towns, is linear. The main difference between the ground plan of the Gdańsk Conurbation and "classi-

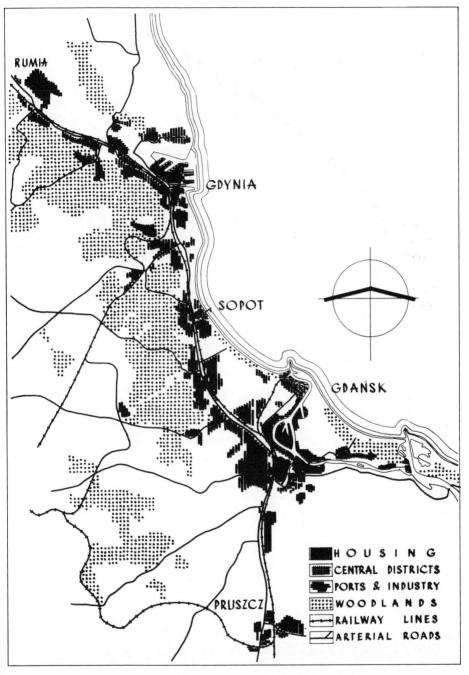

Map 26. Gdańsk-Gdynia Conurbation. Present state

cal" linear conurbation (for example, Soria y Mata's La Ciudad Lineal or N. A. Milyutin's Volgograd[2]) is in the relationship between location of housing and place of employment.

The main concentration of employment in the Gdańsk Conurbation is in the ports, together with the neighboring industrial districts and administrative and trading centers. These are situated more or less at the two opposite poles of the Conurbation, so that many lines of communication are necessary from one end of it to the other. The location of places of employment and of the main city center gives rise to a certain amount of inconvenience. On the other hand, the Gdańsk Conurbation also serves as an example of the advantages which may be derived from an elongated plan for urban areas. For, as in the case of "ribbon" towns, the shape of the present Conurbation provides the inhabitants of the residential districts with opportunity for direct contact with the broad green belt which parallels the main axis of the build-up zone and which is connected by transverse routes to the green coastal belt. This gives the Gdańsk Conurbation a distinct advantage over many other towns of the same size.

Long-range Study

A long-range study based on Dr. B. Malisz' threshold method (see Chapter 2) has been carried out for the Gdańsk Conurbation. It was not restricted by any long-term plan nor based on any terminal date. Its main purpose was to disclose the full potential for the development of the Conurbation. The study included three main elements: analysis of the natural and man-made features, determination of the assumptions for the program, and establishment of several alternatives for physical development, with evaluation of each alternative and conclusion for long-term and five-year plans.

ANALYSIS OF GEOGRAPHICAL CONDITIONS

The analysis of the geographical conditions has been carried out for those terrains where the influence of the Gdańsk Conurbation is predominant, that is, the terrains of existing and planned municipal investments, holiday recreation centers, as well as the whole area within the limits of reasonable access to the two main work regions—the port and industrial centers of Gdańsk and Gdynia. The analysis included the configuration and resistance of the ground, hydrological conditions,

---

[2] Formerly Stalingrad.

farming value of the soil, vegetable cover (woods, natural reserves), climatic conditions, and so forth. The terrains have been classed according to their adaptability for industrial and residential development.

The Conurbation has suitable conditions for the development of port facilities and shipbuilding in the lowlands, especially at Gdańsk. This area, except for the portion that is already built up, is not suitable for housing. That is why the Gdańsk moraine plateau is most important for the physical development of the Conurbation. Its ground, however, has a varied configuration with end moraine, outwash areas, lake channels, river channels, and valleys, which render house construction more difficult; on the other hand the climatic conditions are encouraging.

In considering the geographical features, we next had to deal with the analysis of the thresholds on development barriers, that is, territorial limitations to the development of the towns in the Conurbation. Like every large town, the Gdańsk Conurbation has many barriers to development, with consequent territorial limits. Barriers of minor importance have been eliminated and the remaining barriers have been classified according to their importance.

The study has shown that the most serious limitations to the spatial development of the Conurbation are the problems of developing the

Fig. 46. Gdańsk: The middle part of the city center. Model Plan.
Above left, the reconstruction of the medieval town. Center, the shipping administration center, situated on the Granary Island (*Wyspa Spichrzów*)

transportation system and supplying the towns with water. Of much less importance is the development of the sewerage system and the lines to supply energy, electricity, gas, and remote heating. Within the first limits which cover the area already developed, it is necessary to modernize transportation and to build a new sewage-purification plant replacing the existing obsolete and small facility which lies in the path of future port development. The energy lines also must be modernized.

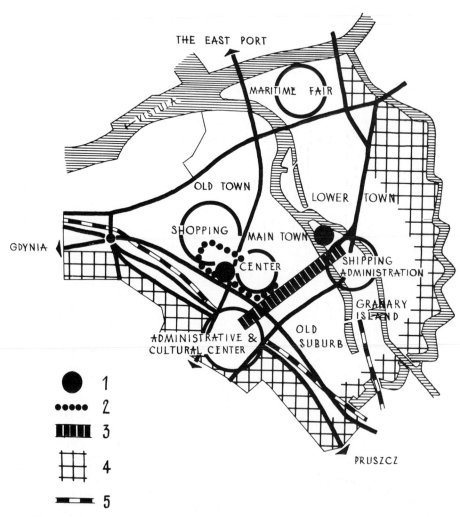

Map 27. City center of Gdańsk
1. Travel offices. 2. Commercial streets. 3. Main axis of urban composition.
4. Green areas. 5. Railroad.

Development beyond the first limit depends on building the first branch of the electric railway southwest of Gdańsk and a new sewage-purification plant on the Gdańsk moraine plateau. These investments would open the lands which lie within the second limitation line. The third line encloses farther lands on the moraine plateau and most probably will not be reached for many years. Development of those lands will require a new circumferential railway.

The development of the water-supply system depends more on the number of inhabitants and the increasing index of water consumption per capita than on the extension of development beyond the limit lines. In any case, the existing and planned ground water-intakes will be insufficient for the 1980 population (long-term plan period). It will be necessary to make the first surface water-intake on the moraine plateau during approximately the next ten years. According to the long-range study further surface water-intakes are recommended. This, however, will not guarantee a full solution of the problem of water supply because of the small quantity of water in the plateau rivers and the great demand for water in agriculture. The necessity of purifying water from the Vistula River and/or evaporating sea water has to be reckoned with.

Next to be dealt with in considering the conditions of the center was an analysis of the possibilities of redeveloping the towns included in the Conurbation. The age, technical condition, usability of the terrain, as well as the functional conditions of the built-up area, were examined. Practical considerations made it necessary to treat the built-up areas in a general manner and to divide them into groups as follows: built-up areas suitable for adaptation beyond the period of the long-term plan, built-up areas suitable for redevelopment with amortization period indicated, low-density areas suitable for more intensive development, built-up areas that should be completely redeveloped.

At this phase of the study it was important to examine the possibility of developing the Conurbation's community center. Taken into consideration were areas within the center with buildings of low value, areas lying next to the existing main community center, and areas which are not built up and which divide the various parts of the Conurbation.

These areas can in the future form the elements of a decentralized community center. The results of analyses of the conditions of the geographical center, of the redevelopment possibilities, and of the "thresholds" have been shown graphically on a map to obtain an image of the areas which are suitable for later development. The map can be described in the words of Dr. Malisz as "a synthesis of development possibilities." This synthesis provides conclusions about the order in which the various areas will be developed in the general development of the town. Thus, it can be useful not only as initial information for the long-range study, but also for setting up a plan for any period.

ASSUMPTIONS FOR THE PROGRAM

The analyses briefly described above made it possible to deal with the next phase of work, making alternative plans for the physical structure. These alternatives could not be worked out without predetermined social and economic assumptions, which are divided into general assumptions for the whole country and specific assumptions for local conditions of the Gdańsk Conurbation. The general assumptions covered development trends of increasing population and urbanization of the country, industrialization of the country, technical progress in transportation systems, and increased urbanization.

On the basis of these, several assumptions have been made for the specific conditions of the Gdańsk Conurbation. It has been assumed that the country's urbanization process will be especially intensive in towns like Gdańsk and Gdynia—larger towns with a favorable geographical position. It is most probable that Poland's foreign trade will increase considerably and more cargo will be handled in the ports. These considerations as well as the ever increasing tonnage of ships call for the reservation of quite large areas for future port development. The introduction of automation into industrial production processes undoubtedly will also take place in the Gdańsk Conurbation but to a smaller extent than in other industrialized towns. The characteristic industry of the seacoast is shipbuilding, which is not very adaptable to automation.

In spite of giving preference to municipal transportation systems, the plan assumes a considerable increase in the number of automobiles and trucks (300 automobiles and 35 trucks per 1,000 inhabitants.) The assumptions do not include any new means of transportation which have not yet been tested sufficiently. The dimensions and structure of the Gdańsk Conurbation have caused most emphasis to be given to modernization of the electric railway, which can take 50,000 passengers per hour on one line when operating at a speed of 50 km. per hour. It will be possible to increase these figures considerably after the introduction of some technical improvements.

ALTERNATIVES FOR PHYSICAL DEVELOPMENT

The specific natural conditions of the Gdańsk Conurbation as well as its present stage of development restrict the possibility of working out various versions for its future physical structure. A compact system developing concentrically around a main center must be rejected immediately. It is also impossible to permit development on the green belts that divide the various parts of the Conurbation. Such a solution would create unfavorable conditions for the well-being of the inhabitants and would complicate the transportation system while making it more expensive. All three versions for the development of the Gdańsk Conurbation which have been worked out by the Town Planning Office of Gdańsk provide for a more or less decentralized system.

The first version (worked out by the team under architect S. Tomaszek) proposes eastward development of the port of Gdańsk and construction of new external basins at the port of Gdynia. Further, this version assumes that 800,000 inhabitants can be housed in the area under present investment. As far as transportation is concerned, a modernized system with trams (Gdańsk), trolleys (Gdynia), and buses, as well as a railway system, has been provided. According to this version, three railway loops with housing estates around them have been provided at the upper terrace. This takes most reasonable advantage of the upper terrace, which lies westward from the present conurbation area, where about 900,000 inhabitants could be located.

The second version (planned under the direction of architect W. Gruszkowski) emphasizes the possibilities of developing the port of Gdańsk and its industrial districts toward the east and south in conjunction with the planned canal. Such a solution permits development of a strip southward from the town center of Gdańsk. This strip would include industrial, transportation, and housing belts parallel to one another. According to this version, a railway loop and one blind line would be built on the upper terrace. Contrary to the other versions, this proposes dense development of the Oksywie plateau, which lies north of Gdynia. According to this version, the Conurbation may be developed in a reasonable manner for 1,500,000 inhabitants.

The third version (worked out by the team directed by architect B. Szermer) provides a different development of the eastern part of Gdańsk. Housing estates are planned on the upper terrace with railway communication. This version gives the most compact solution calculated for 1,200,000 inhabitants.

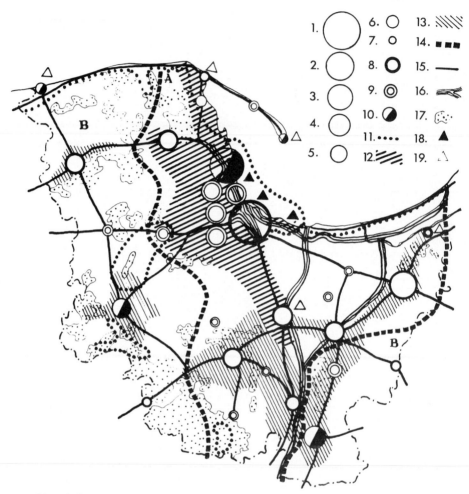

Map 28. Long-range plan of the Gdańsk region

1. Cities with over 300,000 inhabitants. 2. Cities with 200,000–300,000 inhabitants. 3. Cities with 100,000–200,000 inhabitants. 4. Cities with 50,000–100,000 inhabitants. 5. Cities with 20,000–50,000 inhabitants. 6. Cities with 10,000–20,000 inhabitants. 7. Towns with 5,000–10,000 inhabitants.

8. Industrial cities. 9. Service cities. 10. Cities with composite functions. 11. Tourist zones. 12. Highly urbanized zones. 13. Zones with a concentration of nonagricultural population.

14. Boundary of the spatial-economic pattern. 15. Lines of transportation. 16. Inland waterways. 17. Forests. 18. Shipyards and ports. 19. Ports. A. Areas with industrial dominance. B. Areas with agricultural dominance.

All three versions have shown that the privileged geographical position of the Conurbation will give further priority to maritime economy. The development of the Conurbation, however, will be hampered by the complicated physiographical conditions. Therefore, no institutions which are not strictly connected with the ports should be permitted within the Conurbation. Industrial overdevelopment of the Conurbation would create very high expenses for communications and engineering constructions. In addition to such costs overdevelopment would also endanger health conditions (by disturbing the ecological balance). Planned restrictions imposed on the future development of the Conurbation will have a favorable influence on the development of towns in the neighboring region that are distant enough not to be absorbed by the Conurbation.

Long-term Plan

The long-term plan deals with the development of the town (Conurbation) during a twenty-year period. It obviously cannot take advantage of all the possibilities of development given in the long-range study. The economic assumptions for the Gdańsk region have been determined by the development rate of all the branches of national economy. Those data, together with demographic studies, made it possible to determine a hypothetical population of 800,000 for the Conurbation (Figure 47).

The location of the Gdańsk Conurbation is so attractive that tendencies may now be clearly observed toward a much more rapid development than was assumed in the version accepted for the plan. This is a quite common experience, caused by the better economic results attained whenever industrial investments are located in regions which are already developed. The great demand for workers in the rapidly developing maritime economy, which of course has a priority in port towns, will necessitate extensive immigration from outside the Conurbation. On the other hand, the natural conditions mentioned above hinder the unlimited development of the towns around Gdańsk Bay. Thus, according to the recommendations of the plan the development of the Conurbation should be managed so that its population does not exceed 800,000 by 1980. This requires restriction of further development of industrial establishments that are neither closely connected with the maritime economy nor directly serving the population. From the various possibilities of physical development that have been disclosed by the

POPULATION

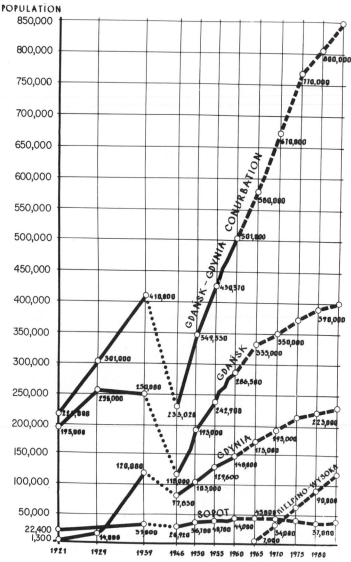

Fig. 47. Gdańsk-Gdynia Conurbation: Population growth

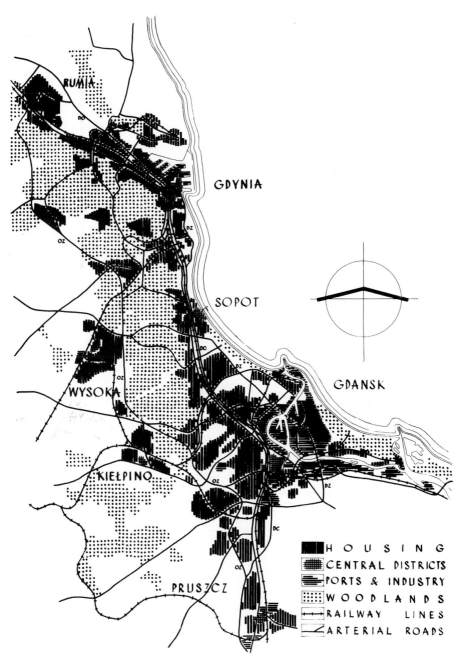

Map 29. Gdańsk-Gdynia Conurbation: Long-term plan

Legend:
- HOUSING
- CENTRAL DISTRICTS
- PORTS & INDUSTRY
- WOODLANDS
- RAILWAY LINES
- ARTERIAL ROADS

Map labels: RUMIA, GDYNIA, SOPOT, WYSOKA, GDANSK, KIEŁPINO, PRUSZCZ

long-range study the authors of the long-term plan have accepted the version which provides the possibility of absorbing the lower terrace and building the first external housing estate on the Gdańsk plateau (Map 29). According to this solution, which provides extra space, the towns will retain their individual character and be prevented from forming one great, amorphous conglomeration. The isolating green belts, which will run at right angles from the seashore, should accommodate sport and recreation centers, individual private gardens, and so forth. The new housing estates on the moraine plateau should reach the western edge of the forests, which will then become parks within the Conurbation.

CHAPTER 6

Postwar Housing Development in Poland

ADAM ANDRZEJEWSKI

HOUSING is one of the most basic and most complicated social problems in Poland. Its postwar development has been determined by a complex set of factors, particularly by:

1. The difficult situation faced by Poland immediately after the war, combined with rapidly growing needs arising from the high birth rate and from urbanization processes. The latter are directly related to changes in the socioeconomic and physical structure as a result of the socialistic industrialization of the country.

2. The limited capital expenditure for housing purposes in relation to needs. The underlying causes of this limitation have been the difficult economic situation immediately after the war, combined with an urgent need to repair war damages, and the necessity in subsequent years to make investments required by national economic development.

3. The necessity for coping simultaneously with several problems— for example, housing needs arising from industrial development, social aims postulated by the housing policy, and alteration of capitalistic building methods to meet socialistic ends.

In view of the recent dynamic changes in economic and social structure and in the goals and methods of housing policy, a brief historical outline of the main housing problems now facing Poland seems necessary.

Origin of the Difficult Housing Situation: Prewar Period, War Damages, Years of Reconstruction

The housing situation in Poland immediately after the war was characterized by an acute shortage of dwellings in relation to the number of inhabitants, by the poor quality of most housing, and by technical dilapidation through wartime neglect and damages. It should be pointed out that there was considerable disparity between housing conditions in different regions, between countryside and towns, and between large and small towns.

The causes of this difficult situation may be sought in the prewar period when Poland was one of the most backward countries in Europe, when the national per capita income was among the lowest and housing conditions among the worst to be found on the continent. In 1931 the average density of occupation was 2.0 persons per room in towns and 3.1 in rural areas. One-room and two-room dwellings accounted for 69 per cent and 87 per cent, respectively, of the total housing stock. Barely 13 per cent of the buildings in urban areas had sewers, only 16 per cent had running water, and 56 per cent of the total had no basic utilities at all, not even electricity. Individual housing conditions depended primarily on a person's financial situation and social class. A large majority of the working people (82 per cent) lived in one- or two-room flats, nearly 71 per cent occupied overcrowded flats containing more than two persons per room.[1]

Housing problems were additionally complicated during and after the war when the extensive changes which the country was undergoing brought new aspects of the problems to the fore. Among these were war damages, shifts of boundaries, and changes in the social and political system.

The western territories of which Poland took possession after the war were more urbanized and had higher housing standards than the territory within the Polish boundaries prior to 1939. Nevertheless, war damages caused either directly in the course of hostilities, or through systematic acts of extermination (the destruction of Jewish districts, the annihilation of ghettos and, following the August uprising, of the city of Warsaw) resulted in a sharp drop in the total housing stock. In all, some one million dwellings with three million rooms, with a total volume of about 12.4 billion cubic feet, were destroyed. Warsaw suffered the highest losses in terms of buildings destroyed (75 per cent of the prewar volume) followed by Wrocław (65 per cent), and Gdańsk (55 per cent). Many other towns also suffered. In rural areas approximately 470,000 farms were destroyed.[2]

---

[1] K. Krzeczkowski, *Kwestia mieszkaniowa w miastach polskich* [Housing Problems in Polish Towns] (Warsaw, 1939). *Concise Statistical Yearbook of Poland 1938* (Warsaw: Central Statistical Office, 1938).

[2] A. Andrzejewski, "Z badań nad sytuacją mieszkaniową w Polsce Ludowej" [Research on the Housing Situation in People's Poland], *Ekonomista*, No. 3, 1957.

At the same time, the population structure was considerably altered. The total loss in population resulting from the war and the Nazi policy of extermination amounted to six million. Another factor in the decrease was the evacuation of the German population from the western territories in the last years of the war, as well as the resettlement action which ensued from the Potsdam agreement. This loss of population was counterbalanced by repatriation of Polish peoples from the eastern territories, the return of persons deported to Germany for forced labor, and the movement of the rural population to towns in which the loss of population had been greatest.

Under these difficult circumstances, where provision of shelter for millions of homeless people was imperative, the government introduced (in 1945) a system of dwelling allocation intended to reshape the housing policy along more just lines and to free it from prewar class discrimination.

Public housing allocation is a form of dwelling regimentation. Except in the case of owner-occupied one-family houses and cooperative flats, dwellings in towns where the regulations were in force could be obtained only by allocation from the municipal authorities. Norms concerning the maximum floor area to be occupied per person were issued.[3] At the same time, rents were fixed at the prewar level. In view of the increase in salaries this actually implied a far-reaching reduction of rents and was of particular social importance. On the other hand, the fixing of rents at too low a level was the source of many future troubles connected, for instance, with the maintenance of buildings.

The public housing allocation policy was also an instrument for reshaping ownership patterns. Although privately owned rental buildings were not nationalized, the scope of the owners' rights was greatly restricted, part of the revenues was removed from owners, and profit was abolished. These measures practically reduced the role of the owner to that of an administrator of the buildings.

Before it was possible for reconstruction work to yield results, the public housing allocation policy greatly assisted in satisfying the most urgent needs and leveling the most striking imbalances. All the government's financial efforts were directed first toward those sections of the

---

[3] Public housing allocation, though in a slightly modified form, is still in force. Certain administrative regulations have been gradually alleviated, and new elements of economic rationing introduced. For instance, the smallest dwellings were exempted from the compulsory housing regulations, higher rents were imposed if the floor area exceeded obligatory norms, and so on.

national economy which were of greatest importance. The reconstruction
of buildings, however, has been undertaken and successfully conducted
by the state, by cooperatives, and by private individuals. Apart from
subsidies granted by the state, other forms of encouragement, such as
exempting reconstructed buildings or flats from the compulsory housing
regulations, have been introduced.

Progressively more intensive reconstruction work carried out between
1946 and 1949 resulted in an increase of 270,000 flats with 810,000
rooms. In rural areas more than 300,000 houses were rebuilt, 230,000 of
them with state aid.[4] During this period a network of agencies concerned
with public housing activities was established. The chief housing agency,
the so-called Workers' Settlements Building Department (ZOR) was set
up, as were State Building Enterprises and Design offices.

Housing in the Period of Industrialization

In 1950 a program of national industrialization was started with a
view to ending the economic backwardness of Poland and creating
a material basis for the development of new social relations.[5] In the long
run this was the only practical way to develop housing activities and to
improve the long-range housing situation, although it should be noted
that new difficulties arose during the early years of the plans because of
the specific demographic situation in Poland.

Beginning in 1950, the housing situation became more acute as a
result of ever growing housing needs. Several factors were responsible.
The rate of natural population increase attained a level of 18.6–19.5 per
mil per annum in the years between 1950 and 1956, the highest in
Europe during the period. The urbanization that accompanied national
industrialization also played its part in increasing the greater demand
for dwellings. After 1956, however, the rate of natural increase gradually declined (to 11.7 per mil in 1962).[6]

The increase in population between the two censuses conducted in
1950 and 1960 amounted to 4.7 million (see Table 10). During that time
the population in towns and urban settlements increased by 4.5 million
and the urban share in the total population grew from 39 per cent

[4] J. Dangel, *Zasoby mieszkaniowe i ludnosc w Polsce w latach 1945–1958* [Housing Stock and
Population in Poland, 1945–1958], Prace Instytutu Budownictwa Mieszkaniowego No. 29,
[Housing Research Institute] (Warsaw, 1960).

[5] The first six-year plan covered the period 1950–1955, followed by two five-year plans
(1956–1960 and 1961–1965).

[6] *Rocznik Statystyczny, 1963* [Statistical Yearbook, 1963], Central Statistical Office.

Table 10. Changes in population and housing stock in Poland, 1946–1960*

Year	Total in millions†	In Towns		Increase Over 1946 Census (%)	
		Millions	%	National total	Towns
Population					
1946	23.9	7.5	31.8	100	100
1950	25.0	9.6	39.0	105	128
1960	29.7	14.1	48.1	124	188
Dwellings					
1946‡	5.05	1.95	38.6	100	100
1950	5.85	2.45	42.0	114	126
1960	7.0	3.55	50.5	139	182
Rooms					
1946	11.5	4.5	39.1	100	100
1950	13.65	6.0	43.7	119	133
1960	17.25	8.9	51.4	150	197

* *Rocznik Statystyczny, 1947, Rocznik Statystyczny, 1963* [Statistical Yearbook 1947, 1963], Główny Urząd Statystyczny [Statistical Central Office], Warsaw.

† Total population also includes persons not included in either the urban or the rural population.

‡ Data under the heading "Total" based on the author's estimates. The 1946 housing census concerned towns only.

to 48.1 per cent.[7] Even if the increase in urban population through bestowal of municipal rights upon some rural communes is disregarded (as being of administrative nature and having no direct impact on the growth of housing needs), urban population increased by more than 3.1 million. Responsible for this was the high birth rate and the migration of rural population to cities, which was particularly high in the first phase of the Six-Year Plan. There was also a high marriage rate: 10.8 per cent in 1950, 9.5 per cent in 1956. Marriage rates have slowly declined up to the present, with a drop to the level of 7.5 per cent in 1962.[8] This seriously affects the fluctuations of housing needs.

The policy of industrialization was on one hand an additional stimulus to the demand for new dwellings. On the other hand it tended to limit the possibilities of housing development in the first period, be-

[7] *Ibid.* Urban population: population of the places legally established as towns and urban settlements.

[8] *Ibid.*

cause it meant the concentration of capital and material means on industrial investments. Not until both production and national income had increased was there an increase in outlay for housing investments.[9]

From the point of view of housing policy there are, as a rule, three phases of industrialization which correspond to the three development plans mentioned previously.[10] The period of intense industrialization in 1950–1955, when rural labor reserves were used, was characterized by a limited growth in outlay for housing purposes and a rapid increase in housing demands resulting from large-scale migrations of people and intense urbanization. The second period, beginning in 1956, was marked by a consolidation and by growth effects of investments begun in previous years. The increase in production was based on an increase in employment to a much lesser extent. The ever growing national income made it possible to accelerate the rate of housing development, which was also assisted by changes in the investment structure. This was accompanied by some decline in housing needs, for demographic reasons. The third period, from 1959–1960 on, has been marked by rapid industrial expansion undertaken with a view to providing employment for persons in the age groups which will begin to enter the labor market in 1965. Competition between investment for housing and for production again came to the fore. Further development of housing was possible through the increase in national income and in labor efficiency. But although the volume of construction grew, there was a stabilization or even a decrease in the share of housing investments in total investment outlays.[11]

According to official statistical data, 1,023,000 flats with 2,824,000 rooms were constructed under the Six-Year Plan and first Five-Year Plan (between 1950 and 1960).[12] About 60 per cent of the newly built dwellings were located within the administrative areas of towns. Besides this, 170,000 rooms were constructed in collective housing for single persons migrating into towns. The dynamics of housing development is characterized by an increase in the average number of flats completed per year during the period 1956–1960. This increase amounted to

---

[9] National income increased between 1950 and 1962 by 135 per cent, housing investments by 332 per cent (data based on constant prices), *Rocznik Statystyczny, 1963.* See also Table 11, p. 159.

[10] See note 5, p. 156.

[11] In the above analysis of general attitude toward housing investments, no attention has been paid to some errors in the general investment policy which led, for example, in the period of the Six-Year Plan to disproportions in the development of the national economy, so that potential possibilities of housing construction were not taken advantage of.

[12] *Rocznik Statystyczny, 1963.*

Table 11. DEVELOPMENT OF HOUSING INVESTMENT AND BUILDING CONSTRUCTION IN POLAND, 1950–1965*

Years	Investment Outlay†		Dwellings completed (in thousands)		Dwellings completed per 1000 inhabitants		per 1000 inhab. incr.
	in billions of lots	% of total of invest-ments	total	in towns	total	in towns	total
1950–1955	39.6	12.3	401.5	235.0	2.6	3.7	135
1956–1960	81.5	19.5	621.9	369.8	4.3	5.6	252
1961–1965‡	97.0	16.0	742.0	550.0	4.8	7.3	400
1951	5.0	11.7	58.5	35.0	2.4	3.5	124
1956	8.5	16.9	90.8	54.0	3.3	4.4	171
1963	19.7	15.9	142.3	107.0	4.6	7.1	402

* *Rocznik Statystyczny, 1963.*

† In terms of 1961 prices.

‡ Estimated.

86 per cent in relation to the previous period (124,400 vs. 66,900 dwellings per year). The execution of the housing plan for 1961–1965 provides for a further 19 per cent increase in the number of dwellings; that is, more than 740,000 dwellings will be built, or an annual average of 148,000.[13]

How were the housing needs of the overflowing population—whose distribution pattern was continually altered—balanced by the housing program? Initially, housing was not adequate for needs. It was only after 1960 that the relationship between housing needs and capacity showed an improvement through an intensification of building and a declining increase of needs. Housing censuses of 1950 and 1960 showed a greater increase in the volume of housing stock than was officially reported. This can be explained by inaccuracy of building statistics, which covered only a part of the whole building activity; recovery of a number of dwellings which had accommodated offices during the general shortage of buildings; and reconstruction of slightly damaged buildings. Over all, housing volume grew at a faster rate than population; the average density of occupation per room considerably decreased.

[13] The increase is not so great as in the first version of the plan, which estimated 180,000 dwellings yearly.

Organization, Planning, and Financing of Housing

Under the Six-Year Plan most housing was constructed (75 per cent) by the state. The share of state-built dwellings amounted to 94 per cent in urban areas, whereas in the countryside it was responsible for only 31 per cent. The chief public investor was the *Workers' Settlements Building Department* (ZOR) with the *Workers' Settlements Building Boards* (DBOR) subordinated to the ZOR. After the abolition of the ZOR, all DBORs were brought under control of local councils. Financial support of the building activities of both the DBORs and the remaining public investors (state institutions and enterprises) was almost entirely based on the principle of government endowment of investors and on subsidies to dwelling occupants. Money from the national budget was allocated to public building activities. Dwelling occupants obtained housing units for very low rents which covered only part of the cost of building maintenance. These rents did not, on the average, exceed 1 or 2 per cent of the family income, thus remaining at the same level as in the old buildings. Most of the cost of maintenance was covered by the state.

Only at the end of 1956, when modifications were made in the over-all economic model, did significant changes in the system of housing economics take place.[14] These modifications tended to preserve the principle of central planning of national economy with simultaneous decentralization of administration. They also tended to base building activity on economic incentives. In this connection the following directives were worked out as new guides to housing policy:

(1) In order to cope with the problems presented by the difficult housing situation it is desirable to draw as much as possible on individual means to finance housing, and gradually to re-establish full payments for services rendered by the public bodies responsible for building maintenance, thereby providing a sound economic basis.

(2) State-financed building is to be expanded. Care should be taken, however, to ensure that flats built by public means are allocated to people whose low incomes and family responsibilities make private housing too expensive.

(3) In order to organize housing activity and production of building materials it is necessary to create conditions for the development of both social and individual initiative, as well as that of local authorities and

[14] A. Andrzejewski, *Polityka mieszkaniowa, zagadnienia ekonomiczne i socjalne* [Housing Policy, Economic and Social Problems] (Warsaw, 1959).

state organizations and enterprises. For this purpose additional capital should be contributed by town councils and enterprises.

(4) The power of the national councils responsible for housing policy, planning and coordination of housing activities, and the allocation of flats in specific areas should be increased. Local councils, however, should at the same time remain the chief investors supervising and managing a substantial part (or, in certain areas, even a majority) of housing.[15]

These directives were aimed at increasing the rate of construction, enlarging the total housing, and reducing the housing shortage—above all, the shortage of separate flats. Of foremost importance, therefore, was the housing-standard policy which postulated a maximum for the number of flats being built and a limitation on building costs.

The development of building is determined within the framework of existing plans. Investment plans for housing constitute a part of the general plan for the development of the national economy. The Five-Year Plan on which the annual plans are based stipulates the extent of public housing and provides material and financial means which enable the plans to be implemented. As far as the individual buildings are concerned, however, the plans give only rough estimates and determine the extent of state aid; the investment plans are worked out on a national scale. The planning of housing is a rather complicated proceeding, since it must take into account not only the requirements resulting from central planning of the development of the national economy, but also the requirements of local plans worked out by local bodies. Localization of investments must also agree with the directives for physical development.

PUBLIC HOUSING

Local councils and the subordinate agencies, the DBORs, are the chief investors for housing built with public funds. Flats constructed by them are allocated to the population by the appropriate municipal authorities. More and more housing is now constructed by industrial enterprises for their workers; but here also general supervision rests with local councils.

Rents on state-constructed flats continue at the level at which they

15 J. Bogusz, *Zasady nowej polityki mieszkaniowe* [Principles of New Housing Policy] (Warsaw, 1958).

Fig. 48. Warsaw: Block of flats. Mokotów cooperative housing estate. Architect: Z. Malicki, 1950 (photo: Central Photographic Archives)

were fixed in 1949 and are therefore still very low. There is a basic payment amounting to 3.6–5.5 *grosze* per square meter of floor area, supplemented by other charges of 55–83 *grosze* per square meter covering a part of maintenance costs.[16] Central heating is paid for separately. In

---

[16] One złoty equals 100 grosze.

addition, a new regulation was issued in 1957 requiring an incoming tenant of a flat built by the state to make a deposit and repay the cost of bathroom installation; in flats sponsored by industrial enterprises, and so forth, the incoming tenant must pay a certain amount in cash. These sums cannot exceed two months' salary of the tenant who, moreover, may pay them in installments.

Building activities carried out by local councils and industrial enterprises are financed from special funds (municipal and plant funds) set

Fig. 49. Warsaw: Block of flats. Koło housing estate. Architects: H. and S. Syrkus, 1950 (photo: Central Photographic Archives)

Fig. 50. Nowa Huta: Block of flats in the central square. Architect: Z. Ptaszycki; realized by ZOR, 1954–1956 (photo: Central Photographic Archives)

Fig. 51. Nowa Huta: Block of flats with shops. Architect: J. Ingarden; realized by the local Council, 1958–1959 (photo: Central Photographic Archives)

up during 1957 and 1958. Revenues from the sale of real estate, houses, and building lots appear in the records of the housing funds of the peoples' councils.[17] These funds also accumulate revenues from the deposits collected upon the allocation of newly built flats and from the sale of buildings to cooperatives, thus recovering for the investors at least part of their investment. At present their basic sources of revenue are budgetary grants.

The industrial housing funds, set up by state enterprises, receive the principal part of their revenues from other special funds of the plants. The amount depends on the economic success of the enterprise, and the money is entirely at the disposal of the workers' self-government. Housing funds are used not only to finance the construction work carried out either directly by the establishments or through commercial contractors, but also as loans granted to individual and cooperative builders. State investors are bound by what are called "standard regulations," prescribing the size and equipment of the flats to be constructed.

COOPERATIVE AND INDIVIDUAL BUILDING

Since private building of a capitalistic nature (that is, the construction of flats to be rented for profit) has been eliminated, two forms of housing activities remain which are carried out at the owners' expense —cooperative and individual building.

Table 12. HOUSING IN POLAND BY TYPES OF INVESTORS, 1950–1965 (IN THOUSANDS OF FLATS)*

Investors	1950–55	1956–60	1961–65†	1951	1956	1963
Public housing (total)	277.0	335.0	384.0	40.7	55.2	73.3
Nat. councils	205.4	201.5	235.0	27.1	38.1	47.7
Cooperatives	0.8	27.3	123.0	0.0	0.8	23.0
Individuals, nonrural population (total)	16.0	93.3	97.0	2.2	8.1	21.0
Aided by state credits	2.0	42.5		0.0	2.6	8.8
Individuals, rural population	108.7	166.4	138.0	15.6	26.7	25.0
Total	401.1	621.9	742.0	58.5	90.8	142.3

* For sources see Table 11.

† Expected.

[17] In order to free themselves from the burden of maintenance, the local councils have also sold some houses.

With state aid, building at the owners' expense has developed rapidly in the last seven years. The rate of increase is greatest in cooperative building, the tradition for which began before 1939 and continued throughout the early years of reconstruction. But in terms of volume, individual building has been and is still greater than cooperative construction. Individuals are allowed to build one-family, or, if they build jointly, four-family houses.

Housing cooperatives fall into three categories: those whose members obtain flats for which they pay rents sufficient to cover the costs involved in self-sufficient maintenance and upkeep of the buildings, through a sinking fund which enables the cooperative first to repay bank credits and then to make major repairs and renovations; those whose members obtain flats on terms approximating owner-occupation; those established for the purpose of organizing the building of one-family houses. Cooperative building, being organized, planned, and socially supervised, is generally considered a social activity. As a result, the housing estate (or neighborhood unit) is now a form of cooperative building which is growing in popularity.[18]

The total number of cooperatives rose between 1956 and 1963 from 299 to 899, and their membership from 44,000 to 258,900.[19] In addition to cooperatives in which membership is open to anyone, there are those linked to one or more plants, whose employees are the only people recruited for membership. Apart from building activity, housing cooperatives also perform social and cultural work. They are affiliated with the National Cooperative Union.

The methods of promoting individual and cooperative building which were developed in 1957–1958 consisted mainly of exempting newly built dwellings from the compulsory housing regulations and providing extensive financial support. The maximum limit of the floor area for the flats, if the building is to be exempt from regulations, has been defined as 110 square meters (or, in certain cases, 140 square meters). The rate of financial aid depends on the type of building ownership and the degree of its social utility.

Groups for cooperative building can receive state loans free of interest or at very low interest rates (1 per cent); these are long-term loans (25–40 years). Cooperatives are also entitled to subsidies that need not

18 W. Kasperski, *Spółdzielczość mieszkaniowa w Polsce* [Housing Cooperatives in Poland] (Warsaw, 1963).

19 *Bulletin of Housing Cooperatives,* Warsaw, 1964.

be repaid, which means that part (20 per cent–40 per cent) of a loan is actually a gift. This support is given if the future owner contributes a sum amounting to 15 per cent–30 per cent of the building costs. Assistance to individual building is more restricted; the privilege of subsidies is not granted, and loans must be repaid within twenty-five years. The upper limit of these loans per flat is fixed annually, small flats being particularly privileged according to the standard policy. The financial aid of the state was further extended in 1965.

As a result of these policies, the total amount of loans granted to individual and cooperative building in the towns has increased rapidly, as follows (in millions of złotys):

1956	153.7
1959	2390.8
1961	2950.0
1963	3470.0

Apart from aid extended by state banks, people building within cooperatives or individually can be given financial support by the enterprise that employs them in the form of a subsidy to cover part of the sum they must contribute.

Building at the owners' expense—individual and cooperative building—has increased more than 300 per cent since 1959. In this time it has accounted for about half of the total number of flats completed. The development of building at the owners' expense helped decentralize local housing investments and develop construction in smaller towns and town-type settlements not yet tackled by the state. In these areas the role of the cooperative movement is growing in importance. The current Five-Year Plan and the one that will follow provide for further expansion of cooperative building. An increasingly greater emphasis will also be placed on building activities of local councils for the low-income group which now has the worst housing conditions. On the other hand, steps have been taken to increase rents from the end of 1965 with simultaneous wage increases.

Housing Forms and Standards

Changes in the organization and structure of housing investment and consideration of housing within the framework of over-all investment plans, while harmonizing these plans with those of physical planning, have made it possible to concentrate housing construction on larger building sites. Thus, it has been possible for housing construction to play a part in shaping the pattern of towns and settlements. Most state and cooperative construction now concerns housing estates which contain social and cultural facilities and shopping centers in addition to dwellings. From the point of view of town planning the construction of such housing estates permitted several new undertakings. Residential quarters in towns destroyed during the war have been remodeled and rebuilt. Towns have been enlarged, following the expansion of industrial development; newly built estates reshape existing quarters and city centers, as well as create new residential quarters in development areas. New towns and administratively independent town-type settlements situated near existing conurbations have been constructed. Historical quarters have been reconstructed so as to preserve the chief elements of the town pattern and the former external appearance of buildings while adapting the interiors to modern requirements.

Fig. 52. Gdańsk: Historical houses in Długi Targ. Reconstructed by ZOR, 1953–1956 (photo: J. Tymiński, Central Photographic Archives)

Fig. 53. Gdańsk: Housing Estate "Jaskółcze." Realized by the local Council, 1960–1961 (photo: E. Uchymiak, Central Photographic Archives)

In certain towns the goals of the town planning policy could not always be achieved because in the early years there was a lack of physical development plans. This might have led to a location of new housing investments which was wrong from the point of view of long-term development. Current economic considerations—such as the necessity of avoiding locations where demolition and clearance of existing buildings were going on—also had to be taken into account.

The remaining area of state, cooperative, and individual building was dispersed. Efforts were made to put new buildings in the spaces between existing buildings. This gives the development a more uniform look and, in economic terms, enables the existing utilities network to be fully used. This policy was realized in the socialized sector of building, but was unsuccessful in private building, which showed considerable dispersal over the outskirts and peripheries of towns and rural areas.

In general, blocks of buildings of several stories are erected in towns by public and municipal authorities. One-family houses are more often encountered in cooperative estates, although even here the percentage is not high. Private building, however, handles this type of construction exclusively.

The free hand of authorities in assigning building sites has greatly helped to implement housing policy. Although ownership of land was left in private hands throughout the country (the only exception being Warsaw, where all land was communized so as to facilitate reconstruction work), state and local bodies obtained extensive areas in the recovered territories. Legislation was enacted providing for expropriation of areas to be used for investment plans.[20]

The size of housing estates varies greatly from town to town depending on the particular program, the amount of land available, and the

[20] In rural areas, compensation rates cover the full value of the land and its development. In towns, owners are usually given a lot in exchange for any lot expropriated, on which they can erect a one-family house. If there was a house on the lot expropriated, an additional sum is granted to cover the cost of erecting a one-family house on the new lot.

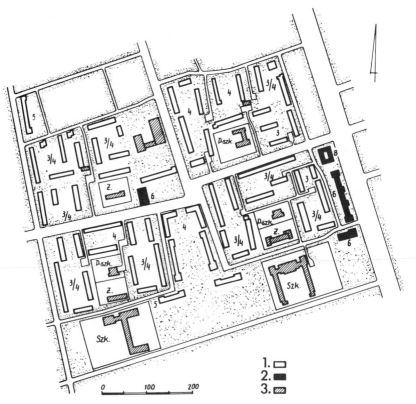

1. ☐
2. ■
3. ▨

Map 30. Plan of housing estate of Mokotów, Warsaw, for 9,000 inhabitants. Warsaw Housing Cooperative (architects: Z. Malicki and S. Tworkowski; completed between 1949 and 1956)

1. Blocks of flats, 3–5 stories. 2. Blocks of flats, 6–8 stories. 3. Service buildings (education, culture, health, trade).

P-szk: nursery schools. Szk: primary schools.

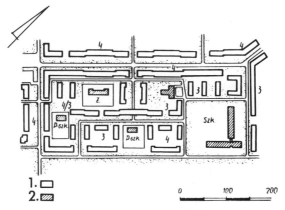

Map 31. Plan of housing estate in Świdnik for 3,800 inhabitants. Realized by ZOR, 1953–1956
    1. Blocks of flats, 3–4 stories. 2. Service buildings
(education, culture, health, trade).
    P-szk: nursery schools. Szk: primary schools.

town planning pattern. The basic planning unit is a neighborhood—
large enough to encompass services and shopping centers catering to the
basic needs of its inhabitants. About 10,000 inhabitants is deemed an
optimal number. The most important services are facilities for children,
such as nursery schools and primary schools; shopping centers for food
and other consumer goods and services; and health centers, including
out-patient clinics and drugstores. A club center is also provided in the
plan. Thus functionally and physically organized, the housing estate is
a basis for the development of social forms of self-management, cooperative forms being held in particularly high esteem.[21] Housing estates are
managed by local bodies and housing committees.

    The programing and design of housing estates is based on town-
planning norms which prescribe the density of development depending
on the zone.[22] There are requirements concerning sunlight and daylight

[21] R. Karłowicz, *Problemy mieszkalnictwa i struktura zespołów mieszkaniowych* [Housing Problems
and the Structure of Housing Estates] (Warsaw, 1962).
I. Rozenberg, *Koszty uzbrojenia terenów osiedlowych o zabudowie wielorodzinnej* [Cost of Equipment
of Terrains Destined for Blocks of Multifamily Flats], Prace Instytutu Budownictwa
Mieszkaniowego No. 33 [Housing Research Institute] (Warsaw, 1962).

[22] For instance, in zones of urban development where 3- and 5-story buildings prevail, the
density of population should not exceed 310–400 persons per hectare of gross housing area,
and in central zones of development it should not exceed 400–700 persons, according
to present housing standards.

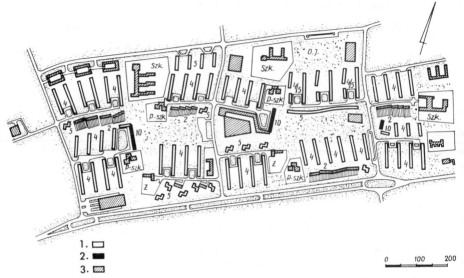

Map 32. Plan of residential district in Bydgoszcz for 17,000 inhabitants; realized
    by the local Council (architect: J. Polak; begun in 1959)
    1. Blocks of flats, 2–5 stories. 2. Blocks of flats, 10 stories. 3. Service buildings
(education, culture, health, trade).
    P-szk: nursery schools. Szk: primary schools.

and norms providing for traffic and parking and prescribing the size of
indispensable services.[23]

Methods for drawing up site plans for blocks of flats and dwellings
are dealt with in separate regulations. Against a background of general
assumptions that permits each family to have a separate flat within which
each resident is actually to have an average of about 118 sq. ft. (11 sq. m.)
of floor area,[24] standards for blocks of flats take into account the type
and size of flats. The minimum and maximum floor area in each category destined for a given housing estate is calculated according to the
demographic structure and the size of family. For economic reasons,
however, rules for average-sized flats have been issued to provide an
index of control for housing estates.

The norm of 118 sq. ft. per person is an average index; it varies with
the size of the flat since it must include appropriate kitchen and sanitary

[23] Green space in dwelling areas must amount to no less than 64.5 sq. ft. (6 sq. m.)
per inhabitant, apart from the open spaces within the housing estate itself: 27–37 sq.
ft. (2.5–3.5 sq. m.) per inhabitant.

[24] In the future it is planned to achieve about 180 sq. ft. (15–16 sq. m.).

equipment. The norm provides for a bathroom, a lavatory, running water, sewerage, and electricity. Gas supply from mains depends on local conditions; central heating is widely used. For economic reasons, buildings constructed in areas only partially developed are less well equipped; in such cases only low buildings are permitted. Even then, projects must be designed with facilities to include the missing installation later on.

These norms refer to state and cooperative building in urban areas. In private building the upper limit of surface area is the only one limited by regulations; it is not to exceed 1,185 sq. ft. (110 sq. m.). When state aid has been given for private building, the surface area cannot

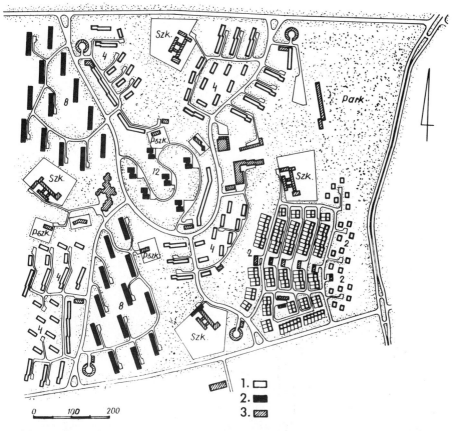

1. ☐
2. ■
3. ▨

0   100   200

Map 33. Plan of residential district in Będzin for 21,000 inhabitants (architects: H. Adamczewska and K. Wejchert; begun in 1958)

1. Blocks of flats, 2–4 stories. 2. Blocks of flats, 8–12 stories. 3. Service buildings (education, culture, health, trade).

P-szk: nursery schools. Szk: primary schools.

Table 13. CATEGORIES OF FLATS ACCORDING TO NORMS FOR
DESIGNING BLOCKS OF FLATS*

Categories (by number of persons)	Floor area	
	sq. ft.	sq. m.
M1	182–215	17–20
M2	258–323	24–30
M3	355–409	33–38
M4	452–516	42–48
M5	548–613	51–57
M6	635–699	59–65
M7	721–764	67–71

* *Monitor Polski*, No. 81, 1959.

exceed 915 sq. ft. (85 sq. m.). Standards for housing built individually with no state aid are lower than for the previously discussed types; the location of such housing in small towns and rural areas is responsible for this fact.

In view of the shortage of capital, the policy of standardization seeks on one hand to maximize the number of dwellings being built. Hence restrictions are imposed on the size of the flat, its equipment, and

Fig. 54. Będzin: One-family houses in the new residential district. Realized by the local Council, 1960–1962

Fig. 55. Gdynia: One-family houses in the Gdynia-Orłowo cooperative housing estates; constructed 1956–1960 (photo: Blażewicz, Central Photographic Archives)

its general cost. On the other hand, it seeks to ensure good dwelling conditions. Therefore, the standards should be viewed against the background of specific economic and housing conditions. But even so, standard dwellings now erected in both urban and rural areas are a considerable improvement on the existing stock, particularly with respect to equipment.

Generally speaking, the standard policy has been the same since the early postwar years.[25] But the method of drawing up plans for housing estates, as well as town planning and architectural concepts, has substantially changed. The housing projects built just after the war made use of the experience acquired during the period between the world wars in cooperative building, which, though quantitatively small, accounted for important achievements in the planning of housing estates. At the same time emphasis was placed on flexible and functional assembly, separation of the housing areas from intense traffic, and the adaptation of building solutions to human needs.

Between 1950 and 1954 the trend in town planning tended to

[25] J. Goryński, *Standardy budowlane—budownictwo mieszkaniowe* [Building Standards—Housing] (Warsaw, 1953).

enhance exterior architectural effects of questionable value at the expense of the utility of dwellings. The architectural concept of making the blocks of flats monumental and ornamenting them was undertaken with no good reasons. The last period, from 1957 on, has been marked by a new appreciation of functional designs for housing estates and of varying heights within developments. There have been many new solutions.[26] The main elements at work are progress in standardizing building types for housing estates and application of mass-production methods in construction. The improvement of construction methods and the introduction of lower costs open new prospects of expansion for the building program.

Changes in the Housing Situation and Development Needs

Trends and rate of changes in the housing situation should be examined with regard to the rapid change in the socioeconomic structure of the country and its effects on housing needs and development. According to the three successive censuses made between 1946 and 1960,[27] total growth in building stock was greater than in that of population (Table 10). As a result, there was a drop in occupation density (the average number of persons per room). The rate at which the decline proceeded varied in urban and rural areas; in the latter occupation density diminished faster, but we should remember that the initial situation was worse. An underlying reason for the change was an increase not only in the number of flats but also in the average size of dwellings. It should be noted that the number of flats per thousand urban inhabitants decreased slightly between 1950 and 1960.

Passing on to the problem of the relationship between the number of flats and the number of inhabitants, we touch upon an essential aspect of the housing situation in Poland—the shortage of separate flats in relation to number of households. In the 1950 census this shortage was estimated to be approximately four to five hundred thousand in towns, assuming such flats to be allocated to half of the single-person households and to all the larger households. In the last ten years, average household size has been increasing in towns (from 2.9 to 3.1 persons); this implies that between 1950 and 1960 the number of households increased at a

[26] M. Kaczorowski, *Zagadnienia ekonomiczne projektowania architektonicznego* [Economic Problems of Architectonic Design] (Warsaw, 1958).

[27] The sources of the census data quoted in this chapter are given in Tables 10 and 15. See also A. Andrzejewski, "Kierunki rozwoju sytuacji mieszkaniowej w Polsce w świetle wyników spisów z lat 1950–1960" [Trends in the Housing Situation in Poland in the Light of Censuses of 1950 and 1960], *Sprawy Mieszkaniowe* (Housing Research Institute, Warsaw), No. 1, 1963.

Table 14. CHANGES IN OCCUPATION DENSITY AND IN SIZE OF DWELLINGS, 1946–1960*

Year	Dwellings per 1000 inhabitants†		Persons per room†		Rooms per Dwelling	
	Poland	Towns	Poland	Towns	Poland	Towns
1946	207	259	2.01	1.67	2.33	2.31
1950	244	266	1.75	1.54	2.34	2.44
1960	245	262	1.66	1.53	2.45	2.50

* Sources: See Table 10.

† Indices were calculated in relation to the population in dwellings. In 1946 this included all population except persons not included in either the urban or rural census (about 0.3 million persons).

slower rate than the total population. In view of the limited extent of building construction and replacements, the shortage of separate dwellings continues in absolute numbers at the same level. As a result, many dwellings accommodated two or even more separate households. Nevertheless, because of the difference in the rate of increase, the proportion of the households per 100 dwellings fell in towns from 132 in 1950 to 123 in 1960.[28] In rural areas the sharing of dwellings by two or more households did not present such an acute problem.

Between 1950 and 1960 urban occupation density did not follow a regular pattern. Changes in intensity of needs and in extent of building activities caused a certain deterioration in the period from 1950 to 1957, due to rapid growth of the urban population and large migrations. In recent years, following a period of stabilization, there has been a gradual improvement in occupation density. Moreover, the differences in the housing situation are fairly sharp from one region to another.[29]

With the changing average occupation density the structure of occupation has also changed. Regional disparity in density decreased as the housing stock increased and the housing policy was implemented. This was assisted by the maintenance of low rents aimed at regulating the allocation of dwellings. Nonetheless, between 1950 and 1960 up to 27.2 per cent of the urban population lived in overcrowded dwellings; in rural areas the figure was 46.4 per cent.[30]

[28] Together with efficiency apartments, the number of dwellings was approximately even to the number of multiperson households. See *Rocznik Statystyczny, 1963.*

[29] W. Litterer-Marwege, *Standard mieszkaniowy w miastach Polski* [Housing Standards in Polish Towns], Prace Instytutu Budownictwa Mieszkaniowego No. 27 [Housing Research Institute] (Warsaw, 1959).

[30] In Poland "overcrowded" means more than two persons per room.

Fig. 56. Warsaw: Blocks of flats in the housing estate Praga II. Architect: J. Geysztor; realized by the local Council in 1960 (photo: I. Rozenberg)

Fig. 57. Warsaw: Blocks of flats in the housing estate of Sady-Warsaw Housing Cooperative. Architect: H. Skibniewska. Constructed in 1961 (photo: B. Miedza, Central Photographic Archives)

At the same time there was an evident improvement in the quality of housing stock and housing conditions. This was the result of a rapid increase in the number of new buildings, much higher building standards, better planning of housing estates, and greater provision of green areas and social and service facilities. In the last census 25.4 per cent of the total housing stock represented building done since the war. It was estimated that 25.6 per cent of the building stock in towns was either completed in the postwar period or entirely reconstructed. In the rural areas the new stock was about 25 per cent. The remaining part of the increase included houses damaged to a lesser extent and repaired and those buildings returned to use for housing purposes.

The rigid standard policy which limited the size of dwellings being built and thus concentrated efforts on the provision of medium-sized dwellings brought about some improvement in the pattern of size of dwellings. The percentage of medium-sized dwellings increased, the percentage of one-room dwellings diminished, and the average size, as already mentioned, increased.

Standard policy on utilities resulted in an improvement of utilities in housing stock. Particularly striking was the increase in lavatory and bathroom equipment, which was relatively rare in prewar dwellings. In 1950, 63.2 per cent of apartments were in buildings with running water;

Fig. 58. Wrocław: Blocks of flats in the reconstructed district of the city between 1959 and 1961 (photo: Central Photographic Archives)

Table 15. CHANGES IN THE SIZE OF DWELLINGS, 1950–1960*

Year	Total dwellings (in thousands)	One	Two	Three	Four	Five and more
Poland						
1950†	5,850	21.5	43.0	23.5	9.0	4.0
1960	7,024	17.5	40.6	26.9	10.8	4.2
Towns						
1950	2,445	21.1	37.5	25.2	11.1	5.1
1960	3,546	17.5	36.8	30.1	11.4	4.2

Header note: Number of rooms (in per cent) spans the One, Two, Three, Four, Five and more columns.

* For sources, see Table 10. See also *Spis Powszechny z dn. 6 grudnia 1960 r.* Ludność, gospodarstwa domowe, mieszkania. Biuletyn Statystyczny, numer specjalny [Census made on December 6, 1960. Population. Households. Flats. Statistical Bulletin. Special Number] (Warsaw: Central Statistical Office, 1962).

† Because of the lack of official data concerning rural dwelling size in 1950, data were supplemented by the author's estimates.

nearly the same percentage were in buildings with sewage pipes; while apartments with inside running water accounted for only 42.2 per cent of the total; those with lavatories accounted for 25.8 per cent, and those with bathrooms for 14.2 per cent. The findings of the 1960 census proved that the number of flats with lavatories increased by 111 per cent, as compared with 1950, and those with bathrooms by 179 per cent.

The evident improvement in housing conditions for the population which inhabited new dwellings[31] was not, however, accompanied by adequate improvement in the prewar housing stock. Measures taken to modernize this housing stock were not carried out on a mass scale, except that many buildings were connected to sewage and water conduits.

The level of housing equipment in rural areas continues to be low. An exception is the provision of electricity which became possible with the electrification of the countryside.

Conclusions and Prospects for Development

In reviewing changes taking place in the housing situation, I have attempted to consider both favorable and unfavorable aspects. A general appraisal of the housing situation cannot disregard the conditions under

[31] A. Andrzejewski, Z. Barszczewska, W. Czeczerda, A. Matejko, W. Malicka, I. Trammer, *Zaludnienie i użytkowanie mieszkań w nowych osiedlach* [Occupation and Use of Dwellings in New Housing Estates], Prace Instytutu Budownictwa Mieszkaniowego No. 23 [Housing Research Institute] (Warsaw, 1958).

which the housing policy was pursued and the relation of this policy to the national economy. From the economic point of view it can be said that housing development—particularly its concentration in underdeveloped regions—hastened industrialization and made it possible to overcome difficulties connected with the intense urbanization process. An important role in solving this problem was played by planned public housing construction.

Following the war, improvement in housing conditions, as determined by social needs, could not be given as much attention as desirable. Housing policy can be credited with important achievements and a considerable improvement has been achieved in comparison both with the prewar and the immediate postwar situation. Nevertheless the reported statistical data adequately show that some key problems of housing policy have not yet been solved in Poland. These are the shortage of separate dwellings, congestion and the poor quality of a major portion of the housing stock, shortage of equipment, and disparity between urban and rural housing conditions and between particular regions. From the point of view of social effects one should stress the importance of elements of the housing policy which leveled disparities in dwelling conditions inherited from the capitalist period. Such elements are the policy of low rents, norms of occupation of dwellings under public control, and standards for new housing.

Under the plan now being implemented, construction of some 140,000–150,000 dwellings yearly (on an average 4.8 dwellings per 1,000 inhabitants) will be completed between 1961 and 1965. This will meet current housing needs and even provide a surplus. Beginning in 1961 and 1962, special steps were taken to meet the needs of that segment of the population that has the worst housing. By 1965 almost all the housing sponsored by local councils is directed toward this end. The ever growing desire for better accommodation resulting from the economic development and the general rise of living standards exerts an additional influence on the housing situation. It creates a strong increase in subjective needs, while it facilitates development of cooperative and individual housing. Such forms of housing are intended to improve the situation of those groups in the population that—because of the higher level of their income—cannot obtain state-built dwellings.

Long-term programs for economic and social development have brought the particular importance of housing problems to the fore. The creation of the general economic base and its further development, as well as the growth of the building industry, permit greater expansion of housing activities. The perspective plan estimates that within its last five years (1975–1980) the number of dwellings completed should amount to an average 12–14 dwellings per thousand inhabitants yearly.[32] The first proposal of the plan, for the period 1965–1970, fixes new housing at about 960,000–970,000 dwellings (about 6 dwellings per thousand inhabitants) yearly.

The above estimates give only a general idea of the building scale that is needed. Such a building program will make it possible not only to overcome the existing shortage and to meet needs arising from urbanization processes and population increase but also to liquidate much poor-quality and substandard housing stock and to raise qualitative and floor area standards. It is assumed that the floor area per person should increase to some 180 sq. ft. (about 16 sq. m.), amounting in terms of density to an average of one person per room.

The building program which envisages this great increase in the number and improvement in the standard of dwellings will create conditions for a thorough remodeling and expansion of towns and rural settlements, and for improvements in the system of meeting housing needs according to principles of social policy.

[32]W. Nieciuński, "Uwagi w sprawie perspektywicznego programu budownictwa mieszkaniowego w miastach na lata 1961–1980" [Remarks on the Perspective Housing Program in Towns 1961–1980], *Miasto*, No. 1, 1961.

CHAPTER 7

Sociological Implications of Urban Planning

Janusz Ziółkowski

THE phrase "sociological implications of planning" in its most general sense signifies the existence of social conditions which determine or influence the procedure called urban or regional planning; it also suggests that this procedure has definite consequences for social life. But urban planning is "social"—if we may say so—in its own right. It is a social activity performed by a set of people representing a specific social background, a "culture" (in the broad, anthropological sense); it is based, like all planning, on values, selection of goals, and expectations of results. Physical planning, although concerned with shaping the material reality around us, basically deals with human beings. There is a deeply humanistic side to the planner's work. He builds in order to satisfy human needs and desires and to fulfill human aspirations.

The problem of the sociological implications of such planning may be approached either in terms of the *objective* phenomena and processes that take place in connection with planning, or in terms of the *subjective* consciousness of the actors involved in this process.

It is in the objective sense that we speak of the social determinants and social consequences of urban or regional planning. The socio-economic structure of a particular society, the level of its economic development, the existing political system and social philosophy—all determining physical planning—exist objectively, that is, independently of social awareness. The same is true of the social consequences of planning. Physical planning is not only dependent on social conditions; the reverse is also true—planning has a great influence on social life in all its aspects. And this influence is again "objective." The development of individuals and social groups, the establishment of social ties, the psychic satisfaction that is created or hindered by the spatial organization of the region, town, or neighborhood unit may occur without people being conscious of all the factors influencing social behavior in a spatial setting.

The great importance of the objective processes connected with urban planning is clearly evident in Poland, a country whose whole social and economic life is based on the principle of planning. Urban planning is not an autonomous process in Poland; here, as in other countries where there is national ownership of the means of production, physical planning is closely linked to economic and social planning. The forces released by central planning activities permeate all spheres of life.

We are inclined sometimes to think about planning in slightly metaphysical terms. Let us make it clear that people are always involved— both as subjects and as objects of planning. Human beings and their consciousness are inseparable. Indeed, human evolution in general may be characterized by the steady growth of reflexive awareness. The process of "hominization," as the late Teilhard de Chardin called it, brought into being on our planet a "noösphere," "the psychically reflexive human surface."[1] I should like to dwell on this human side of the problem,[2] which implies consideration of a "self-conscious" type of behavior. The object of my analysis will be the main actors in urban planning, the planners themselves.

The sociological problems connected with the category of people called "planners" and with their profession[3] are very broad indeed. The problem to be examined is rather limited in scope: how are social factors reflected in the planners' consciousness, and what is the impact of this on their work? Or in other words, to what degree are planners endowed with "sociological imagination," to use the expression of the late C. Wright Mills.[4]

Our epoch is characterized by a very high, and still increasing, degree of "sociological imagination." This applies not only to sciences dealing with man (social sciences and humanities) but also to natural

---

[1] P. Teilhard de Chardin, "The Antiquity and World Expansion of Human Culture," in W. L. Thomas, Jr., ed., *Man's Role in Changing the Face of the Earth* (Chicago: The University of Chicago Press, 1956), pp. 103–104.

[2] The tendency to consider individuals as a central focus of attention has received in contemporary sociology the name "hominocentrism": see H. D. Lasswell and A. Kaplan, *Power and Society* (New Haven: Yale University Press, 1950), p. 24.

[3] See in this respect B. Kaye, *The Development of the Architectural Profession in Great Britain: A Sociological Study* (London: Allen & Unwin, 1960).

[4] *The Sociological Imagination* (New York: Oxford University Press, 1959).

and technical disciplines.[5] Increasingly, the conviction is gaining ground that apart from purely physical phenomena (such as day following night and so forth) everything happening on this globe, being to a lesser or greater degree subject to human intervention, has social roots and consequences, is a functional part of the social order, and is related to the social structure. "Sociological" thinking is becoming an essential part of contemporary man's self-knowledge.

In the realm of physical planning there are, it appears, four elements in the planner's sociological consciousness: (1) awareness that in creating a spatial framework for human life he performs a social function of enormous significance; that planning is "social" at the core; (2) awareness of a necessity to become acquainted in a systematic way with social reality, to gather all relevant data about the community and society as a whole in order to trace trends of development of social groups and institutions, and to learn about human values and preferences; (3) awareness that his work has profound social consequences, furthering or hampering fulfillment of human desires, the achievement of men's goals, and the solution of their problems; (4) awareness that his activities, his views, ideas, and values, are determined by his social and cultural background and group affiliations.

It should be noted that these elements of the planner's consciousness are abstract constructions. In empirical reality the particular elements may be not so clear-cut, they may often overlap and intermix. Taken as a whole, they constitute an "ideal type" of the planner's consciousness. The aim of typology in the social sciences is purely heuristic. "Types" are conceptual constructions for "ordering," comparing, and comprehending the concrete data.[6] The ideal type "in its conceptual purity . . . cannot be found empirically anywhere in reality."[7] Such a presumption

---

[5] Let us mention just one example: medicine, where, according to A. Leslie Banks and J. Hislop ("Sanitation Practices and Disease Control in Extending and Improving Areas for Human Habitation," in Thomas, *op. cit.,* p. 820), "it is possible to see the transition in emphasis from the physical and the biological to the social environment, for many current 'medical' problems are now recognized to be medico-social or, indeed, socio-medical in character." See also B. J. Stern, *Social Factors in Medical Progress* (New York: Columbia University Press, 1927); an extensive bibliography can be found in G. G. Reader and Mary E. W. Goss, "The Sociology of Medicine," in R. K. Merton, *et al.,* eds., *Sociology Today: Problems and Prospects* (New York: Basic Books, 1959).

[6] See J. C. McKinney, "The Role of Constructive Typology in Scientific Sociological Analysis," *Social Forces,* XXVIII, March, 1950, and the same author's "Constructive Typology and Social Research," in J. T. Doby, ed., *An Introduction to Social Research* (Harrisburg, Pa.: Stackpole, 1954).

[7] M. Weber, *The Methodology of the Social Sciences* (Glencoe, Ill.: The Free Press, 1949), p. 90.

as regards the "planner's mentality"[8] may be considered unjustified. Surely, there are planners whose "sociological imagination" includes all the four elements. Nevertheless, this situation can be very usefully treated as an "ideal-type" construct, from which the empirical cases deviate to a greater or lesser extent.

Some further reservations should be made. This is not a systematic study of the planner's consciousness in which all the sophisticated methods of contemporary sociology are used. It is rather a series of impressions based on observation of the planner's "sociological imagination" as it reveals itself in words and deeds (the statements, the organizational initiatives, and, most difficult to discover, the traces of "sociological imagination" in actual urban planning). The difficulty is that consciousness does not always determine social behavior. The latter can also be directed by a stereotyped way of thinking, or sociological fashion, which may be a boon as well as a curse for the development of scientific discipline.

Bearing this in mind, let us examine the particular elements of the planner's consciousness, each of them involving a different kind of "sociological imagination."

I. The idea that a city is more than a technical accomplishment seems to be as old as the art of city-building itself. Hippodamus was not only—as far as we can judge—the first city planner in the Western world; according to Aristotle, he also projected a social utopia.[9] "Most cities of the historical past can be interpreted as expression of a way of life."[10] The Athenian Agora, where the whole public life of the town was concentrated (the original meaning of "agora" was "gatherings"), and Fort Agra of the Great Mogul with its Divan-I-Am, beyond which no ordinary man ever penetrated, reflect the Greek type of democracy and the despotism of the East. The domination of the cathedral, the castle, the guild halls, or the town hall in the spatial layout of medieval towns reflects the hierarchy of values of that epoch. The burghers' houses of the self-governing towns of medieval Europe, almost equal

[8] This is an expression used by H. Orlans in his *Stevenage: A Sociological Study of a New Town* (London: Routledge and Kegan Paul, 1952).

[9] R. Turner, *The Great Cultural Traditions* (New York: McGraw-Hill, 1941), I, p. 479. See also E. A. Gutkind, *Revolution of Environment* (London: Routledge and Kegan Paul, 1946), pp. 27–29; L. Mumford, *The Culture of Cities* (New York: Harcourt, Brace, 1938), p. 504.

[10] S. Riemer, *The Modern City: An Introduction to Urban Sociology* (New York: Prentice-Hall, 1952), p. 437.

with respect to the size of plot and height of the building, reveal the egalitarian tendencies within the mercantile social stratum.[11]

But it was not until the time of Ebenezer Howard[12] and Patrick Geddes[13] at the turn of the last century that the idea of the social function of town planning was expressed in an explicit form. This was, needless to say, a result of the industrial revolution, which intensified the process of urbanization on a scale unprecedented in human history, and which induced town planners to seek solutions to problems raised by this new and tremendous challenge. For both Howard and Geddes the construction of a city was, first of all, a social problem. From their concerns sprang the tradition of regarding the city as a human group, a social organization and institution. The tendency to look for man in the city —which can be seen in the work of the greatest figures in architecture and urban planning, such as Frank Lloyd Wright,[14] Jean Le Corbusier,[15] Walter Gropius,[16] and Siegfried Giedion,[17]—found its climax in the passionate cry, "The city is the people."[18]

For the Polish school of town planning the sociological approach was typical from the very beginning. In the nineteen-twenties J. Chmielewski was advocating the closest collaboration between town planning and sociology. He was in favor of introducing "the social criterion" into urban design on the widest scale. Chmielewski's work remained chiefly theoretical.[19] The link between theory and practice was established in the same decade when T. Toeplitz and his colleagues founded the

---

[11] The examples are taken from the author's paper "Human Environment and Civilization: Human and Social Evolution" delivered at the Twenty-sixth World Congress of the International Federation for Housing and Planning (Paris, September 2–9, 1962).

[12] See his *Tomorrow: A Peaceful Path to Real Reform* (London, 1898), reprinted as *Garden Cities of To-morrow* (Cambridge, Mass.: MIT Paperbacks, 1965).

[13] Especially in his *Cities in Evolution,* rev. ed. (London: Williams & Norgate, 1949); see also "Civics as Applied Sociology," in *Sociological Papers* (London, 1905).

[14] Especially in his *An Autobiography* (New York: Longmans Green, 1932); see also F. L. Wright and B. Brownell, *Architecture and Modern Life* (New York: Longmans Green, 1932).

[15] See his *Urbanisme. Collection de l'Esprit Nouveau* (Paris, 1925); *Concerning Town Planning* (London: The Architectural Press, 1947); *When the Cathedrals Were White* (New York: Reynal and Hitchcock, 1947).

[16] See his *The New Architecture and the Bauhaus* (London: Faber and Faber, 1935).

[17] See his *Mechanization Takes Command* (New York: Oxford University Press, 1948).

[18] This is the title of H. S. Churchill's book: *The City Is the People* (New York: Reynal and Hitchcock, 1945).

[19] The most representative of his views are presented in a book written with S. Syrkus, *Warszawa funkcjonalna* [Functional Warsaw] (Warsaw: 1937).

Polish Association for Housing Reform. Their forum for discussion was the journal *Dom, Osiedle, Mieszkanie (House, Housing Estate, Dwelling)*, and the ideas expressed there were put into practice by the Warsaw Housing Cooperative and the Social Enterprise for Construction.

At the core of the activity of the whole group was the notion of "social urbanism." One aim was to build "the dwellings most needed socially"; the other was to create small residential units, as socio-culturally self-sufficient as possible, where strong emotional ties among members and attitudes of mutual help and solidarity could arise.[20] Housing estates based on these aims were built in Żoliborz and Mokotów, suburbs of Warsaw. About the Żoliborz cooperative, which housed 4,000 people, one of its members, S. Ossowski, an eminent Polish sociologist, wrote:

[It] had developed . . . manifold . . . economic and social activities which were carefully planned by the elected body and subject to the criticism of all members, and which included schools, artistic and discussion clubs, scientific lectures, and experimental theater. It had succeeded in creating certain forms of social life in which people who were diverse in their social opinions took part.[21]

What was striking about the Warsaw Housing Cooperative was the homogeneous character of the ideology of its members. Both the Warsaw Cooperative and the Association for Housing Reform were socialistically inclined. Their activity was a form of social protest against the indifference of the existing political system to the most socially handicapped part of the population.

The activities of the Warsaw Cooperative were carried on even during the Nazi occupation—of course, in a clandestine manner. Lectures were given[22] and plans designed for future settlements in which "social cohesion among inhabitants would be stronger than anything known in history."

[20] The principles upon which this project was based were very close to C. A. Perry's neighborhood-unit formula, but the Polish experiment was carried out independently. The first housing cooperative in Warsaw was built in 1923. It was in the same year that Perry presented the nucleus of his idea in a paper, "A Community Unit in City Planning and Development," at the joint meeting of the National Community Center Association and the American Sociological Association. It took its definite form in *Housing for the Machine Age* (New York: Russel Sage Foundation, 1939).

[21] *Social Conditions and Social Consequences of Social Planning*, Transactions of the Fourth World Congress of Sociology (London: International Sociological Association, 1959), p. 204.

[22] For instance, by Helena Syrkus to the workers of the Social Enterprise for Construction and to the staff of the Warsaw Housing Cooperative in 1941; the title of this lecture was "The Social Housing Estate against the Background of the Quarter, the City, and the Region."

The new political system after the war brought great social change. Along with the democratization of the whole society, conditions were created for "democratization of the city area," in the phrase of two architects, Helena and S. Syrkus.[23] Together with B. Brukalska they were the main proponents of the "sociological" approach to town planning just after the war. Symptomatic is the title of Mrs. Brukalska's book, which gives the fullest outline of the ideas of "social urbanism": *The Social Principles of Housing Estates Design.*[24]

Opportunities for putting the sociological principles of town planning into practice were enhanced enormously by the foundation in 1948 of the Board of Worker Settlements (BWS). Earlier efforts had been planned and carried out by individuals or small groups of dedicated people. Now there was a state establishment having at its disposal all the capabilities of a planned economy. In the Six-Year Plan (1950–1955) alone, the BWS was expected to provide 75 per cent of the total dwelling space. The activities of the BWS have been social ones par excellence, and not only because there have been social ideas (to which we shall return later) underlying the construction of workers' housing estates. Provision of adequate dwelling conditions for people in a socialist country undergoing rapid industrialization and urbanization has been considered the state's responsibility. This principle has been put into effect on a mass scale; for many years (until 1958, when small initial deposits were introduced) a new dwelling was a sort of a gift from the state, with rent constituting but a slight percentage of the family budget.

Another factor that stimulated social rebuilding was the enormous amount of war destruction. The heaviest damages were sustained in the Western Territories, where the total destruction in towns reached 54 per cent of all buildings. Rapid, efficient, and broad action was called for. Ironically, war damages also provided a unique opportunity not only for reconstruction according to the old pattern (in city areas of historic interest), but also for reshaping cities along the lines laid down by the Socialist state. The reconstruction of Polish cities aroused great national enthusiasm. It was watched with close interest and evoked lively discussion. The press was full of architectural terms, detailed descriptions of individual projects, and so forth. Architects and urban planners found themselves suddenly at the center of the nation's attention. They

[23] "Budownictwo doświadczalne" [Experimental Construction], *Dom, Osiedle, Mieszkanie,* No. 6–8, 1946.

[24] *Zasady społeczne projektowania osiedli mieszkaniowych* (Warsaw: 1948).

were subject to both assiduous social protection and rigid social control. It is not usual elsewhere for the highest state authorities to take part in the discussion (almost the elaboration) of a particular scheme, and to reach the final decision concerning it, as was the case with the East-West route in Warsaw in 1948, with the Old Town in Warsaw, in Poznań, in Gdańsk, and so on. Neither is it usual to subject designs to criticism at public exhibitions, where a sort of a plebiscite is held, which is the normal practice in the Polish capital and in many other cities.

II. Hand in hand with awareness of the social character of urban planning goes the conviction that the urban planner is able to perform his function effectively only if he is aware of all the complexity of human nature and the social world around him. Here an obvious need arises for the planner to learn the facts concerning the individuals and social groups destined to live in the spatial framework created by him. This raises certain questions: what facts does he need? and how should they be collected?

In answering the second question first we shall be able to clarify the first one. The attitude of urban planners toward social reality for many decades might best be depicted in the phrase "every planner his own sociologist." The science of society, sociology, is rather young; it was not born until the eighteen-thirties. But gradually it was felt that casual observation of social life and reflection upon the facts of one's experience was not enough. What was really needed was to collect the facts that are relevant to a coherent theoretical framework—systematic, professional investigation of community life, existing social groups, norms, institutions, and values. This is the role of sociology. In the contemporary world ever increasing hope for proper solutions to all the complicated problems of human environment is placed in the science of society.

The first question has been answered in an unsurpassed manner by an eminent American sociologist, the late Louis Wirth—one of the most ardent advocates of the closest cooperation between urban planning and sociology—in his lecture "Sociological Factors in Urban Design."[25] For him "the function of design is to create, by rational means, the physical form to enable men to achieve as close an approximation to the solution of their problems and the fulfillment of their hopes as their resources,

---

[25] Delivered at the Convention Seminars of the American Institute of Architects (Salt Lake City, June 25, 1948).

their creative imagination, and their disciplined intelligence allow."[26] The crucial problems, as well as the most obvious questions about sociodemographic structure, which a design poses for the urban planner may be formulated, according to Wirth, as follows: first of all, do we need cities at all? Then, why do people wish to live in cities? Do they obtain from city life what they hope to obtain? What are the assets and liabilities of city life? Which are the most fundamental and which are the secondary values in the value scheme of the people who enlist the planner's services? What are the relative advantages of the central city, the suburbs, the satellite towns, and the urban periphery for the satisfaction of human needs and for the provision of the essential functions to supply these needs? What are the structure and function of the family and what are the trends of its future development? Can a neighborhood exist in cities? Into what social groups do people in cities congregate to satisfy their various sociopsychic needs? What is the nature of social intercourse in the city? What is the impact of the mobility and heterogeneity of city people on urban design?

It is, of course, not possible to achieve anything like a general consensus regarding the nature and range of social factors in urban design, and the extent to which they determine the planner's work. Each case is individual and requires individual treatment. But none of these questions can be ignored in responsible town planning.

The degree to which the planner feels he has to turn to the sociologist varies from country to country. In some, the two disciplines hardly tolerate each other, in others they form the closest alliance. Examples of the latter situation, so it seems, at least, are the United States, France, and the United Kingdom, where the advice of eminent sociologists is sought and respected by urban planners (where, indeed, they are planners themselves). Among the most important figures are Lewis Mumford[27] in the United States, Paul Chombart de Lauwe[28] in France, and Ruth Glass[29] in England.

Poland represents a special case. In the interwar period, when the

[26] E. Wirth Marvick and A. J. Reiss, Jr., eds., *Community Life and Social Policy: Selected Papers by Louis Wirth* (Chicago: The University of Chicago Press, 1956), p. 285.

[27] See especially *Technics and Civilization* (New York: Harcourt, Brace, 1934); *The Culture of Cities* (New York: Harcourt, Brace, 1938); *City Development* (New York: Harcourt, Brace, 1945); *The City in History* (New York: Harcourt, Brace, 1961).

[28] See his *Paris et l'agglomeration parisienne* (Paris: Presses Universitaire de France, 1952), 2 vol.; *Famille et habitation* (Paris: Presses Universitaires de France, 1960).

[29] See especially *The Social Background of a Plan: A Study of Middlesborough* (London: Routledge and Kegan Paul, 1948).

country "had the most highly organized and productive center of sociology in Europe,"[30] successful attempts were made to create a *rapproachment* between urban planning and sociology. These were due mainly to the energy and zeal of S. Rychliński, the pupil of the noted economist and sociologist, L. Krzywicki. In an amazing series of articles and books, written between 1933 and 1939, as if in anticipation of his untimely death (killed by the Nazis in 1944), Rychliński attempted to lay the sociological foundations for an urban development policy.[31] The gap caused by his death was hard to fill. Immediately after the war the leading Polish sociologist, S. Ossowski, wrote some theoretical studies on the spatial aspects of social life.[32] Unfortunately, his attention was diverted very soon from this field of sociological analysis. The years after 1956, marked by the revival of sociological studies (both theoretical and empirical), have also been characterized by growing interest in urban sociology and by organizational initiatives aimed at bringing urban planning and sociology closer together. One source of these changes, to be sure, lies in social life itself. Poland has become industrialized and urbanized very rapidly. The percentage of urban population rose from 27.2 in 1931 to 48.1 in 1960. Many hundred thousands of people have been involved in the migration to cities. Housing construction, rebuilding of destroyed cities, building of new towns, and urban renewal in general have reached unprecedented dimensions. The pursuit of these goals has been possible only through a joint effort of planners and social scientists.

Thus, when the Polish Academy of Sciences created two committees to work on coordinating and sponsoring research in regional and urban planning—the Committee for Space Economy and Regional Planning

---

[30] T. Abel, "Sociology in Postwar Poland," *American Sociological Review,* XV, February, 1950, p. 104.

[31] Here are the most relevant studies from Rychliński's rich heritage: "Przebudowa wspolczesnego miasta" [The Renewal of the Contemporary City], *Droga,* 1933; "Socjologia miasta" [Urban Sociology], *Przegląd Socjologicany,* III, 1935; "Warszawa jako stolica Polski" [Warsaw as Poland's Capital], *Warszawa,* 1936; "Założenia polityki urbanistycznej" [The Principles of Town Planning Policy], *Samorząd Terytorialny,* 1937. Rychliński's interest in urban sociology was stimulated by his stay in the United States on a Rockefeller Foundation grant in 1934. In connection therewith see his *"Rozpad sąsiedztwa w mieście amerykánskim"* [Breakup of the Neighborhood in the American City], *Przegląd Sosjologiczny,* III, 1935; "Przeobrażenia społeczne w Stanach Zjednoczonych A. P. na tle urbanizacji" [Social Change in the United States against the Background of Urbanization], *Warszawa,* 1937.

[32] "Socjologia i urbanistyka" [Sociology and City Planning], *Problemy,* No. 1, 1945; "Organizacja przestrzeni i życie społeczne w przyszłych osiedlach" [Spatial Organization and Social Life in Future Housing Estates], *Wiedza i Życie,* No. 1, 1946.

(in 1958) and the Committee for Building, City Planning, and Architecture (in 1959)—extensive opportunities for sociological research were provided in connection with them. The main center of sociological research in Poland, however, is the Institute of Philosophy and Sociology at the Polish Academy of Sciences. There, as a result of reorganization in 1962, the Urban Sociology Center was created.

Sociological research is also being carried on in the Institute for Town Planning and Architecture, and in the Housing Institute. Recently established is the Institute for Research on Architecture, City Planning, and Building of the Ministry of University and Polytechnic Education, which gathers together professors and research workers from various technological institutes and universities. Urban sociology, too, plays a substantial role in the research work of the sociology departments at the universities of Warsaw, Kraków, Łódź, and Poznań, as well as at the Catholic University of Lublin. Most active in the sociological study connected with urban planning, both in the academic field and outside it, have been A. Matejko,[33] S. Nowakowski,[34] Z. Pióro,[35] W. Piotrowski,[36] P. Rybicki,[37] and J. Turowski.[38] Since 1960 sociology has been taught at the Warsaw Institute of Technology as a part of the general curriculum for undergraduates in the Department of Architecture. Lectures in sociology have also been given at the two-year postgraduate courses in city and regional planning at institutes of technology in Warsaw, Kraków, and Gdańsk. Finally, professional sociologists have been employed recently in town planning centers on the regional, subregional, and city levels.

The most remarkable event in this area, however, was a seminar on "Sociology and Town Planning" in Kazimierz, May 25–28, 1960,[39] organized by the governmental Committee for Building, City Planning,

---

[33] See "Socjologiczne aspekty budownictwa mieszkaniowego" [Sociological Aspects of Housing Construction], *Przegląd Socjologiczny,* XII, 1958.

[34] See "Hotel robotniczy na tle procesów urbanizacji i industrializacji" [The Workers Hostel in the Light of Urbanization and Industrialization Processes], *Przegląd Socjologiczny,* XII, 1958.

[35] See *Ekologia społeczna w urbanistyce* [Social Ecology in City Planning] (Warsaw: 1962).

[36] See "Z badań ekologicznej struktury miasta Łodzi" [Some Ecological Aspects of the City of Łódź], *Przegląd Socjologiczny,* XV/2, 1961.

[37] See "Problematyka środowiska miejskiego" [Problems of the Urban Milieu], *Przegląd Socjologiczny,* XIV/1, 1960.

[38] See "Urbanizacja świata: Z zagadnień socjologii miasta" [Urbanization of the World: Problems of Urban Sociology], *Zeszyty Naukowe Katolickiego Uniwersytetu Lubelskiego,* No. 4, 1961, p. 2.

[39] See "The Bulletin of the Committee for Building, City Planning, and Architecture" [in Polish], No. 12, 1960.

and Architecture and by the Institute for Town Planning and Architecture. It was a large gathering of all noted specialists in town planning and urban sociology in the country. From abroad came Professor Paul Chombart de Lauwe, of the Centre National de la Recherche Scientifique, Paris, and Professor S. Groenman, of the University of Utrecht. The aims of the seminar were: (1) to promote cooperation and stimulate discussion between town planners and sociologists, (2) to review and evaluate sociological studies from the point of view of the planners' needs, (3) to suggest new and vital problems for sociological research, (4) to determine the role of the sociologist in the planning process, and (5) to elaborate an organizational scheme for joint education and research in town planning and urban sociology.

The significance of the seminar was enormous. It was the first event of this kind in Poland. The initiative came from the community of planners, whose high level of "sociological imagination" was reflected by the idea and borne out by the lively and fruitful discussion. As regards the planner's consciousness of his need for sociological knowledge, the discussion centered around two comprehensive questions. First, what does the town planner expect from the sociologist?[40] (Here we evidenced a slight shift of emphasis from the original question: what sociological facts does the planner need?) Second, what can the sociologist offer the planner? Many important problems were touched upon, such as the role of the sociologist in particular phases of urban design. The one problem, however, that came to the fore is whether the sociologist is to remain an abstract scientist or is to enter the field of practice. It was rather obvious that the planners wanted the sociologist to be not only an aloof scientist investigating social reality *as it is,* but also a policy-maker, venturing statements about what *should* be done. The sociologists, on the other hand, showed considerable reluctance to adopt this position.

This discussion is still going on, and the controversy is far from being settled. Nevertheless, the vast majority of sociologists cannot help strongly believing that their usefulness to society as a functional whole is much greater if they stay within the sphere of intellectual activity which we call "science."[41] There is also some misunderstanding con-

[40] This was the title of one of the main papers at the seminar, written by B. Malisz and Z. Pióro.

[41] These remarks are taken from the author's paper delivered at the plenary session of the Committee for Building, City Planning, and Architecture of the Polish Academy of Sciences (Warsaw, June 15, 1961): "The Future Development of Architecture and Physical Planning in the Light of Sociological Problems," *Miasto,* 2, 1962.

cerning the alleged gap between theory and practice. The nature of science lies in enunciating scientific laws. "Every scientific law asserts subsistence of recurrent association or regular connection of certain conditions and events."[42] To put it in other words, whenever conditions *A* occur, event *B* follows. The ultimate aim of science is to predict the course of events. The more "theoretical" science is, the more able it is to predict, and the greater is its practical usefulness. Sociology is still far from the degree of theoretical capability possessed by the natural sciences. Social planning based on the conviction that social phenomena can be controlled if the laws governing them are known is still in its initial phase. But as the methods of sociology improve, as a firm body of sociological knowledge is established, and as sociological theory is developed, the ability of the science of society to transform social reality will grow constantly.

I cannot here resist the temptation to quote again the sage remarks of Louis Wirth:

It is important to point out the limitations of the sociologist in connection with the tasks of practical administration and the formulation of social policies. Here, as elsewhere in science, it is not the function of the sociologist to tell the world what *should* be done, but rather how the world's will *can* be done. Alluring as the role of prophet or statesman may be, the sociologist, insofar as he wishes to remain within his province and to avoid playing the role of a charlatan or quack, must content himself with the more modest task of saying: If you do this, these in the light of our present knowledge are the probable consequences; or if you wish to do this, these are the most efficient measures thus far discovered of accomplishing your end. Our general theoretical knowledge furnishes the basis for these tentative hypothetical predictions. This theoretical knowledge must be supplemented by the concrete data pertaining to the given situation to make it relevant to a specific problem.[43]

III. Let us turn now to the planner's awareness of the social consequences connected with his work. It has at least two aspects. First, there is a consciousness of the staggering responsibility of the planner's activity. The material things created by him are going to endure. It is in part the durability of esthetic and functional values that worries him. Even more important is his awareness that a particular project (a house, a railway station, an airport, a department store, a campus, a neighbor-

---

[42] E. Zilsel, "Physics and the Problem of Historico-Sociological Laws," in H. Feigl and M. Brodbeck, eds., *Readings in the Philosophy of Science* (New York: Appleton-Century-Crofts, 1953), p. 715.

[43] "Regional Research in Relation to Social Planning," in *Community Life and Social Policy*, p. 296.

hood unit) is bound to mold human behavior, to encourage or deter a
given way of life, to cause states of frustration or contribute to developing a happy, balanced human creature. The planner has to anticipate
all this. He has to take man and society not as they are now, but
as they will be in the near or distant future. He must, therefore, be a
man of vision. Without creative imagination his work would be impossible, but to his despair he is fully aware of the discrepancy between
present knowledge and the future needs of society and future forms of
social life. Hence his impatience with the sociologist's prudence in the
prediction of forthcoming events. It is not an accident that the theme of
the recent Twenty-sixth World Congress of the International Federation
for Housing and Planning was "Human Environment and Civilization,"
with special stress on the trends of development of our industrial and
urbanized civilization.

Second, there is an awareness of the way in which the accepted
sociological principles underlying the planner's creative activity really
work in a given spatial setting. Assuming that this type of consciousness
is a widespread phenomenon, we could imagine the phases of the planning procedure as (1) elaboration of sociological premises, (2) the process of design based on them, as well as on premises taken from other
fields, and (3) thorough examination of the practical working of the
design. Unfortunately, this is more a postulate than an acknowledged
procedure. It sometimes seems that the planner's interest in the sociological aspect of his particular piece of work is extinguished once the design is completed. His interest reawakens when he turns to the next
project. Then he is compelled to compare the results of the previous
projects with present expectations, and to make new guesses about the
future.

Undoubtedly, this summary is grossly oversimplified and unfair to
the planner. Besides, he may well argue that an examination of the social
consequences of planning is definitely the sociologist's business. But the
point is not who is to make the investigation. The crux of the matter
does not lie in an *ad hoc* elaboration of some sociological principles or in
an *ex post facto* investigation of social relations in the long-range spatial
setting. What is absolutely necessary is the closest collaboration of planner
and sociologist in the first and the third phases of the above-mentioned
procedure (the second one, the design itself, is the planner's undisputed
domain). From the methodological point of view it is equivalent to the
hypothesis-verification method. A carefully prepared set of sociological
premises referring to a specific case constitutes the hypothesis, and the

practice of social life in given conditions created by the planner's design provides a verification of these hypothetical premises.

In Poland, as in most other countries, only a few such projects have been made so far. To put it more correctly, in none of these cases was there an all-embracing plan that attempted to go step-by-step through all the phases of planning, and to deal afterward with the immediate social consequences. To my knowledge, the only project which is going to meet these conditions is one for a Warsaw neighborhood unit now under way at the Intercenter for Basic Problems of Building, City Planning, and Architecture. Both town planners and sociologists are taking part in it. The first step will be the sociologists' theoretical analysis of the neighborhood unit as a social system. Then the sociological hypotheses will emerge in a joint discussion with the town planners. The latter will elaborate the so-called socioeconomic program of the unit. During the next phase the accepted principles will be applied in the design of the housing estate. After construction is completed, the hypotheses will undergo verification through a systematic observation of social behavior in the neighborhood unit.

The main sociological problems which will be tackled by the study are: What is the nature of social ties in the neighborhood units? Does physical (spatial) neighborhood lead in an urban setting to social neighborhood? Does neighborliness more easily arise in socially heterogenous or homogeneous units? What is the participation of inhabitants in the voluntary associational groups in the settlements and outside it? What is the degree of sociocultural self-containment in the neighborhood unit?

IV. The last element of the planner's consciousness to be analyzed is connected with the fact that urban design, like every form of intellectual activity, is determined by social conditions. It is now generally acknowledged that "thought, besides being a proper subject matter for logic and psychology, becomes fully comprehensible only if it is viewed sociologically."[44] The view that human thought is conditioned by social existence (an idea, to be sure, of Marxist origin[45]) has given rise to a new branch of sociology—the sociology of knowledge.

It is a truism, indeed, to say that the planner is influenced by the

[44] L. Wirth, preface to K. Mannheim, "Ideology and Utopia," in *Community Life and Social Policy, op. cit.,* p. 50.

[45] According to R. K. Merton, one of the most eminent American sociologists, "a central point of agreement in all approaches to the sociology of knowledge is the thesis that thought has an existential basis. . . . Marxism is the storm-center of *Wissenssoziologie.*" "Sociology of Knowledge," in G. Gurvitch and W. E. Moore, eds., *Twentieth-Century Sociology* (New York: Philosophical Library, 1945), p. 373.

civilization of which he is part; by the way of life of his nation, by its tradition and sociopolitical system; by his class affiliation; and by his professional interests. The planner's "ideology" is formed under the influence of all these factors, and it reveals itself in many ways. The planner approves or disapproves of the spreading of urbanization; he accepts or rejects the contemporary city as a form of social organization and a spatial framework for social life;[46] he yearns for the rural way of life, trying to re-create the neighborly relations characteristic of rural communities in the cities,[47] or he despises it; he is in favor of a socially heterogeneous neighborhood unit or he prefers a socially homogeneous community.[48] In reference to these and many other choices he is expressing value-judgments. Like any other intellectual, he is not free of bias and prejudice. He may be aware of the ideological flavor of his views, or, as happens more often, he may act without regard for those considerations. But without tracing his judgments to their ideological roots in society, without dragging the latter into the light of day, he cannot raise his art to a higher level of methodological maturity. This is the only way in which the limitations of the planner's views can become apparent in his own eyes, and in which deformations can be avoided in the future. Once he has undergone such a mental operation, his *Weltanschauung* and whole intellectual activity will never be the same.

Now, what is the Polish planner's "ideology"? I shall restrict myself to two traits only, since it would be impossible to investigate this immense question in a short article. First there is the fact that the Polish planner is extremely oriented toward history. This preoccupation with Poland's past, which sometimes puzzles foreign visitors, reflects the nation's bitter war experiences, when the very biological existence of the Polish nation was threatened and its cultural heritage was drastically diminished, not so much by the wartime fighting as by the Nazi Occupation's deliberate destruction. One realized with horror how very few material evidences

---

[46] The most characteristic in this respect are views of Frank Lloyd Wright, especially his conception of "Broadacre City."

[47] The nostalgia for the rural way of life seems to be at the bottom of the conception of the neighborhood unit. See R. Dewey, "The Neighborhood, Urban Ecology, and City Planners," *American Sociological Review*, XV, August, 1950; the author remorselessly exposes the hidden motives lying behind the American planners' approach to the neighborhood unit. See also the stimulating article by N. Dennis, "The Popularity of the Neighborhood Community Idea," *The Sociological Review* [British], VI, December, 1958.

[48] Typical for this controversy are the articles by R. Isaacs, "Are Neighborhoods Possible?" *Journal of Housing*, V, July, 1948; "The Neighborhood Unit as an Instrument for Segregation," *Journal of Housing*, V, August, 1948.

of Poland's thousand-year-old history were left. This is particularly true of architecture. Kraków was the only historical city that escaped damage. Hence the nationwide, and amazingly rapid—for a poor and devastated country—reconstruction of historical monuments. During this immediate postwar period the planner was both influencing and being influenced by the course of events. He was an independent actor grasping an initiative; at the same time he was a medium sensitive to the nation's emotions, which found an outlet through his work. His enthusiasm was not checked by the fact that this reconstruction went against the rigid rules of economy (rebuilding being far more expensive than the building of new structures), or by the fact that the reconstructed monuments were in fact in many cases completely new creations.

Very typical for this attitude, which prevailed especially in the period 1945–1955, was the response to the reconstruction of the Old Town in Warsaw.

The rebuilding of the quarter [the Old Town] expressed, above all, a vehement social protest against the very idea of liquidating the oldest part of Warsaw. This emotional background, this new positive relation of the nation to its culture and history, was behind the completely new practice of rebuilding—or strictly speaking, reconstructing—historical areas. This is a practice unprecedented in history and defying the principles of protection and conservation of historical monuments. . . . Between the conservators and the crowds wandering to the ravaged Old Town, just to see what has happened to the beloved "Starówka," stronger and stronger bonds are being developed.[49]

The other characteristic of the Polish planner's ideology may be found in his defense of social democratization and an egalitarian model of social relations. Since 1945 he has been a member of a society undergoing profound political and socioeconomic changes. Industrialization, urbanization, growing spatial and social mobility, cultural "revolution," the introduction of social services on a large scale—these are the phenomena that are now resulting in widespread attitudes of social egalitarianism. At the core of these attitudes is the simple truth that people are equal as in regard to their basic needs, desires, and aims and in their right to satisfy them. The planner cannot avoid being greatly influenced by this view. As a matter of fact, he did not have to be convinced of it. Social radicalism was common among Polish planners before the war, when the Warsaw Housing Cooperative was active.

[49] J. Zachwatowicz, *et. al., Stare Miasto w Warszawie: Odbudowa* [The Old Town in Warsaw: The Reconstruction] (Warsaw, 1956), p. 6.

The egalitarian outlook is reflected in the planner's conception of the neighborhood unit. All Polish planners share the convictions that, when a human environment is shaped, social segregation should be avoided, that the neighborhood unit should be socially mixed, re-creating as far as possible the social, occupational, economic, and even age structure of society as a whole.[50] They are not misled by the illusion that merely mixing people from different social milieux will lead automatically to intimate contacts, or in other words that spatial neighborhood will result in social neighborhood. Manifest neighborliness,[51] such as visiting and spending free time together, is bound to be established through social relations based on common professions and interests, similar cultural levels, and so on. But the planners feel that opportunities should be provided for developing neighborly ties among inhabitants: if not for the adults, at least for the children, this typical community bases their relations on the neighborhood principle and ignore all social barriers. Creating a sociocultural heterogeneous neighborhood unit, and through this, a school of social life for the younger generation, has been perhaps the main achievement of Polish planners, in spite of the many shortcomings associated with housing estates in Poland, such as high density, and inadequate floor space.

The egalitarian principle is also visible in housing standards. The difference between particular housing estates is practically negligible. Within a given neighborhood unit there is no difference in standards at all. Individual flats may be larger or smaller, according to the number of occupants, but all the equipment and facilities are the same. High officials and intellectuals live together with the rank and file in the same housing estate, in the same apartment house, and enjoy—or suffer from —the same dwelling standard (the only difference being an additional room for some professional categories, such as physicians, artists, university professors, and higher civil servants).

This does not mean that ecological laws do not obtain in Poland, that there is no segregation along sociovocational lines, and no competition to get into the "right" area in the city. But the segregational and competitive process occurs not so much among the individuals as among institutions, such as factories, offices, and educational and cultural establishments, which, after the Board of Worker Settlements, are the main

[50] It is really not necessary to quote all the statements of Polish planners supporting my thesis. The literature is too large.

[51] This is the expression used by P. H. Mann: "The Concept of Neighborliness," *The American Journal of Sociology*, LX, September, 1954.

housing investors (usually acting through a cooperative system). A housing estate (or a part of it) belonging to the same establishment may also be a highly heterogeneous unit, reflecting all the vocational and sociocultural variety of the staff.

To discover that the planner's mentality has been formed by given social conditions, to trace back the social roots of his "ideology," to discover how it finds its expression in urban planning is much easier than to detect whether the planner himself is aware of all these factors. The scattered and incidental utterances and published statements coming from the planners' community are highly inadequate as a source of scientific information. Here a detailed, methodical investigation of the planner's consciousness is needed. But this is still a *pium desideratum* (in Poland at least). In advocating this investigation, may I be allowed to venture an impressionistic guess that the fourth element of the planner's consciousness mentioned above is by far the least, not only in Poland but elsewhere as well. The planner's "sociological" consciousness consisting of the four elements may be conceived as a pyramid. The first element, being most common, forms the base. Ascending, the strata of the planner's "sociological" consciousness become narrower. And yet, as time goes on, these elements that have thus far been unimportant are likely to play a decisive role in the planner's work.

CHAPTER 8

A View of Architectural Theory

BOHDAN PNIEWSKI

MOST architects and critics of architecture today base their work on entirely subjective premises, in spite of the fact that general principles of the art are current and widely accented. Individual tastes and points of view—lacking any objective foundation—seem to be decisive factors. When a creative effort or a critical utterance is found to be in accord with some objective principle of architectural art, it is almost invariably an accidental coincidence.

Against such a background of fanciful designs and criticisms governed by whim, doubts arise about the existence of any objective rules by which to appraise architectural works. One is forced to doubt the possibility of establishing rules of architectural composition. We are trying to overcome these doubts. Poland is one of the few countries in which institutions have been founded to undertake research in the principles and rules of architectural composition. The work is progressing, but it is too early to attempt a report on its progress. It is possible, however, to present the initial concepts upon which the program of research is based.

Our primary assumption is that Polish architecture represents a segment of world architecture, and that it is developing in close relation to world architecture. Modern architecture has not evolved laws about composition. One is tempted even to claim that chaos reigns over ideas, definitions, and programs of research in this field. Nevertheless, certain peculiarities and trends based on national tradition and culture are definitely developing in various countries. In some instances, as they evolve, these peculiarities may lead to the birth of a style. This, however, depends on many factors, including time and political and economic stability. Propitious combination of all the necessary elements is not likely to be easy or simple. One must remember that artistic thought cannot always catch up with the tremendous technical and economic progress being made in our era.

Considering the problems of architectural composition in Poland in relation to world trends in architecture, one must make a short survey of such trends—as we see them. We know that in England a concept of monumental synthetic integration of architecture, sculpture, and painting is being worked out. In America solutions to technical and organizational problems of construction have attained such a high level that, quite naturally, one notices the preponderance of structural drafts over compositional designs. It should be stated that the highest achievements of Frank Lloyd Wright have not been overshadowed by anything new. When he says that architecture is a material expression of the needs, the abilities, and the feelings of the age in which it is created and that it must be proportioned, harmonious, and functional, he states an accepted truth. His claim that architectural detail should be the logical issue of the architectural composition and not an end in itself is true. No composition can be good unless this truth is accepted. But neither Frank Lloyd Wright himself nor his followers have taken up the task of making the principles which they advocate into a set of rules.

Italy's brilliant Pier Luigi Nervi commands both technical knowledge and compositional genius. He is giving Italian architecture the luster and splendor of a modern Renaissance. The success of his architectural works is primarily a result of his structural design, which, intricate as it is, possesses an evident clarity, and of the unusual forms he presents, which are a direct consequence of the structural properties of reinforced concrete. From his early Stadium in Florence to the Olympic Stadium in Rome, he appears to be interested first of all in the solution of structural problems. He claims that a correct solution of structural problems, aided by what he calls "static intuition," is all that is needed to give esthetic value to any construction. When he speaks about "static intuition," however, he emphatically states that it has nothing to do with nebulous, mystical esthetics, but is the result of true knowledge and of a masterly grasp of the art of architecture. On the other hand, when Nervi presents his theoretical views he does not say how one should correlate structural and compositional elements, nor does he say whether science or art should dominate in the solution of architectural problems.

Le Corbusier has had a stronger influence not only as a form-giver but also on the thinking of the younger generation of architects than any other master of modern architecture. His genius explains this influence, in part, but there is an additional explanation in the fact that his works are to be found in all parts of the world and in most metropolises: New York, Paris, Moscow, Tokyo, Chandigarh (India). Architects of many countries have had the opportunity to see the works of Le Corbusier. In view of the passionate quality of his teaching and his personality, Le Corbusier might have had still stronger influence were it not for a certain disappointment felt by those who noticed the incongruity between the teachings of the master and the application of them to his own designs.

The contributions of Le Corbusier to the basic problems of the theory of architectural composition are not many. His "Modular"—worked on during the war—is a table of harmonious measures based on the human scale, to be applied both in architecture and in the construction of machinery. This is an important step toward the unification of measures in the world. But his main contributions are in the field of town planning. Le Corbusier is also responsible for the appointment of the Committee for the Establishment of Harmony in the Mechanical Civilization after the Triennale at Milan. The work of this Committee might possibly have important effects.

Problems of the theory of composition are also being considered by the Institute of the Theory and History of Architecture in the Soviet Union, where work is progressing. The basic assertion of the Institute is that works of architecture should express by artistic means their specific functions, since the concept of architecture should not be construed exclusively in terms of esthetic values; utility instead should be the dominant factor.

An entirely new development in architecture—in Poland and elsewhere—is the importance of industrial buildings and industrial interiors, which comprise 85 per cent of all new studies. The new problems arising with industrial construction affect the stability of conditions required for the crystallization of a modern style, and thereby delay its birth. Architectural activities in Poland are being influenced by those architects and trends described above. It is thus necessary to know what problems face practicing architects and theoreticians of architecture in all countries, and Poland in particular.

We believe the most pressing problem is that of finding the proper correlation of modern technical knowledge and architecture. This is a rather complex task in the face of the dynamic development of technical knowledge today. The structural possibilities ensuing from technology are approaching their culmination, while we have to deal with the art of architecture, in which—as in all arts—everything belongs to a superstructure not existing in the physical universe. We assert that architecture exists as an abstract notion and must be transformed into physical existence as part of a new, hitherto unknown Nature. True architecture, correct architecture, must be an inherent continuation of Nature. Thus approaching one of the first problems of our inquiries into the theory of architectural composition, we see that architecture cannot be merely the technology of building. On the other hand, we believe that a way must be found to ensure the coexistence of architecture as an art with the highest structural achievements and the technology of building, for they are two inseparable parts of one whole.

The concept of architecture as an inherent continuation of Nature is one of our basic premises, but we are equally persuaded that architecture mirrors the character and the culture of a nation. We shall return to this subject in connection with the compositional problems of choosing a situation for a work of architecture.

Proportion is one of the basic theoretical problems of the art of architecture. This is a problem of relations—numerically or geometrically expressed—by which we are able to judge the correctness of architectural composition. Correct proportions are the first quality by which we appreciate the artistic expression of a work of art. Of course, any composition may show an apparent irregularity in linear or surface relations, but such deviations from regularity may be admitted within certain limits of tolerance, and may be justified by technical or optical considerations. In connection with the varying degree of conformity to established principles, we may venture to differentiate between architectural works in which the principles are clearly and consistently observed and those in which no regularity is observable but which are nevertheless unquestionably great architectural works. Architecture seeking perfection would designate the former, powerful architecture the latter.

Compositional ideas are born under the influence either of rational thought or of emotions. Rational influences lead to regularity and consistency. The rational architect, in fixing the proportions of his work, seeks order and unity. In such circumstances perfect architecture may be created. When emotions take the upper hand, the structural clarity, the use of materials in accordance with their properties, the static adequacy of their use—all such considerations become secondary. The brilliance of the work of art created thus depends on its dynamic effect, often a disturbing effect, which—if significant and unique—marks the birth of powerful architecture.

The rational basis of creativeness is perfectible and may eventually lead to as near an approach to perfection as may be expected.

Logos and pathos! Perfect or powerful architecture: we wish to discover in which direction present-day architectural creativity is bound. Perfect architecture was created by great architects of the past in their monumental buildings. Apart from sacred buildings, this type of architecture included castles, palaces, and public buildings; usually it exemplified compositional integration of architectural grandeur, space, and landscape.

Perfect or powerful architecture: both are adverse to architectural performance based on whim and fancy and both stimulate continuous inquiries into the theory of composition, as well as into the meaning of architecture. The image of architecture corresponding to the social needs of the time in which it was created is tantamount to the meaning of architecture. But, as in all arts, there is also an aim in architecture, which is to express beauty. What is needed to evoke beauty in architecture? A completeness of work is necessary. This means that all problems are solved and all decisions taken. The elements of the work must be attuned and correlated to the whole as organically as they are in a human body or in a tree or flower. The work of architecture is beautiful when its proportions are adjusted to a logical order forming a unity with its environment. The interior measurements of the work must also express its inner unity, and must be logically ordered.

Finally, to be beautiful architecture must be splendid. It must bear the mark of the architect's genius; it must reflect his inner light, which —through the medium of materials and forms—others must be able to apprehend clearly.

Equally important is the solution of the compositional problem. A thematic idea, a conception of thematic motive, or a combination of two or three basic architectural forms (the surface, the perpendicular, the mass) is the initial stimulus for the development of a composition. The shape matures through juxtaposition of simple and complex main forms, and through the elaboration of these main forms into an external image of the composition.

The main motive may spring either from the development of the surface (Palazzo della Cancelleria), or of the perpendicular (Campanile of St. Mark), or of the mass (Notre-Dame). In each of the above examples the whole composition is subordinated to one main thought and idea. Correctness is attained when the idea is legible. The correctness of the whole composition depends on the visible clarity of the principle which rules the juxtaposition of forms, and on the consistency of adherence to the adopted principle.

An important factor in the attainment of a correct composition is the clearly visualized unity of composition and structure. The principles of composition and the modes of procedure in structural designing should be considered therefore as parallel matters. They are strictly inter-dependent. In a work of architecture one must compose a hierarchy with strict subservience of all elements to the main formal motive. In struc-tural design all elements are equally important as they pertain to the technology of architecture.

What else is needed to create good architecture? One must consider problems of the plan, the location, the expressiveness, the image, as well as those of function and economy.

The solution of the plan must be considered from three viewpoints of composition: the purity of the plan, the proportions of the whole, and the correlation of interior proportions. The purity of the plan requires the use of a homogeneous structural pattern throughout. Should a divergent structural pattern be introduced, the elements of the plan affected by this must be distinctly separated from the rest. The plan is pure when heterogeneous structures do not intersect each other. For good results plans should be conceived not so much on the principle of sym-metry as on the principle of balanced arrangement of elements. When considering proportions of the plan as a whole, one must have in mind the careful and proper correlation of the length to the depth. Deviations necessitated by functional requirements are admissible. Correlation of interior spatial proportions is an inherent compositional problem.

Solution of the compositional problems of the location in which a work of architecture is to be erected is an important factor. It influences the development of architecture and expresses the national traits and the culture of the people. If a nation has a culture it will have its own com-position as well, for architecture is the expression of national culture. The influences of other cultures are usually quite evident. Sources for prefer-ences in the choice of architectural locations may be found not only in the culture of a nation but also in the mentality of the people and in the regional customs. An analysis of the compositional preferences of various nations indicates these differences. The French, Italian, Russian, English, Polish and other compositions all have their particular traits. Le Nôtre emphasizes the seemingly endless axis of the landscape composition of Versailles, while the Italians make their axes shorter and close their side views with unexpected vistas (Boboli Gardens). The situation of the Polish Royal Palace at Łazienki shows a compositional principle different from both the French and the Italian; it becomes discernible only when one walks through the side lanes of the park.

The main entrances to castles and palaces in the West are placed on the axes of the roads leading to them. Polish architecture from its beginnings has avoided such a direct approach to dwellings. The entrance has always been hidden and placed on the side or at the back, with access from the inner court. This reflects early customs of protection against enemy invasions. Later, although the entrance was frequently accentuated by detail such as columns, no direct access was provided. One still had to make a tour around a circular court.

The correct solution for locating a work of architecture is attained when architecture develops from its environment, whether natural landscape or surrounding architecture. The importance of the correct composition of the location comes from the fact that all architectural works are built on the earth and are lighted by the sun—two obvious facts to be considered. One must remember that the character of the composition from the north is determined by the outline of the work of architecture against a light background. The silhouette can have apertures which let in the light of the south. The sky will be light-hued. From the south, the composition should offer the play of projecting detail, of partitions, of shadows cast by it and falling on it. The sky in the background will usually be darker. The west side admits warm colors, including reds, while the east side takes cold colors, including green, and allows deeply cut details.

If architecture is to fulfill its mission of assisting the harmonious development of man, if it is to be the proper expression of his creative abilities, it should present from every viewpoint a unity with the surrounding nature. To be more precise, the image of architecture must be perceived as a totality comprising town and country.

The image of architecture should include the solution of architectural composition, of locational problems, of proportions and beauty. It also includes the correlation of orthogonal plans and views to the plans and views of green spaces. Moreover, esthetic values should be regulated so that every phenomenon will support the human imagination, by facilitating associations that link the whole with its parts and the parts with the whole.

The expressiveness of architecture, on the other hand, reflects the individual decision of the architect with regard to his work. The formal means of expression are many. The great forms contain smaller forms which can be variously arranged and brought into a chosen order. These smaller forms comprise in their turn a wealth of architectural detail and textural varieties. Naturally, the use of detail does not mean the absurd repetition of the well-known forms of extant styles.

The correctness of architecture includes the functional usefulness of the building, answering the requirements of the owner. It also includes economical use of materials and of money. Our age gives ample opportunity for economical building; the new structure materials and new engineering and finishing possibilities promise continuous cost reductions. The development of technical knowledge appears to open unlimited possibilities, and the apogee (see below) is almost within reach.

We have defined one of the oldest problems with which architects have been faced as the problem of apogee. This is the problem: building materials have strength and endurance as well as dimensional limits. Timber used for building wooden houses or churches in Poland does not exceed a length of twelve meters. The strength of bricks or stone limits the height of piers and walls. Tension perimeters determine the size of vaults. In some Gothic temples, miscalculation of the dimensional or resistance limits of materials brought about catastrophic results (as in the cathedral at Beauvais). Today we can assess structural possibilities with great accuracy, and we are able to tax the materials we use to their limit. New materials—and even such known materials as concrete reinforced with better cement, better steel—have extended limits in strength and durability. New structures appear, of very thin reinforced concrete and shells. The use of new materials should lead to the culmination of possibilities. Some of the known materials have already attained their apogee. For example, the spacing of columns in ancient Greece did not exceed four meters with the use of marble architraves, for the architraves could not be longer. The columns were increased in height, but the spacing between columns never exceeded four meters. Today, however, the wonderful reinforced-concrete structures are yet far from culmination. The strength and durability of steel also continually increases.

Concisely summarized, these are the problems which we set ourselves to solve, in order to introduce better order into architecture.

The question arises: what are the qualities required of a modern architect? Leon Battista Alberti said: "Him I call an architect who with the aid of unfailing and magnificent Art and Method is able to design in Thought and by Measure, as well as to execute by deed all these works of supreme beauty which can be accepted for the use of mankind."

Alberti's claim that an architect should be able to "execute by deed" his composition is fully valid today. We cannot imagine a contemporary architect who lacks a good knowledge of the properties of new materials and of their use in building. Today, even a medium-sized building presents so many special problems that it becomes necessary for the architect to be able to make use of information and of methods supplied by contemporary science. We need only mention mathematics and sociology as examples. He must also be ready to work with a team of specialized assistants.

To study the means of eliminating haphazard and erratic architectural performance and to help the development of true creativeness, an institution was established in Warsaw, the Institute for Research on Architecture, City Planning, and Building of the Ministry for University and Polytechnic Education. The program of the Institute is as complex as the problems of architecture, city planning, and building which await solution. The same financial means, however, which go into the creation of improper architecture could be better employed for the creation of good architecture—and this is our aim. The chief task of the Institute is the elaboration of bases for theories of architecture, of city planning, and of building. It is hoped that the results of this work may orient architects in their complex creative activities. At some later date we expect to undertake the education of young architects so that properly formed talents will be available to engage in the harmonious development of architecture in all parts of Poland.

In our work on the problems of the theory of architecture we wish not only to retain the elements of beauty that issue from the culture and character of our people, but also to ensure their lively development. It is possible that with time eventually elements of a new order and a new style may emerge. Obviously this will not be an easy process. We are thus also interested in securing the help of all branches of science and technical knowledge that touch, (however lightly), upon architecture, in order to eliminate errors from architectural design. The problems of physics, chemistry, building structures, and statics are included in our program in so far as they are relevant. We are especially interested in static modeling, because we believe that the approach to the apogee of the strength and durability of materials, and the use of new materials, will open new possibilities for architectural composition and for the economy of building.

All our studies and research are conducted with constant reference to social problems. We consider architecture to be the art of creating the most important values for mankind. Our program, therefore, includes the study of demographic, social, economic, and recreational problems.

The Spatial Planning Act*
of January 31, 1961

Section I
General Regulations

Art. 1. 1. The objects of spatial planning are to ensure proper development of individual areas of the country, taking into account mutual bonds and the interests of the entire country; to establish correct spatial interrelations between production and service facilities in these areas; thereby to create conditions for the expansion of production for meeting the various needs of the population and for protection of the natural resources and values of the country.

2. The task of spatial planning is to establish the land utilization for individual areas and the manner of their development for definite purposes, taking into account current needs and future ones issuing from the program adopted for economic and social development.

3. Dispositions mentioned in items 1 and 2 should be based on long-term [perspective] national economic plans,[1] on short-term national economic plans,[2] and on results given by a study of the natural, demographic, and social conditions of the given area and on indispensable technical preparation.

Art. 2. 1. Spatial planning is undertaken:

1) For the area of the entire country—within the framework of the long-term national economic plan;

2) For areas of particular voivodships or parts thereof—within the framework of the long-term national economic plans of the voivodships or parts thereof, called in these regulations "regional plans";

---

* *Official Journal*, No. 7/61, p. 47 (unofficial translation). Article 42 has not been included since it prescribes the changes necessary for acts previous to this one and are concerned with quite formal matters.

[1] At present for fifteen years.

[2] For five years.

3) For areas of individual settlement units or parts thereof, and in specific cases, for areas not settlement units—within the framework of local plans for physical development, further called "local plans."

A settlement unit in the meaning of this act is a town or urban settlement, village, or other place which constitutes a concentration of dwellings and, in conjunction with production and service facilities, forms a definite environment for the life of the population.

ART. 3.   1. Plans for spatial development may be prepared:

1) for a period overrunning the period set for the long-term national economic plan, with particular attention to the period set for this plan and distinguished from the period of the short-term national economic plan [long-range study];

2) for a period conforming to the period of the long-term national economic plan with particular consideration for the period of the short-term national economic plan [long-term plans];

3) for a period conforming to the current period and the next period of the short-term national economic plan [stage plans].

2. Plans for spatial development are subject to a periodic analysis of the assumptions and decisions adopted therein; conforming to the results of the analysis, the competent agencies for preparing the plans execute the respective actualization of the plans. Changes introduced into the plans issuing from their actualization are presented for the approval of proper agencies.

ART. 4. In addition to the plans mentioned in Art. 2.1.3, and jointly with projects for building investments, plans are prepared for the development of building lots or areas destined for building investment, called in further regulations "implementation plans."

ART. 5.   1. The central state administrative agencies are:

1) Planning Commission of the Council of Ministers [Komisja Planowania przy Radzie Ministrów]: within the domain of spatial development of the entire country and regional plans;

2) Committee for Building, City Planning, and Architecture [Komitet Budownictwa, Urbanistyki i Architektury[3]]: within the domain of local plans.

---

[3] Whenever the Committee for Building, City Planning, and Architecture or its agencies or the Chairman of this Committee is referred to in this Act, the Ministry of Building or its agencies or the Minister must be understood, respectively, because of changes made in agencies of the central government in 1963.

2. The voivodship or county agencies for local spatial planning are the competent departments of the voivodship or county praesidia of the people's councils [Prezydia Rad Narodowych].

3. The competent agencies of the praesidia of the people's councils prepare regional and local plans on the basis of their own documentation and also the documentation presented by central and local state administrative agencies, the proper cooperative organizations, scientific institutions, and scientific research centers.

4. The proper scientific institutions undertake research and scientific studies indispensable to the solution of problems in spatial planning conforming to the programs coordinated with the central administrative agencies for matters pertaining to spatial planning.

Section II
REGIONAL PLANS

ART. 6.   1. Regional plans define the trends for the general economic and social development of the given area, the manner and stages of their implementation, the principles for the allocation of production forces and service facilities, the shaping of the settlement network, the distribution of the population, and the designation of areas for definite purposes.

2. The regional plans are prepared for a period conforming to the period of the long-term national economic plan with special consideration for the period of the following short-term national economic plan. Simultaneous with the preparation of draft regional plans, agencies responsible for their preparation undertake a study of the assumptions and hypotheses for spatial development and especially for the allocation of the principal investments in the given area for the period of the following long-term national economic plan.

ART. 7.   1. Regional plans are prepared as general plans and as detailed plans.

2. A general regional plan is prepared for every voivodship. In principle, such a plan conforms to the area of the administrative boundaries of the voivodship. A general plan for a definite area which does not conform to the boundaries of the voivodship may be prepared subsequent to the approval of the Chairman of the Planning Commission of the Council of Ministers and the praesidium of the voivodship people's council concerned.

3. Joint regional plans are made for areas of cities having the rank of a voivodship and for areas of the voivodship in which such a city lies.

4. Detailed regional plans are made for areas constituting a part of the voivodship or part of adjacent voivodships where the implementation of large investments is envisaged, or other economic activities fundamentally affecting the economic development of such an area.

ART. 8. 1. Draft regional plans are prepared by the voivodship agencies of economic planning.

2. Commissions summoned by the competent voivodship people's councils, primarily composed of representatives of the state administrative agencies, scientific institutions, and competent professional experts, participate in the work of preparing the regional plans, as far as the basic principles of such plans are concerned.

3. If the regional plan covers areas of voivodships and cities having the rank of voivodships or areas constituting two or more voivodships, a special commission is nominated by the praesidium of the people's council whose agency prepares the given plan in agreement with the praesidia of the proper voivodship people's councils.

4. The commissions mentioned in items 2 and 3 are proposing, advisory, and consultative organs. The composition of the commissions should be agreed upon with the Chairman of the Planning Commission of the Council of Ministers.

ART. 9. 1. Regional plans, after coordinating with the respective state administrative agencies, are resolved by the proper voivodship and, in cases defined in Art. 7.3, by voivodship and municipal people's councils as motions for the Council of Ministers [Rada Ministrów].

2. Regional plans adopted by the respective people's councils are subject to opinion passed upon them by the Planning Commission of the Council of Ministers and the Committee for Building, City Planning, and Architecture.

3. The Council of Ministers approves the principal elements of regional plans.

ART. 10. Expenses incurred for the preparation of regional plans are covered from the budget of the voivodship people's councils whose areas are included in the plans.

ART. 11. 1. Regional plans constitute the base for the elaboration of local plans for physical development.

2. On the basis of regional plans the proper agencies issue decisions

relative to the general location of building investments. Such decisions approximately define the site where investment is to be made and, in case of linear investments, the route.

ART. 12. The Chairman of the Planning Commission of the Council of Ministers, in agreement with the Chairman of the Committee for Building, City Planning, and Architecture, defines the detailed order, principles, and method of elaboration and coordination of general and detailed plans and also the procedure of fixing general locations.

Section III
LOCAL PLANS FOR SPATIAL DEVELOPMENT

ART. 13. Local plans for spatial development are:

1) Master plans for spatial development of settlement units called in further regulations of this act "master plans" and plans for the spatial development of areas constituting groups [systems] of settlement units;

2) detailed plans for the spatial development of parts of settlement units and, in justified cases, the whole of such units, called in further regulations of this Act "detailed plans."

ART. 14. 1. The master plan defines in a general manner the basic trends and scale of development and the principles of the spatial development of the area for the entire perspective-planning period, and also the program and manner of the spatial development of the settlement unit during the following short-term national economic plan.

2. A master plan should in principle be prepared for all the periods envisaged in Art. 3. The master plan for small towns and urban settlements and villages can be prepared as a long-term and stage plan or as a stage plan alone.

3. The master plan constitutes the base for the development of the area and for establishing investment needs in the area of the given unit. It includes the basic instructions for working out the detailed plans for this area and defines the areas requiring such preparation and their order.

4. The draft master plan should be prepared for the entire area included in the development intended for the given settlement unit. In justified cases, the master plan may also be prepared for a particular part of the city. The master plan for rural areas includes the area

of land designated for farming, the area to be built up, and the areas designated for social and other purposes.

ART. 15. 1. In principle, master plans should be prepared for all settlement units.

2. The order of the settlement units for which plans are to be prepared is established by the praesidia of the people's councils whose agencies are responsible for preparing such plans. Master plans for settlement units which are being reconstructed, redeveloped, or newly planned should be prepared before beginning such reconstruction, redevelopment, or new building.

ART. 16. Plans for spatial development of a group [system] of settlement units are prepared when such group of settlement units is already in existence or in the phase of being built in the given area, which—owing to the functional links—constitutes an economic and spatial whole. In particular, such plans should be prepared for areas of groups of industrial and port towns and urban settlements, settlement units lying in the suburban zone of large cities, rural settlement units within the framework of the counties or parts thereof, health resorts, recreational and tourist resorts, etc.

ART. 17. 1. A detailed plan is prepared for part of the area of a settlement unit, envisaged for development [building, reconstruction, redevelopment] during the current and following period of the short-term national economic plan.

2. A detailed plan for the spatial development of small towns, urban settlements, and villages can be prepared jointly with the master plan for the area of the entire unit.

3. A detailed plan defines in detail the designation of areas for particular purposes, delineates the boundary lines of the areas, fixes the principles for the development and technical equipment facilities of the area, delineates the frontage line and the permissible height of the buildings and—if necessary—other conditions and instructions relative to the shaping of buildings.

4. As regards rural areas, a detailed plan is prepared only for the areas designated for building purposes.

ART. 18. 1. The detailed plan is prepared in reference to the master plan.

2. If an urgent necessity to prepare the detailed plan arises and there is no approved master plan, the detailed plan should then be

worked out adapting it to the preliminary assumptions fixed for the master plan.

ART. 19.   1. Draft master plans for towns and urban settlements and plans for groups of settlement units are prepared by the respective voivodship agencies of local spatial planning. Draft master plans of other settlement units and draft detailed plans are prepared by the county agencies of spatial planning.

2. The praesidia of voivodship people's councils can assign the preparation of master plans of towns and settlements and plans for groups of rural settlement units to the respective county agencies for spatial planning.

3. The Chairman of the Committee for Building, City Planning, and Architecture can define which of the draft local plans for spatial development must be accepted by him before being submitted for approval.

4. The voivodship agencies for local spatial planning may define which of the drafts of the local plans for physical development, prepared by the county agencies must, before being approved, be accepted by the voivodship agency for local spatial planning.

ART. 20.   Draft local plans are subject to coordination with the concerned departments of the praesidia of the people's councils and the local agencies of the state administration which are not subordinate to people's councils. If agreement is not reached, the decision is submitted to the respective central agencies.

ART. 21.   1. A pronouncement of the opinion of the praesidium of the respective people's council [town, urban settlement, or village and in cities divided into districts: district council] should be made on each draft master plan before it is presented for approval.

2. Before an opinion is pronounced on the draft master plan, a discussion of the principles of the plan should be arranged by the respective agency of the praesidium with the representatives of the socialized economic units, social and professional organizations, interested private persons. Remarks reported should be taken into consideration before pronouncing opinion and before approving the plan.

3. The draft master plan of the village should be examined at a village meeting before being presented for approval. Remarks and inferences relative to the draft plan announced at the village meeting—after an opinion has been pronounced by the praesidium of the village

people's council—should be presented to the decision of the praesidium of the county people's council.

ART. 22. 1. The draft detailed plans—after being coordinated and before being presented for approval—should be displayed to public view at the seat of the praesidium of the respective people's council [municipal, district, urban settlement, or village] for a period of 14 days.

2. Notices relative to the display of the draft plan to public view should be announced by the proper agency of the praesidium of the people's council in the local newspaper and on the notice board of the praesidium of the respective people's council.

3. During the period when the draft plan is on display, socialized economic units, social and professional organizations, and interested official and private persons may submit their remarks and proposals to the praesidium of the people's council.

4. Remarks and proposals should be examined by the agency of the people's council responsible for preparing the draft plan and should be presented to the praesidium of the people's council responsible for approving the plan.

ART. 23. 1. Master plans for villages and plans for groups of village settlement units are approved by the praesidia of the county people's councils, other master plans and plans for groups of settlements by the praesidia of the voivodship people's councils.

2. Detailed plans are approved by the praesidia of the county people's councils.

3. The Council of Ministers defines which of the local plans will be presented to the Council of Ministers for acceptance with regard to the fundamental elements of such plans. Such plans are presented to the Council of Ministers after an opinion has been pronounced by the Chairman of the Committee for Building, City Planning, and Architecture and by the Chairman of the Planning Commission of the Council of Ministers.

ART. 24. 1. The decisions of the praesidium of the people's council relative to the approval of the local plans are published in the Official Journal of the voivodship people's council and announced on the notice board of the praesidium of the respective people's council [village, municipal, or urban settlement]. Furthermore an announcement should be made relative to the approval of the plan, in the local newspaper.

2. The announcements mentioned in item 1 should indicate those

agencies of the praesidium of the people's council which are obliged to render the plan accessible to view and to give information. If plans are unavailable for view because of regulations relative to state secrets, the respective agency for spatial planning is obliged to inform those concerned, at their request, of such provisions of the plan as pertain to their interests.

ART. 25. 1. Local plans go into force the day the act relative to the approval of the given plan is published in the voivodship Official Journal.

2. Alterations in the plan may be made only after receiving the consent for such from the agency which approved the plan. Such alterations cannot include any changes in the fundamental elements of the plan. Such alterations can only be introduced in the procedure fixed for preparing, coordinating, and approving of plans.

ART. 26. Expenses incurred in the preparation of the local draft plans are to be covered from the budget of the people's councils whose agencies are responsible for the preparation of such plans.

ART. 27. The Council of Ministers will issue by way of regulation detailed prescriptions relative to coordination of draft plans [Art. 20], pronouncements of opinion on the draft plans by praesidia of people's councils, instituting discussions on the principles of the plan, examining master draft village plans at village meetings [Art. 21], and the display of detailed draft plans for viewing, submitting, and examining remarks and proposals relative to the plan [Art. 22].

ART. 28. The Chairman of the Committee for Building, City Planning, and Architecture, in agreement with the Chairman of the Planning Commission of the Council of Ministers and the ministers concerned, will issue detailed instructions for the preparation of local plans for spatial development, fixing:

1) contents in detail of the local plans for spatial development;
2) method, procedure, and form for the elaboration of plans;
3) instructions, guidelines, and standards for the elaboration of the plans.

ART. 29. 1. Drafts for local plans for spatial development may be prepared by persons professionally qualified, whose qualifications have been confirmed by proper agencies.

2. The Chairman of the Committee for Building, City Planning,

and Architecture, in agreement with the ministers concerned, will determine by way of regulation:

1) the kind of higher studies required for confirmation of qualifications;
2) extent, duration, and manner of acquiring practice;
3) procedure of issuing certificates relative to confirmation of qualifications and method of filing the names of persons who have received such certificates.

Section IV
THE COMPETENCE OF AGENCIES FOR SPATIAL PLANNING IN MATTERS PERTAINING TO THE UTILIZATION OF LAND

ART. 30. 1. Matters pertaining to the utilization of specific land belong to the competence of agencies for local spatial planning.

2. In particular, agencies for spatial planning:

1) determine the detailed location of building investments, defining the building lot or area on which the investment is to be made and—if necessary—the city planning conditions which should be fulfilled when making the investment;
2) express their consent to a change in the manner in which the land is to be utilized without making any investment in it, fixing—as needed—the conditions which must be met when the manner of utilizations is changed;
3) determine the protective zones and manner of development if there are no other competent agencies stipulated in the particular regulations pertaining to such matters.

3. Units of the socialized economy, official persons not being units of the socialized economy, and private persons are obliged to obtain decisions pertaining to matters mentioned in item 2, points 1 and 2. Decisions pertaining to matters mentioned in item 2, points 2 and 3, are issued ex officio or upon request of persons concerned.

ART. 31. 1. The basis for making decisions in matters mentioned in Art. 30.2.1 is an approved plan for spatial development.

2. If an urgent need arises to issue a decision pertaining to a detailed location in areas for which there is no approved plan, the proper agency makes the decision on the basis of materials already in possession for the plan, supplemented by indispensable data and after coordination with the agencies concerned. In matters pertaining to detailed location of private investments, the voivodship agency for spatial planning can,

at the request of the county spatial planning agency competent to issue such decision, postpone issuing such a decision up to the time the plan is approved but not for longer than three years.

Art. 32.   1. Matters pertaining to the determination of detailed location of investment and matters pertaining to changes in the manner of land utilization in areas in which no investment is made belong to the competence of the county agency for spatial planning if a particular regulation does not envisage the competence of the voivodship agency.

2. In the absence of an approved local plan for spatial development, the elaboration of which belongs to the voivodship agency for spatial planning, the draft of the decision pertaining to detailed location of investment requires the acceptance of the voivodship agency for spatial planning.

Art. 33. Matters mentioned in Art. 30.2.3 belong to the agencies for local spatial planning responsible for fixing the detailed location of building objects requiring the delimitation of a protective zone.

Art. 34. The Council of Ministers will define by way of regulation, the minimum distances which must be maintained in respect to public roads, railway lines, and airfields when issuing decisions pertaining to detailed location of building investments.

Art. 35. The Chairman of the Committee for Building, City Planning, and Architecture will issue detailed regulations establishing the principles and procedure of issuing decisions in matters mentioned in Art. 30.2; such regulations define the investments which do not require obtaining a decision for detailed location and the cases where a change in the manner of land utilization, where no investments are made, require the permission of agencies for spatial planning and furthermore define the investments for which decisions pertaining to location are issued by the voivodship agencies for spatial planning.

Section V
IMPLEMENTATION PLANS

Art. 36. Implementation plans are elaborated:
1) for individual building lots as plans for the development of such lots or plans for locating the building objects;
2) for areas destined to be built up by one investor or by a group of investors—as part of the plan for the building investment.

Art. 37.   1. The basis for preparing the draft implementation plan is an approved detailed plan for spatial development of a settlement unit and a fixed decision relative to location.

2. If the implementation plan of Art. 36.2 includes areas for which there is no approved detailed plan for spatial development, the investor is obliged to elaborate a draft of such a plan for the area included in the location of the given investment on the basis of instructions given by the competent agency for local spatial planning. The draft of such a plan is subject to coordination and approval in conformity with the generally obligatory instructions.

Art. 38. Principles for the elaboration of implementation plans and the procedure of their coordination and approval are established by the Chairman of the Committee for Building, City Planning, and Architecture in agreement with the ministers concerned.

Art. 39. Expenses incurred in the elaboration of the implementation plans and the detailed plans for spatial development in Art. 37.2 are borne by the investor.

Section VI
Temporary and Final Regulations

Art. 40. Plans for the spatial development of towns, urban settlements, and villages approved before the present act came into force are considered local plans for spatial development in the meaning of the present act.

Art. 41.   1. Whenever mention is made of voivodship people's councils and their praesidia or the voivodship agencies for economic planning and voivodship agencies for local spatial planning, it also refers to the respective people's councils of towns having the rank of voivodships, the praesidia of such councils; and whenever mention is made of county people's councils and their praesidia, of county agencies for spatial planning, it also refers to the respective municipal people's councils of cities constituting municipal counties, district people's councils of cities having the rank of voivodships, the praesidia of such councils and their respective agencies.

2. The praesidia of people's councils of cities having the rank of voivodships may transmit to the praesidia of county people's councils and their agencies those functions pertaining to spatial planning which,

in the light of the regulations of this act with regard to areas of the voivodship, belong to the functions of county praesidia of people's councils and their agencies.

.   .   .   .

ART. 43.   1. The act of April 2, 1946, pertaining to a planned spatial development of the country, becomes ineffective [*Official Journal*, No. 16, p. 109].

2. The day that the regulations are issued on the basis of Art. 34, the following become ineffective:

1) Art. 1, 2, 3, and 4 of the act of March 13, 1934, relative to the removal of buildings, warehouses, trees, and earthworks from railway lines, protective antifire belts, and antisnow screens [*Official Journal*, No. 28, p. 220];

2) Art. 15 of the act of October 7, 1921, relative to regulations with regard to order and discipline on public highways [*Official Journal*, No. 89, p. 656, with subsequent alterations].

ART. 44. The act will become effective six months from the day on which it was published.

Chairman of the State Council [*Rada Państwa*]:
A. ZAWADZKI
Secretary of the State Council: J. HORODECKI

Town Planning Standards

Part 1.

Data from the "Provisional Town Planning Standards," 1951[*]

These standards are primarily intended for the development of vacant land, *i.e.,* new cities and city expansion. Where redevelopment is needed, special studies must be made.

The regulations are given in fifteen chapters:

1. Housing areas
2. School grounds
3. Cultural and art institutions
4. Health services
5. Government administration
6. Social services
7. Commerce
8. Restaurants and other dining facilities
9. Handicrafts
10. Local industries (supply)
11. Streets and squares
12. Parking and garages
13. Green areas
14. Utilities networks
15. Sample table of land use in the settlement area
16. List of area and volume indices for public utility installations

Introductory Remarks

The area of the city can be divided into:

1. Land adjusted for building purposes
2. Other land

Developed land for building purposes consists of:

1. The settlement area, which contains:
   a. Housing areas, blocks of homes and other
   b. Public utility areas
   c. Green areas
   d. Area for streets and squares

* Selected, prepared, and translated by Bolesław Malisz.

2. Other adjusted land:
  a. Industrial and commercial
  b. Communal utilities grounds (connected with utilities networks)
  c. Major public utility sources or works, outside the developed land
  d. Major thoroughfares and other external communication facilities

The residential area is divided into:

1. A high-density residential area
2. A low-density residential area with detached and semidetached houses

The standards relate only to the high-density residential areas.

The standards for the housing area . . . relating to programing and zoning in residential districts are based on a long-term standard, assuming a net living area of 9 m² per inhabitant. In the present type of housing construction, this corresponds to 20 m² gross floor area and to 73.5 m³ per inhabitant . . . For the intermediate period, during which only 7 m² of net floor area are available (corresponding to 15.5 m² of gross floor area and 57.5 m³ per inhabitant), no change should be made in standards for residential service facilities. These will be more intensively used during the intermediate period.

A block of housing includes primarily:

1. The ground coverage of houses, measured within the outside walls
2. Green and recreational areas, for block residents only
3. Service courtyards, pedestrian walks, and internal streets
4. Areas for nurseries, kindergartens, and other service facilities for block residents only

The residential zones are:

Zone I: detached and semidetached houses, average site 280 m²
Zone II: multifamily houses of two stories
Zone III: multifamily houses of three stories
Zone IV: multifamily houses of four stories

Zone V: multifamily houses of five–eight stories
Zone VI: multifamily houses of over eight stories
Zone 0: built-up rural areas, site 1,000 m²

Table 16. STANDARDS FOR CONSTRUCTING HOUSING BLOCKS

Zone	Floor area ratio*			Per cent of site coverage			Net population density (inhab./hectare)		
	Min.	Med.	Max.	Min.	Med.	Max.	Min.	Med.	Max.
I	0.29	0.40	0.55	19.3	23.3	27.5	145	200	275
II	0.47	0.55	0.64	23.5	27.5	32.0	235	275	320
III	0.65	0.80	0.90	21.7	26.6	30.0	325	400	450
IV	0.78	0.94	1.08	19.5	23.5	27.0	390	470	540
V	1.07	1.17	1.45	15.3	16.7	20.7	535	585	725
VI	1.10	1.31	1.56	11.0	13.1	15.6	550	655	780

$$\text{* Floor area ratio} = \frac{\text{ground coverage of buildings} \times \text{no. of stories}}{\text{1 hectare}}$$

The preferred floor area ratios, per cent of site coverage, and net population densities are given in the middle columns in Table 16. Higher indices, up to the maximum, may be used in partially developed blocks with a high floor-area ratio to conform with existing conditions. Lower indices, down to the minimum, can be used in partially developed blocks to save detached houses in good repair.

Within the intermediate period, assuming 15.5 m² gross floor area in houses, the indices for net population density on land used for housing purposes should be multiplied by 1.3 ($= 20.0 : 15.5$).

(An example from the service standards: *Primary Schools*)
Primary schools include children from age 7 to 14. These standards are based on the assumption that this age group constitutes 14 per cent of the population. In practice, corrections will be necessary. The primary school comprises seven grades. There are forty children in each classroom. Three types of such schools are possible:

Type I: tripled school for 840 children, serving 6,000 inhabitants
Type II: doubled school for 560 children, serving 4,000 inhabitants
Type III: single school for 280 children, serving 2,000 inhabitants

In a tripled school there are three parallel classes for each grade, and in a doubled school there are two parallel classes for each grade. Type III (single school) will be used only when the range of the school-service area would be more than R = 1.5 km. In the long-term-plan period this type will be changed into a doubled school. In small towns it is advisable to combine the school site with the recreation grounds of the town. . . . The school site should be so located that children going to school need not cross streets. To use the schoolgrounds more efficiently, groups of two schools are advisable. When the school is situated near the public playgrounds the site size can be diminished by 10 per cent to 20 per cent.

Table 17. STANDARDS FOR PRIMARY SCHOOLS

Primary schools	Number of pupils	Site size		Volume		Range	Employ-ment
		hectares	M²/child	Gross m³	m³/child		
Type I	840	1.25	15.0	13,860	16.5	1.0	32
Type II	560	1.23	22.0	9520	17.0	1.0	22
Type III	280	1.00	35.7	4900	17.5	1.0	12

Green spaces: The specially developed green areas in cities should be provided according to the following standards, in m² per inhabitant.

Table 18. STANDARDS FOR GREEN AREAS*

Type	City population (in thousands)				
	5	15	50	100	250
Within the settlement area:					
Parks	–	–	3.0	3.5	4.0
Wooded parks	5.0	6.0	3.5	4.5	5.5
Boulevards, promenades	–	1.0	1.5	2.0	2.0
Green squares	2.0	2.0	2.0	2.0	2.5
Total	7.0	9.0	10.0	12.0	14.0
Outside the settlement area:					
Allotment gardens	–	2.0	3.0	3.5	4.0
Cemeteries	3.5	3.0	2.0	2.0	2.0

* The model table of land use in high-density residential areas is not included in this draft. It will follow Table 18 above in the publication of the standards.

Part 2.

Data from "Regulation fifteen" of the President of the Committee for Building, City Planning, and Architecture, 1961

(relating to the major standard indices for programing housing estates for the period 1961–1965).*

The provisional standards from the year 1951 (see Appendix II, 1) had to be revised and corrected. New standards have been prepared by the Institute of Town Planning and Architecture. Regulation fifteen is based on a part of these new standards.

I. *General Remarks*

1. The purpose of the regulation, constituting a basis for:
   a. Preparing and approving draft detailed plans, programing, designing implementation plans for residential districts in the period 1961–1965.
   b. Defining the relationship between local physical-development plans (both master plans and detailed plans) and implementation plans.

2. Application of the regulation, obligatory for:
   a. New housing estates, built-up into multifamily houses
   b. Parts of new built-up areas in multifamily houses
   c. For redeveloped residential districts these regulations are suggestions only.

3. Definition of a housing estate (*i.e.* a neighborhood unit): A housing estate constitutes the basic unit of the structure of the residential area. It is the smallest unit for which a program of basic services and green spaces should be prepared. A housing estate is bounded by the rights-of-way of arteries or boundary lines of land in other use. The size of a housing estate (neighborhood), *i.e.* the number of inhabitants, its ground coverage, depends on specific local conditions . . . theoretically the proper size is 10,000 inhabitants. The number of inhabitants should be linked to the school facilities.

* Selected, prepared, and translated by Bolesław Malisz.

By a housing estate of multifamily houses, it is understood that no more than 10 per cent of the area is designated for individual houses (detached and semidetached dwellings).

The area of the housing estate includes:

1. Net residential land (used for dwelling purposes)
2. Basic neighborhood service facilities on their own sites
3. The common garden, when not provided elsewhere by the master plan
4. Access to community service facilities
5. The internal roads, walks, etc. for internal communication

II. *Standards for local planning*

Table 19. GROSS FLOOR-AREA RATIOS (F.A.R.) AND POPULATION DENSITY FOR HOUSING ESTATES

Type of Housing estate		Buildings of 3–5 stories (Net F.A.R.: 0.70–0.95)		High-rise buildings (Net F.A.R.: 0.95–1.20)	
No. of inhabitants					
Age group		Gross F.A.R.	Pop./ha.	Gross F.A.R.	Pop./ha.
A. Under 5000	0–14 is 30% or more. Female employment is more than 50% of total	0.52–0.64	310–380	n/a	n/a
B1. Over 5000	0–14 is no more than 30%. Female employment is no more than 50% of total. Situated about 500 m. from district service center and from open green space	0.53–0.65	330–400	0.67–0.76	400–470
B2. Under 5000	0–14 is 30% or more. (Other conditions as in A)	0.53–0.65	330–400	0.67–0.76	400–470
C. Over 5000	0–14 is 30% or more. Situated more than 500 m. from district service center and from open green space (Other conditions as in A)	0.50–0.60	300–360	0.60–0.67	360–400

III. *Principles for designing site coverage of housing estates*

Required standards for site coverage depend on the average number of stories, the height, width, and length of houses.

Table 20. STANDARDS FOR SITE COVERAGE OF HOUSING ESTATES

Average number of stories	Net floor-area ratio
3–4	0.70–0.80
4–5	0.80–0.95
over 5	0.95–1.20

To calculate the number of inhabitants from the net floor-area ratio, the following figures for floor space per inhabitant should be used:

14.7 m² living space + 0.4 services space = 15.1 m² housing space.

Table 21. USEFUL SURFACE AREA OF FLATS

Average number of stories	Density of useful surface area (m²/ha.)
3–4	5110–5840
4–5	5840–6935
over 5	6935–8760

The standards for useful surface area of flats are based on the assumption that the useful surface area is 75% of the total surface area of the house.

The regulations also give detailed prescriptions for providing for sufficient sunlight.

IV. *The basic services within a housing estate*

(This chapter gives all necessary data for programming basic neighborhood service facilities.)

nurseries	basic handicraft workshops	garages and parking areas
kindergartens	restaurant and dining facilities	central heating plant
primary schools	basic health services	local administration offices
shops for daily needs		common garden

City Planning

Table 22. STANDARDS FOR CHILDREN'S FACILITIES

Facility	Per cent of population in age group served	Per cent of users in age group*	Number of seats	Site size (ha.)
Nurseries	7–9	10–20	55	0.25
			80	0.35
Kindergartens	8–10	40–60	60	0.30
			90	0.40
			120	0.48
Primary schools	12–16	use made of the school: 1.25†	7 classes	1.00
			11 classes	1.22
			15 classes	1.25

* Based on per cent of female employment 30%–60%.

† On the assumption that in the present period one of four schools will be used twofold, this means that the total number of users will be 1.25 greater than the number of seats in each school.

Regional Planning

Part Two

Commentary and Orientation

JACK C. FISHER
WOJCIECH MORAWSKI

IN Poland, as elsewhere, regional planning is a relatively new, dynamic discipline of learning and subject for economic-administrative practice.[1] Like city planning, it is a component of the broader notion of spatial planning. A number of issues in regional planning, however, including the scope and definition of the term itself, its place as a scientific field, and its research tools, are to a large extent unresolved. There are still no accepted definitions of regional planning in professional literature, and views on the scope and purpose of this kind of planning diverge widely among various countries. Therefore, an effort is made in Part Two to reflect the view of regional planning current in scientific circles and economic and administrative agencies in Poland.

The first chapter of this section describes the spatial changes in economic activities that have taken place since the war. Against this background of spatial studies, Józef Zaremba, the Director for Regional Planning of the Planning Commission, describes the basic theory and methods upon which Polish regional planning rests. Three case studies, selected to provide examples of regional development in areas with different economic structures, are presented. Two chapters deal with problems of rural development and water resources. The activities of a scientific committee designated to develop new methods of planning and to improve understanding of the development pattern in Poland are described, with a review of the results of several of its studies.

To introduce the reader to the subject we will concentrate on three issues: the concept of "region," relations between regional planning and economic planning, and the differentiation between regional planning and territorial planning.

We must treat the idea of "region" in a narrow, practical sense, as a spatial unit adopted by regional administrative organs as the subject

---

[1] Regional planning traditions in Poland go back to the nineteen-twenties; see Chapter 10.

for studies and projections. The extent of the discussion in Poland of the concept of "region" in its wider sense prohibits treatment here. We can only invite interested readers to study the relevant literature.[2] In its practical sense a "region" in Poland usually means the area of a voivodship.[3] In some cases part of a voivodship may be considered a region or sections of adjacent voivodships may be regarded as one region, that is, as the subject for regional planning.[4] It is also an accepted practice in the planning process to combine several voivodships in superregional or macroregional systems when their common analysis is expected to produce sounder studies and conclusions. Thus, while regional planning benefits from, and is linked to, the administrative divisions of the country, regional planners are assured of the flexibility indispensable to determining the study and the program area. Although it makes use of the statistical data and organizational basis of the administrative units, regional planning is not hampered by having to follow strictly administrative divisions, when the method might handicap the work.

As in the case of city planning, close integration with economic planning is a notably characteristic feature of Polish regional planning. The explanation for establishing such close links between spatial and economic planning was presented in the commentary and orientation to

[2] Without attempting to cover the bibliography in Polish literature on the problem we wish to draw the reader's attention to some important articles on theoretical problems of regionalization, especially to those available in English:

Dziewoński, Kazimierz. "Economic Regionalization," *Geographia Polonica,* Jan., 1964 (Polish Scientific Publishers), 171–185.

———. "Geographical Research for Regional Planning in Poland," *Problems of Applied Geography, Proceedings of the Anglo-Polish Seminar* (Nieborow, Sept. 1959, Geographical Studies No. 25, Polish Academy of Sciences, Institute of Geography) (Warsaw: P. W. N., 1961), 17–28.

———. "Problems of Regional Structure of Poland," *Przegląd Geograficzny (Polish Geographical Review),* XXXII, Suppl. (Warsaw: P. W. N., 1960), 115–125.

———. "Theoretical Problems in the Development of Economic Regions," *Regional Science Association, Papers,* VIII (1962) (The Hague: European Congress, 1961), 43–54.

———. "Theoretical Problems in the Development of Economic Regions (within one country), II," *ibid.,* X (1963) (Zurich: European Congress, 1962), 51–60.

Secomski, Kazimierz. *Wstęp do teorii rozmieszczenia sił wytwórczych* [An Introduction to the Theory of Location of Productive Forces] (Warsaw: P. W. N., 1956). In Polish only.

Wróbel, Andrzej. "Study of Economic Regional Structure," *Przegląd Geograficzny, op. cit.,* 127–132.

[3] The area of the particular voivodships (excluding the five major cities) ranges from 9,500 sq. km. to 29,400 sq. km. The population of the voivodships (excluding the five major cities) ranges from 0.7 million to 3.4 million inhabitants.

[4] Appendix I, *Spatial Planning Act,* Art. 2.1.2. and Art. 7.

Part One; here we will discuss the practical aspect of the connection. Two fundamental concerns in Polish regional planning should be emphasized: the spatial determination and coordination of economic and social tasks adopted for the whole country in the long-term, or perspective, national economic plans; and the exposition of possibilities created by the natural environment and infrastructure as well as the exposition of economic and social requirements in the particular regions.

The two concerns seem to reflect opposing tendencies. The first shows the supremacy of the macrospatial pattern (the area and economy of the whole country) over the microspatial (the regions and their economies), with some concession to the regional pattern for spatial coordination of the plans embodied in the general economic program. The second trend seems to emphasize the microspatial pattern. There is evident an inherent struggle between the macrospatial pattern, representing trends formulated generally at a central level by the various sectors of the national economy, and the microspatial pattern, expressing a regional point of view in projecting economic growth in the various spatial units. The supremacy of central economic planning is a fact; it allocates optimal tasks within the framework of available means. It is expected to create realistic limits for estimating regional growth.

These statements, however, do not fully explain the relationship of national to regional planning. There are ample possibilities for regional planning to influence general economic decisions. Regional planners can suggest possibilities for development of the national economy in particular regions (for example, those offered by natural resources, infrastructure, and balance of manpower); they can determine direct and indirect expenditures which the national economy must meet to achieve the programed development of productive potential in particular groups and sectors of given regions; and they can offer analyses of basic economic and sociological parameters in a regional cross-section, revealing problems that require solution.

The influence of the regional viewpoint on decisions reached at the macroeconomic level is exerted through appropriate stages of the planning process. In problems of spatial and economic reconstruction, regional planning is seen through long-term plans, embracing periods of fifteen to twenty years and even more in some cases. Plans for such a period have the character of a long-range study, with reciprocal flow of information, postulates, tasks, and designs between central and regional centers of planning and administration. The effectiveness of this flow is ensured by the institutional pattern. The Planning Commission of the

Council of Ministers, the state's central authority for economic planning, also treats the over-all problems of regional planning, including functional control over the voivodships' Regional Plan Workshops.

It would be incorrect to assume that the present system has succeeded in eliminating the conflict between macrospatial and microspatial economic patterns. This system has substantial advantages in that it creates conditions in which conflict among measurable economic variables may be revealed, and thus it should be able to confine the conflict within the discipline of the planning process, and allow optimum conditions for both general and partial patterns to be anticipated.

Although regional planning has a dependent relation to national economic planning, territorial planning is a constituent part of economic planning, and thus differs from regional planning. All economic planning can be divided into central planning—dependent on the central authority of the Planning Commission and the ministries—and territorial planning—dependent on the local authority of the people's councils. Territorial planning is used in two spheres: to take immediate and direct action in response to economic issues with a high degree of local determinability and to economic issues that require adaptation to actual conditions in particular voivodships and counties; and to take indirect action in response to centrally controlled economic issues.

Territorial planning has direct responsibility in certain basic fields, such as: agriculture (generally as a whole), commodity distribution in commerce, municipal economy (urban transportation, water-supply and sewerage systems, gas supply, hotel management, laundry management, city maintenance), and housing management. Local industry (small-scale works producing mainly for the local market), education (elementary and secondary schools), health services, and social security programs are included. At the voivodship level a balance of employment, expenditures, and personal incomes, should be achieved, as well as the productive potential of the building enterprises. The indirect responsibility of territorial planning is the regional coordination of the plans of all the economic units in the voivodship. To carry out this function, centrally planned units give voivodship authorities a number of control data describing their activity. The regional balances mentioned above must be coordinated, but other tasks are also performed: ensuring the appropriate means to finance supplementary investment projects; initiating and realizing investment projects shared by various users (especially construction of common social-welfare and cultural services, railway sidings,

warehouses, water-supply projects, sewage-treatment projects, and so on);
and facilitating cooperation between nonbasic industry and basic
industry, which is planned centrally.

Regional planning differs from territorial planning in several ways:

Time: Territorial plans are prepared for periods of one and five
years; regional plans are prepared for a perspective period of fifteen or
twenty years, with five-year stage plans.

Subject Matter: Territorial planning essentially deals with only those
social and economic phenomena of a given area (voivodship or county)
that have a high degree of local determinability; regional planning
treats *all* social and economic phenomena of a given study area. Regional
planning deals with all problems (production, raw materials, cooperation, employment, space, and so on) of any major industry (a steel factory, for example) as well as with problems of small local factories (such
as a bottling plant). Territorial planning has no over-all responsibility
for basic industry, which is guided by central authorities, but only for
certain aspects of basic industry, such as construction of sidings or
warehouses shared by several users. On the other hand, all the problems
of the nonbasic industries enter the national economic plan or national
statistics via territorial cross-sections.

Methodology and Character of Process: Territorial planning concentrates
primarily (but not solely) on the problem of *how much.* Regional planning emphasizes *where* and *why.* Territorial planning is mainly an
administrative document prepared according to central instructions,
while regional planning is primarily a scientific study or work of research.

Planning Agency: Territorial plans are prepared by the voivodships'
planning commissions; regional plans are prepared by special planning
teams which draw on the particular competence of the various sciences.
In the Planning Commission of the Council of Ministers regional planning is under the Department of Perspective Planning, which coordinates long-term plans. In the same Commission territorial planning is
under the Department of Territorial Economy, which coordinates one-
year and five-year plans for all the voivodships.

Despite these considerable differences in target, scope, and method,
there are distinct connections and correlations between regional and
territorial planning. In a number of ways territorial planning constitutes
a statistical inventory base for regional planning. Conversely, the five-
year stages of the long-term regional plans are interpreted as guides or
directives for territorial planning.

CHAPTER 9

Postwar Changes in the Polish Economic and Social Structure

Kazimierz Dziewoński
Stanisław Leszczycki

Poland's Position in 1945

THE whole social and economic structure of Poland, especially its spatial economy, is now being changed as a result of rapid industrialization and intensive urbanization. A comprehensive picture of these changes requires a brief description of Poland's position immediately after the war.

In spite of very heavy losses, the result of both fierce fighting and ruinous enemy occupation, the Polish nation came out of the war as a strongly unified, integrated community. The great tribulations suffered under Nazi rule and the large migratory movements, both voluntary and compulsory, had broken all traditional, regional, social, cultural, national, and religious barriers. Before the war Poland had been characterized by the existence of large and strong national minorities (amounting to about one-third of the whole population). As a consequence of the cession of eastern territories, inhabited mainly by Ukrainians, White Russians, and Lithuanians, the extermination of the Jewish population, and also of the flight of the majority of Germans and, later on, the repatriation of the remaining Germans, the state is now inhabited almost solely by Poles. Members of other nationalities, now widely dispersed, do not amount to more than several hundred thousand, that is, less than 1 per cent of the total population. Moreover, within the national population, the postwar social and economic revolution—expressed, among several ways, by the nationalization of industry and commerce—resulted in the far-reaching equalization of living conditions. The classless society is already emerging from the turmoil of these changes. *This well-integrated community* is the basic fact of postwar Poland.

243

Shifts in the national territory were paralleled by changes in population structure. The cession to the U.S.S.R. of about 180,000 sq. km., that is 46.3 per cent of the prewar territory, and the return of about 103,000 sq. km. of the former Polish land on the western side mean that the whole area has been diminished by about 77,000 sq. km., or by 19.8 per cent. The configuration of the state, however, is now much more integrated. Poland is almost circular in shape. The length of her frontiers diminished from 5,529 km. to 3,538 km., or by about 36 per cent, and the index of "compactness" as expressed by the relation between the frontiers and the area included within diminished from 14.2 to 11.3 km. per 1,000 sq. km. At the same time the character of Poland's frontiers became more advantageous. The length of seacoast was increased from 140 to 524 km., or from 2.5 per cent to 14.8 per cent of all frontiers. Moreover, the whole interior economic structure was improved. The most important industrial and economic section of the country—the Upper Silesian Coal Basin—which before the war had been a border region split between neighboring states, was reunited in 1945. Therefore, the integration of the national territory is the second important fact of postwar Poland.

The third fact is the existence of disparities in geographical environment, particularly in the location of natural resources and sites of their use, as well as disparities in the distribution of the accumulated capital as expressed in the basic investment for both production and service.

Generally, all known and exploited important mineral resources were concentrated in the south in 1945, along the foothills of the Sudeten and Carpathian Mountains. Less important deposits existed in the southern Holy Cross (Swiętokrzyskie) Mountains. This is the area where older, prequaternary deposits are found near the surface. The best soils and the most propitious climatic conditions are also in the southern parts of the country outside the mountainous areas—in the Odra valley, on the northern side of the upper Vistula, and in the southern part of the Lublin region. The distribution of basic investments in 1945, although somewhat disturbed by the war, still correspond to the twentieth-century division of the whole country among three great and powerful empires, each with different social and economic policies. The German part of the country was characterized by comparatively balanced development; the Russian section, although partly industrialized, was extremely deficient in services; the Austrian section, on the other hand, though it had well-developed services, especially in the cultural area, was not industrialized at all. All three regions were backward and underdeveloped sections of the empires in which they were incorporated. Geographically, the number and importance of industrial plants diminished sharply from the southwestern to the northwestern parts of the country, while the quantity and quality of services diminished to the southeast and east.

War devastation was concentrated in Warsaw, which was deliberately destroyed by the Nazis, and in the western and northern regions where heavy fighting had taken place in the final months of the war.

In the years immediately after the war, up to about 1950, efforts were concentrated on starting production in the remaining factories and on abandoned or uncultivated farms; the reorganization of disrupted services, especially the communal ones; and the reconstruction of destroyed buildings and plants, wherever it was still possible. This obviously was the most effective economic policy for the time, but it did not introduce any serious changes into the spatial structure of the country. The period of postwar reconstruction, however, was already clearly coming to a close about 1949, and the time was ripe for undertaking much more ambitious plans for the complete redevelopment of the country on the basis of strong industrialization and urbanization. Those plans which had been prepared and discussed since 1947, were finally approved as the Six-Year Plan (for the years 1950–1955) and later extended in the form of two five-year plans (1956–1960 and 1961–1965).

The period that has passed since the inauguration of this great effort is long enough to permit a critical appreciation of the results achieved, of the gains and losses.

Industrialization of Poland in the Years 1950–1960

In 1960 the growth index of the national income as compared to 1950 was 208, that is, national income was more than twice as large as in 1950. A similar growth index for total industrial production, however, reached the figure of 338, well over three times as much as in 1950. At the same time industrial employment grew from 2,050,000 workers in 1950 to 3,012,000 in 1960; this growth index is only about 150. Figures concerning the parallel although slower growth of the population are also interesting. The number of industrial workers per thousand inhabitants was about 52 in 1946; in 1950 about 82; and in 1960 about 109.[1] Among the principal products, coal production rose from 78 million tons in 1950 to 106.6 million tons in 1961; electric

---

[1] In 1937, within the old boundary lines of the state, this figure was only 25.

power from 8.3 million to 32.2 billion kw-hr; steel from 2.5 million to 7.2 million tons; cement from 1.3 million to 7.4 million tons; sulphuric acid from 180,000 to 794,000 tons; sugar from 506,000 to 1,508,000 tons; cotton textiles from 325 million to 710 million meters, and so on. Production of many new goods, such as automobiles, different types of machines, machine tools, electrical railway equipment, and ships, was also either started or organized on a basically different scale. The quality of goods has also been steadily rising.

CHANGES IN PRODUCTION

The growth of industrial production was accomplished by changes in the structure, size, and type of industrial plants. In Poland, as in many other countries experiencing rapid industrialization, the role played by smaller industrial establishments is declining in importance and larger plants employing greater numbers of workers are being erected. The smallest plants (those having fewer than four workers) employed about 986,000 people before the war (data for 1937), that is, 41 per cent of all industrial workers. In 1957 this figure dropped to 247,000, or to merely 8 per cent of all industrial workers. The decrease in the number of such establishments was caused by wartime destruction and changes in the economic and social structure of Polish industry after World War II. Some plants were united into cooperatives, some were reorganized and developed into larger units as state industries, and a great number of antiquated ones were closed. Still, in 1960 there were almost 9,000 private industrial establishments, and the number of private craftsmen's workshops amounted to nearly 106,000.

At the same time changes occurred in the total industrial structure. The changes in the relative importance of particular industries are a good illustration of this evolution. From 1950 to 1960 the share of industry in the means of production rose from 47.4 per cent to 54.5 per cent of the total industrial output; machine industries from 2.3 per cent to 6.1 per cent; electrotechnical industries from 1.5 per cent to 4.1 per cent; transportation industries from 3.2 per cent to 7.4 per cent; metal industries from 2.2 per cent to 4.7 per cent; and chemical industries from 3.9 per cent to 6.2 per cent. Other industries have decreased in relative importance and their participation in the total industrial production has diminished: extractive industries from 9.0 per cent to 4.8 per cent; fuels from 10.2 per cent to 5.8 per cent; ferrous metallurgy from 6.9 per cent to 6.2 per cent; textiles from 13.4 per cent to 12.3 per cent; and foodstuffs from 38.3 per cent to 28.1 per cent.

Since 1950 employment has risen: in fuel industries by 38.4 per cent; in electric-power stations by 13.1 per cent; in ferrous metallurgy by 26.7 per cent; in nonferrous metallurgy by 32 per cent; in machine industries by 81 per cent; in electrotechnical industries by 191 per cent; in transportation by 100.9 per cent; in metal products by 107.3 per cent; in chemicals by 48.7 per cent; in building materials by 65.1 per cent; in wood industries by 23.8 per cent; in textiles by 8.1 per cent; and in foods by 62.9 per cent. In percentages of total industrial employment, the changes for 1950–1960 were as follows: fuels from 12.8 per cent to 12.1 per cent; ferrous metallurgy from 5.8 per cent to 4.3 per cent; in machine industries from 6.2 per cent to 7.7 per cent; in electrotechnical industries from 2.0 per cent to 4.0 per cent; in transportation from 5.3 per cent to 7.2 per cent; in textile industries from 16.9 per cent to 12.9 per cent; and in food industries from 11.1 per cent to 12.3 per cent.

Poland is very rich in coal deposits, which are concentrated in Upper Silesia and around Wałbrzych in Lower Silesia. The extraction of steam coal is done in the central core of the Upper Silesian Coal Basin, and the industry is being extended in southern and eastern directions. New coal shafts are under construction in the upper valley of the Vistula. In spite of the wealth of coal seams, however, there is a definite deficiency of coking coal. Numerous new mines for coking coal are being developed in the south between the Ostravian and the Upper Silesian Coal basins on the Czechoslovakian border at the Rybnik Coal Basin. At the same time all coking coal from the vicinity of Wałbrzych is taken to steel mills in and around the Upper Silesian Industrial District and in return large amounts of steam coal from Upper Silesia are transported back to power stations in Wałbrzych. There is a definite lack of oil. Intensive geological searches for oil are being made both in the Carpathians and, for the first time with some success, in the Polish lowlands. Large deposits of natural gas have already been struck in the lowlands at the foot of the subcarpathian hills, a western extension of the well-known deposits in the Dniestr Valley in the eastern Carpathians. Important amounts of gas from these last deposits are also imported across the frontier.

In the future large quantities of oil will be imported by means of a special pipeline from Soviet Russia—from the area of the so-called "Second Baku" in Baszkiria. This pipeline crosses the whole of central Poland and will serve two great petrochemical works, one in Poland, at Płock in the valley of the lower Vistula, and another in eastern Germany, at Schwedt, on the left bank of the lower Odra.

Enormous changes are now being made in the location of electric-power stations. For a long while all plants were concentrated in the central part of the Upper Silesian Coal Basin. Several plants situated outside the Basin in the vicinity of big cities were also based on Upper Silesian coal. In the years 1950–1960 several new stations were constructed on the outer fringe of the Upper Silesian Coal Basin and in central Poland. In ten years production has trebled. At present new, very large power stations are being built in the lowlands on the basis of lignite. Already two new centers of power production are in existence: in Turoszów, in Lower Silesia, on the frontier between Poland, Czechoslovakia, and East Germany, and in the Konin area to the north of Łódź, halfway between Warsaw and Poznań. At least two others are planned: one on the Oder below Wrocław, and one to the south of Łódź in the vicinity of Bełchatów. In a few years one-third of all electricity will be produced outside Upper Silesia, and this proportion will continue to grow. Water-power stations do not at present play an important role in the Polish economy. In view of the wealth of coal deposits in Poland and the general technological progress lately achieved in the efficiency of steam-power stations, prospects are limited. They have a continuing important function, however, as a reserve for peak hours in the consumption of energy. In consequence, water-power stations are now built whenever big reservoirs are being constructed for some other reasons, such as for flood control and for storage of water. Two main areas for such water-power stations are clearly established: in the Carpathians and on the lower Vistula. At present big reservoirs are under construction on the San River in the mountains and on the lower Vistula in Włocławek.

Basic steel plants, concentrated since the end of the nineteenth century in the Upper Silesian Industrial District, are at present being developed in the large regional centers around Upper Silesia, in Kraków and Częstochowa. They are based on Upper Silesian coal, local limestone, and iron ore imported from Krivoi Rog in the Ukraine. Polish low-grade ores extracted in the district of Częstochowa, in the Swiętokrzyskie Mountains and recently also in the district of Łęczyca, north of Łódź, are also used together with other high-grade ores. The steel-processing plants are more widely spread throughout the country —the most modern ones being in Warsaw, Ostrowiec, and Stalowa Wola. Several important plants are located in the western part ᵒᶠ Upper Silesia, outside the coal basin.

Nonferrous metallurgy is only partly developed. Zinc was the traditional product of the northern part of the Upper Silesian district, once the world's most important source of this metal. Its present development, however, is hampered by the slow depletion of the ore deposits. A completely new area of production is copper. The exploitation of rather low-grade ores in Lower Silesia was organized during the war by Germans. It has been extended in the last ten years; mines have been enlarged, new ones constructed around Bolesławiec, and a copper mill built in Legnica. But a real change came with the discovery of new and richer seams halfway between Legnica and Głogów. By about 1970 Poland will have become a very important European producer and even exporter of copper. Aluminum is produced in a new plant in the vicinity of Kraków on the basis of electricity made from Upper Silesian coal and bauxite brought in from Hungary. Another plant is under construction in Konin (in central Poland) on the basis of electricity produced from local lignites and both Polish and imported clay.

Machine and metal industries, although concentrated in large and medium-sized cities, are the most evenly distributed throughout the country. The growth of machine industries characterizes the planned changes in the development of national economy. With the chemical industry it is already playing an increasingly important role in foreign trade, and its traditional structure is being altered. Previously the main Polish export goods were food, wood, and coal, but now wood products and coal are receding in importance. Although machine and metal industries are evenly distributed, various regions specialize in particular goods. Shipbuilding, for example, is concentrated on the coast, especially in and around the large seaports of the Vistula and Odra estuaries. Railroad equipment is produced in the western and southern parts of the country.

Chemical industries are at present growing rapidly both in number and size. In the future they are to be the leading branch of industrial production. Several large industrial combines spread throughout the country, involved in the production of multiple basic materials, are either being enlarged or being constructed. Among these are the factories of Kędzierzyn and Oświęcim in the outer ring of the Upper Silesian Industrial District as well as the plants of Tarnów, Brzeg Dolny, Gorzów, and Tarnobrzeg, and also those for which construction was recently started in Płock and Puławy. Among the several new developments are the production of sulphuric acid from recently discovered very rich ores in the vicinity of Sandomierz, and the above-mentioned big petrochemical works in Płock, whose products will serve as a basis for the production of all kinds of artificial fibers.

Pharmaceuticals also play an important role, with rather large factories in Warsaw, Kraków, and Pabianice (in the vicinity of Łódź).

Cellulose and paper production is closely connected with both the chemical industries and the forestry and wood industries. A dominating factor in this development is Poland's present deficiency of wood, caused by the growing consumption of wood products and their derivatives, and the depletion of forest resources during the war and in the postwar reconstruction period. There is now definite need for the economical use of our wood resources. In building, construction wood has already been practically eliminated, and there is a constant effort to supersede the use of wood in mines. More cellulose is necessary for the production of paper and a search for sources other than wood is now going on. Several modern paper and cellulose factories are now being constructed, mainly in northern Poland where the forests are still able to supply the necessary materials, but also in the southeastern part where there are large afforested areas which have still not been fully exploited because they lock proper transportation facilities.

Increase in the production of building materials is important because all investments and investment plans depend on it. Poland is a country rich in building materials, practically independent from imports. But the modernization of the building industry and the constantly growing scale of its tasks make great demands on production capacity in this area. The production of bricks has grown from 182 million bricks in 1937 to 696 million in 1947, 1,426 million in 1950, and 3,489 million in 1960, but the role of bricks as a material is diminishing. The production of cement has grown from 1.7 million tons in 1937 and 1.5 million in 1947 to 6.6 million tons in 1960. Cement is also an important export product. An interesting side of brick and cement production is the requirement of very large shipments over long distances. In this field there is a serious gap between production and consumption. Large brickworks are concentrated in the western parts of the country, where extensive deposits of tertiary clay come to the surface, while the quaternary deposits accessible in other parts of the country are rather small and widely dispersed. In Upper Silesia the materials excavated in coal-mining make possible an extensive and rather cheap production of brick, which, however, is all consumed locally. In fact, the large scale of its industrial investments and new housing has forced Upper

Silesia to import brick from other regions—although it represents the strongest intensity of brick production in the country. Cement works, although more concentrated and therefore represented by a smaller number of plants, are fairly evenly spread over the southern part of the country. Indeed, they were originally located with a view toward the regionalization of cement supplies. It was found better, however, to concentrate on the production of limited types of cement in specific plants, and, as a result, these products are now traveling all over the country.

The production of gypsum prefabricated materials was recently organized in the valley of the Nida on the basis of very rich surface seams of gypsum. Lower Silesia and, to some extent, the district of Kraków and Kielce specialize in the production of all kinds of road and building materials, using basalt and granite rock, various types of limestone, and sandstone. To supply northern regions deficient in stone and clay, the production of sandlime bricks is being strongly developed.

The remaining branches of production (food, textiles, clothing, and so on) are directly connected with consumption—in fact, they provide the main consumer goods. As a result their development is closely connected to the structure of consumption, which has also changed.

Two primary factors determined the character of consumption in postwar Poland. First, general prewar living conditions, although sharply differing from one social class to another, were on the average low. There were very distinct differences between urban and rural areas. The war and the postwar social revolution brought about a strong leveling of these differences. The Polish community is at present an equalitarian one and any elevation in standards of living has to apply to the whole population.

The second factor is connected to wartime devastation. As a result of the war, all accumulated consumer goods were either used up or completely destroyed. Consequently, some basic needs had to be supplied on a mass scale; there were sharp changes in patterns of consumption when, after primary needs were satisfied in one direction, the whole population turned to another. In the beginning it was clothing, later on furniture and all kinds of lasting domestic goods; now television sets, refrigerators, and motorcycles or automobiles are slowly coming to the front. Meanwhile, great deficiencies in housing and communal services continue, despite the steady, although slow, rise in the level of living conditions—which again is expressed in changes in the character and structure of needs in consumer goods. A demand for better quality

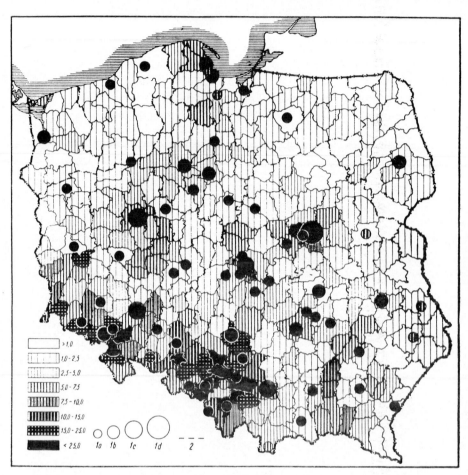

Map 34. Number of employees in industries and handicrafts per square kilometer as of December 31, 1956 (first appeared in *Polish Geographical Review,* XXXI, 1, 1959)

1a. Cities with 75,000 inhabitants. 1b. Cities with 75,000–300,000 inhabitants. 1c. Cities with 300,000–1,000,000 inhabitants. 1d. Cities with over 1,000,000 inhabitants. 2. Boundaries of the voivodships.

is taking the place of the former rather frantic search for any goods satisfying basic needs.

This shift has had an especially strong influence on the program of food production, forming the basis for the development of a more intensive agricultural economy as well as of food-processing industries. Intensification and specialization of agricultural production are, however, seriously impeded by the extreme fragmentation of land on peasant homesteads and farms. The necessity for some kind of unification and the creation of larger productive units in agriculture is generally recognized. Originally some mistakes were made in organizing units into cooperative farms under administrative pressure, but these policies have been abandoned and every effort is being made to create economic and social conditions propitious for the voluntary development of socialist forms of agricultural production. These efforts involve the diffusion of general education and technical knowledge, financial aid to communal agricultural enterprises, and mechanization of production. Some good results have already been obtained. The level of agricultural production has risen by about 50 per cent from 1949 and it is already higher than before the war. Animal husbandry is increasing much faster than plant production. The percentage of land under specialized industrial crops like sugar beets and tobacco has almost doubled.

The progress achieved, however, varies from one region to another, and disparities resulting from the long tripartite division of the country still persist. The most intensive agriculture and the best over-all results have been achieved in the regions of Opole (Upper Silesia), Poznań, Bydgoszcz (Greater Poland), and Wrocław (Lower Silesia), as well as around Warsaw. Steady progress is also characteristic in areas with good soil in the regions of southeastern Poland (the regions of Lublin, Rzeszów, and Kielce, and in part of Kraków). There is extensive production with good results from efficient labor in the northern part of the country, along the seacoast. New processing plants, erected mostly in the eastern and northern regions, are already helping in the growth of specialized commercial agricultural production there. The export of special processed foods is again expanding, forming an important part of the foreign trade.

In textile and clothing as well as in leather industries the changing structure of consumption involves greater diversification of production and improvements in quality. The changes have made it necessary to reorganize the smaller productive plants along with the large ones that concentrate on mass production. As a result, all the factories producing both for the national market and for export are much more diversified than other branches of industry.

In textiles other factors influence the location of new factories. One is the need to replace traditionally imported raw materials, such as cotton and wool, by artificial fibers. This need has connected the textile industry more closely to certain large chemical combines. Another important locational factor may be found in the necessity for the modernization of existing factories, which date mostly from the end of the nineteenth century and the beginning of this one; some represent even older technologies. In the interwar period, with its great economic depression, as well as in the period immediately after the war, when reconstruction absorbed all available means for new investments, the problem of modernization was overlooked. In the Six-year Plan (1950–1955) several new plants were proposed and at least partly constructed. But there is still discussion over two alternative solutions: to modernize old and build new factories in the traditional centers of the textile industry (primarily in and around Łódź), or to locate them in other parts of the country that are still only slightly industrialized.

Strong arguments exist both for and against the location of new factories in the Łódź district, where the water supply is deficient but where an enormous army of trained workers is available. With full automation of production employment will be extremely diminished, and if the new factories are located in other areas, Łódź might become an area of permanent unemployment. One solution of this problem is to diversify the local structure of industry, introducing other industries (such as machine or electrical ones) that consume less water. Still at least some of the new textile factories should and will be located in the near vicinity of Łódź.

REGIONAL DEVELOPMENT PROBLEMS

This discussion of the future development of the Łódź area has already turned our attention from specific to regional problems. Obviously all locational questions bring up the general problems of regional distribution of production and the spatial structure of industrialization. From this point of view Poland may be divided into several characteristic zones.

The most important industrial area of Poland is formed by the Upper Silesian and Kraków Industrial Region, where at present about 30 per cent of the total value of industrial production and about 25 per

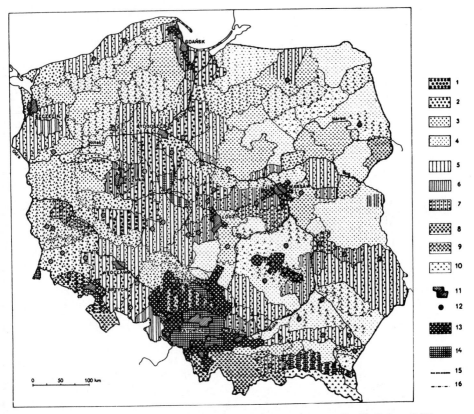

Map 35. Poland: Zones of different types of regional economy (by K. Dziewoński).
Intensity of agricultural production in conventional grain units as common
denominator

1. Very high (over 25 units per ha.). 2. High (20–25 units per ha.). 3. Average (12.5–20 units per ha.). 4. Low (under 12.5 units per ha.). 5. Cultivation of
industrial crops strongly developed. 6. Vegetable crops strongly developed. 7. Culture of fruit trees strongly developed. 8. Mountainous areas characterized by
well-developed forestry, tourist economy, and stock breeding. 9. Areas of forest
economy. 10. Areas of deteriorated forest economy. 11. Areas of metropolitan
economy or intensive industrial development. 12. More important industrial
centers with over 20,000 inhabitants. 13. Suburban zones, with extensive commuting to work, and in industry with widely developed large factories and other
plants. 14. Areas of intensive underground or open mining. 15. Boundaries of the
state. 16. Boundaries of the voivodships.

cent of industrial employment is concentrated. This region is composed of (1) a central core where growth is limited, in principle, to the modernization of existing plants; (2) an inner belt, which has the greatest growth of production because of the presence of new coal mines (in the southern part), important new power stations and metallurgical plants, and two very big chemical combines (Oświęcim and Kędzierzyn); and (3) an outer belt where several important regional centers (Kraków, Częstochowa, Opole, Racibórz, and Bielsko–Biała) are undergoing rapid industrial growth. Thus the growth in size of an important industrial area is connected to the decentralization of its inner core. This process is not dissimilar to that which may be observed in France in connection with the decentralization of the Paris region.

The other important industrial districts of Poland are much smaller in size. Among them three should be mentioned by name: the Łódź district, described earlier, whose existence and at present very limited industrial development are due to the concentration of manpower; the Warsaw Metropolitan Area, now expanding on the basis of the important consumer market in the nation's capital; and the Sudeten district, whose existence depends at present on the exploitation of its varied mineral resources and on the traditional diversified processing industries (textiles, chemicals, machines).

Besides these industrial districts, there are various industrialized zones. They differ from the industrial districts in their less dense industrial development, larger concentration of industries being limited to a few points connected usually to large or medium-sized towns. Among the industrial zones should be mentioned the areas around Gdańsk (shipbuilding industries), Wrocław (machines and electronics), and Bydgoszcz (machine chemicals, wood products) as well as the Kamienna Valley (the so-called Old Polish Industrial District dominated by steel-processing and machine industries). The industrialized areas are characterized by numerous dispersed industrial enterprises with very few points of larger concentration. They include such areas as Greater Poland (corresponding more or less to the Poznań voivodship), Little Poland (corresponding more or less to the eastern part of the Kraków voivodship and the whole Rzeszów voivodship), as well as the northwestern part of the Wrocław voivodship and the southern part of the Zielona Góra voivodship. The remaining parts of Poland possess only a few industrial centers, usually in the largest cities such as Szczecin, Lublin, and Białystok.

The growing mining areas connected with the extraction of lignite

Map 36. Poland: Industrial districts and areas

A. Industrial Districts: 1. Silesian-Kraków. a. Subdistrict Upper Silesia—Górnośląski. b. Subdistrict Kraków. c. Subdistrict Bielsk. d. Subdistrict Częstochowa. 2. Łódź. 3. Warsaw. 4. Sudety. a. Subdistrict Jelenia Góra. b. Subdistrict Wałbrzych. c. Subdistrict Swidnica. d. Subdistrict Kłodzko.

B. Industrial Areas: 5. Gdańsk. 6. Bydgoszcz. 7. Wrocław. a. Region of Wrocław. b. Region of Legnica. 8. Opole. 9. Old Polish (Starapolski) Industrial Area.

C. Industrialized Areas: 10. Tarnów–Rzeszów. a. Region of Tarnów–Mielec. b. Region of Tarnobrzeg. c. Region of Rzeszów. 11. Zgorzelec–Zielona Góra. a. Region of Zgorzelec. b. Region of Zielona Góra. 12. Poznań. 13. Submontane (podkarpacki) industrialized area. D. Major new industrial investments. E. More important industrial centers. F. Boundaries of voivodships. G. Boundaries of districts and areas. H. Boundaries of subdistricts and regions.

(around Konin in central Poland and Turoszów in Lower Silesia), copper ores (between Legnica, Bolesławiec, and Głogów in Lower Silesia), and sulphur ores (in the vicinity of Sandomierz) will probably become industrial districts in the future, but the intensity of their potential industrial development is not yet clearly defined.

Process of Urbanization in the Years 1950–1960[2]

In contemporary economic and social growth urbanization complements industrialization. The phenomenon of urbanization—the growth of towns both in number and in size is not new in Poland, which possesses a long social and economic history and old traditions of urban life.[3] Although the growth of urban population in Poland throughout the nineteenth and twentieth centuries (Table 2), was interrupted several times by great wars and other social and economic upheavals, it has continued steadily and at an increasing rate. In the past ten years it has been especially great, as the direct result of the planned industrialization of the national economy. In fact no greater growth has been observed except in Soviet Russia in 1926–1939, when it was caused by the collectivization and industrialization of the agricultural economy.

From 1950 to 1960 the increase in urban population in Poland totaled up to 450,000 persons annually, while from 1870 to 1900 it amounted only to about 75,000. The present increase in urban growth has been almost equal to the total natural population increase; in the interwar period it was below 60 per cent, and at the end of the nineteenth century below 36 per cent of the total natural increase. Moreover, in the prewar years about 100,000 inhabitants (mostly from the countryside) left Poland annually, that is, emigration was then greater than the migration from rural areas to towns. At present emigration is practically nonexistent, the number of persons leaving the country annually being limited to a few thousand. (In 1957–1958, however, the size of both emigration and immigration from abroad was definitely larger.) Thus, the present movement to the cities is greater than both urbanization and emigration together in the past.

URBAN GROWTH

Present urban growth is heterogeneous in origin and structure. Generally speaking, it is composed of four elements: natural increase,

[2] For the preparation of this section materials presented at the second Anglo-Polish Geographical Seminar were used.

[3] See Chapter 1.

influx from the countryside, repatriation from abroad, and change of administrative status (*i.e.* alteration of urban boundaries and creation of new towns). Data collected and published for the years 1950–1959 indicate that natural increase was responsible for 40.9 per cent of the total urban growth; migration from rural areas for 19.0 per cent; immigration for about 1.0 per cent; and changes in administrative status for the remaining 40.0 per cent.

The most characteristic of these indices is that of natural increase. Usually it is assumed that the index of natural increase for urban areas is well below the same index for rural areas and, as a result, below the average for the whole country. This was certainly true before the war, when the urban index was about half the rural one (8.4 per cent as against 16.7 per cent in 1931–1932). But in the postwar years indices for urban and rural areas were practically the same. Only in the last few years has the rural index again gained over the urban one, although the difference so far is not as great as before the war (in 1960, 16 per cent and 13 per cent). This high rate of natural growth has several causes. Among them are the fall in the death rate (the result of the improvement in sanitary conditions) and the postwar compensatory increase in the number of births. Economic factors, however, should not be omitted as they are probably the most important. The general rise in living conditions, at first a result of the changes brought about by the social revolution and later increased through great progress in the industrialization of the country, played the decisive role. A specific influence was exerted by the educational policies of the present government. When practically all costs of education on all levels are covered by government funds, parents are released from otherwise heavy financial burdens and worries.

The growth of towns as a result of the influx of rural population was, according to the statistical data, comparatively small. It was still great enough to deprive the rural areas of all natural increase of manpower. In the future it is expected that this tendency will continue, probably even at an increased rate. There are, however, obvious limits to such migrations. At present, in spite of war losses, there is very definite overemployment (or hidden unemployment) in Polish agriculture, especially in the central part of the country. This overemployment has already diminished, and with continuing emigration of rural population the stage will be reached where it will turn into underemployment. The advent of difficulties due to deficits in manpower will probably be the starting point for more mechanization and socialization in agriculture.

It will also mean that the importance of rural unemployment as a factor of urban growth will diminish in the future.

The most disputable—although obvious and potent—sources of increase in indices of urbanization are the changes in administrative status, especially with reference to municipal boundaries. This factor should not be omitted. At the worst these legal changes were no more than a recognition of realities. The inclusion of these changes in statistical data has in fact been overdue: the urbanization had already taken place. In other cases the change of administrative status marks new developments in town construction or at least in urban housing.

DISTRIBUTION OF URBAN POPULATION

As in all other countries the urban population of Poland is not evenly distributed. There is a great diversity of function, character, status, and size in our towns and cities.

Graphs for Polish towns, collated nationally and regionally on a double logarithmic scale, according to the city rank-size rule, demonstrate rather remarkable regularities and characteristics. First of all, the graph for all Polish towns in 1960 has an exceptionally regular shape, forming almost a straight line. According to probability interpretation this shows an ideally balanced structure of urban networks without almost any strong influence of deforming forces. The same graph for 1950 shows some evidences of the underdevelopment at the left end of the curve. This is a reflection of the destruction of Warsaw and of its uncompleted reconstruction.

Norton Ginsburg, in the *Atlas of Economic Development* (University of Chicago Press, 1961), presented some comparative maps of urban population. One in particular deals with the problem of the primacy of the largest city. The measure used is the ratio of the population of the largest city to the total population of the four largest cities in the given country. The data on which the map is based shows that Poland takes fifth place (after Italy, Saudi Arabia, Bechuanaland, and Syria, and before Canada, Spain, and Yugoslavia) among the countries with the least developed primacy of the main urban center.

The regional graphs for Poland may be grouped into three classes: (1) the regular graphs characteristic for areas of an evenly developed urban network with slight preponderance of the main urban center (the voivodships of Katowice, Kraków, Poznań, Wrocław, and Szczecin); (2) the skewed graphs characteristic for areas where the main urban center is growing at the expense of others, especially middle-sized towns (the voivodships of Warsaw, Łódź, Gdańsk, Bydgoszcz, Lublin, Białystok and, in lesser degree, Rzeszów, Olsztyn, and Opole); and (3) the irregular graphs characteristic for areas without clearly crystallized main urban centers (the voivodships of Kielce, Koszalin, and Zielona Góra). In fact, in these last areas the largest city is not the seat of the voivodship administration. As a result, within the generally balanced urban network certain areas of smaller and greater irregularities may be distinguished.

Geographically, the central, eastern, and northeastern parts of the country show marked growth of the largest cities at the expense of smaller towns. Areas without clearly crystallized main urban centers are located between or on the peripheries of the regions with a well-balanced urban network.

Problems parallel to that of the primacy of the largest city are those of the density of towns of various types and classes of importance. This density, however, is extremely variable. The general density of towns, for instance, varies by voivodships from 11.6 to 36.8 inhabitants per thousand square kilometers (the average density being 22.7) and the density of towns of over 5,000 inhabitants from 6.0 to 27.4 (with an average of 12.5). The greatest densities are characteristic of the western and southern regions, the lowest for the eastern, northern, and central ones. Greater densities of the urban network are clearly connected with areas of stronger intensity of the regional economy and also with wealth of natural resources, both mineral and agricultural.

An additional aspect of the urban network is found in the journeys to work. Partial analysis of statistical data indicate that this phenomenon is extremely complicated. In some cases, longer journeys to work represent only the first, passing stage of urbanization. Usually the large industrial plants were only lately concentrated in a few places, and large centers have developed from an earlier pattern of dispersed manufactures and/or even older industrial trades and handicrafts; in the southern parts of the country, for instance, commuters form a permanent feature of the urban settlement. In the southeastern, central, and northern parts of Poland the second explanation applies. There the long trip to work is perhaps a temporary phenomenon which will vanish in the future when housing difficulties in the towns are completely overcome and the industrial population moves in from the countryside to newly developed residential districts. The western parts of the country, especially Lower Silesia, are characterized by almost complete absence of long trips to work.

DISPARITIES IN URBAN DEVELOPMENT

Among the many differentiations of towns, the sociological ones have special importance. The present state of research allows only limited, rather loose conclusions. Four basic types of urban societies are, however, clearly defined. They result from the general division into young and old communities, varying in terms of the age structure of the population, its origin, and its degree of integration. This basic division is clearly connected, on the one hand, with the great postwar migrations and, on the other, with the migrations of rural population to urban areas. The general types of urban societies may be defined as follows: (1) comparatively well-developed towns with considerable capital investment, inhabited by a population of stabilized age structure, typical of slow and evolutionary urban growth; (2) well-developed and invested towns, inhabited by a young population, in the main newly arrived from the countryside, passing through processes of social integration, with an age structure typical of new urban centers; (3) underdeveloped and badly invested towns, inhabited by a population forming a stagnant urban society, deformed by the emigration of the more active elements (the age group from 20 to 40); and (4) new towns still under construction, with a mixed population, mainly of rural origin, passing through processes of social integration, with an age structure typical of young urban societies. Type 2 is characteristic for almost all towns in the western and northern territories recovered after the war. Type 1 is dominant among the larger cities of central and southern Poland, while type 3 prevails among the small rural towns and also among towns of the old industrial district of Łódź. Type 4 occurs in the new industrial developments of the last ten years, especially in the belt around the Upper Silesian Industrial District and in the southeastern part of the country.

All these differences in urban network are further complicated by disparities among urban buildings and communal equipment and their use. The natural resources for production of building materials, varying regionally and locally, have deeply influenced the morphology of Polish towns. Areas deficient in building stones and the richer deposits of clay suitable for brickmaking preserved the tradition of wooden construction in housing right up to the last war. As a result their towns are characterized by low and widely dispersed development. These tendencies were greatly enhanced by the historical processes of settlement. At the present moment, in spite of great changes brought by planned reconstruction, the differences are still easily visible. The towns in the areas of the

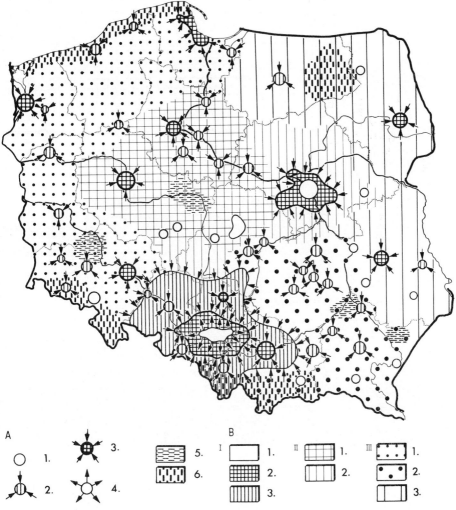

Map 38. Poland: Processes of urbanization, 1950–1960 (first appeared in *Polish Geographical Review,* XXXIV, 3, 1962)

A. Main urban centers and areas. 1. Limited growth. 2. Heavy growth. 3. Very heavy growth. 4. Signs of decentralization. 5. New mining areas. 6. Areas of mass tourism.

B. Zones of urban growth. I. Heavily urbanized areas. 1. Conurbations metropolitan areas. 2. Areas of direct deglomeration. 3. Areas of indirect deglomeration. II. Areas of decreasing growth of urbanization. 1. Areas of balanced structure. 2. Areas of deformed structure. III. Areas of strong urbanization. 1. Areas of balanced structure. 2. Areas of growth of middle-sized cities. 3. Areas of concentration in larger cities.

ancient so-called Congress Kingdom (the central and eastern part of the country which belonged to the Russian Empire from 1815 to 1917) are still poorly equipped and only loosely integrated into coherent urban entities. The towns in the south, and especially the southwestern industrialized regions, are on the whole more densely developed (in terms of both percentage of built-up areas and height of buildings) than in any other part of the country. But the high quality of communal equipment and services (sewerage, water supply, gas and electric grid, mass urban transport) ensures satisfactory sometimes even good living conditions, while the industrial towns of central Poland (around Łódź and elsewhere), lacking the necessary communal services, have always been characterized by very bad housing conditions.

As already mentioned, the diversified network of urban settlements is changing and the changes are not proportionally or evenly spread. Although there are no areas where the urban population has diminished (there are, however, a few sporadic cases of small towns with decreasing population), the whole central part of Poland (the voivodships of Łódź, Katowice, Poznań, Bydgoszcz, Opole, and Warsaw) in comparison with the remaining areas is characterized by a slower, below-average rate of growth. This represents a change from the prewar situation, especially from the nineteenth century, when progress in urbanization was greatest in the central areas—in the Upper Silesian Industrial District and around Warsaw, Łódź, Poznań, and Bydgoszcz. Moreover, the rate of change in towns of different size groups varied in different regions. In some places the development of all towns was parallel, in fact balanced; in other places towns of one specific class, whether large, middle-sized, or small, were growing faster than those of other classes. The final distribution of growth was more diversified than a first glance might notice. Generally, proportional growth of towns of all classes was evident in the territories recovered after the war (in some areas the growth of small towns was even greater than that of larger ones). In the eastern voivodships urban growth was concentrated to a high degree in the main city; middle-sized towns developed the most in the southeastern regions. There were several reasons for these differences. First, planned industrialization created possibilities of development for specific areas and centers; second, the rates of natural growth varied from one region to another, the western and northern ones having the highest indices; finally, the differences in housing and in living conditions, generally affected the attractiveness of various areas and towns.

One additional fact should also be noted. The southern voivodships of Katowice, Opole, and (at least partly) Kraków together formed an integrated economic region and their urban networks developed in a characteristically interrelated manner. There, three concentric zones can be distinctly distinguished. The central core, composed of at present nineteen cities with about 1.5 million inhabitants, forms a classical mining and industrial conurbation—the traditional Upper Silesian Industrial District—whose rate of growth is rapidly decreasing (well under the national average). The first ring or belt includes areas of the greatest present development—mining, industrial, and urban. This development is not, however, territorially continuous but occurs in a series of middle-sized towns and industrial settlements. Within this area new satellite towns for the overspill population from the central area are under construction. The second or outer belt is composed of several large districts, each developing around a large main urban center of distinct industrial and cultural character. Here planned industrial development is greatest and the urban growth is also very marked and well above average, although less than within the inner ring.

A similar development is taking place in the metropolitan area of Warsaw but there the full stage of decentralization has not yet been reached. So far only two concentric zones can be distinguished—a central core, which is the city of Warsaw itself, and the suburban zone. But there are signs of new developments in the outer area—some subregional urban centers such as Płock and Siedlce are showing signs of increased rates of growth in comparison to other similar towns.

MIGRATION

The complex processes of urbanization, apparent especially in their geographical structure, result from past migrations and are the basis for future migrations. These migrations are more complex than is usually assumed. Parallel to the movements from rural to urban areas there exist strong migrations back to the countryside and between various towns, industrial settlements, or agricultural communities. Migrations also take time. This may be observed within social groups such as families and sometimes involve more than one generation.

A cursory analysis of the geographical distribution of migrations shows that in contemporary Poland there are at least three distinct types of movements from rural to urban areas. First, we have those migrations which are the consequence and extension of postwar resettlement, in particular in the recovered territories. Familial and cultural relations between the places of former and present habitation remain and influence migrations in spite of distances. There are, for instance, strong mutual migrations, both temporary and permanent, between the voivodships of Wrocław and Kielce, Lublin, and Rzeszów, although they are not adjacent and are separated by the very distinct and attractive migratory area of the Upper Silesian and Kraków region. The second form of migration is local, to the developed industrial towns and settlements from the adjacent rural areas. Sometimes the first stage of such migration takes the form of the journey to work. The third form of migration originates within the areas characterized otherwise by a great deficit in manpower. There the recruitment has to be organized from more distant places, in particular from agricultural districts of the country which are still overpopulated. It should be stressed that this last form of migration is usually an organized one that is economically and socially rather costly.

CHARACTERISTICS OF POLISH URBANIZATION

To sum up all these data and conclusions, it is possible to define the present trend of urbanization in Poland as typical for countries with existing traditions of urban life, passing through a period of very intensive modern industrialization characteristic of the planned socialist development of the national economy. Urbanization trends are more rational and structurally more balanced here, however, than in other countries. This is revealed in the limited growth of the main urban center (the capital) and in the existence and development of numerous large and middle-sized towns, as well as in the vitality of small towns. Moreover, there are some specific characteristic elements both in the existing network and in its present changes. These are caused by:

(1) The variability of the geographical environment, and especially of the distribution of natural resources;

(2) Differences in the length of time taken to develop settlements, especially from the point of view of the density of the settlement network; based on the distribution of "gród" (burgh) organization dating from the early Middle Ages, the network was fully developed in Silesia in the twelfth, thirteenth, and fourteenth centuries, in Greater and Little Poland as well as in Pomerania between the thirteenth and fourteenth centuries, in Masovia in the fourteenth, fifteenth, and sixteenth centuries, and in Podlasie, Lakeland, and Mazurian in the sixteenth, or in some areas even in the eighteenth century;

(3) The great differences in function and size of towns between various regions, created by the development of industrial towns and

settlements from the second half of the eighteenth century right up to our times;

(4) The division of the whole territory of Poland into three parts, incorporated for about 150 years into three empires completely different in political, social, and economic structure;

(5) The differences in the population structure of various parts of the country, resulting from the postwar resettlement and recent migrations.

All these factors have found expression in the existing and dynamically developing regional structure of the urban network. Certain definite settlement regions may be distinguished: (1) the Upper Silesian and Kraków region with its specific territorial structure, already described; (2) a heterogeneous zone of below-average urbanization, including the voivodships of Łódź, Poznań, Bydgoszcz, and Warsaw, including the entire metropolitan area of Warsaw; (3) a zone of great urbanization intensity, which includes three different kinds of areas: (*a*) one of balanced development of the urban network (the western and northern voivodships), (*b*) an area of the greatest growth of medium-sized towns and limited growth or even stagnation of small towns (the voivodships of Rzeszów and Kielce as well as the eastern part of the voivodship of Kraków), and (*c*) an area of increasing concentration of urban population in the main urban center (the voivodships of Białystok and Lublin).

Poland's Position in 1962 and Future Prospects

Together, the industrial structure and the urban structure make up the regional structure of Poland. There is one very large industrial region whose center is formed by the most important concentration of urban population in the country—the Upper Silesian conurbation. Its internal spatial structure has already been described.[4] There is another large-scale region on the seacoast, characterized by a maritime economy and only just emerging as a distinct entity. Its two main industrial and urban areas—which are seaports and cities—are grouped around the estuaries of the Odra (Szczecin and Świnoujście) and the Vistula (Gdańsk, Gdynia, and several smaller cities). The present and future growth of sea traffic, of shipbuilding industries, and of the processing of products imported and exported by sea forms the basis for plans for the construction of another great seaport halfway between Szczecin and Gdańsk, in the vicinity of the city of Koszalin.

[4] Chapter 4.

All the other larger regions, although smaller than those already mentioned, correspond at present to the main administrative division of the country into voivodships. In a socialist country whose economy is based on national ownership of the basic means of production (at present in industry, commerce, and transport) the administrative units play an important and active economic role. In fact, part of the nationalized industries are in the hands of regional and even local authorities, whose function thus is to produce as well as to rule. Consequently, there is a strong tendency to integrate economic life on the voivodship level.

Within various voivodships there are naturally other regional divisions, mostly on the next lower administrative level, that of individual *powiats* (counties). But in many cases several counties are integrated according to their specific functions and structure into larger entities (though still smaller than voivodships). Among these are the Warsaw Metropolitan Area, composed of the capital city and surrounding five counties, and various industrial districts, such as Łódź and that of the Sudeten Mountains.

New elements are brought into the regional structure by capital investments for the exploitation of newly discovered mineral resources— lignite, copper, iron, and sulphur ores. These investments are made frequently in the frontier areas of two or even more voivodships. Evidently new regional units are being created which in the future may seriously change the economic and also, therefore, the administrative division of the country. Whether this will involve the creation of new voivodships or only a change in the boundaries of the existing ones is not yet clear. It partly depends on what concentration of industries and population will follow the opening of new mining areas. Otherwise it is planned that the location of new industries will take place within the existing urban network, with a strong stress being laid on the development of middle-sized cities within the less urbanized parts of the country, especially in the east and in the north; and also on limited and controlled growth and decentralization of main urban centers, especially of Warsaw and Upper Silesia.

The picture of contemporary Poland presented here seems—in view of the progress achieved since 1945—to be positive and optimistic. Our economy is growing at a steady rate, the basic processes of industrialization and urbanization are developing under control with slow but real elimination of past deficiencies and without too many new disproportions. It has been said that at present Poland is already moving from the stage of "take-off" to the stage of "industrial maturity," and as a result is increasingly able to sustain her own growth. This is important because it means that for the first time the growth of the economy and its diversification increase the importance of foreign trade. Hence the desire for the development of the international division of labor.

With all our achievements, the standard of living is still unsatisfactory and low. In our spatial economy there are some serious disparities. The average national income per capita varies in the poorest and richest regions in a ratio of 1:3. The government policies for planned economy are able, by the division of the national income, to diminish this difference to the ratio of 1:2. Nevertheless, these differences, especially irritating in an equalitarian society, do exist. The efficiency of economic development demands that development be differentiated according to the potentialities of geographical environment and natural resources, as well as demanding full use of existing unequally distributed productive and service investments. At the same time, social justice demands equal opportunity of work and of living conditions for everyone without reference to his location.

It may seem that a simple solution of the problem would be in the distribution of population proportional to the wealth of the natural resources. But even bypassing such problems as the changing technological values and unequal knowledge of the location of those resources as well as the differences in the accessibility and basic investments of various regions, such a distribution would not solve the difficulties. There would still be the advantages of centralization and the disparities in age and social structure which must arise between areas losing and gaining in population. At the same time, the problems of decentralization of the most congested areas and the redevelopment of older industrial and urban centers are already increasing in importance. As a result, careful and balanced economic and spatial planning within the general national plan, defining specific means and ends of future development, are necessary for all regions.

CHAPTER 10

Regional Planning in Poland: Theory, Methods, and Results

JÓZEF ZAREMBA

Development of Regional Planning

THE present state of regional planning in Poland and its theoretical basis and methods are the result of evolving research that dates back to the nineteen-twenties. Regional planning was developed on the basis of building laws, as an extension of urban planning ideas. Originally it was intended to be an auxiliary instrument in working out problems connected with the physical development of cities; it later developed into a higher level of physical planning. Town planners realized that since a city cannot be isolated from its environment, urban physical planning should be specifically connected to the socioeconomic processes occurring in the adjoining areas with which the life of the city is closely linked. The planners soon concluded that it was essential to elaborate plans for the physical development of a city on a broader, regional basis and that there was a justified need to work out a spatial composition for an entire region.

THE PREWAR PERIOD

Such ideas were first applied in Warsaw in 1930, when the Warsaw Regional Plan Office was established on the basis of the provisions of the building law. Later, with the organization of work on plans for physical development, regional planning offices and commissions were set up for other large cities (Łódź, Poznań, and the Upper Silesian industrial-urban agglomeration) and for the coastal areas affected by the construction of the port and city of Gdynia. These offices and commissions were to make regional plans for the spatial development of land as a basis for planned management, following a general design. The establishment of such offices and commissions created the proper ground for

271

wide-scale development of research in new ideas and techniques for regional planning.

Functional Warsaw, the study published in 1936 by J. Chmielewski and S. Syrkus, marked an important step forward in regional research; it became an incentive to the development of a physical planning method for the country's larger cities. It contained the first formulation of the conception of the Warsaw Metropolitan Area. The authors of the study were the first to oppose the existing conception that the functions of a large city or capital should be concentrated within a single cramped area. As substitute they presented the idea of a decentralized network of settlements. Their plan took into account the geographical and natural advantages of the region, and defined the purpose, directions, and degree of land use, creating out of a large city and its environs a functional entity of a higher order. At that time this was a creative, progressive, and forthright conception, especially since its authors based it on strictly defined theoretical assumptions. The crux of it lay in the principle of functionalism and closely related methods for determining the potential traffic flow, which would require an adequate transportation network. The points of intersection of the traffic pattern, modified by physiographical conditions, defined the layout of the settlement network.

The theoretical and methodological premises of the study played an important role in postwar research on the development of the Warsaw urban complex and the Warsaw region, as well as in analogous work in other regions of the country such as the Gdańsk Bay port-city agglomeration, the Upper Silesian Industrial District, and the Łódź city complex. It also strongly influenced physical planning for the country as a whole.

In the thirties the idea was put forward that it would be particularly useful to extend regional planning to encompass as many parts of Poland as possible, including less urbanized regions with diverse natural, geographical, and economic conditions. Extension was facilitated both by definite needs in town planning research and by geographical research of increasing practical importance, carried out mainly by the Jagiellonian University's Geographical Center in Kraków.

Regional plan offices for the Podhale (Tatra foothills), western Beskid, and Huculszczyzna districts were formed in 1934. These are all mountain regions offering great tourist and holiday attractions. Following changes in the building law, eleven regional planning commissions and offices, covering over 40 per cent of the country's territory, were established by special decree of the Minister of Internal Affairs in 1937.

It was no great step to enlarge this regional concept to one of national physical planning. Before World War II a National Planning Office had been set up in the Finance Minister's Office, where studies on the location of basic economic phenomena were undertaken. These were to have served as a basis for the elaboration of an investment program to cover several years.

Work began on the plan for the so-called Central Industrial District, at the fork of the Vistula and San rivers and the adjoining areas, and intensive industrialization of the region was initiated. Many of the preliminary materials for this plan were destroyed during the war, as was much other material for regional plans; only fragments were available after the war.

Regional planning was undertaken on a very wide scale in the prewar years, in spite of the fact that theoretical and methodical research was not highly developed. The typical regional planning process covered: (1) a lengthy study of the natural and geographical conditions, made in order to determine the suitability of the land for various development purposes; (2) an inventory of population distribution and structure and the degree of development and structure of land use and ownership; (3) an analysis of these findings, arranged on appropriate maps and charts, aimed at determining the location for basic facilities, socioeconomic phenomena, and land use—in order to ascertain the compatibility of existing land use with natural and geographical conditions and functional connections; (4) suggestions for the concepts of the plan; (5) the plan itself: its general premises and detailed projections, which determined the functions of the region, proposals for investment programs, housing development, and zoning.

Since almost half of the country's territory was to have been covered by these plans, there was a need to coordinate this work in a plan for the physical development of the entire country. It was assumed that the various regions should perform not only specific regional functions, but also national ones and should link together to form greater entity. Without work on a national scale it would be impossible to obtain the correct directives for developing particular regions. In practice, however, with a few fragmentary exceptions, such directives themselves were impossible, since—as is well known—socioeconomic life in prewar Poland was burdened with disparities and required radical, far-reaching social and cultural transformation. The authorities at that time exerted themselves to avoid such changes, so that the work of the National Planning Office was of a strictly internal character and used only partially. Under such conditions, regional planning ideas were primarily an expression of the inventiveness of regional planners and the scientific research-workers cooperating with them, who could not know whether, or in what way, their studies and conceptions would ever be put into practice.

Not a single regional project had been completed by 1939; nevertheless studies and projects on plans for the Warsaw and Łódź regions, the Upper Silesian Basin, the seacoast, and Podhale region were considerably advanced. Work on plans for other regions was still in the early stages of development. Unfortunately, most of these studies were destroyed during the war.

CRITIQUE OF PREWAR PLANNING

Prewar regional planning did not exert any specific influence on investment trends and spatial change, nor did it become an instrument of the spatial coordination of investments. In the first place, as mentioned above, not a single regional project was finished prior to the outbreak of the war. Had one been finished it is improbable that it would have been given full legal status. These plans—in accordance with their schematic conceptions—were a valuable result of lengthy studies and displayed a predominantly technical character (although during the preliminary studies there appeared many complicated socioeconomic and political problems to which the regional planners could not find a solution). The plans did not anticipate any economic substantiation of their proposals nor outline any policy for their realization. They were not linked to the program of investments planned by the various economic units and could not become an effective instrument in the spatial coordination of investment-building activity. Studies of these prewar regional plans did, however, facilitate some decisions.

In this respect we must stress that regional planning in prewar Poland made possible a better knowledge of the various parts of the country. It uncovered many unknown and valuable properties of the regions and brought into the open numerous social, economic, and technical problems that required solution. It also helped to accentuate disparities in the socioeconomic level of development—not only between various regions, but also within regions. Substantial differences were discovered between the degree of knowledge of the natural and geographical resources and of the social and economic relations in the different parts of the country. Much earlier regional research had been of a haphazard, uncoordinated character which required a basic change.

Prewar regional planning played yet another role, perhaps the most important: pioneering new planning methods. It brought together the work of various specialists, including (in addition to architects) geographers, naturalists, engineers of various branches (such as geodesists), farm specialists, economists, sociologists and lawyers. This guaranteed further creative evolution in regional and town planning.

All this work was interrupted by the outbreak of the war and the dark days of the Nazi occupation of Poland, during which most of the studies and initial material compiled were destroyed and many prominent workers were killed in battle or murdered by the Germans. During the Occupation a small group of people, former members of the large body of regional and town planners, tried to continue work on certain studies and research in the hope that it would be of some help after the war. Unfortunately, very little even of this work survived, but among the fragments which remained were certain studies of the Warsaw region and the conception of the Warsaw Metropolitan Area.

PERIOD OF POSTWAR RECONSTRUCTION OF THE NATIONAL ECONOMY

The development of regional planning in postwar People's Poland took place under completely different social and political conditions than those prevailing before the war. The most important task placed before the nation by the new socialist government in the immediate postwar years was the reconstruction of the country from the enormous devastation of the war, during which Poland lost 38 per cent of her entire national wealth; over six million people were either killed during the hostilities or died in Nazi concentration camps. This basic task was formulated in the Three-Year Plan of Economic Reconstruction in the years 1947–1949. It was carried out under a great socioeconomic transformation and demographic changes connected mainly with the postwar migrations and the repopulation of the territories regained in the west and north of the country. It was carried out in the period when the national administration was being formed and the first methodological premises of economic and physical planning were being outlined.

The principle of unity and correlation of physical planning at all levels (national plan, regional and local plans, town development plans) derived from prewar experience, and was applied not only in the organization of the physical planning administration, but also in its legal foundations and methods of work. The Central Physical Planning Office was established in 1945 as an organ of the Reconstruction Ministry, as were the fourteen regional physical planning offices subordinate to it. The territorial jurisdiction of each of the latter embraced a

voivodship. A decree on the planned physical development of the country was issued in 1946. It outlined the scope of physical planning and
defined the principles, contents, and goals for the national physical
development plans and for the regional and local plans. It also established the hierarchical relationship of the regional plans to the national
plan and of the local plans to the regional plans.

The obligation to base plans of a lower level on the provisions contained in plans of a higher level, set by the decree, demanded broad-
scale and intensive work. Taking into account the war destructions, the
urgent necessity of reconstructing towns and villages, and the fact that
Poland's frontiers had been altered, one can see that such work, though
far from perfect, was deeply justified. From the beginning, the people
responsible for the job were aware that elaboration of fully mature
plans would call for lengthy studies and require time. But they knew
that even partial studies, especially the making and analysis of physical
inventories, would allow for more appropriate location decisions during
the Three-Year Plan of Economic Reconstruction. Furthermore, this
work could be used in the following national plan.

In the years 1945–1949 all regional planning offices were engaged
primarily in drawing up inventories based on data provided by various
temporary commissions, by the results of the February, 1946, national
census, and by earlier publications. Work was started on elaboration of
regional plans for the economically more important regions of the
country. In the studies the main emphasis was on problems concerning
war losses sustained by the basic municipal installations, the transportation network, production installations, and housing resources. Other
problems that were emphasized concerned the natural and geographical
conditions of the regions, the distribution of the forces of production,
the settlement network, and the population. Such studies constituted a
basis for the formulation of working hypotheses for local plans, indispensable for the reconstruction of destroyed cities. By 1949 over 400
simplified master city plans had been drawn up with the help of such
regional studies. They proved very useful in practice.

The most important regional studies of problems in the reconstruction of the country were concentrated in regions that had a particularly
important role in the national economy: the Upper Silesian Coal Basin
(now fully within the boundaries of Poland), the Gdańsk Bay region,
the Wałbrzych Coal District (the Sudeten Mountains), the cities of
Warsaw and Łódź and their environs, and the midwestern part of
Kraków voivodship. Studies were also initiated on regional experimental
plans for the Pyrzyce-Gryfino-Myślibórz agricultural subregion, extend-

ing to the east and south of Szczecin along the Odra River, and for the farming regions of the Tomaszów and Hrubieszów districts in Lublin voivodship, in the eastern part of the country.

Studies on the physical development of the whole country and work on directives for the regional plans were centered at that time in the Central Physical Planning Office. Studies for the national plan were published in 1947 and 1948 in two successive editions of the *Atlas of the National Plan Study* and a volume of monographs. The section of these studies dealing with natural and geographical conditions was mainly a compilation and summation of various, mostly older, monographs, while the inventory section put much more emphasis on the postwar picture. The third part introduced and outlined major directions of development and the functional division of the country into regions with particular emphasis on the transportation pattern and the main features of the settlement network. The methods employed were a continuation of those used before the war.

The backbone of the national plan was to have been the pattern of traffic flows between those areas which were most important nationally in economics, geographical location, existing investments, and population figures. The pattern of traffic flow determined the zones of potential activity; at their points of intersection were located the existing, or potential, centers of production and services.

This theoretical scheme, modified by analyses of geographical and natural conditions, led to the concept of dividing the territory of the country according to various uses, in order to determine the optimum directions for decentralizing those conurbations then excessively concentrated, such as the Upper Silesian Coal Basin, and also to define the principles for the regionalization of the country. Efforts were made to create a conceptual framework for the settlement network based on the "pattern of flows," by using regional and local studies and Christaller's theoretical scheme.

The initial conception of the physical development of the country (the national plan) was elaborated in line with the above theoretical and methodological premises on the basis of two principal assumptions. First, in the long-term physical plan (25–30 years) there appeared three stages of socioeconomic development—the first, covering several years, was defined as the "reconstruction period"; the second, somewhat longer, as the "industrialization period"; the third, the longest, as the "urbanization period." It was assumed that the detailed plans for the physical development of the country and the various regions would follow these stages. Second, work on physical development plans was to be carried out by using the successive-approximations method, which allows for increasingly precise compilation of data and more exact documentation of the conception, and for its verification and correction.

Studies on the national physical development plan and on the regional plans, elaborated in 1945–1949, served as a basis for issuing guidelines to the local plans. They also helped in working out a concept for the location of production in the Six-Year national economic plan for 1950–1955, and studies on changes in the administrative division of the country.

The introductory, perspective idea of regionalization elaborated in the "national plan" was partly realized in 1950 with the establishment of three new voivodships (Koszalin, Zielona Góra, and Opole) and substantial boundary changes introduced in several other voivodships.

THE SIX-YEAR-PLAN PERIOD OF BUILDING THE BASES OF SOCIALISM IN PEOPLE'S POLAND

Accomplishment of the tasks laid down in the Three-Year Plan of Economic Reconstruction was successfully completed in 1949. Shortly before the acceptance of the new Six-Year Plan of development of the national economy, for 1950–1955, important organizational changes in the structure of the state authority and the apparatus of management were introduced. A bill was passed by the Sejm (the Polish parliament) which stipulated the establishment of people's councils and their praesidia as local elected organs of people's power. Changes in the central state apparatus consisted in the formation of several ministries for the various industries and branches of production to replace the single existing ministry, and the creation of a strong coordinating economic planning apparatus: the State Economic Planning Commission. This was accompanied by the liquidation of the Central Planning Office and the Central Physical Planning Office.

Since then, research in physical planning to embrace the whole country has been carried on within the organizational framework of economic planning. The basis for this decision was that regional planning on a national scale had been recognized as one of the methods of economic planning especially useful in planning the distribution of productive forces and the interregional division of work. Physical planning on a local scale (for towns and settlements), which is of a more technical character, has been subordinated to the city planning, architecture, and building authorities.

The changes introduced at that time into physical and economic planning were the result both of criticism concerning the working methods of the immediate postwar period, and of an expressed desire to bring about improvements in face of the tremendous tasks outlined in the Six-Year National Plan—called the plan for building the foundations of socialism.

Criticism directed toward previous methods of physical planning on all levels, from political, economic, and organizational standpoints, focused attention first of all on the indivisibility of the problems connected with physical and economic planning; it questioned the effectiveness of physical conceptions elaborated without concrete directives from economic plans and without a searching study of the economic effects which might support the proposed solutions. The functionalism scheme and the "patterns-of-direction" scheme applied in prewar Poland and too rigorously observed in the early postwar period also came under strong criticism, though they were not denied certain valuable qualities. It must be emphasized that the divergences between economic and physical planning in the early postwar years resulted, in the first place, from the fact that the proposed physical plans covered socioeconomic and physical changes to be carried out within some 25 to 30 years; while the first national plan covered a period of only three years.

The year 1950 marked the opening of a new stage in physical planning which lasted until 1957. The criticism of working methods and the organizational changes at that time not only affected the evolution of methods, but also concentrated qualified forces on the most important problems connected with the tasks laid down in the Six-Year Plan. Therefore, research in physical planning was concentrated on the elaboration of plans for areas of concentrated building investment. In such areas a regional plan was urgently necessary as a foundation for the spatial coordination of investments set by the directives for plans of towns and settlements destined for expansion. This work was carried out in various organizational steps, such as through placing orders with the various designing offices.

With this work, during the years 1950–1957, the territorial scope of work on regional plans was considerably narrowed.[1] Among other things, work was stopped on regional plans for entire voivodships, excepting the Kraków voivodship, for which an experimental plan was worked out. Regional studies essential for the realization of the Six-Year Plan were prepared in the first years of this period, and in the following years the requirements of the following Five-Year Plan for 1956–1960

[1] We may enumerate for example the Upper Silesian Industrial District, the region of Warsaw, the Low Ground of the Vistula River Delta, the region of Gdańsk-Gdynia, the Old Polish Basin, the regions of Łódź, Bydgoszcz, Kraków, etc.

were taken into consideration. Work on the plan for national physical development was limited to only the most essential needs.

Among the more important studies made in this period were those concerning the location of production and population anticipated for 1970, taking into consideration both vocational and settlement structure. These in turn served as a basis for the elaboration of development studies for all the major Polish cities. Development studies for the smaller towns and settlements located within the territory embraced by regional plans could then be formulated on the basis of regional materials. In town development studies for the remaining towns and settlements, use was made of economic directives available from the local sources of economic planning.

Regional planning work in 1950–1957 included the elaboration of draft plans for fourteen different, mainly key regions of the country, designated in the plans for the years 1950–1955 and 1956–1960 as areas of increased investment in industry, transportation, and housing construction. Initial studies were undertaken at the same time for seven other areas. In this way about one-third of the entire area of the country was embraced by regional plans or studies. Of particular importance in this work were the economic directives of the national economic plans, especially those parts dealing with the development of the main branches of production and the more important investment projects, together with their expected general location and certain technical and economic indices. These were subjected to constant modification and correction as statistical data was gathered.

In general, at least four basic requirements had to be fulfilled for every regional plan:

(1) An estimate had to be made (on the basis of comprehensive inventory studies and their analysis, among other things) of the long-range effects of the anticipated planned investments.

(2) An effort had to be made to elaborate those basic economic and spatial solutions which would guarantee the best possible conditions for the development of production in the region, and would allow for the creation of proper conditions of work, living, and leisure and the cultural development of the people. Such solutions would, in effect, lead to the attainment of the desired structural and qualitative changes within the region, satisfying certain clearly defined sociopolitical aims.

(3) Those requirements necessitated inclusion, as a vital section of any such plan, of a concept of the spatial composition of the whole region, together with a program for all the accompanying essential in-

vestments and a definition of the various types of land use in the region, for the distant as well as the immediate future.

(4) The draft plan had to be internally balanced and externally connected with plans for neighboring regions. The elaboration of plans for fourteen areas of the country—differing in natural and geographical conditions, in character and intensity of development, in functions of national importance and further possibilities of development—constituted a valuable source of knowledge. Much experience was gained in seeking the best methods of analysis and research and in the solution of problems with different regional specifics.

Especially valuable experience came from working out studies on regional plans for the Upper Silesian Industrial District,[2] the city of Warsaw (general plan), the Żuławy region in the Vistula delta[3] (Gdańsk voivodship), the Staropolskie Basin (Kielce voivodship), the Kraków voivodship,[4] and also many others. The plan for the Upper Silesian Industrial District was the first to be passed by the government in a special decree in 1953.

Regional Planning in the Prospect Period of Development of the National Economy

Three distinct periods can be distinguished in the evolution of regional planning in Poland up to 1957. Given the diverse conditions and socioeconomic and political needs, regional planning fulfilled in each period the tasks facing it, shaping at the same time its own methods of work. The periods were that prior to the outbreak of World War II in 1939, the postwar years from 1945 to 1949, corresponding to the economic reconstruction of the country, and a second postwar period, from 1950 to 1957, which saw the implementation of the Six-Year Plan for building the foundations of socialism. At the end of this, the country embarked on the Five-Year Plan of economic development for the years 1956–1960.

The present period, which started in 1957, has come to be considered a fourth stage in the evolution of regional planning, integrally linked to the full range of problems of the country's socioeconomic development. This period is characterized by the rapid growth of a social demand for studies and research in regional planning. Since 1957 there has been a

[2] See Chapter 11.

[3] The regional plan for the Żuławy delta of the Vistula River was finally passed in a government decree in 1961.

[4] See Chapter 12.

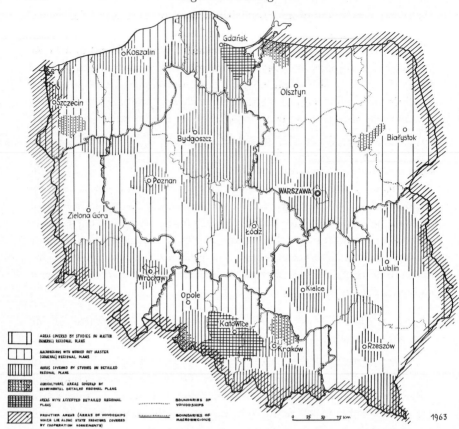

Map 39. Regional planning in Poland

noticeable constant growth of interest on the part of the people and the central and local authorities in regional planning as an important instrument of local policy. This has characteristically been accompanied by heightened activity in regional research aimed at a more thorough knowledge of the various parts of the country—their physiography, internal and economic structure, territorial division of work, socioeconomic function in the national economy, and the like. Regional knowledge has stimulated work on the theory and methods of regional planning, and on theories of settlement network location.

GROWING NEED FOR REGIONAL RESEARCH AND PLANNING METHODS

Simultaneously, research on the physical development of the whole country has entered a new phase. In a desire to coordinate this work the Committee for the Physical Development of the Country was set up at the Praesidium of the Polish Academy of Sciences. This Committee, working in close cooperation with the planning organs and various scientific and research centers and institutes, developed on a wide front research studies on Poland's physiography, the evolution and present structure of industry, building, demography, settlement network, and transportation; and also on interregional economic relations, territorial division of labor, and regional distribution of the national income. In addition, the first attempts to elaborate an economic theory of regional development were undertaken, introducing among other things econometric and accounting methods into physical research.

These developments have had four main sources. The first is the need to carry out the systematic research and analysis essential for planning and socioeconomic policy resulting from the great quantitative and qualitative changes that occurred in the physical structure of the national economy with the realization of the national economic plans.

As is known, the agricultural and industrial character of the Polish economy before 1945 was radically transformed in the postwar period, and Poland became a rapidly developing industrial and agricultural nation. Though this process did not take place uniformly throughout the country, important structural changes occurred in every region, and the existing disproportions in economic development were considerably leveled out. As a result of great internal migrations in the years 1945–1950—connected with the exchange of population of the western and northern territories, and also the movements of population from country to town, characteristic of all regions of Poland (due mainly to the extension of old and construction of new industrial districts and centers)—there was great differentiation of the population in terms of age and place of residence. The western and northern parts of Poland in particular became regions of predominantly productive age-groups and also large numbers of children and youth. These phenomena are of principal importance for the future socioeconomic development of the country, especially since in the regions with young populations the natural increase of population will remain relatively greater, as is shown by demographic forecasts up to 1980.

The industrialization processes in Poland were accompanied by intensive urbanization. The latter's scope and dynamics can be seen from Table 23.

Population increase in industry according to districts in the years 1946–1956 is shown on Map 40. New interregional ties and relations appeared during the country's postwar economic development, and the old territorial division of labor and functions changed.

These and other phenomena require constant research and elaborate

Table 23. POPULATION GROWTH IN POLAND

Population	1946	1950	Growth index 1946/1950	1960	Growth index 1950/1960
Total (in millions)	23.9	25.0	105	29.7	119
Urban (in millions)	7.5	9.6	128	14.1	147
Urban (in per cent)	31.8	38.0		48.1	

analysis if the proper subjects for further physical and regional planning are to be found. This problem is especially important since within the unchanged area of the country, dynamic processes of growth in the economy, population, and in towns will continue to occur; these in turn will expose many important and complicated problems.

There is, however, a second source of social demand for regional planning. The planned process of decentralized management of the national economy was considerably extended after 1956 and is still going on. Decentralization has increased the people's councils' scope of authority and responsibility for the overall socioeconomic development of their regions. The people's councils have come to consider regional planning and the analysis of the results of research and construction essential tools of their work and a foundation for important economic decisions.

The third source of social demand for planning was the introduction in 1957 of long-range, or perspective, plans of development of the national economy. Work on a perspective plan was first undertaken for a fifteen-year period (1961–1975) and then for a twenty-year period (up to 1980). The basic tasks of perspective plans were defined in 1957: they should outline all the basic problems, directions, and proportions of the national economic development with particular emphasis on structural and qualitative changes. Similar work for the period up to 1980 was undertaken in all the socialist countries that are members of the Council for Mutual Economic Aid. Perspective plans in these countries, mutually related and increasingly precise with the successive-approximations method, are becoming a foundation for long-range agreements for international specialization, cooperation, and division of labor. They have also served as a basis for the elaboration of stage plans covering a period of a few years.

Work on the long-range plan for the development of the Polish national economy brought into the open many methodological problems for regional planning. On the agenda appeared, among others, problems connected with the long-range development of all the economic regions in Poland, their future functions, and their role in the development of the entire national economy. Particular attention was focused on regional planning as an essential instrument in perspective planning. It was emphasized that the inclusion of regional planning in work on the development of the perspective plan for the national economy leads to further improvement in research methods, and consequently greater social and economic effectiveness. It is also helpful in the formulation of the plan's targets and their realization.

The fourth source of growing social demand for research in regional planning is the ever increasing cooperation between the members of the Council for Mutual Economic Aid. The formation of the Regional and Town Planning Section within the framework of the Permanent Building Commission of the Council for Mutual Economic Aid constituted an organizational expression of this cooperation in the field of regional planning. This Section undertook intensive work primarily to improve the methods of solving important tasks that face regional planning and problems revealed by the general perspective plans, including similar and mutual problems. The Section gave special attention to the important new question of coordinating regional plans for key boundary regions divided by national frontiers. This type of work was first undertaken in 1959 by Poland and Czechoslovakia, thus providing an example in the complex coordination of regional plans for the Upper Silesian Industrial District (Poland) and the neighboring Ostrowsko-Karwiński District (Czechoslovakia). Following this successful and useful venture, similar work was extended to other regions.

The basic principles of the international socialist division of labor, accepted in June 1962 at the meeting of representatives of Communist and workers' parties of the Council's member-countries, are of paramount importance for the future development of regional planning methods, and for the organization of scientific research work.

The substance of these principles lies in the linking of international specialization of production with the whole economic complex, and thus creating the most effective and harmonious development of the economies of the individual socialist countries. The socialist division of labor, expressed in the specialization of production in the various countries, also affects the functions and specializations of the various economic regions within each country. Thus it affects also the internal, territorial division of labor, the functions and trends of long-range development of the individual regions, and the over-all regionalization of the country. Regional planning, in its very concept long-range and comprehensive, can well assist to realize the principles of the international socialist division of labor by developing the economy and culture of each country and the socialist community of nations. This assistance is made more effective by extending the scope of work, streamlining the methods, improving cooperation with science, increasing staff sizes, and improving their professional qualifications.

In the light of the principles of the international socialist division of labor, the various member-countries of the socialist community (with the exception of the U.S.S.R., because of its large area) should be treated as political and economic regions, for which regional plan schemes of a general character and on a large scale are essential. In Poland this sort of plan is known as the "national plan." The U.S.S.R. is divided into so-called economic and administrative regions, for which regional plan schemes are elaborated.

The regional aspect of the international socialist division of work expresses itself both by locating products destined for exchange within the trade agreements and by distributing certain investment projects, to increase the productive power of particular industries. It is specifically involved with the (heavy) manufacturing industry, where there is the greatest possibility for specializing production and for cooperation. Coordinating various networks such as railroads, highways, pipelines, and high-power lines also has a regional aspect. We cite, for example, the construction of a pipeline system for the transportation of oil from the U.S.S.R. to Poland, across Poland to the German Democratic Republic, and from the U.S.S.R. to Czechoslovakia and the Hungarian People's Republic. The petrochemical complex now under construction in Płock on the Vistula River is supplied through pipelines with raw materials coming from the U.S.S.R. for manufacturing.

LEGAL, ADMINISTRATIVE, AND RESEARCH INNOVATIONS

The accomplishment of the tasks of regional planning after 1957, as presented above, required changes in the legal foundations of regional planning, organizational changes, and outlines for new methods of work. In 1961 the Sejm passed The Spatial Planning Act.[5] This Act regulates the planned spatial development of the nation, regions, towns, settlements, and villages. Taking into account past experience and methodological results of spatial planning, the Act tied it very closely to economic planning, making possible total planning for the development

[5] See Appendix I.

of the various parts of the country. It established that regional plans should be perspective economic plans, within the framework of which the spatial plan for the development of the region is worked out, just as the plan for the spatial development of the whole country is elaborated within the framework of the perspective plan for the development of the national economy.[6]

This integration of economic and spatial planning on a national and regional scale constitutes an achievement of methodological and practical importance. From the provisions of the Act regional plans, like master plans, are now elaborated for all voivodships simultaneously, following the program of the national economic perspective plan and also as specific regional plans for parts of a voivodship or for areas comprising parts of neighboring voivodships. In this way the voivodship has been accepted as the basic economic and administrative region, having complex connections with the over-all development of the national economy. General coordination is effected through the national economic perspective plan.

Following a special decree issued by the Council of Ministers, regional plan research departments were established in all the voivodship economic planning commissions in 1961 and 1962.[7] These departments employ some 350 workers with higher degrees, including economists, economic geographers, physiographers, engineers of various branches, and sociologists. A special department for raising the professional qualifications for regional planning of employees in research departments capable of training annually some 30 to 35 postgraduates, was set up in the School for Planning and Statistics in Warsaw.

Regional planning in Poland does not have its own scientific research institute, but does closely cooperate with and receive far-reaching assistance from the Praesidium of the Committee for Space Economy and Regional Planning in the Polish Academy of Sciences. Through the effective coordination of scientific research work, including theoretical studies, problems crucial to the national economy, and questions

[6] "1. Regional plans define the trends for the general economic and social development of the given area, the manner and stages of their implementation, the principles for the allocation of production forces and service facilities, the shaping of the settlement network, the distribution of the population, and the designation of areas for definite purposes. 2. The regional plans are prepared for a period conforming to the period of the long-term national economic plan with special consideration for the period of the following short-term national economic plan." *The Spatial Planning Act of 1961,* Arts. 6.1 and 6.2.

[7] "Draft regional plans are prepared by the voivodship agencies of economic planning." *The Spatial Planning Act of 1961,* Art. 8.1.

connected with the international socialist division of labor, the Committee has gained much experience over the past several years. Its achievements are now used in regional planning work. The Committee is divided into several Commissions: Physiographical, Location of Production, Economic Regions, Population and Demography, and Regional Planning Methodology.

PERSPECTIVE PLANNING

The introduction of perspective plans into the system of national economic plans is vital for further development of regional planning methods and the effectiveness of regional plans. Now each regional plan, as a component of the perspective plan for the development of the national economy, can be very closely correlated with the perspective plan.

For this reason every regional plan is elaborated according to the same outline and methodological structure. This outline is flexible enough to include the specific features and the problems of the given region; it also constitutes a basis for comparing and analyzing all regional plans as far as basic figures, proportions, and interrelations are concerned. From the methodological point of view, the regional plan can be divided into three parts. The first contains the results of research on the main national economic functions, past and present, of the given area. Further material, compiled in over-all regional studies, defines the undeveloped, or insufficiently used resources of raw material, the reserves of production and service capacities, manpower, organization, and the like. This research also points up basic internal structural disparities and contradictions requiring correction, and shows potentials for all-round long-range socioeconomic development. Concrete suggestions for the development of the plan, stemming from the analysis carried out so far, together with a substantiation from economics and an outline of the basic problems to be solved, form the final element of the first part of the regional plan, which has a predominantly explorative character.

The second part is composed mainly of general program outlines and documentation. It develops the regional plan by subject areas, presenting a comprehensive approach to each area. This is elaborated from the directives and concrete data contained in the perspective economic plan for the given area. It takes into account the results of the studies and suggestions contained in the first part of the regional plan. It defines and describes, among other topics, the planned internal and territorial allocation of labor and services, the spatial structure, the methods and stages of long-range development, the investments of an economic and technical nature substantially affecting the further development of the region. It also deals with the planned distribution of production and service installations in conjunction with the proposals for the expansion of the urban and rural settlement network, the various objectives of land use, and the social costs and envisaged social effects of the plan. The regional draft plan must also be linked to regional plans drawn up for adjoining areas and must define those tasks requiring interregional coordination.

The third part of the regional plan contains a list of the key problems which require solution within a defined period of time as a precondition for the realization of the whole program. These problems can include many issues which will have to be solved by present economic policies. In this part are also regional suggestions for the perspective plan of national economic development and postulates for scientific research and documentation work essential for further detailed solutions envisaged in the plan. Some of the studies postulated are indispensable as a basis for assessing alternative or differing solutions proposed in the plan and selecting the most propitious variant.

It must be emphasized that every regional plan should be balanced both internally *and* within the framework of the perspective plan of national economic development for the period covered, and that its main stages should be placed within clearly defined time limits. At present, plans are balanced for the period 1961–1980, with transitional points in 1965, 1970, and 1975.

During the elaboration of regional plans and also of the national physical development plan, studies ranging beyond the period of the current perspective plan are also made. These cover only problems for which developmental hypotheses must embrace a longer period of time. In particular, such studies deal with the expansion of the raw-material base, the population, and the settlement network, water management, location of basic investments, and the like. Work on regional plans of this kind was well advanced much earlier. It was carried out in the *regional plan research departments* at the *voivodship economic planning commissions* for all the voivodships, certain groups of voivodships, many industrial areas and districts, regions containing new raw materials, large urban regions, and so on.

NATIONAL AND MACROREGIONAL PLANNING

Work on a plan for the physical development of the whole territory of Poland is done within the framework of studies on the perspective plan of national economic development. The crux of the work on this plan is that it makes possible the over-all examination and analysis of many aspects (for example, from the point of view of the location of existing and potential reserves). Among these are the present pattern of the country's physical structure, the functions and economics of the various regions, the interregional division of labor, the regional distribution of gross and per capita national income, and the exploration and analysis of the physical connections with the territory of neighboring countries.

Based on the results of such research and analysis, and on the results of regional studies and the contents of the plan for the perspective development of the national economy, plans for Poland's long-range physical structure are developed. Particular emphasis is laid on: (1) the distribution of large and medium industry according to type and industrial complexes, (2) the power network pattern, (3) the regionalization of agriculture and forestry, (4) the basic transportation network, (5) the main services network, (6) the main recreation and tourist areas, (7) the distribution of population and the settlement network, (8) the main centers of the water economy, (9) conservation, (10) lines of external transportation connections, and (11) the principles of internal territorial division of labor. A plan for the regionalization of the country, with an outline of the functions of the particular regions, is to emerge as a synthesis of this work.

Alternative solutions are drawn up for many of the elements contained in the plan for the country's physical development. These include, in particular, alternative sites for all sorts of industrial development projects, basic water-development projects, and the expansion of the settlement network.

It must be stressed that this work is carried out through the use of two different methods—the balance-sheet method and the method of successive approximations. Geographical and cartographical methods have also found wide application in this work. The plan for the physical development of the country and the studies for it are drawn up on unified maps and charts with a scale, mainly, of 1:500,000.

The plan for the physical development of the country, or the studies for the plan, are of principal importance in drawing up the list of objectives for the regional plans. As mentioned above, the voivodship has been accepted as the basic economic and administrative unit in regional planning in Poland. This allows regional planning to embrace the entire territory of the country. All the voivodship regional plans are drawn up at the same time; geographical methods are used to make maps and charts with a scale of 1 : 200,000 and 1 : 100,000.

During the work on voivodship regional plans it turned out that a closer examination and analysis of the existing intervoivodship connections and other economic and spatial correlations were essential; with the material gathered by such analysis, it was possible to uncover problems that would require joint solution. This led to *regional plans,* grouping several neighboring voivodships which together form specific macroregions. A typical example of such a region is that formed by the coastal voivodships, in which the maritime economy and its long-range program of development is the linking element. The principal aim of the regional plan for this macroregion is to define the territorial division of labor and the functions of the coastal areas and their hinterlands. The elaboration of such a general plan allows, in turn, for drawing up a supplementary set of objectives for the individual regional plans for the coastal voivodships.

As for the regions of Gdańsk-Gdynia, Szczecin-Świnoujście, and Koszalin, such a plan has been the basis for determining the objectives of development and specialization of the shipyard industry, the character of the ports with respect to commodity structure and specialization of shipments, as well as the cooperating functions of the industrial centers situated in the hinterland of the shipyard industry.

The area taken up by Katowice voivodship, and, bordering on it, Kraków and Opole voivodships, is another example of a macroregion. As is well known, the largest Polish industrial district and the largest industrial-urban agglomeration has developed in the central part of this huge area on the basis of the existing hard coal deposits. Other large industrial districts adjoin the Kraków and Opole voivodships and together form an industrial complex which is destined for further intensive investment and development in the perspective plan. This development will bring many complicated problems requiring a comprehensive solution. The greatest problems are those of labor supply, location for basic investments in the various branches of the economy, complex problems of water economy, territorial division of labor, cooperation and specialization, and also distribution of the population and development of the settlement network.

Regional plans for such macroregions are usually drawn up on maps and charts at a scale of 1:300,000. The whole territory of the country is divided into six macroregions.

The third category of regional plans in Poland consists of the detailed plans for areas comprising part of one voivodship or parts of neighboring voivodships. The boundaries of such regions are delineated during work on regional voivodship plans. Detailed regional plans are shown on maps and charts in a scale of 1:50,000 or 1:25,000—depending on the size and character of the area. This scale makes it possible for the detailed regional plans to define many of the region's technical problems.

Detailed regional plans are of great importance for planning the construction and reconstruction of towns and villages and also for determining the sites of basic investments. It is expected that within two or three years these plans will embrace some two-thirds of the country's territory, beginning with those areas where there is the most urgent need. Regional plans, and especially detailed plans, are worked out in close collaboration with the voivodship town planning offices using their data on conditions and development opportunities for each of the various towns, settlements, and villages.

OTHER TYPES OF REGIONAL PLANNING

Detailed regional plans are also drawn up for various areas of the country which can be differentiated according to production specialization, character of land development, and direction of planned expansion. These plans can be divided into several groups.

The first group includes areas with raw materials; these are designated in the short-term (5 years) and perspective (15–20 years) plans of national economic development for complex expansion through land development and the exploitation of mineral resources of national importance. Included here are, among others, the Rybnik Coal Basin, the Konin-Łęczyca mining and power district, the Tarnobrzeg sulphur district, the Turoszów coal and power district, and the Legnica-Głogów copper district. For these districts, regional plans balanced in detail for 1980 have either already been drawn up or are now in process.

The second group embraces large city and industrial-urban centers with their complicated range of socioeconomic, spatial, and technical problems. With their hinterlands, these require correct and economically feasible locations for production and service installations, and the creation of essential conditions for expansion of production and services to meet the needs of the population. As a rule, the following problems exist:

reconstruction of industry and modification of its structure, reconstruction of the transportation network and installations, and decongestion and limitation of excessive expansion. Inevitably, a host of other equally complex issues arise. This group of plans embraces the regions of Warsaw, Łódź, Kraków-Nowa Huta, Szczecin-Świnoujście, Wrocław, the Upper Silesian Industrial District, and many others. Top priority is given to detailed regional plans for key regions of this type, since further intensive investment and reconstruction is envisaged for them.

The third group of detailed regional plans is made up of areas which demand speedy definition of their principles of development and physical coordination of investments, in view of the growth of large industrial complexes and the construction of basic water-supply systems and transportation installations anticipated in the short-term and perspective plans of national economic development. Included in this group should be the Płock region of the Vistula River (construction of a petrochemical complex), the lower Vistula belt (construction of the Vistula Cascade and of many water-consuming plants), the Kielce region (construction of numerous industrial plants in Kielce and the immediate neighborhood), and the like. Work on regional plans for such regions is urgent.

The fourth group comprises areas less active and economically less developed. Their expansion depends primarily on developing local resources in particular local natural and geographical and labor resources. Typical examples of such areas are the Kurpie region in the middle Narew River drainage area (the northern part of the Warsaw voivodship), and the region covering part of the Kashubian districts in the Gdańsk voivodship. Work on several regional plans for such areas is under way.

The fifth group, on the whole closely connected with the last, covers areas with a predominantly agricultural economy. The need to reshape Poland's predominantly small-scale commodity agriculture into large-scale commodity socialist agriculture of high productivity requires time, an appropriate regional economic policy, large investment outlays for farming and building construction in the villages, industry, and services, and also large-scale and systematic organizational work with social backing and assistance. In the streamlining of agriculture, reconstructing the undesirably shaped and excessively dispersed village settlement network is a special assignment, which calls for gradual rebuilding and concentration. This is why detailed regional plans for farming areas are considered urgent and important. The complicated, diverse problems for such regional plans and the need to acquire the proper experience

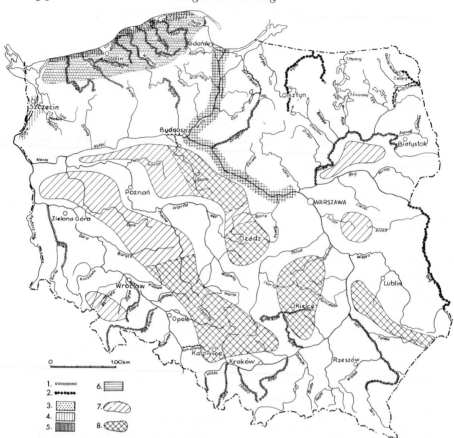

Map 41. General plan for restrictive industrial employment
  1. Rivers, reserves of clear water for residential and industrial use. 2. Rivers, frontier waters under special protection. 3. Zone appropriate for industries causing heavy water pollution. 4. Zone appropriate for chemical industry. 5. Zone for eventual location of plants with radioactive discharge. 6. Zone appropriate for cellulose industry. 7. Area deficient in surface water. 8. Area deficient in surface and underground water.

has been the motive underlying the decision to develop experimental regional plans for six selected typical farming districts in several different regions. These districts vary in structure of farmsteads, natural and geographical conditions, level of farm productivity, settlement network, general level of agriculture, and so on. Conclusions drawn from this work should help to advance regional planning methods in Poland's agricultural regions. In addition to the experimental plans, detailed regional plans are being drawn up for several important agricultural areas, such as the Wieprz-Krzna canal hinterland (Lublin voivodship), the Pyrzyce district (Szczecin voivodship), and the Żuławy delta of the Vistula (this plan has been drawn up and passed).

The sixth group covers recreational, tourist, and spa areas of national importance, such as the Tatra Mountains, the Dunajec valley, the Poprad valley (Kraków voivodship), the Karkonosze Mountains (Wrocław voivodship), the Mazurian Lake district (Olsztyn voivodship), and the seaside recreational area.

The rising recreational and tourist trend—involving not only urban and rural populations, but increasing numbers of foreign tourists—and the expansion of health resorts require proper development of these regions, and the improvement of hotel, camping, and sports facilities. The elaboration of regional plans for such areas is important but it has not been possible for detailed regional planning to cover all of them.

Some of the areas for which detailed regional plans are elaborated lie along the national frontier. The development of cooperation in the realm of regional planning with the U.S.S.R., Czechoslovakia, and the German Democratic Republic has also facilitated coordination of work on detailed regional plans for frontier areas, especially those for which plans for expansion, division of labor, mutual investment, and so on, require consultation and cooperative research.

The Relation of Regional Planning to the Future Development of Poland

As already mentioned, in Poland the regional plan is understood as a complex perspective economic plan for the given area, taking into account all the physical problems involved. This makes possible the extensive use of geographical methods, in addition to economic analyses from which spatial correlations are made. These latter methods aim at discovering variations in the expansion planned for various areas at given times, and disclosing the location of underdeveloped areas with a view to their future rational utilization. Such methods are of basic importance in the analysis of the present state of economic development in the region, as well as in planning its future development. Studies for regional plans, as well as the completed projects, are composed of descriptive text, tables, and cartographic sections.

Detailed regional plans differ from the master plans in degree of detail, contents, justifications, and documentation. This difference is reflected, for instance, in the scale of the maps used in such planning. In effect, detailed regional plans display a predominance of technical elements.

The introduction of perspective plans for development of the national economy has made it possible to give the regional plans a proper foundation in the studies and data pertaining to the entire country. These larger-scale studies determine the over-all long-range proportions of the separate branches of the national economy and balance them for the entire country. They also permit the coordination of regional plans with the indices defining the planned level and distribution of the national income, and the level of the standard of living.

Simultaneous work on the perspective plan—carried out by means of the successive-approximations method, especially in balancing the needs and capabilities of the national economy—gives regional planning the task of exploring and analyzing these needs within the voivodships and other regions, and also that of making suggestions for the perspective plan.

The role played by regional plans is all the more important since the perspective plan for the years 1961–1980 anticipates far-reaching economic transformations connected with the structure of socialism; these will bring out important new tasks for regional planning.

According to the version of the perspective plan elaborated in 1962, Poland's population should increase from 30 million in 1962 to 38 million in 1980, of which some 22–23 million will be living in towns. The huge urbanization process (considering Polish conditions) anticipated in the plans will involve a growth of eight million in the number of urbanites as a result of the natural increase of population and migration from country to town. The perspective plan envisages a several-fold rise in industrial output, accompanied by the construction of many new plants and industrial districts, and the modernization and extension of existing ones. This expansion of industry will be accompanied by a re-shaping of agriculture into up-to-date socialist agriculture. The perspective plan also provides for a considerable rise in the standard of living, a factor which will be reflected in part by an increased housing supply and improved standard of housing construction.

The planned socialist transformation of the national economy will be not only quantitative, but also, and primarily, qualitative. Without great qualitative changes (modern technology and techniques in industry, building, agriculture, and transport; qualified personnel, scientific organization of work), which are the precondition for the attainment of high productivity, the quantitative tasks would be impossible to fulfill. The physical-economic structure and the spatial division of labor, when viewed in the light of the perspective plan, assumes prime importance;

for dynamic economic and population growth and expansion of the settlement network will be occurring in heretofore unchanged areas of the country.

Definite specialization in production and services will be the guiding factor in expanding national functions. At the same time, the potential raw material resources, the natural and geographical environment, the unexpected production reserves, and labor resources will be of special importance in shaping these functions.

The data given here for the sake of illustration throw a light on the diverse problems which are being studied and analyzed during elaboration of regional plans. At the present stage of work on the perspective plan, regional planning is faced with two principal problems: the need to define and justify the consequences of achieving the roughly accepted goals of the perspective plan for the level of economic development, the vocational and social structure, and the standards of living of the various regions; and the need to point out and define the requirements and capabilities of the various regions (with particular emphasis on all sorts of reserves), which will prove the correctness of the data used in the perspective plan or else will serve as a basis for its correction.

The method of successive approximations and the principle of periodical revision of plans (as a rule, every five years) enables us to perfect the envisaged solutions and to introduce essential supplementary changes.

In the light of this discussion of the current state, methods, contents, and directions of regional planning in Poland there becomes evident the particular role of science in explaining and solving the many complex natural, economic, social, and technical problems facing regional planning. Regional planning without science and theory would be a blind venture. That is why international exchange of experience can be highly fruitful for regional planning methods and techniques, and why they in turn can serve the cause of international cooperation and *rapprochement*. For these reasons, regional planning in Poland has a lively interest in the progress of regional planning methods and their scientific and theoretical foundations in all countries, regardless of their political and social systems. It is why Polish regional planners take an active part in the work of international institutions engaged in research on regional planning and related disciplines.

CHAPTER 11

Regional Planning in the
Upper Silesian Industrial District

RYSZARD SZMITKE

TADEUSZ ZIELIŃSKI

Sketch of the Economic Development of Upper Silesia

THE intensive economic development of Upper Silesia, particularly that part known as the Upper Silesian Coal Basin, began in the eighteenth and nineteenth centuries, when coal became the fundamental basis of power for industry. It was in this basin that geological conditions advantageous for coal mining were found.

The establishment and development here of many other branches of industry followed the enlargement of the railway network at the close of the nineteenth century. The proximity of the coal basin as well as the profit derived from a large labor force and sales market were deciding factors for locating them here. Simultaneous with the growing concentration of production was the enlargement of settlements. The old towns—Bytom, Gliwice, Mysłowice, and Będzin—as well as settlements like Zabrze, Świętochłowice, Chorzów and Dąbrowa grew rapidly.

It is necessary to stress that the manner and progress of economic and spatial development were not even throughout Upper Silesia. For many years this region had been divided among three different states (Germany, Russia, and Austria) and subsequently between two, Germany and Poland. Besides, geological conditions in the separate parts of the region varied greatly. It may be stated that generally the prewar development of Upper Silesia was not directed by a common interest and long-term planning, but by a spontaneous and fairly arbitrary exploitation of natural resources. The many negative consequences of this development could be observed in chaotic forms of spatial economy and in subsequent problems of space utilization. The degradation of the natural advantage of geographical environment of the region occurred at the same time. It was thus impossible to outline a uniform plan to embrace the whole region, particularly in view of the prevailing political and legal structure. During World War II all mining and other industries of Upper Silesia were excessively exploited. Therefore, despite the relatively light damage caused directly by war, the renewed operation of the productive forces of the region and the correction of wartime negligence required large investments—not only in industry but also in communal, social, and cultural services.

Need for a Regional Plan: Its Aims, Tasks, and Range

Its economic importance and specific geological conditions had caused the Upper Silesian Industrial District to be the subject of studies for spatial planning long before World War II; unfortunately these undertakings were prevented by the political and legal structure of the nation from yielding satisfactory results. It was only the merger in 1945 of the formerly separate parts of the region within the state boundaries of Poland, the socialization of heavy industry and large rural estates, and finally, the introduction of the principle of economic planning that created the possibility of outlining new development schemes for this important area. These schemes were based upon broad and profoundly analyzed conceptions of regional planning.

During the years 1945–1949 regional investigations and planning studies, undertaken within the Office of Regional Planning, were mainly concentrated on problems of inventory studies, the network of settlements, the distribution of population and productive forces, housing, the communications network, war damages, and on a recognition of the geographical and geological conditions of the region with particular view to their usefulness in mining. At that time regional planning was in a stage of preliminary organization, and its relation to long-term economic planning was unstable. Thus, the planning studies were not yet able to give full and satisfactory results. Nevertheless the data obtained from them took into consideration the fundamental structure of the region and made possible an outline of a preliminary, schematic conception of regional planning which expressed the principles of decentralization of industry and settlements, as well as the fundamental principles of recultivation and restoration of the region. But this was only an ideal plan, and the correct principles formulated in it could not be transferred—given the current planning organization—to binding directives for investment activity. This possibility emerged only after the reorganization of regional planning in 1949 connected it more closely to economic planning.

In 1950 a committee was formed by the State Planning Commission whose purpose was to outline a regional plan of the Upper Silesian Industrial District; in 1951 a special Regional Planning Laboratory was established as an administrative agency of this committee. The need for such careful organization, which made it possible to obtain a full development of consequent planning studies in the Upper Silesian Industrial District, was recognized in the directives of the Six-Year Plan for national economic development. According to the plan, this district was to be a region of great investment activity to increase productive potential and continually ameliorate the living conditions of the population.

The activities planned met with many difficulties because of the extraordinarily complicated economic and spatial structure of the region, itself a result of planless economy in the past.

The factors which compose this specific structure may be grouped as follows: (1) The size and scope of productive establishments is seen in the great concentration of industrial works. There are mines, foundries, machine and metal works, electric-power plants, chemical factories, and others. In addition, there are diverse auxiliary establishments such as condensed arteries of railways and roads and power-transmission networks. (2) The settlements are very concentrated, which is seen in the uncommon congestion in big industrial towns. These directly adjoin one another in a relatively small area with a well-developed, but accidental, network of communications and community services. (3) Acute conflicts have arisen between the development of mining and other industries or settlements. This is found, on the one hand, in the blocking of coal and ore deposits by existing buildings or developing investments on the surface and, on the other hand, in a restriction of the scope of building activities in favor of an easy exploitation of the natural riches. (4) Water supply is limited—a result of natural conditions of the Odra-Vistula watershed. The problem is intensified by mining and the development requirements of the industry and the population. (5) The violent and uncontrolled development of industry and settlements have caused chaos in the spatial organization, which is augmented by the effects of economic, social, and political relations in the past. These relations can be seen in the mixture of industrial and residential buildings and in the complex communications network, as well as in the faulty urban structure. (6) Natural resources have been destroyed. In addition to devastation of the landscape and deforestation of the area's central region, this is found in the amassing of useless soil and industrial waste matter, such as heaps of cinder, stones, remaining open sandpits, and ground depressions. Moreover, large industrial operations constantly contaminate the air with smoke, dust, and chemical exhalations, and the flow of filthy industrial waste waters impairs the climatic conditions of the region beyond permissible limits.

With these factors exposed it became clear that any investment activity which does not involve a penetrating analysis of all of them may give rise to dangerous mistakes and that only a comprehensive plan, based upon a long-term program of economic development, can create a basis for coordinating planned investments. The aim of the planners was therefore to outline correct ends and means for economic development and to point out possibilities and means for gradual reconstruction and sanitation of the region. They also had to create a basis for the establishment of a good location policy for planned investments.

These aims have been stated as two principal points of the directives issued by the State Planning Commission, in which conclusions from previous studies have been used in a general way to set the tasks of the plan. The first is the creation of conditions for the full development of the productive forces of the region, concomitant with a limitation on the growth of manufacturing industry which does not depend upon local raw materials and a gradual decentralization of the existing factories of such industry. The living conditions of the population were to be ameliorated by reconstructing present towns and creating new towns and settlements, set apart from the detrimental influences of industry, mainly on the outskirts of the Coal Basin. Other activities were to include purification of the air, afforestation of useless soil, and creation of a network of recreational parks and sport facilities. The transportation facilities were to be improved.

To remedy existing disproportions and faults as well as to promote an economic, spatial, and social integration of the whole area, it was also necessary to take into consideration the hitherto prevailing differences between the various parts of the region.

The regional planning work which concerned the Upper Silesian Industrial District was undertaken after a detailed definition of the planned area was achieved in accord with the results of a general analysis of the situation of the region on a larger scale. The whole area embraced by the plan has been divided into two parts. Area "A" includes the predominantly urbanized central part of the Coal Basin with an area of about 700 sq. km. and with about 1,850,000 inhabitants. The average density of this area was about 2,000 inhabitants per sq. km. in comparison with 293 inhabitants per sq. km. in the voivodship and about

80 inhabitants per sq. km. in Poland. Area "B" surrounds area "A." It is destined for future location of industry and settlements and embraces an area of about 1,700 sq. km. with about 310,000 inhabitants. The average density of area "B" amounted to only 182 inhabitants per sq. km. (all above data from 1950).

The elaboration of the regional plan included a descriptive section and 50 maps scaled from 1 : 300,000 to 1 : 1,000. For the fundamental conceptions, a scale of 1 : 50,000 was used. Larger scales were applied only in relation to particular settlements in order to provide an illustration of specific problems. The essential elaboration of the plan was based upon many individual supplements including among others a regional plan for vegetation, a study of the Odra-Vistula canal, and a study of transportation.

Essential Problems of the Regional Plan

The factors discussed above, which determine the specific spatial and economic structure of the region as well as the aims and tasks of the plan, also define its chief problems. Briefly, it may be stated that the fundamental problems of production have been studied with a view to the establishment of a *production profile* that is more specialized and better adapted to the natural conditions of the region. In the future this would guarantee rational use of the coal and zinc ores and would preserve the possibility of developing industry directly dependent upon these raw materials. Because of the planned enlargement of the mining operations, other industry must be limited in its development, or even removed or eliminated.

Such an economic policy is viable because the region suffers from a great deficit of workers, water, farm products, and open terrain for reasonable extension of the dwelling area. Moreover, the policy is a result of the planned changes in the distribution of productive forces in Poland. One of the most significant spatial problems of the region is that of establishing a rational and correct distribution of settlements and other buildings in relation to the present and planned sphere of coal and zinc mining. It should be noted here that area "A" is almost entirely undermined by extensive exploitation, which has caused a continuing deformation of the surface that limits the scope of building activities. On the other hand, existing buildings reduce the possibilities for a full use of coal and ore deposits.

Within the scope of this short article it is possible only to describe some of the most important specific problems of the plan.

Coal and zinc mining. According to the national directives increased coal output for 1970 is needed, independent of an increase in the productive potential of the existing mines. The erection of new mines and substantial enlargement of the mining area are included in the plan. On the basis of detailed studies of geological and mining conditions, the areas of future mining have been outlined and the location of new mines has been generally fixed. In further supplements to the plan the views of the Ministry of Mining concerning planned employment, and the requirements of transportation, electric power, water and gas supplies were taken into consideration. These supplements were used for a study and outline of a "sphere of mining protection" in the planned area; in order to discover what must be done, a more detailed picture of the conflict between the existing and planned mining and surface building was sought. For the same purpose, the zones of ground deformation caused by mining operations have also been defined. The studies have prompted the Ministry of Mining to undertake many investigations into present and expected influence of geology and mining in the region.

The initial results of the studies have enabled the Ministry of Mining to formulate precise requirements for dwelling areas, according to regional concepts for the location of towns and settlements. Moreover, areas without coal or zinc deposits and areas not intended for mining exploitation have been afforded the opportunity of unrestricted planning.

The regional plan directs that the mines of the region, which in 1950 made up 85 per cent of the total Polish coal production, must enlarge their production in conjunction with the erection of new mines and a planned increase in production through further mechanization. In 1950 the region's mining of lead and zinc ores made up about 90 per cent of the total production output of these ores in Poland. Here the planned increase in production and employment up to 1970 is about 10 per cent.

Closely connected to the development of mining is the problem of sand use. A widely applied procedure in coal mining is to fill up exhausted seams with sand, and this calls for large-scale production and delivery of sand. Formerly the sand fields were arbitrarily dispersed over the whole region, and their steady enlargement led to a devastation of the landscape, principally to the deforestation of the area. The premises of the regional plan required that digging of sand within the region be stopped or restricted in favor of the use of sand from outside the region—from the so-called "Błędów desert." This meant laying a new "sand railroad," a special railway line with numerous branch lines built exclusively for delivery of sand to the mines.

Another problem connected to the development of mining and industry is that of the cinder piles. During the earlier unplanned development, heaps of cinders, stones, and other waste matter from mines or smelting-ovens grew up in the area. As a result of planning activities a complete inventory of these heaps has been prepared, the possibilities of their use have been estimated, and principles for the future location of such heaps has been outlined. The existing old heaps will be used either for the production of building materials or will be forested; future waste products will be located on selected sites, primarily with a view to filling up the remaining open sand pits.

Manufacturing industry. There are in the region about 200 large and average-size plants, chiefly steel mills, machine and chemical factories, and about 500 smaller factories. The regional plan tends toward reduction of that manufacturing industry which does not depend upon local raw materials.

Transportation. The volume of freight transport in the planned region makes up more than 42 per cent of Poland's total freight transport. The region has the greatest density of railroad and road networks in Poland. Moreover, it has a very extensive network of mass transportation facilities; yet this does not fully cover the growing needs of the region. The fault lies with the chaotic transportation system, itself a result of the previous political division of the region and the repeated change of political boundaries. The regional plan includes suggestions for improving the railroad network. One is to eliminate heavy freight transport from the principal central line. Such traffic will be diverted to the new ring-line system, especially made for it. The other plan is to convert the Silesian Knot or railroad junction to electricity and adapt its development to new dwelling centers such as Tychy, Pyskowice, Radzionków, Tarnowskie Góry.

The plan suggests rebuilding and considerably extending the road and tramway network in order to improve communications between formerly separated parts of the region and also to connect employment centers with dwelling and recreation sites. At the same time, it would correct street systems in the principal towns of the region.

Agriculture. The region is not self-sufficient in farm products and must depend upon other regions. Therefore, a considerable intensification of agriculture is outlined by the plan in order to reduce the most acute shortages in fresh milk, vegetables, and soft fruits, which do not bear long transportation. It must be noted that individual vegetable gardens, leased by the local authorities to the working population, are of particular importance in the urbanized part of the region.

Forestry. The wooded areas constitute about 25 per cent of the total region, but the central part (about 300 square kilometers) is almost entirely devastated. The plan suggests a considerable increase in forestation in the central areas; moreover, some forest parks and recreation sites are planned around area "A."

Dwelling areas. In the central part of the region 84 per cent of the area is covered by towns which house 95 per cent of the population of area "A." In peripheral area "B," towns cover only 11 per cent of the area and house 25 per cent of the zone's population. The plan requires sanitation, rebuilding, and a slight extension of towns in area "A," with simultaneous reduction of the existing density of inhabitants per room. It also requires the creation of new towns and settlements (mainly upon the outskirts of area "A" and within area "B") along the principal transportation lines. The most important of these new or intensively de-

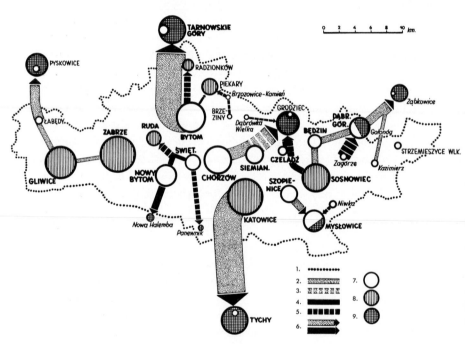

Map 42. GOP deglomeration plan, prepared in 1953 (scale of cities by thousands of inhabitants)

1. Boundary of zone "A"—according to first phase of the regional plan. 2. Existing railroad connections. 3. Planned railroad connections. 4. Existing tram connections. 5. Planned tram connections. 6. Flow of population to be deglomerated (1 mm. = 2,500 inhabitants). 7. Existing cities—reconstructed. 8. Existing cities—reconstructed and partially extended. 9. New towns.

veloped towns are Nowe Tychy (planned to hold about 120,000 inhabitants), Pyskowice and Nowa Dąbrowa (about 40,000 inhabitants each), Radzionków and Tarnowskie Góry (about 60,000 to 80,000 inhabitants each).

This scheme will reduce growth of settlements in the central undermined part of the region in favor of development in the outside zone, which will function as a new dwelling area for the region. Expansion of the net of settlements under the principle of decentralization has already been realized in Nowe Tychy, Pyskowice, and Nowa Dąbrowa, not to mention some smaller settlements developing on the outskirts of area "A."

Water supply and sewerage. The region is situated on the Odra-Vistula watershed which is not large enough to supply present peak demand. Moreover, much water is lost through mining operations and industrial sewage. There is also a vast requirement of water for industry and, of course, for the needs of the population. All the needs cause a continuing lack of water. The yield of the springs and water-supply systems of the region barely meets 60 per cent of its needs. For this reason, and in view of increased future requirements, the plans suggest the necessity for building new water-supply stations outside the region. One of these, the great water dam at Goczałkowice, has already been completed.

Parks. As mentioned earlier, the regional plan is paralleled by a plan for parks. After preliminary studies of soil and climatic conditions, plans have been made for a network of recreation parks and sports accommodations. Many of the principal objectives of the plan have been realized today—the Central Park of Chorzów, the park for Gliwice and Zabrze, the park for the eastern towns of the region, and others.

Government Acceptance of the Principles of the Regional Plan

ITS USEFULNESS FOR SUBSEQUENT PLANNING AND RESEARCH WORK

The regional plan of the Upper Silesian Industrial District was prepared and elaborated in 1951 and 1952. It was officially accepted and endorsed in 1953 by a separate act of the government and thus became a basis for the general economic and spatial policy which governs the region. It also outlined principles of future detailed investigations and planning, which have been fully developed in various respects.

Based upon the regional plan, general designs have been prepared for all towns and settlements in area "A" as well as for the most important ones in area "B"; full consideration has been given to the specific conditions of the region and their economic and geographical correlations. These local plans extended the provisions of the regional plan and go more fully into problems of demography, settlements, social services, transportation, and parks, and at the same time provide operative schedules for the first phase, 1960–1965.

Serious layout work has also been done by the Ministry of Communal Services in the preparation of short-range and general perspective plans along specialized lines such as development of the local transportation network, water-supply lines, sewerage, sewage-disposal plants, and street cleaning.

Of the utmost importance for further planning activity will be the results of scientific research being carried out by a special Committee of the Polish Academy of Sciences. It concerns building methods in areas already exploited by mining or being exploited, intensification of agricultural production through the use of sewage and so-called waste heat, problems of local climate (particularly the struggle against pollution of air and of waste waters), the use of cinder piles, and the cultivation of barren lands.

In conclusion, it may be stated that today this planning and investigatory activity is in a steady state of development which embraces the whole voivodship.

CHAPTER 12

Regional Planning in the Kraków Voivodship

JERZY KRUCZAŁA

THE Kraków region has at present one of the highest rates of economic growth in the country. It is also notable geographically: the Tatra mountains here are the highest in the country. The region contains important natural resources, such as coal, salt, zinc, and other minerals. Poland's greatest river, the Vistula, flows through the area. Historically, this part of the country was second to none, for in former times Kraków was the capital of Poland. Today it is second only to Warsaw as a cultural center. Thus natural features, history, and present importance combine to make this one of the most interesting regions of Poland.

Before World War II the region was noted for its low economic level and for overpopulation in the rural areas. A large percentage of those persons who emigrated from Poland to the United States, Brazil, and France came from this area. Regional planning here has a difficult task in view of past neglect, the rate of economic growth, the natural features, and the cultural characteristics of the region.

Brief Description of the Region

The Kraków region is in the southern part of Poland. To the south it borders on Czechoslovakia, to the west on the Katowice voivodship, to the north on the Kielce voivodship, and to the east on the Rzeszów voivodship. There is an administrative division between the city of Kraków and the Kraków voivodship, the latter consisting of seventeen administrative districts and four towns. The whole region covers 15,500 sq. km., 5 per cent of the total area of Poland. The population (1960 data) is 2,468,000, which is 8.3 per cent of the total population of the country. The density of population—approximately 160 per sq. km.—is much greater than the average for the country of 95 per sq. km.

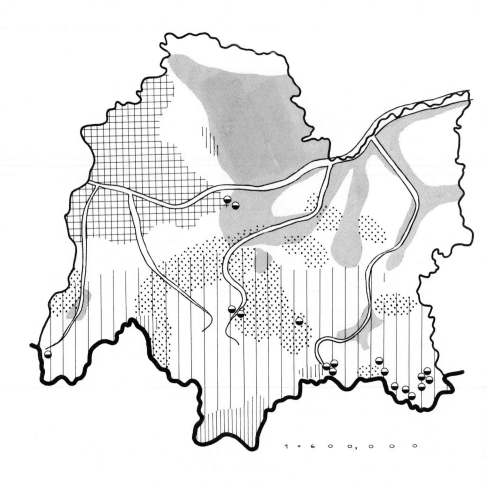

1 = 6 0 0, 0 0 0

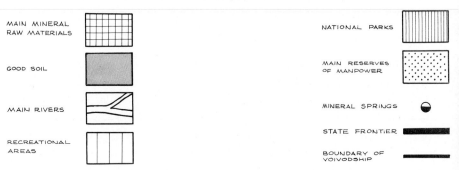

MAIN MINERAL RAW MATERIALS		NATIONAL PARKS	
GOOD SOIL		MAIN RESERVES OF MANPOWER	
MAIN RIVERS		MINERAL SPRINGS	
RECREATIONAL AREAS		STATE FRONTIER	
		BOUNDARY OF VOIVODSHIP	

Map 43. Kraków Voivodship, Master Regional Plan: Natural resources and manpower reserve

The climate differs considerably from that of the rest of Poland. Precipitation is much heavier, the winters are longer and more severe, and the snow remains longer. Good soil is to be found along the Vistula and to the north of Kraków. Mountain soil of a poorer quality covers the greater, southern part of the region (Map 43). In the west-center of the region there are rich seams of coal, amounting to over 20 per cent of all the coal in Poland, as well as seams of zinc and lead ore, and salt deposits. Many of the less important raw materials, such as limestone, sand, gravel, and porphyry, are found in the western districts. The greatest forest areas are in the mountain districts, where woods cover 26.2 per cent of the surface. The rivers, most of which have their sources in the mountains, have abundant water, but unfortunately the water level is not stable. In the south there are many mineral springs. The beauty of the landscape is another particular feature of the mountain areas (Figure 59). Recently, holiday resorts serving the whole of Poland have been developed here, especially in the south.

Although the prewar overpopulation is now being corrected, there is still a large surplus of manpower in the rural areas (Map 43). Fifty-five per cent of the employed population work on the land, and 45 per cent are in nonagricultural occupations. The number of employed per-

Fig. 59. Kraków Voivodship: View of the landscape near the mountain areas

sons is rising fast, especially in industry, where the figures have risen
from 90,600 in 1938 to 285,000 in 1963. Industry is the main basis of
economic development in this region, growth being particularly noticeable in the chemical, electrical, and metallurgical industries. Industrial
growth has been more rapid in the Kraków region than in many other
parts of Poland. For example, 17 per cent of the total sum invested in
industry by the state in 1957 went to this region, and 15.3 per cent of
the total in 1960.

The economic development of the area is uneven. (The economic

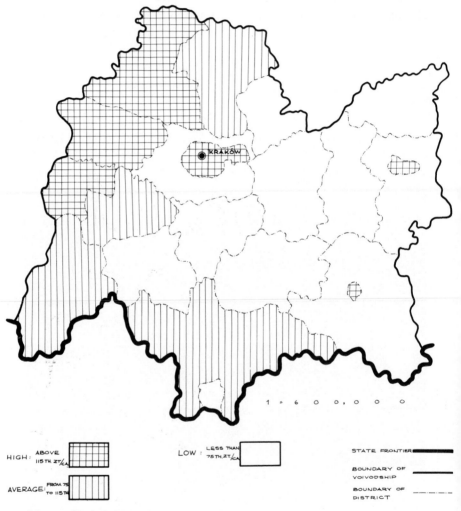

Map 44. Kraków Voivodship, Master Regional Plan: National income per capita
(in thousands of złotys)

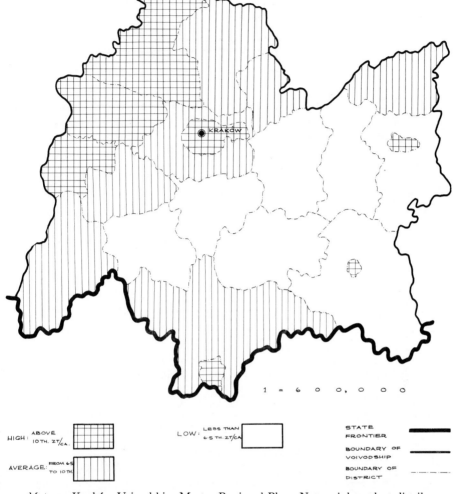

1 = 6 0 0, 0 0 0

HIGH: ABOVE 10 TH. ZŁ/CA.   LOW: LESS THAN 6·5 TH. ZŁ/CA   STATE FRONTIER

AVERAGE: FROM 6·5 TO 10 TH.   BOUNDARY OF VOIVODSHIP

BOUNDARY OF DISTRICT

Map 45. Kraków Voivodship, Master Regional Plan: Net social product distributed per capita (in thousands of złotys)

effects of this disparity, and the distribution of the national income and the income of the inhabitants of this region are illustrated in Maps 44 and 45.) Until recently, industry has been concentrated chiefly in the west-central part of the area, and in the Tarnów district, but more and more industrial works are now being built in other parts of the region. Where the soil is good, there was intensive farming; in the hilly and mountain areas there was mostly mixed farming. In these districts agriculture was very often accompanied by forestry, small-scale industry, and steadily growing health resorts and recreational services.

The principal city of the region is Kraków, which now has nearly 500,000 inhabitants, as compared with 240,000 in 1939. Most of the towns of over 10,000 inhabitants are concentrated in the western part of the region (where new towns are also rising), along a line running from Kraków eastward, and in the mountain valleys.

National Importance of the Kraków Region

Certain branches of industry in the Kraków region are of great importance to the country as a whole. In 1958 this area produced 22 per cent of all the electricity in the country, more than 20 per cent of the nonferrous metals, about 16 per cent of the building materials, and 14 per cent of the chemicals. Kraków industry is increasing steadily.

The Kraków region is growing in popularity as a recreation center for the whole of Poland. The area contains four of the seven national parks, and about 16 per cent of the country's spas, convalescent homes, and sanatoria, while the number of tourists is increasing by leaps and bounds.

Moreover, Kraków's role in the development of education, learning, and culture in Poland is an important one. The region has eleven centers of higher education with 32,500 students, 15.3 per cent of all the students in Poland. A quarter of all the museums in the country are located in the region.

The Evolution of Planning in the Kraków Region

Studies in regional planning were carried out in the Kraków region both before the war[1] and during the years 1945–1948. The first detailed regional plan was drawn up in 1949–1950 for the west-central part of the region, an area covering 3,000 square kilometers. Other plans of the same type were drawn up in the following years. In 1952–1955 the first experimental general regional plan, covering 15,500 square kilometers, was made. Over the years, planning methods have undergone an evolution, some features of which are listed below.

(1) Early planning consisted mainly of geographical studies, in which propositions concerning the economic planning of the area were put forward. Gradually, however, the plans came to contain more proposals for the future; in the later stages, plans were made for the development and location of all the important branches of the economy.

(2) In the beginning, the projects very often concerned only details or particular elements of the region's economy. As time went on, these

[1] For example, S. Leszczycki, *Podhale Region* (Kraków, 1938).

projects were replaced by more general plans, laying down the lines of economic development for whole areas—that is, covering all the elements in the economy of a given area. Simultaneously, the plans were made more flexible, in that alternative plans were produced.

(3) The physical and economic elements of planning were brought closer to each other, whereas in the early plans the geographic elements predominated, in the later plans economic elements played a more important part; and later still there was a happy balance between geographic and economic elements.

(4) Improvements in planning methods were gradually introduced so that now many different scientists and scientific institutions cooperate in this work, and teamwork is increasingly the rule. For example, after twenty-four individual studies on raw materials had been made, a group of specialists drew up a joint geological study of the raw materials of a given area. Growing emphasis is being placed on obtaining more and more precise results from these studies, and the planning office is now in constant contact with a large number of scientists and scientific institutions.

(5) There is increasing integration of the internal elements of the plan, as well as coordination of the plan for Kraków voivodship with the plans for neighboring areas.

(6) Efforts have been made in the later work to expand those elements which ensure the usefulness of the plans, especially in town planning and location policy. There have been large-scale preliminary studies of existing conditions and in the actual plans more space has been devoted to those practical elements which are essential to carrying out the projects.

(7) After the importance of economic elements had been recognized, there was a growing tendency for the studies and plans to take into consideration the noneconomic elements of people's lives.

(8) Elements which in the early plans were scarcely taken into consideration, since they were thought to be in the domain of medium-term rather than long-term plans, have now acquired greater importance.

(9) Lately there has been some stress on economic calculations. Despite the inherent difficulties, attempts have been made to calculate the national income for each region (both the gross national product created and the net social product distributed) and to calculate the fixed assets. The plans can then be judged in terms of their effectiveness in relation to an increase in national or in personal income.

(10) An interesting experiment which may be described here was

the drawing-up of a general regional plan of Kraków before such plans had been officially undertaken in Poland at all. A general plan was drawn up for the whole voivodship, an area several times larger than the areas which had previously been subjected to planning. For the sake of experiment it was decided that the plan should be based on the assumption that there would be full employment of all available manpower up to 1975, and that overcrowding of the rural areas would be abolished. This program was then compared with the possibilities for developing industries which could provide new employment and the services which would be necessary to meet the needs of the growing population. The "autarchy" assumed in the plan enabled its authors to show what would be the maximum requirements of the Kraków voivodship for available jobs, as well as the other consequences of population growth in a large area. It also enabled the planners to indicate the many different possibilities for the development of the region, and to put forward suggestions for zoning.

(11) The regular work of the Kraków regional planning office now includes theoretical studies of the region and of methods of regional planning. Experiments are carried out, foreign literature on the subject is studied, discussions are held with visitors to the planning office, and members of the staff are sent to gain further experience in planning offices in other parts of Poland and abroad.

Regional Plan of the Kraków Voivodship

The first version of the regional plan, which covers the period 1961–1980, was drawn up in 1961. Emphasis was placed on strict precision as to the aims of the plan and the interrelations between the different elements. The plan is based on a projection of the optimal growth of regional income, which consists mainly of an increase in production, as well as of a growth in supraregional services. It is expected that by expanding recreational facilities for vacationers from all of Poland as well as for foreign tourists (boardinghouses, hotels, hostels, spas, winter sports centers, etc.) it will be possible to increase the income of the region.

A 4.7-fold growth of industry is planned. This is based on studies of the distribution and extent of raw materials, on analysis of the present position of industry, and on a study of the possibilities for locating new processing factories. The highest growth indices in the plan are those for coal production, metallurgy, the production of metal ores (zinc), the electrical and chemical industries (both based on coal), and the engineering industry (in which an increase of 9.5 is planned), which depends on the metallurgical industry and on the supply of manpower. The plans for transport have been drawn up with the future location of production in mind.

Special importance is attached to increasing agricultural production in order to supply the growing industrial centers with perishable foodstuffs such as vegetables, milk, and fruits.

Construction is to be of an extent to guarantee that the investment programs can be carried out successfully.

A study has been made of various elements of physical planning and of the distribution of the per capita income of the population in the various parts of the region. The plan provides that the average incomes in the various parts of the region will be leveled out as far as possible, to give the smallest possible range between the various districts. The size of the per capita income in the various districts will depend mainly on the level of production and the extent of supraregional services.

Since the distribution of good soil, as well as of the raw materials on which industrial development is based, is uneven, it was impossible to plan an even distribution of the forces of production. To attain equality of per capita income of the inhabitants of different parts of the region despite the different production possibilities of the parts, it was assumed that there would have to be migration of manpower. It was planned that migration should be chiefly to those areas with greater possibilities for industrial development—that is, to the west and north of the region, as well as to the towns situated in the mountain valleys, where some development of industry was planned. It was assumed that the migrants would come principally from the rural population in the southern part of the region, where the opportunities for increased production and employment are small in comparison with the manpower resources. In this part of the voivodship, however, migratory tendencies will be countered by the development of the supraregional services mentioned earlier.

The above calculations were made on the basis of predictions as to the growth of population and manpower. It was taken that through natural increase over the period of the plan the population would grow from 2,550,000 to 3,400,000.

The program for the development of services and of consumption, which will bring about an improvement in income and standard of living, is a large one. The extent of this program will depend on the level of the regional income as well as on the per capita income of the voivodship's inhabitants.

The following goals have been set for the region:

(1) *Density of housing.* In the towns one person, and in the country areas 1.36 persons per room will call for the construction of about 1,000,000 rooms.

(2) *Public services.* It is assumed that a large percentage of the population will make use of public services such as local transport, water-supply systems, sewerage systems, etc.

(3) *Commerce.* Annual consumption per capita is expected to be as follows:

meat and meat products	57 kg.
milk and milk products	540 kg.
fats (excluding butter)	25 kg.
eggs	215 kg.
vegetables (fresh and processed)	130 kg.
fruit (fresh and processed)	70 kg.

(4) *Education, health, and culture.* Similarly high targets have been set in these areas.

The location of services and public utilities is dependent on the dwelling pattern of the region, which in turn depends on the location of those elements which lead to the formation of human settlements: of industrial and agricultural production in the first place, but also of recreational and administrative services. It is planned that cultural and recreational facilities will be distributed more or less evenly throughout all parts of the region. Especially in the rural areas, public utilities and other services will be provided to encourage the development of selected villages.

As far as noneconomic aims are concerned, the plan provides for improvement of the ecological conditions of human life. In plans for the location of industry, more attention will be paid to the avoidance of water and air pollution. Green belts will isolate industrial from housing areas: there will be no building of houses or service facilities for the population in these belts. In areas which are to be devoted to the regeneration of the physical and mental abilities of the people, there will be no development of industry or other installations that might have an unfavorable effect on living conditions. Especially in the areas near towns the beauty of the countryside will be preserved.

These provisions for the attainment of noneconomic aims provide a correction to the earlier plans, which aimed only at maximum production. For example, the scheme for exploiting the sand deposits near the Jaworzno Colliery was given up in order to preserve the woods surrounding the town. If the woods had been cut down, the people of Jaworzno would for years have been deprived of a pleasant place in which to spend their leisure time, and the countryside would have been made ugly.

The general aim of the regional plan was taken to be the drafting of principles for the physical plan and the formulation of directives for other sections of planning—urban planning, for example. The first step of the physical plan was to denote the various economic zones of the region and coordinate them with the various transportation networks. This process gives us the static plan; the dynamic plan is based on the principles adopted for regional operations.

The region was divided into three main zones (Map 46) according to their dominant economic function—industrial, agricultural, or agricultural-recreational. In decisions between different investment projects, the dominating function was the decisive factor in determining whether first place be given to industry, agriculture, or services.

As Map 46 shows, the plan indicates an industrial zone (A) in the west and the central part of the voivodship; an agricultural zone (B) in the north where the soil is best and around the biggest industrial centers, and an agricultural-recreational zone (C) in the south, which has the best conditions for recreation.

The transportation network considered in the plan includes the main lines of communication within the region itself, between the Kraków region and other regions, and directly through the region.

The delineation of the economic zones and of the road and rail networks was coordinated with the plans for the neighboring voivodships of Katowice, Kielce, and Rzeszów. In view of the importance of the frontier between Poland and Czechoslovakia, the plans for the frontier areas were included in a simplified, detailed regional plan drawn up jointly by the regional planners of Kraków and Bratislawa (Czechoslovakia). This plan was designed to ensure coordination, especially for transportation, water supplies (the river watersheds are divided by the frontier), adjacent national parks, and recreational facilities.

The planning of regional transportation operations is concerned with the direction of both commercial and passenger traffic, covering operations on an interregional scale, within the main zones of the region, and on a local scale. For example, the planners studied probable tourist movements between Poland and Czechoslovakia in the frontier zone, freight transport between the Kraków region and Silesia, the extent and direction of transportation of food from the agricultural to the industrial

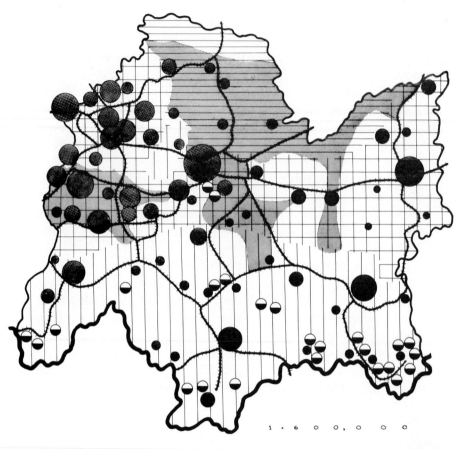

1 · 6 0 0 , 0 0 0

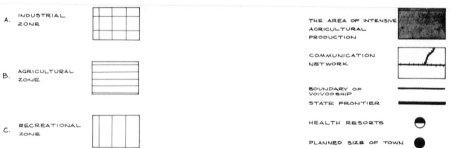

A. INDUSTRIAL
   ZONE

THE AREA OF INTENSIVE
AGRICULTURAL
PRODUCTION

COMMUNICATION
NETWORK

B. AGRICULTURAL
   ZONE

BOUNDARY OF
VOIVODSHIP

STATE FRONTIER

C. RECREATIONAL
   ZONE

HEALTH RESORTS

PLANNED SIZE OF TOWN

Map 46. Kraków Voivodship, Master Regional Plan: Zoning

zone, passenger traffic to recreational areas, and so on. On the local scale the studies were chiefly concerned with transportation to and from work, and for leisure activities. Another of the operational plans deals with water supplies.

A great deal of attention has also been given to the network of towns and villages. Studies in this area provide the data necessary for city planning. Table 24 gives projected town population figures for 1980.

The main functions of each town and the type of industrial works to be located there have been defined, as well as the spheres of influence, the network of roads and railway lines in the region, and some of the important economic indices.

The plan concludes with provisions for carrying out in detail the investment program so as to ensure attainment of the principal aims.

Large maps on a scale of 1:100,000 and 1:200,000 illustrate the elements on which the plans are based. There are soil maps, geological maps, maps giving the distribution of raw materials, the location of industrial and agricultural production, the development of villages, and so on.

As far as regional plans are concerned, the graphic method has various functions. It is useful, for example, in studying the location of human settlements; it is a means of illustrating the program for the development of industry, and it serves to present the general plan for the agricultural development of the area. The most important of the maps is that which combines all the others to give a composite picture of all aspects of the plan.

Apart from the general regional plan for the whole voivodship, detailed plans have also been drawn up for the parts of the voivodship—for instance, the industrial area in the west-central part of the region, the Sub-Tatras, the area of intensive agricultural production, and the Tatra National Park (Map 47).

Table 24. POPULATION IN TOWNS, 1960–1980

	Number of inhabitants	
Town	1960	1980
Tarnów	71,500	105,000
Oświęcim	24,000	100,000
Jaworzno	53,000	72,000
N. Targ	16,700	30,000
Szczucin		15,000

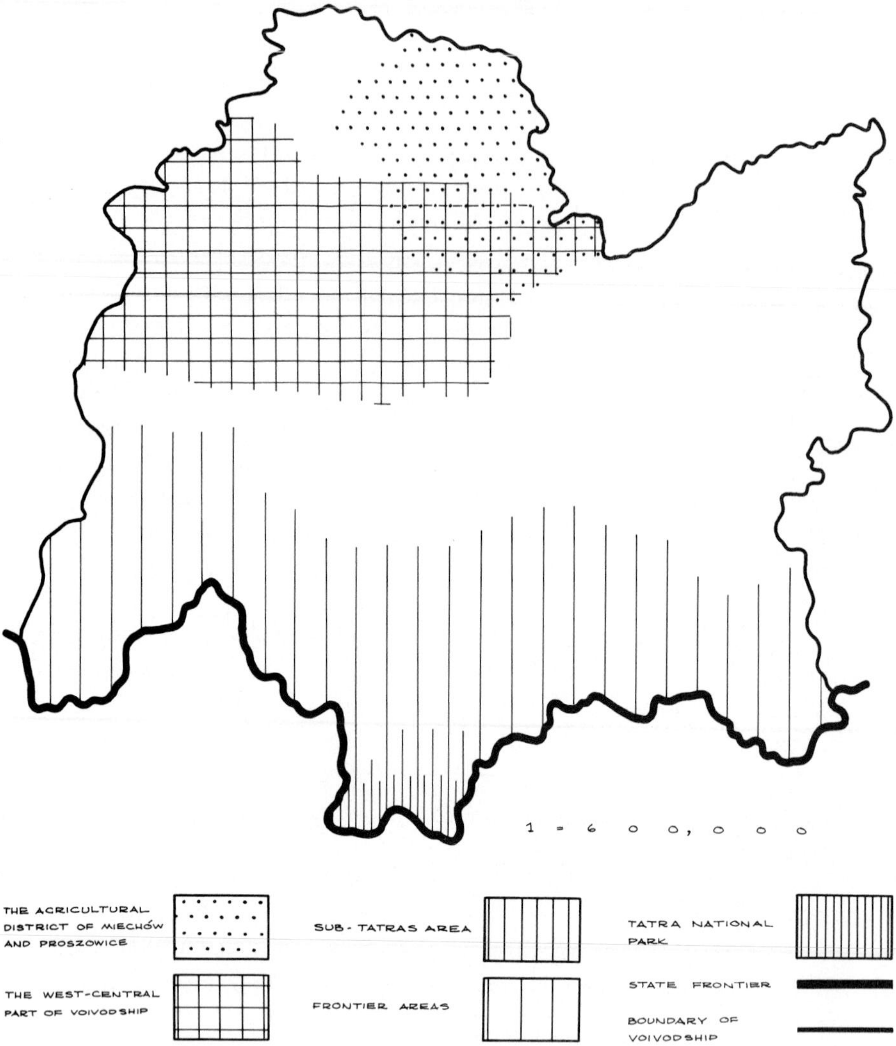

Map 47. Kraków Voivodship, Master Regional Plan: Areas covered by detailed regional plans

The principal aim of the plan for the industrial area was to ensure proper exploitation of the rich mineral resources—coal, zinc, economically valuable rocks, and so on. Extensive studies were made of the mineral resources, the location of housing, the transportation network, water supplies, and demographic conditions. The plan contains projects for the zones where minerals are extracted, the zones where industry is connected with supplies of raw materials, the distribution of housing in the areas which are of least value for mining, the green belts protecting the residential areas from the harmful effects of industry, and the recreation zones. The aim of the transportation plan is to ensure the efficient transport of both goods and passengers. The plan for the water-supply system is important. The services plan will provide for improvement in living conditions. The program is based on demographic predictions, and on estimates of future manpower, water supplies, and so on.

The plan for the Sub-Tatras was designed to lay the foundations for the correct development and physical planning of this recreational area, the only one in Poland which contains mountains with a height of over 2,500 meters (Figure 60). The Tatras are visited by over one million people a year. According to the plans, facilities for tourism, recreation, and sports will be on a scale appropriate to the relatively small size of this mountain area. All economic activities that are incompatible with or unrelated to the main function of the area will be eliminated. Both transportation facilities and tourist services will be spread out along the foot of the mountains to provide bases for excursions into the mountains. This marks an important change from the past, since there was a tendency (Figure 61) for investment to be concentrated in the town of Zakopane in the middle of this belt. This led to the overcrowding of Zakopane and the middle section of the Tatras (Map 48).

Fig. 60. View of the Tatras

The main task of the detailed regional plan for the area of intensive agricultural production is the localization of agricultural production so as to make maximum use of the good soil and to supply the neighboring industrial areas with vegetables, fruit, milk, and other perishable foodstuffs. The most difficult part of this plan is that concerned with the creation of suitable conditions for the development of agricultural production. Plans have to be made for road expansion, for the provision of services connected with the mechanization of agriculture, for drainage and irrigation, for agricultural schools, for appropriate fiscal and social policy, and so on. Provision must also be made for raising the per capita income of the population to the highest possible level, and for satisfying the needs of the population to the highest possible degree by, for instance, ensuring sufficient numbers of well-located shops and other services and setting a high standard for public utilities, health services, education, and cultural facilities.

The chief aim of the plan for the Tatra National Park is to protect nature in this most beautiful part of the country, as well as to plan facilities for the 1.5 million tourists who will visit the area every year. The plan for this area will determine the limited number and location of hostels and camping sites up in the mountains. It is more desirable that hostels and camps be built at the foot of the mountains, outside the Na-

Fig. 61. Tourist area of Zakopane at the foot of the Tatras

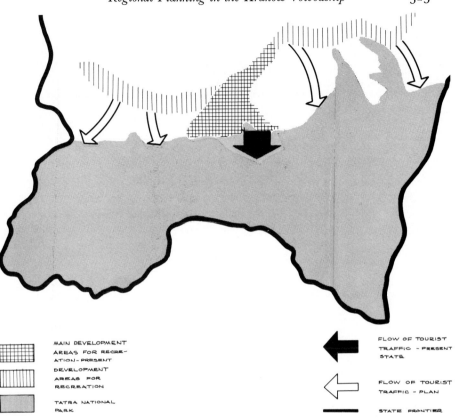

MAIN DEVELOPMENT
AREAS FOR RECRE-
ATION - PRESENT

DEVELOPMENT
AREAS FOR
RECREATION

TATRA NATIONAL
PARK

FLOW OF TOURIST
TRAFFIC - PRESENT
STATE

FLOW OF TOURIST
TRAFFIC - PLAN

STATE FRONTIER

Map 48. Kraków Voivodship, Master Regional Plan: Sub-Tatras region planned
  spatial structure

tional Park, at spots which would provide suitable starting points for
excursions into the mountains. The plan for the National Park sets forth a
number of desiderata as regards the physical plans for the adjacent
areas, which it treats as a protected zone. For instance, it proposes that
the area nearest the mountains be protected by limitations on technical
use. It also proposes a more distant, basic protected zone, in which the
provision and location of services would be determined in relation to the
supposed tourist capacity of the Tatras and the location of roads and foot-
paths. The plan for the Tatra National Park is coordinated with similar
plans for the Czechoslovak part of the Tatras, constituting an international plan for the Tatras as one natural area.

CHAPTER 13

Regional Planning in the Białystok Voivodship

BOGUSŁAW WEŁPA

Description of the Voivodship

THE Białystok voivodship lies in the northeastern part of Poland. It covers an area of 23,145.6 sq. km., about 7.4 per cent of the total territory of the country, and has a population of 1,115,500, that is some 3.7 per cent of the total number of inhabitants in Poland.

Historically political conditions were not favorable to the development of the area which today lies within the territory of Białystok voivodship. Up to World War I the area of the voivodship was divided among the Tsarist Empire, the Kingdom of Poland, and the Kingdom of Prussia. In principle, these were all frontier territories. The larger cities in them were dependent mainly on military garrisons and administration, the only exception being the Białystok region, which was incorporated into the Tsarist Empire. The introduction by the Tsarist authorities of duties on commodity imports from the Kingdom of Poland to Russia (following the 1831 Uprising) allowed for the development in this region of a textile industry working mainly for the Russian market. This industry was almost completely destroyed during the last war.

The ravages of the war, however, did not affect industry alone. The transportation and services networks and installations were also heavily damaged, and there was a considerable drop in the population. The number of inhabitants in the present territory of Białystok voivodship decreased from some 1,300,000[1] in 1939 to 941,000 in 1946. The urban population decreased from some 340,000[2] in 1939 to 176,000 in 1946— in other words almost by half. The number of inhabitants in the capital

[1] Author's own estimates.

[2] Author's own estimates.

city of Białystok, dropped from 100,000 to 56,000 in the same period.

This population decrease—which is quite understandable when one takes into account the fact that war losses were particularly acute in all sections of the economy except agriculture—affected, above all the non-agricultural population, which fell in the period between 1931/33 and 1950 from 395,000 to 244,000; its share in the total population figures for the whole voivodship dropped from 33.2 to 26 per cent. In the immediate postwar period this proportion was probably even lower, though the actual figures are not known, because of the lack of reliable data. Certain conclusions can, however, be reached from the available statistics of employment in industry. In 1950 some 24,200 people were employed in industry, against only 10,200 in 1946. This would suggest that the nonagricultural population must have been even smaller than existing figures suggest.

The years 1950–1960 brought evidence of a marked improvement in economic standards in the voivodship. Many new industrial plants were built, including the two large textile plants in Białystok and Zambrów —this being a continuation of the region's old traditions of textile manufacturing; hundreds of kilometers of roads with improved surfaces were built or rebuilt; and there were scores of cultural, social, and communal projects.

Basic changes occurred, especially, within the city of Białystok. The city center was completely rebuilt, and various new housing estates were constructed. As a result, the prewar town, which was predominantly built of wood and much of which had been destroyed during the hostilities, received a complete facelifting; its appearance was radically changed, and the number of inhabitants soon surpassed 120,000. The former functions of an industrial and administrative center were preserved but, the city also became a center of science, with the Medical Academy and the Higher Engineering School. It must be emphasized that all these changes were the result of the realization of the first postwar studies dedicated to the transformation of Białystok into a strong regional center.

In spite of the changes, however, the Białystok voivodship still ranks among the most underdeveloped in Poland. Out of a total population of 1,115,500 at the end of 1961, 775,000 lived in the country, and only 340,400 in the towns. The density of population in the Białystok voivodship was 48 inhabitants per sq. km., that is, about half the average for the whole country.

Agriculture remains the main source of income for the voivodship's inhabitants, and 62.5 per cent of the population derives a living from farming. The amount of urban employment is rather insignificant, and this is best evidenced by the share of the urban population in the overall population figure for the whole voivodship—a bare 30 per cent. Besides the city of Białystok, with 120,000 inhabitants at present, there are practically no large towns in the voivodship, and the next largest town, Elk, has a population of only 23,000, that is, one-sixth that of Białystok.

The voivodship is also very poorly industrialized. Only 43 per every 1,000 inhabitants work in industry (the average for Poland is 105) and the overwhelming majority of the industrial establishments are concentrated either in Białystok itself, or in its immediate neighborhood.

The transportation network is still insufficiently developed in comparison with other regions of the country. In the Białystok voivodship there are only 21.4 km. of roads with hard surfaces (against a national average of 34.2), and 4.7 km. of railway lines (against a national average of 8.6) per 100 sq. km.

The level of agricultural production, in terms of both productivity and soil utilization, is low, and in some parts of the voivodship the three-field rotation system of soil cultivation is still used.

As a result of poor industrialization and the still widely applied old methods of farming, and although the average density of population is only half the national average, Białystok voivodship is an area with a surplus of manpower (unskilled labor). This population migrates to other voivodships (mainly to Upper Silesia and Warsaw) in search of work.

Past Planning Studies

Until recently, the character of the Białystok voivodship did not seem to justify the institution of studies or regional plans of major importance. Nevertheless work on a regional plan for the voivodship had been undertaken and studies completed in the years 1945–1949. As in the case of other voivodships, these studies were of an experimental character, which is understandable when one considers that they were undertaken in the immediate postwar period. They were accompanied, however, by studies dealing generally with such practical problems as the transportation network, the settlement network, and the location of industry. Some of these were later utilized in work on the Six-Year Plan (1950–1955). After this, right up to 1957, no more plans of any major importance for the whole voivodship were elaborated. There were only two regional plans, embracing smaller areas. The first, "The Wizna Regional

Plan," was worked out in 1954 in connection with the planned construction of a power station operating on the rich local peat deposits in the so-called "Wizna Swamps"; the second, "The Regional Plan for the Gołdap District," was elaborated in 1955—its basic provision was the precise definition of an agricultural development program for the Gołdap district, taking into account the development of all sorts of services, the processing industry, the settlement network, and the like.

In addition to these studies, the southern part of the voivodship was included in studies for the "Bug River Valley Regional Plan" carried out in connection with the current project for constructing a line of locks and hydroelectric power stations on the Bug River. The abandonment, or postponement, of this project, however, prevented the plan from bringing any great advantages to the region.

Work on regional voivodship plans undertaken on new principles in 1957 was different in both character and importance. The new plans constituted an integral part of the perspective plan for the development of the national economy. They were based on both national proportions and development trends, and on the all-round knowledge of the conditions prevailing in the voivodship; therefore they could postulate the most correct line for the region's development under existing conditions. The character of the Białystok voivodship, so different from the industrialized southern voivodships, which were comparatively well equipped with raw materials, was necessarily reflected in the structure of the regional plan.

Long-term Regional Plan

The final "Premises of the Białystok Voivodship Regional Plan for the Years 1961–1980" contains seven chapters and includes both an appraisal of the present state of development of the voivodship and a program for its further development, as well as statistical table and maps. The table of contents of this work provides a fairly good indication of the problems covered by the regional plan for the voivodship, and it is therefore reproduced here: (1) Appraisal of the present state of the voivodship's economy. (2) Demographic conditions and employment in the years 1961–1980. (3) Development program of commodity production and supraregional services in the perspective plan, 1961–1980. (4) Problems connected with the present structure and standard of living of the population and the directions of development in the perspective plan, 1961–1980. (5) Development of the settlement network and the more important settlement complexes in the perspective plan, 1961–1980. (6) Program of basic investments and conditions of realization in the perspective plan, 1961–1980. (7) Summary.

BASIC PROBLEMS AND PREMISES

In the first place, the basic task facing the plan was not (as, for example, in the Warsaw region or the Upper Silesian Industrial District) to limit the rise in industrial employment and curtail urban population increases, but to encourage all the possible factors which might help to attract industry and arrest the population outflow which had been continuing over the past decades. The second basic task, and perhaps the most important in view of the agricultural character of the voivodship, was to work out a program for reorganizing the structure of agriculture, from the point of view of both the site of farmsteads and the lines of production.

Closely linked with both these tasks are important problems in the reconstruction of the settlement network, transportation facilities, and the like.

One of the basic premises of the regional plan was the assumption that differences between the living conditions prevailing in the voivodship and the national average anticipated for the period covered by the perspective plan should be narrowed down as much as possible. Previously, the Białystok voivodship had been last among all the voivodships in terms of both gross income and average real income per capita. The second basic premise was the assumption that the outflow of manpower would have to be checked because it had detrimental effects, such as the deformation of the population's age structure (since the outflow was mainly of the younger population) and the withdrawal from the area of the people with greatest initiative—precisely those people who would decide to seek residence elsewhere.

PROPOSALS OF THE PLAN

Population. Anticipating a further, but insignificant outflow of the population during the entire period covered by the perspective plan (2,000–3,000 annually), the Białystok voivodship regional plan envisages decisive changes in the vocational structure of the population and its distribution. In the first place, the decrease of the agricultural population by some 15 per cent is assumed—achieved mainly as a result of the reshaping of agriculture. The share of the agricultural population in the over-all population figure is to decrease from 62.5 per cent in 1961 to some 41.0 in 1980. This will occur as a result of an approximately two-fold increase of the nonagricultural population, which is to be brought about by the development of industry and other nonagricultural branches of the economy.

Linked very closely with changes in the vocational structure of the

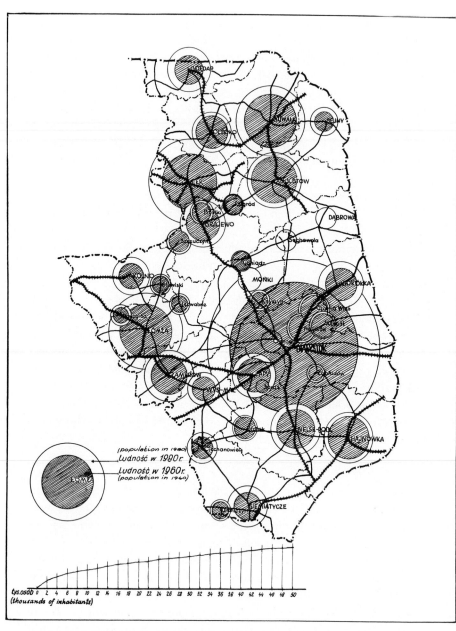

Map 49. Białystok Voivodship: Settlements (in thousands of inhabitants)

population, as provided for in the plan, is the considerable danger of deforming the age structure of the agricultural population, which might later lead to manpower difficulties in the countryside. In actual fact this deformation is already apparent today. For instance, only 4.9 per cent of the nonagricultural population in the voivodship is over 60 years of age, while 13.1 per cent of the agricultural population is over 60; in the age-group from 25 to 34 years old, 20.1 per cent are nonagricultural and 13.3 per cent are agricultural. As a result of this disparity, further work on the regional plan needs to include a very searching analysis of the possibilities of maintaining the decrease of the agricultural population while allowing only desirable changes in the age structure of this population.

Industry. The accepted premises of long-term industrial development in the voivodship postulate an approximately sixfold rise in industrial production and an approximately threefold rise in industrial employment. This projected rise in employment is based on the expectation that there would be a continuing desire to guarantee jobs fully for the growing labor force and for the manpower being released from the countryside.

Postulates concerning the various types of industry were worked out on the basis of an elaborate and careful analysis of prevailing local conditions, particularly the geographical environment, with special emphasis on local mineral, agricultural, and forest raw material resources. Also taken into consideration were manufacturing traditions; this found expression, for instance, in plans envisaging extensive development of the textile industry. The planners also considered transportation connections and the possibilities of power supply. The latter problem is rather important, since the voivodship lies far from the country's major power-producing centers and does not possess its own natural power resources. (At one time the suggestion of building a peat-fired power station ("Wizna") was put forward; but this idea was soon dropped, primarily because of the possibility of more profitable utilization of existing peat resources.) This fact places a decisive obstacle in the way of even considering the possibility of establishing any power-consuming industries in the region.

As far as other branches of industry are concerned, a very detailed analysis of the possibilities for developing industries based on local raw material resources was made. And so, for instance, the perspective plans anticipate the construction of several processing plants in connection with the outlined intensification of agricultural production. Their location has been drawn up on the basis of hypothetical balances of agricultural surpluses. An exact study of the location of building-materials plants was also carried out. Taken into consideration were amounts and sources of raw materials and anticipated demands. Detailed attention was also given to the timber industry.

Substantially less care was devoted to the elaboration of plans for other branches of industry. There was the possibility of eliminating certain types of plants, mainly because conditions were not conductive to their development, including the already-mentioned power-consuming plants and those which use up large quantities of raw materials or semifinished products which have to be transported from other parts of the country. It was thus difficult to give an unequivocal and precise definition of the types of plants which absolutely had to be set up for these industries. Nevertheless, the first attempts at planning have already been made, and some of the plans have already been used in determining the location of new plants in the long-term economic plans.

Agriculture. The development program for backward agricultural practices is based on an attempt to divide the voivodship into economic districts on the basis of an analysis of soil, climatic, and physiographical conditions. This has led to defining four economic and production districts with different forms of agricultural production, directions of development, and general level of organization of agricultural production.

Plans elaborated on the basis of this division postulate a number of basic changes, as a result of which the over-all level of agricultural production in the voivodship will rise more than twofold.

The substantial changes to be made in soil utilization are based principally on studies of the division of farm production according to districts. These changes will tend to decrease the acreage taken up by cereals and potatoes and greatly increase the acreage of industrial and fodder crops. This anticipated expansion of agricultural production and, in particular, the increasing share of fodder crops will bring about an almost threefold rise in livestock herds per 100 hectares of arable land and an almost equally great increase in the number of pigs. The anticipated mechanization of agriculture, particularly of field work and transportation, will allow for a threefold decrease in the number of horses. At present there are as many as 14.9 horses per every 100 hectares of arable land. Naturally the figures laid down in the regional plan differ from district to district; in certain instances a differentiation has been made for even smaller areas.

It is practically impossible to discuss here all the issues embraced by

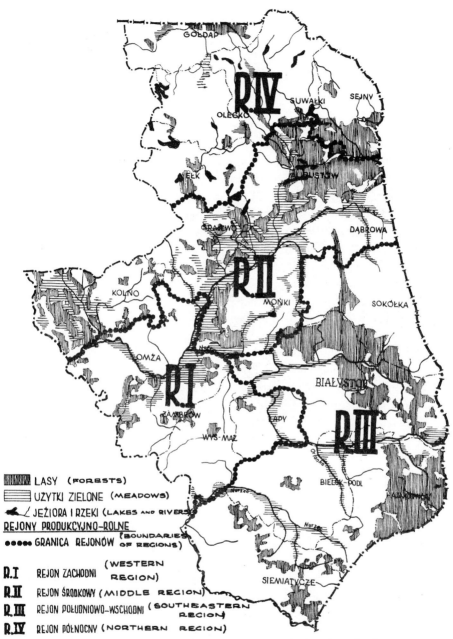

LASS (FORESTS)

UZYTKI ZIELONE (MEADOWS)

JEZIORA I RZEKI (LAKES AND RIVERS)

REJONY PRODUKCYJNO-ROLNE

●●●●● GRANICA REJONÓW (BOUNDARIES OF REGIONS)

R.I REJON ZACHODNI (WESTERN REGION)

R.II REJON ŚRODKOWY (MIDDLE REGION)

R.III REJON POŁUDNIOWO-WSCHODNI (SOUTHEASTERN REGION)

R.IV REJON PÓŁNOCNY (NORTHERN REGION)

Map 50. Białystok Voivodship: Regions of agricultural production

the plan. Nevertheless it must be stated that in addition to the problems already mentioned—including that of water purification, which is of vital importance in the Białystok voivodship and has been elaborated in great detail—the plan also covers such problems as seed production, organization of zootechnic and veterinary services, and the economic building program.

Forestry. Since the voivodship contains several large and important forest complexes—including the Białowieża Forest, internationally famous for its bison and elk reservation—forestry problems are given ample consideration in the regional plan. Among matters analyzed in particular detail are problems of water improvement in forests, the construction of forest roads, afforestation, and the exploitation of forests according to the provisions of development plans for the timber industry.

Transportation. Because of the present low density of the transportation network, the plan gives much space to an analysis of its development. Estimates of the total future extent of tasks in transportation, together with a breakdown for the various means of transportation, provide a point of departure for estimating the development needs of the network. The analysis considers simultaneously the problem of providing adequate connections between the countryside and the main centers of gravity in the towns and the need for developing main lines of regional and national importance. While, as a result of these studies, the provisions of the plan for the expansion of the railway network anticipate the construction of only one section, and this of national rather than of regional importance. The program is a very rich one in road construction. It proposes raising the density of hard-surface roads from 21.4 km. to 35.5 km. per 100 sq. km. in the voivodship.

In addition to the railway and road network, the regional plan also contains proposals for the expansion of waterways which is to be accomplished, in the main, by making certain rivers navigable.

Services. In view of the present low rate of service installations the regional plan devoted much attention to this problem, in some cases providing extremely detailed solutions and even determining the location of certain clearly defined projects in the perspective plan. For instance, the location of homes for the aged and of welfare homes is laid down in detail. A full program for extending the present range of vacation facilities has been mapped out. This includes almost everything, from selecting sites for hotels, rest homes, hostels, and camp grounds to proposing additions to the existing network of roads in connection with the development of tourism, and suggesting locations for gasoline and service stations.

The settlement network. In the regional plan for the Białystok voivodship the problems of the settlement network have been worked out separately for the towns and for the countryside. But while the issues connected with the town network have been elaborated in great detail, so far the proposals for the village settlements have been limited to several general premises and to drawing up a network of supravillage centers. No doubt the factor that hampered the proper elaboration of this topic was the general problem of transforming Polish agriculture from small-scale to large-scale commodity farming.

As far as the expansion of the town network is concerned, in addition to the twofold increase in the population of Białystok envisaged over a twenty-year period, the plan anticipates the expansion of several city centers (Ełk, Łomża, Suwałki) to 35,000–50,000 inhabitants and a considerable development of all the district centers. The plan also envisages the creation of two new towns and the removal of city rights from two others (Choroszcz and Suraż).

DEVELOPMENT OF THE SUBREGIONS

The basic premises and problems of the Białystok voivodship regional plan, described above, provide a general idea of its character and specific properties. This brief review may be concluded by a short description of the already-mentioned geographical subregions in terms of their basic developmental tendencies. These subregions have been established on the basis of differing natural and economic conditions, in order especially to visualize the possibilities of locating industry.

Subregion of the city of Białystok. The main developmental directions are substantial expansions of the capital city, Białystok, from 120,000 to some 230,000 inhabitants by 1980; extension of supraregional and regional services, particularly higher and primary education, culture, and health services; continued development of the textile, machine, and metallurgical industries; and formation of a suburban supply zone.

Northern subregion. The main directions of development include expansion of the city of Ełk from its present 23,000 inhabitants to some 50,000 in 1980. Ełk is destined to become the principal city of this subregion. Development of the machine, food-processing, and textile industries in the larger city complexes of the subregion (Ełk, Suwałki, Grajewo) is expected. In farm production development of cattle-rearing

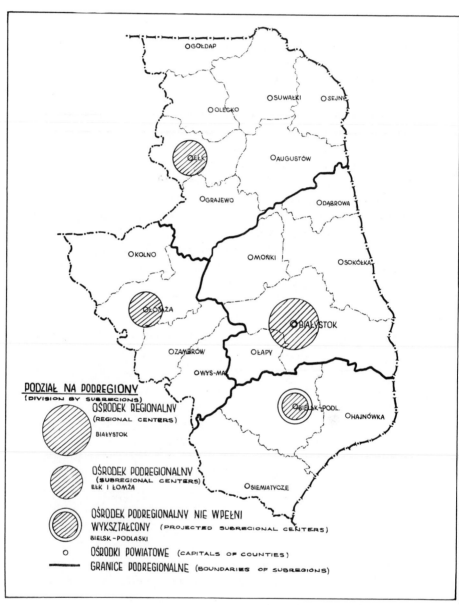

Map 51. Białystok Voivodship: Division by subregions

for increased dairy production will be substantial. Tourist facilities will be extended in the subregion, particularly in the area of the Suwalsko-Augustowskie Lakes district.

Western subregion. The main directions of development are expansion of the subregion's principal city, Łomża, to some 40,000 inhabitants; intensification of agricultural production, with particular emphasis on stud cattle; expansion of food-processing, metallurgical, and textile industries, mainly in Łomża.

Southern subregion. A characteristic feature of this subregion, both as present and in the perspective plan, is the lack of a center with a subregional character. The main directions of development are rapid expansion of agricultural production, with cereal cultivation and cattle-breeding predominating and expansion of the building-materials industry on the basis of local raw materials (chalk, clay, sand).

CHAPTER 14

Water Economy in Poland*

ALEKSANDER TUSZKO

THE conception of water economy has recently been acquiring a two-fold aspect—first as embracing the economic, administrative, technical, and biological considerations involved in state husbandry of water, second as a separate branch of learning lying at the juncture of natural, geophysical, technological, and economic sciences and tying them together.

The primary purpose of water economy is deliberately and purposefully to subordinate natural water circulation to human needs, relating requirements to resources by impounding the greatest possible quantity of precipitation and allowing it to return to the sea in the manner which provides the greatest social benefit. Rational husbandry of water resources to cover present and future needs should be based on a long-range plan for the development of the national economy, for water plays a major role in the maintenance of life and associated production processes.

The complicated modes of coexistence of societies in our day confront water economy with tasks that are much harder to accomplish than those of even the recent past. Technological and economic advances in recent decades have been characterized by the speedy growth of heavy and light industries, including those industries that are heavy users of water.

The growth of populations and higher consumption per capita have resulted in an increased demand for food. This necessitates intensification of agricultural production and the development of livestock farming. There is also an increase in electric consumption, and this consumption per capita is often regarded as an index of the economic development of a country. We have been witness to an intensive search for new sources of power; atomic power is now coming on the scene.

* Reprinted from the *International Journal of Agrarian Affairs,* II, 6 (1960), with permission of the Institute of Agrarian Affairs, University of Oxford, England.

Modern means of transportation such as railways, road haulage, and most recently air transport have been developing.

As a result, water is becoming relatively more important as a raw material, as a biological agent, than it is as a material for which substitutes can be found. Therefore, in the plan for the utilization of water resources priority is given to satisfying the needs of the centers of habitation, agriculture, and industry in all those spheres where water has no substitute today and where there is unlikely to be a substitute in the future.

Nevertheless, water power gives great benefits in comparison with thermal and even nuclear power because of its constant and indestructible reserves which are regenerated by the cycle of water circulation in nature; and at the same time it saves such valuable raw materials as coal and oil. Water power should therefore be fully utilized in every country where the supply of these resources is smaller than the needs. Also, waterways should be adapted to the requirements of modern navigation wherever this is economically justified in the complex planning of water routes.

The trends of administrative forms for water economy are beginning to exceed the bounds of individual countries. It is necessary to maintain the principle of complexity in interconnected balances of water needs and resources in vast areas, linking the uses of water for power, navigation, and other purposes, and having consideration for the far-reaching influence of the water economy on the natural system of water distribution. As a result of all these factors, rivers which have been eagerly chosen as state frontiers, dividing countries and nations, are becoming arteries that unite people because of their community of interests.

The Water Supply of Poland

Poland has an area of 312,520 sq. km. and a population of over 30 million (1961 figures). It lies in the Sarmatian lowlands within the great European lowlands where the influences of various climates meet and clash—in the main, oceanic from the west and continental from the east. The climate is therefore marked by unstable weather, fluctuations of temperature, and variations in atmospheric pressure. Almost the entire country lies within the basins of the Vistula and Odra rivers. The Vistula river basin covers 174,300 sq. km. (55.9 per cent of the total area of the country) and the river basin of the Odra 106,200 sq. km. (34.1 per cent), other Baltic river basins occupying 30,000 sq. km. (9.9 per cent). The remaining 0.1 per cent drains into the Black Sea. The water supply comes mainly from rainfall. Only a small proportion of water flows through rivers from the neighboring countries of Czechoslovakia, the Ukraine, and Byelorussia. In this Poland differs from countries like Hungary, Germany, and Rumania in which the rivers bring large quantities of water from areas beyond their frontiers.

The quantity of precipitation in an average year amounts to 186 billion cu. m., corresponding to an average rainfall of 597 mm. for all Poland. The distribution of precipitation is uneven, so that the mountains have from 800 to 1,500 mm. and the lowlands from 450 to 550 mm.

Only 5 billion cu. m. flow into Poland from rivers in other countries. The difference between the inflow of 191 cu. km. and the discharge of 58 cu. km. is used up mainly to promote the life of plants, humans, and animals. Part of the water evaporates unproductively. Agriculture and forestry use about 155 cu. km. and are therefore the main users of the rainfall.

Water resources vary from one area to another. The average coefficient of flow in the mountain areas, for instance, is as high as 14 liters per sec. per sq. km. In the lowlands this drops to 3–4 liters per sec. per sq. km. The range of flows in the various months is quite large. In the case of mountain streams, for instance, the flows vary by several hundred per cent.

The irregular discharge of water in different years and months and the irregular distribution of water resources in the country make it difficult to utilize the apparently large volumes of water which hitherto have been flowing unused to the seas. Enormous quantities of water are discharged at times of spate and floods, but the average flows, particularly in the lowlands, are in many cases already insufficient to meet the demand. In years of drought the flows in the rivers in critical months amount to 20 per cent–30 per cent of the average flows. Therefore with unregulated water husbandry only part of the resources in the rivers and streams can be used directly.

Calculations show that about 36.6 cu. km. of water sink into the surface soil, and about 76.5 cu. km. sink deeper. The former part of this water constitutes an underground reservoir which feeds the rivers and streams during periods of less precipitation and smaller inflows; the latter, which seeps deeper into the soil and cannot flow back into the rivers and streams, constitutes a store from which some of the water can be regained by pumping. Roughly speaking, approximately 25 cu. km. of surface water feed the rivers and streams and about 33 cu. km. find the way into the rivers from the underground reservoirs with some time lag. Of the above 25 cu. km. about 20 cu. km. are discharged at time of spate, and it is precisely this water that not only brings no economic benefit, but also causes damage in the river valleys and destroys the beds of rivers and streams.

Present and Prospective Needs

SETTLEMENTS AND INDUSTRY

In 1950 Poland's total population was 25 million and by 1957 it had risen to 28.5 million. In the postwar period Poland has had one of the highest natural rates of population increase in Europe, averaging 1.75 per cent per annum in the years 1950–1954 and going as high as 1.9 per cent in 1955. It has been calculated that in 1975 the population will be 38 million. In 1957, of the total of 28.5 million, 13 million lived in the towns and cities and the remaining 15 million in the countryside.

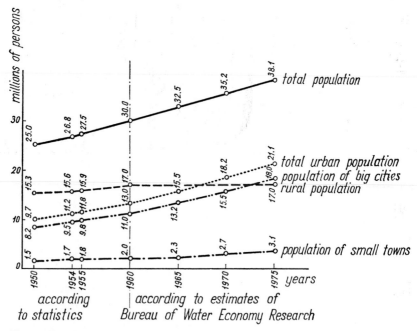

Fig. 62. Population of Poland: 1950–1975

Population data presented here are based on studies carried out before 1959. In the following years new studies were executed and additional data gathered. More recent estimates of expected future population in Poland are presented in the article by K. Secomski. (Ed. note.)

The urban population in 1975 is expected to number 21 million—*i.e.,* 53 per cent of the total—and the rural population 17 million.

As these figures show, the necessary development of the towns and cities confronts the national economy with a big and responsible job within the next twenty years in order to maintain rational economic development. In view of the growth of the urban population it is necessary that waterworks considerably increase the volume of water they provide for the inhabitants, the municipalities, and the light industries which usually consume between 20 per cent and 35 per cent of the piped water.

The amount of water used per capita per day varies with the sanitation facilities and with the extent to which small industries use piped water. This ranges from 30 liters (in houses without water mains and sewerage systems) to 250 or even 400 liters per day per person where houses have sewerage systems and all the facilities for the full use of hot and cold water. According to estimates, waterworks will have to provide about 4.5 million cu. m. of water to towns per day in 1975, compared with 0.53 million in 1950 and 0.88 million in 1954.

The minimum requirements for piped water for the countryside have been put at approximately 0.5 million cu. m. per day. This should be supplied by group water mains.

In total, therefore, apart from industry, the piped-water requirements in 1975 are estimated at approximately 5 million cu. m. per day, or 1.8 billion cu. m. per annum. This means an almost sixfold increase in comparison with 1954, which is not surprising considering that in 1950 about 40 per cent of all urban residents were without piped water.

Industry needs incomparably greater quantities of water. In the mid-nineteenth century the rapid expansion of industry began in Poland as elsewhere. Huge coal and metallurgical centers came into being in Silesia, a textile industry grew up in Łódź and its environs, various manufacturing industries were established in Warsaw, Radom, Kielce and Częstochowa. After World War II, however, industrialization proceeded at a much faster rate and the problems of water supply and sewage disposal have become increasingly difficult.

The long-range plan for the development of the water economy worked out by the Water Economy Committee of the Polish Academy of Sciences estimates that consumption of water for industrial purposes in 1975 will most probably exceed 11 million cu. m. daily—*i.e.,* about 4 cu. km. per annum. This means that the demand for water will be trebled in the period from 1950 to 1975, since the daily industrial water consumption in 1952 amounted to 3.5 million cu. m.

In the final account the demand for water in the towns, countryside, and industries in 1975 has been estimated at 7.02 cu. km. per annum, compared with 2.25 in 1950; this gives an increase of 4.77 cu. km., of which 3.82 cu. km. will be discharged into open waters as sewage; the remainder, 0.95 cu. km., will evaporate, reducing the flow in the rivers.

The great consumption of water by industry necessitates the introduction of planned husbandry of water and the appropriate siting of industry near abundant sources—for instance, on big rivers. Transfers of large quantities of water over considerable distances obviously involve heavy costs in the construction of canals or aqueducts with pumping stations.

Such siting is not always possible since many other factors must be considered in setting up new industrial centers or expanding existing ones. These include a whole number of economic factors as well as the development dynamics of large centers of habitation. As a result such industrial centers as Upper Silesia and Łódź are in watershed areas which do not have sufficient supplies of water of their own.

In such cases the problem must be faced of transferring water stored in areas with surpluses to areas with shortages. It appears that at present about 70 per cent of the towns in the country lie in areas that are entirely without surface streams and rivers or else with small ones with basins not exceeding 1,000 sq. km. in area. In 1975 there will be 158 large towns so placed (65 per cent of the total) and they will have half the total urban population.

Difficulties exist already in providing sufficient water for the population and for industry. Upper Silesia, Łódź, Wałbrzych, and others, suffer from shortages. Map 52 shows the supplies in the main towns and industrial establishments in 1950, and the difficulties encountered at that time in satisfying the demand. The areas of the arrows indicate, according to a chosen scale, the water required. Shading and dots down to solid black have been employed to indicate increasing difficulties in providing water; white indicates the possibility of completely satisfying the demand. Map 53 illustrates the difficulties expected with water supplies in 1975. There will be new deficit areas and the situation will have become worse in present areas of shortage. Along the Vistula and Odra watersheds there will be a disastrous situation unless huge transfers of water are effected.

The increase of demands by industry and settlements in 1975 compared with 1950 amounts approximately to 5 billion cu. m. per annum, of which about 4 billion will be discharged into the rivers as sewage. The remaining 1 billion cu. m. will evaporate as an irretrievable loss, reducing the flow of water in the streams and rivers.

Water supplied to towns and countryside brings with it the problem of disposal of municipal and industrial effluent water. Surface waters—rivers and lakes—have some capacity for self-purification. This capacity is limited, however. If the waters are overloaded with an excessive proportion of effluent in relation to the flow of water or to its surface area then, in extreme cases, biological life in the waters may disappear and

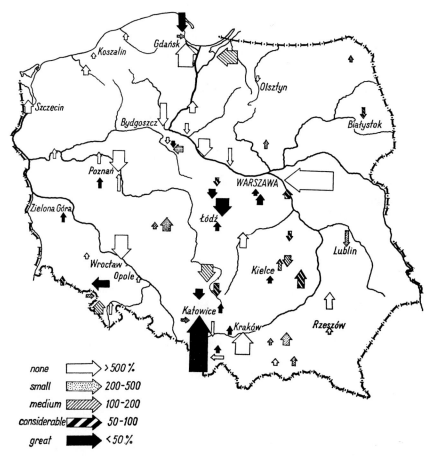

Map 52. Scale of difficulties with water supplies in 1950

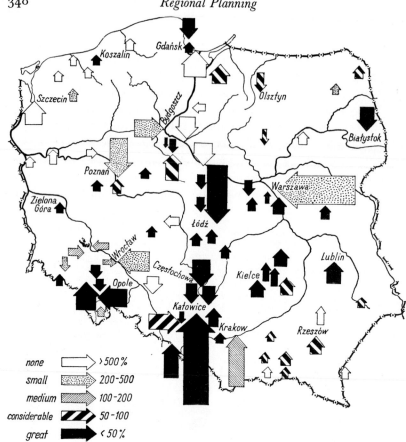

Map 53. Estimated scale of difficulties with water supplies by 1975

the capacity for self-purification be lost. In such cases the rivers are turned into huge sewers, and lakes into sewage reservoirs. The water in them becomes unfit for use not only for the direct needs of man but often for industry and agriculture as well. In many countries, including Poland, the problem of pollution of surface waters is becoming increasingly urgent.

The Bureau of Water Economy Studies at the Polish Academy of Sciences has done research on the pollution of Polish rivers during the low-water period in summertime, when the rate of flow is low. The Bureau determined the ratio of the flow of water to the quantity of sewage added per 24 hours at various points. From calculations made for 1950 it appears that 64 per cent of all sewage was directed to the streams and rivers which do not have large flows at low-water time and in most cases the sewage was discharged into the rivers unpurified. Sewage handling is still unorganized and insufficiently controlled. This has led to a disastrous situation today on such rivers as the Przemsza, Kłodnica, upper Odra, and a number of others. Of sixty-six towns in the Vistula river basin which have sewerage systems, forty-four have no plant at all for purifying sewage.

In the Odra river basin most of the purification plants that exist are not in operation. The situation in industry is even worse in this respect, as many enterprises discharge highly injurious sewage into the rivers without any purification whatever.

Map 54 illustrates pollution of rivers in 1950. The circles in white stand for good rivers, and the darkening of the circles represents pro-

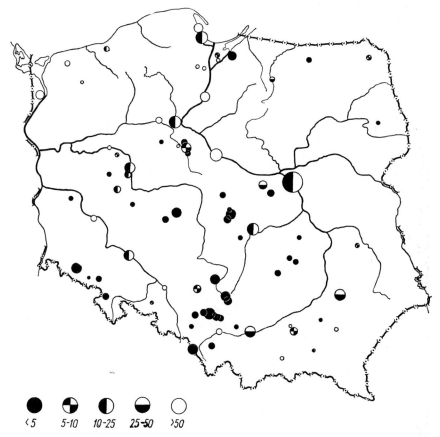

●	⊕	◑	◒	○
‹5	5-10	10-25	25-50	›50

Map 54. Ratio of mean monthly low-water flow Q 75% in the receiver to the quantity of urban and industrial effluents in 1950

gressive worsening of the situation, black standing for a disastrous situation. There are clearly centers of pollution in Silesia, in the Łódź area, and elsewhere. If sewage continues to flow unpurified into rivers, in twenty years, with the expansion of towns and industries, we shall have a situation as pictured in Map 55. There would then be a very dangerous situation since all forms of life would disappear even in the large rivers. Without exaggeration it can be said that while man once fled from rivers in fear of floods, rivers polluted with sewage would prove to be even more dangerous, as it would be more difficult to purify the rivers than to control the floods. The water economy has the great job of building sewage-purification plants which twenty years from now should have a capacity on a national scale of 100 cu. m. per second, or about 9 million cu. m. of sewage daily.

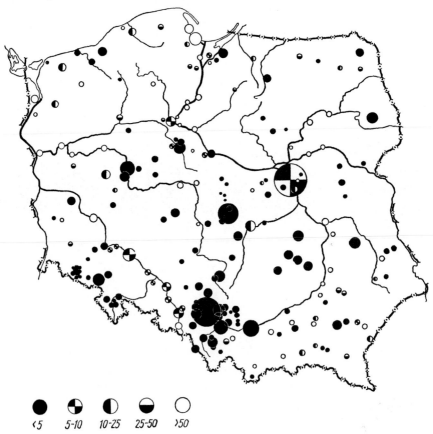

●	◕	◑	◒	○
‹5	5-10	10-25	25-50	›50

Map 55. Estimated ratio of mean monthly low-water flow Q 75% in the receiver to the quantity of urban and industrial effluents in 1975

Agricultural and industrial utilization of sewage should go hand in hand with purification. Agriculture can benefit by directing part of the sewage, especially town sewage, to the fields and meadows as fertilizer, while industry can retrieve valuable materials which are at present lost in effluent.

AGRICULTURE AND FORESTRY

The population of the world today numbers about 2.5 billion and twenty-five years from now it will have grown to 3.5 or 4 billion. In order to ensure better food and clothing for this enormous number of people agricultural output must increase by from 3 per cent to 4 per cent per annum—faster than the expected rate of growth of population. It is not strange, therefore, that each national state strives for self-sufficiency in satisfying the fundamental needs of its citizens.

In accordance with the principle of self-sufficiency in staple food supplies and with a specific diet, the size of the total population is limited by the volume of these commodities required. This in turn determines the necessary dimensions of the agricultural and stock-farming output. The expected growth of agricultural output to provide for the increase in population entails intensifying agriculture, which increases the water requirements of plants and animals. Therefore, before the water economy can be expected to undertake tasks imposed by the future requirements of agriculture and forestry, the future water needs of these sectors must first be established. Further, the effects of this increased use of water on the flow in the streams and rivers must be determined, for a good part of the water used by plants transpires into the air.

Analysis of the present consumption of food in Poland shows that although it does not differ much from that in neighboring countries so far as calories are concerned, the diet cannot be regarded as satisfactory, for it contains too many bulky foods such as potatoes and bread and too little meat, fat, sugar, fruit and vegetables (Figure 63).

The prospect is that by 1975, for which the basis of a water-economy plan is being worked out, food supplies will have to be increased not only to satisfy the population growth but also to accommodate a highly desirable change in the pattern of nutrition. Increases in output necessary to satisfy the demand for agricultural produce, according to the estimates of the Bureau of Water Economy Studies at the Polish Academy of Sciences, are presented in Table 25.

The planned expansion of stock farming and the associated increase

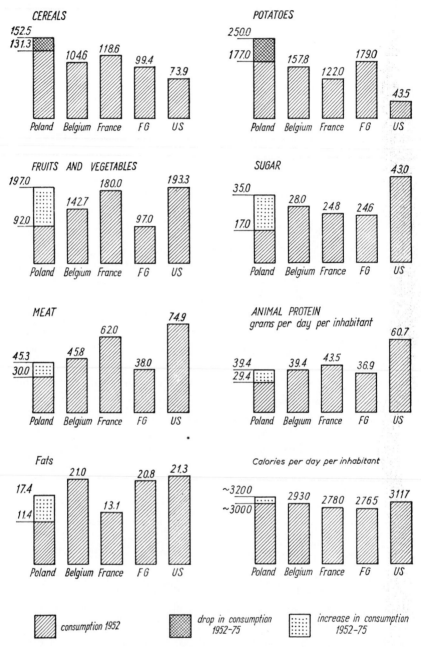

Fig. 63. Daily food consumption per person in grams

Table 25. GROWTH OF OUTPUT NECESSARY TO SATISFY DEMAND, 1952-1975

Produce	Unit	1952	1975	Increase	Increase per cent
Wheat	mlns. tons	1.80	4.35	2.55	142
Rye	mlns. tons	6.00	8.40	2.40	40
Potatoes	mlns. tons	29.40	42.90	13.50	46
Sugar-beet	mlns. tons	6.60	12.60	6.00	91
Hay	mlns. tons	9.60	23.70	14.10	145
Cattle	mlns. of head	7.20	12.90	5.70	79
Hogs	mlns. of head	9.75	14.20	4.45	46
Meat	mlns. tons	0.90	1.95	1.05	117
Lard	mlns. tons	0.17	0.32	0.15	88
Milk	mlns. tons	8.80	20.30	11.50	132

in fodder produced from meadows are dependent in the first place on the provision of adequate volumes of water for irrigation. It appears that about 4 million hectares of meadow should be worked more intensively. Calculations of the Bureau of Water Economy Studies show that 8 billion cu. m. of water will have to be used for irrigation in a year of medium dryness and even more in a drought year. A considerable proportion of the water earmarked for irrigation will evaporate and this will reduce the flow of the rivers, mainly in the vegetative period during which the flow of many of the rivers is insufficient even today. Taking into account the increased evaporation due to intensification of agriculture on arable land and the increase of areas under forest, it appears that the total irretrievable losses reach approximately 10 billion cu. m.

Calculations show that the smallest proportion of the loss in discharge (17 per cent) is accounted for by the forests. Tilled fields account for 33 per cent, while the largest loss is from meadows—50 per cent. These figures, of course, relate to the proportions set in the Plan. In order to determine their influence on the low-water flows during the four summer months, these irretrievable losses have been computed, the result being 5.5 cu. km. for an average year and 7.1 cu. km. for an average dry year.

Water Consumers

WATER-POWER INDUSTRY

In the postwar period the development of the power industry the world over has been proceeding at an accelerated pace. The average capacity added each year in selected countries in the years 1945–1955 is given below:

Table 26. AVERAGE POWER CAPACITY ADDED ANNUALLY, 1945–1955

Nation	Per cent	Nation	Per cent
USSR	17	France	13
Italy	15	Belgium	13
Austria	14	Sweden	6
Poland	13.5	Switzerland	4.6

These figures show that countries that have lagged behind Switzerland, Sweden, or Belgium in the production of electricity are displaying an unmistakable tendency to catch up. Since the last war Poland has made great strides, generating 21.5 billion kw-hr in 1957 compared with 5.8 billion kw-hr in 1946. In comparison with the electricity consumption per capita in other countries, this is not a large amount. In Sweden, for instance, the figure in 1953 was 3,121 kw-hr per inhabitant; in Switzerland, 2,800; in the German Democratic Republic, 1,340; in Belgium, 1,130; in Czechoslovakia, 580; in the U.S.S.R., 660; and in Poland, 546 kw-hr per inhabitant (760 kw-hr in 1957). Poland, however, is a country with relatively small water-power resources and their utilization is insignificant. Map 56 shows the water-power resources of Europe and the extent to which they were exploited in 1953.

It can be seen there that the water-power resources of such a small country as Norway are as great as 104 billion kw-hr, 20 per cent of the resources being used. Poland is a long way down the list, behind Rumania and Germany, with 13 billion kw-hr, of which only 4 per cent is being used at present.

Rivers in Poland do not have large falls like those in the Alps, in Scandinavia, and in the Caucasus. Dams have been built, like that at Rożnów on the River Dunajec which impounds water to a depth of 30 m. The power is utilized by a hydroelectric station with an installed capacity of 50 million-watts (50,000 kw). The hydroelectric station at Dychów also uses a head of 30 m., obtained by means of a small rise in head level resulting from a weir across the Bobra River, and the exploitation of the drop of a long section of the river (about 30 km.) by a canal cut across a loop formed by the river. The open canal that brings water to the turbine house has a minimum gradient and a length of 10 km. The water-power resources are distributed as shown in Map 57. It

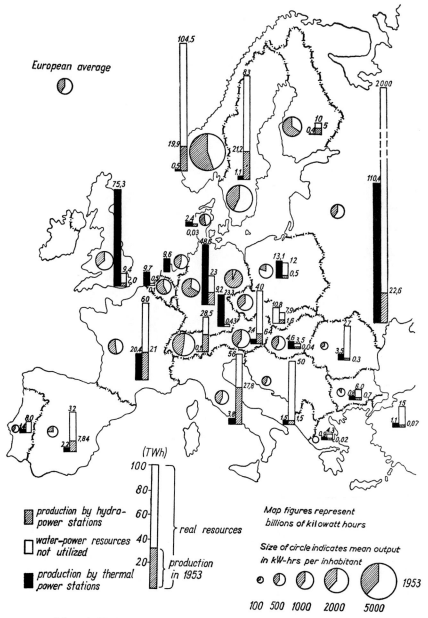

European average

(TWh)

- 100
- 80
- 60
- 40
- 20

real resources

production in 1953

production by hydro-power stations

water-power resources not utilized

production by thermal power stations

Map figures represent billions of kilowatt hours

Size of circle indicates mean output in kW-hrs per inhabitant

100 500 1000 2000 5000

1953

Map 56. Electricity production and water-power resources, 1953

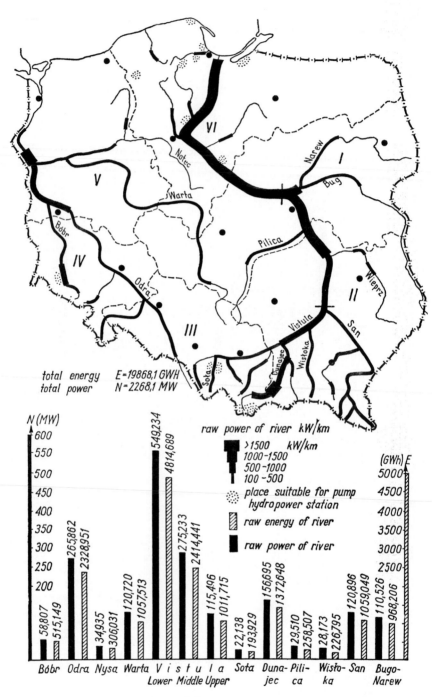

Map 57. Water-power resources

is planned to build reservoirs and cascades on Polish rivers in the next twenty years to make it possible to use water power to generate 7 billion kw-hr per annum.

WATER TRANSPORT

The state of waterways in Poland has not been satisfactory to date. As a result of constant fluctuations in the waters of the uncontrolled rivers there are significant changes in the depth of navigable channels. Generally speaking, they do not meet the requirements of rational modern navigation. Man-made waterways (canals) or canalized sectors of rivers together with the uncontrolled rivers have been neglected for years and do not form a system of waterways adapted to the transport needs of the country as do the splendidly developed systems of France and Germany. The volume of goods carried by inland waterways and the magnitude of the work done by Polish waterways is insignificant in comparison with traffic in railway goods.

Table 27 gives comparative data concerning the ratio of length of waterways to length of railway lines and the ratio of goods carried in tons and work in ton-kilometers for water navigation and railways in Poland and several other European countries. From the table it appears that the distribution of our waterways and railway lines in relation to the area of the country is similar to that of France. The volume of goods carried and work done by the waterways, however, is altogether different in the two countries. In France goods-traffic on the waterways reaches 52.5 million tons and 8.3 billion ton-kilometers, whereas in Poland the comparable figures are barely 4.85 million tons and 570 million ton-kilometers. Water transport in France carries 31 per cent as much goods as the railways; in Poland, on the other hand, the proportion is a mere 2.2 per cent. The figures speak only too eloquently of the neglect of the rivers, which in their present state cannot be considered even partially as waterways capable of transporting large volumes of goods.

The question arises, however, whether in view of the growth of other large-scale means of transport such as railways and motor haulage, the construction and improvement of the waterway system in Poland is not out of date. It appears that in other countries which have dense networks of railways and motor roads, water transport has been continuing to grow, as pictured in Figure 64 (France).

It appears from the work of the Polish Bureau of Water Economy Studies that in working out over-all integrated solutions for the water

Table 27. GOODS CARRIED BY INLAND WATERWAYS AND RAILWAYS IN 1954 AND COMPARISON OF RATIOS OF LENGTH OF WATERWAYS AND RAILWAYS AND RATIO OF GOODS CARRIED BY NAVIGATION AND RAIL

Countries	Area in thousands of sq. km.	Length of inland waterways				Unit	Traffic		Navigation traffic as percentage of railway traffic	Navigation traffic as percentage of railway + navigation traffic
		Length of railways		Length of waterways as percentage of length of railways	Length of waterways as percentage of length of railways + waterways		Navigation	Railways		
		Total in hundreds of km.	in km. per sq. km.							
Belgium	31	1,569 / 4,980	5.1 / 16.0	31.9	24	million tons / billion ton-km.	51.1 / 4.1	62.5 / 5.6	82 / 73	45 / 42.3
France	551	7,807 / 39,800	1.42 / 7.5	19.0	16.4	million tons / billion ton-km.	52.5 / 8.3	169.3 / 41.5	31 / 20	23.7 / 15.8
Federal Germany	245	4,900 / 31,500	2 / 12.4	15.4	13.4	million tons / billion ton-km.	109.4 / 25	229.0 / 51.6	48 / 48	32.2 / 32.6
Poland	312	4,500 / 23,090	1.44 / 7.5	19.2	16.3	million tons / billion ton-km.	4.848 / 0.574	221.9 / 48.2	2.2 / 1.2	2.1 / 1.6

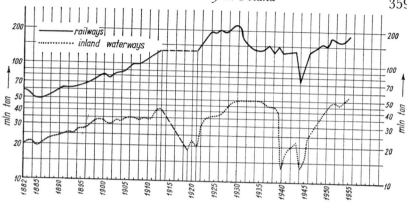

Fig. 64. Growth of railways and inland waterways in France

economy of the country, we can create a system of waterways, in particular:

(1) a 1,000-ton waterway along the Vistula from the outlet of the Przemsza to Nowa Huta with canalization of the Przemsza to Mysłowice;

(2) a 600-ton waterway along the Vistula from Nowa Huta to Sandomierz;

(3) a 1,000-ton waterway along the Vistula from Warsaw to Gdańsk, including the Żerań-Zegrze Canal;

(4) a 1,000-ton Central Canal linking the Upper Silesian Industrial District with the Vistula at localities between Włocławek and Płock via Częstochowa and Łódź;

(5) a 600-ton waterway along the Odra River from Racibórz to Szczecin;

(6) a 600-ton waterway from the Vistula to the Odra (via Bydgoszcz);

(7) a 600-ton transit waterway (as part of the east–west waterway system) running along the Bug River from Brześć to the outlet of the Vistula;

(8) a 600-ton branch from Racibórz along the Odra to Morawska Ostrava, with a prospect of an outlet into the Danube river basin.

The development of Poland's waterways into a navigable system will make possible convenient transport at low cost in domestic and foreign traffic. Poland will cease to be a bottleneck between the highly developed system of waterways of the west and the rapidly growing waterways of the east.

The connection of the waterways provided by the Bug and Vistula rivers, the Central Canal and the Odra River, with an outlet into the Danube river basin, will open up tremendous commercial vistas for the north–south route, giving in Polish territory the equivalent of the western Rhine–Main Danube Canal. Poland has all the natural prerequisites for becoming a country linking together waterways of the west, east and, south to serve common interests.

Floods

From 1310 to 1955, a period of almost 650 years, eighty-two serious floods were recorded in the Odra river basin, most of them major disasters. Flooding by the Vistula and its tributaries, especially the mountain tributaries, has been more common and much more violent, thus causing even more damage than the Odra.

Flood statistics of the Vistula river basin are less detailed than those for the Odra basin, but detailed material can be found concerning the Żuławy district on the lower Vistula, which at one time was the area in greatest danger of flooding. In the past 625 years there have been 132 floods (on the average once every five years) when the swollen waters of the Vistula burst the levees and flooded the areas that had been protected. Construction of levees along the lower Vistula to protect the Żuławy area began in the eighteenth century. The areas most exposed to floods today are those in the Małopolska region where the Carpathian tributaries of the Vistula add a great deal of water. The greatest such disaster in this century occurred in 1934. The raging waters flooded about 100,000 hectares of land where the Danube joins the Vistula and the levees were washed away in a number of places. The resulting damage was estimated at 75 million złotys in the currency of that time.

Water economy in Poland has a major task in improving the protection against floods, mainly active protection, that is by the construction of reservoirs with a total impounding capacity of 4 billion cu. m. and by afforesting the slopes and mountains, as well as by passive protection, that is river-control work, especially on mountain streams, and additions to levees.

Perspective Plan and Trends of Development of the Water Economy in Poland

In both the south and north of Poland are areas where water needs can be satisfied by local resources and where surplus water can be impounded for transfer to areas with short supplies. Particularly favorable hydrological and topographical conditions for storing water are to be found in the southern part of the country in the Carpathian foothills and to some extent in the Sudeten Mountains (Map 58).

The distribution of water resources indicates that the Carpathian foothill area should play a special role in improving the water economy over large regions of the country. This area has a large annual rainfall (21 cu. km.) and suitable run-off which amounts to 9 cu. km. Though it accounts for only one-eighth of the area of the Vistula basin it provides almost one-third of the outflow of the entire basin. The rhythm of the annual swelling of the rivers in this area makes possible more rational use of the storage capacity of reservoirs built in the Carpathians than is possible in the case of valley reservoirs, since the waters in this area rise in the summer as well as in the spring.

The mountain areas should become the principal water stores, with huge volumes of pure healthy water.

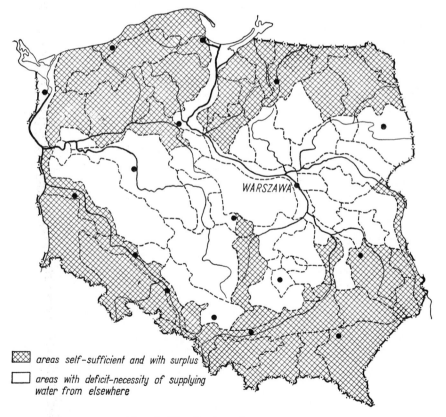

areas self-sufficient and with surplus

areas with deficit-necessity of supplying water from elsewhere

Map 58. Distribution of water resources

Water is in short supply in large areas in the Wielkopolska-Kujawy and Mazowsze-Podlesie plains, in the Vistula and Odra watersheds and the Silesian highlands.

If the water economy is to meet the needs of the various sectors of the national economy, a numer of fundamental investments will be necessary. A picture of the Poland of the future is taking place: a whole system of reservoirs is being built in the Carpathian foothills; reservoirs are going up on the Soła, Skawa, Raba, Dunajec, Poprad, Wisłoka, Wisłok, and San rivers with a total storage capacity of approximately 3.5 billion cu. m. The water from these reservoirs is intended in the first place to cover shortages during low-water periods on the Vistula, and will ensure a reserve for industry, partly in Silesia and partly in the industrial region which is growing up along the upper Vistula. The impounding of water during high-water periods will make for better flood protection in the valley of the Vistula and its tributaries. The water will also be harnessed to generate electricity (700 million kw-hr per annum). Forest areas will be increased, which will help slow down the run-off of surface water and protect the soil against erosion.

In order to accelerate the rate of growth of settlements and industry in the valley of the upper Vistula from the Przemsza to the San, an upper Vistula cascade will be built and the Przemsza canalized. This will ensure supplies of water for industry and the transport of coal from Silesia for this area. Hydroelectric power stations will be built at the falls produced by the cascades. On the middle reaches of the Vistula, at present the most untamed stretch of the river, a reservoir will be built. It will work together with the Carpathian reservoirs to even out the flow on the Vistula for the needs of the centers of habitation, industry, and agriculture. The canalization of the middle reaches of the Vistula will not take place, however, until a late date.

The cascades of the lower Vistula will be used mainly for power, but will also be designed to increase supplies of water for industry and agriculture. The power stations of the cascades will utilize water power to produce about 4.5 billion kw-hr of electricity per year. All the cascades of the Vistula will have locks for letting through vessels of a deadweight of up to 1,000 tons. A modern waterway for the transport of goods will thus come into being.

The Bug will be canalized from Brześć to its outlet. The resulting waterway will comprise the eastern section of the east–west route. It will make one huge transport system of European waterways going from west to east.

The waters of the Bug impounded in reservoirs will serve agriculture and even out the flow of the river. They will also produce electricity. In the northeastern region in the Mazurian Lakes district the waters impounded by raising the level of the lakes will be transferred for irrigation purposes in the Narew river basin.

A central canal, 300 kilometers long, will be built running westward from the Vistula between Płock and Włocławek, through the Łódź and Częstochowa regions, reaching Silesia to join the canalized Przemsza in the Mysłowice region. The canal will be the backbone of Poland's water economy. The water pumped from the Vistula into this canal at the rate of 100 cu. m. per sec. will make it possible to fill many economic needs; farms will get 800 million cu. m. of water for irrigating crops. This water will be distributed by means of streams in the areas with short supplies.

The canal built to join the lower reaches of the Vistula with the main part of the Upper Silesian Industrial District can be easily adapted for navigation without high costs. The central canal will then take over transport of coal to many centers of industry and habitation along its banks as well as in the Vistula river valley from Włocławek to Gdańsk, together with coal exported through Gdańsk. This canal will connect the east–west and north–south waterways.

The key role in the Odra river basin will be played by a reservoir, to hold about 700 million cu. m., which is to be built in the vicinity of Racibórz. The water from this reservoir will ensure supplies to the Odra River during dry periods, thus enabling modern navigation to continue even below the canalized reaches of the river. Supplies of water will be guaranteed for farmers for irrigating adjoining areas. Reservoirs will also be built on the tributaries of the Odra in the Sudeten Mountains. The utilization of the impounded waters by hydroelectric power stations will produce 160 million kw-hr of electricity per annum.

With the realization of the Water Economy Plan (Map 59) the total storage capacity of reservoirs will rise to 9 billion cu. m. The water from these reservoirs will fully cover the needs of the population, industry, and agriculture. The irrigation of meadows will enable an increase in hay crops from 25 to 57 quintals per hectare from an area of approximately 4 million hectares. The irrigation of tilled land coupled with proper farming based on the newest developments of science and agricultural engineering will help to increase crops to a sufficient degree to cover the demand for food.

I class waterway
II class waterway
planned navigable canal
existing navigable canal
transfers of water
industrial effluents
canalizing weir
peak-pump power station

△ planned lowland reservoir
▲ existing lowland reservoir
◩ planned mountain reservoir
◪ existing mountain reservoir
◭ planned power reservoir
◮ planned impounding reservoir, primarily for power

Map 59. The water economy plan

The water-power resources of the rivers will be utilized to a high degree by hydroelectric power stations which, with a total peak capacity of approximately 1,900 mw., will produce about 7 billion kw-hr per annum. There will be reserves of water for industry, towns, and settlements; the rivers and canals will bring the water to the large industrial centers. The agricultural utilization of sewage and special sewage-purification plants will protect the rivers and canals from contamination. New waterways with a total length of 2,200 km. will come into being to transport about 25 million tons of goods per annum. At the same time, flood protection will be increased.

CHAPTER 15

Rural Planning in Poland

Marian Benko

Introduction

BEFORE we approach the actual problems of rural planning in Poland, it may be useful to present some data on the rural regions and their economic and demographic situation. The data characterize the situation as of 1961–1962.

The total area of the country is 312,520 sq. km.; 65 per cent of this (approximately 20,321,000 hectares) is agricultural land, and about 25 per cent (7,750,000 hectares) forest. Out of a total population amounting to over 30 million persons in 1961, approximately 15.5 million persons (that is, over 51 per cent) were living in rural settlements. During the last decade, the population increase in Poland has been between 440,000 and 530,000 persons per year. In 1960 over 11,200,000 persons (over 38 per cent of the total population) were living from agriculture. Farm units, divided into two groups, in June, 1961, had reached the following figures: state and cooperative farms—about 10,220 units with a total area of approximately 3,320,000 hectares (2,700,000 hectares of this being agricultural land); and individual farmholdings—about 3.6 million units with an area of 19,473,000 hectares (17,552,000 hectares of agricultural land); many of these farmholdings are associated within more than 25,000 rural cooperatives called "kółka rolnicze."

The figures quoted above can serve as evidence of:

(1) A relatively high population density, approaching 100 inhabitants per sq. km. This is higher than the European average (87 inhabitants per sq. km. in 1960).

(2) A high population index for agricultural land, amounting to approximately 150 persons per 100 hectares.

(3) A very high agricultural population index—about 55 persons per 100 hectares of agricultural land.

(4) Great segmentation of the farmholding structure, especially in terms of individual farms, the average area of these units being 5

hectares. It is to be remarked that nearly 63 per cent of the farms have a total area of less than 5 hectares, while about 26 per cent have an area of from 5 to 10 hectares.

This gives an idea of the complex economic and social problems in our villages. Of course, some important changes have resulted from the reconstruction of the economic system in Poland within the framework of the socialistic economy. Some of these changes are shown in Table 28, illustrating the population pattern in Poland with regard to the source of subsistence in different periods.

Table 28. CHANGES IN PROPORTION

Population	Prewar	1950	1960
Agricultural (per cent)	60	47	38
Nonagricultural (per cent)	40	53	62

The increase in the population depending upon nonagricultural occupations has been caused by the rapid industrialization of the country after World War II. It is expected that further progress in industrialization will lead by 1980–1985 to (1) a marked decrease in the population living from agriculture; (2) the maintenance—presumably without notable changes—of the population residing in villages; (3) a considerable extension of the towns so as to enable them to accommodate the total natural population increase; and (4) a change in the character of the rural population, with a percentage decrease in the agricultural group in favor of the group depending upon work in industry and services.

During the war the Polish rural economy suffered immense damage. Among the heavy losses were the destruction of livestock, approximately 470,000 ruined farms, tens of thousands of square kilometers lying waste. A great part of these losses has been made up during the reconstruction period; this is shown by the production indices, which are perceptibly higher than the prewar figures.

The land under grain, amounting in 1946 to 10 million hectares only (as the result of the war devastations), had already risen by 1950 to 15 million hectares and exceeds at present 15.3 million hectares. The corresponding figures for the culture of potatoes are: 1946, 1.66 million hectares, 1950, 2.6 million hectares, and 1960, 2.8 million hectares; for sugar beets: 1946, 170,000 hectares, 1950, 287,000 hectares, and 1960, 420,000 hectares. The four fundamental cereals (wheat, rye, barley and oats) which yielded 13.7 quintals per hectare annually in the prewar period (1934–1938) within the present boundaries of Poland, yielded during 1947–1949 an average of less than 12 quintals per hectare, but rose by 1961 to 18 quintals per hectare.

The total head of cattle, 3.9 million in 1946, mounted in 1961 to about 9.2 million, approaching the prewar figure. The number of swine, amounting in 1938 to approximately 9.7 million, fell in 1946 to 2.7 million but rose during the following years and reached the figure of 13.4 million in 1961. The production of meat, amounting to about 900,000 tons in 1938, decreased to 312,000 tons in 1946, yet rose by 1961 to 1,800,000 tons—twice as much as before the war.

These few examples illustrate the increase in agricultural production. Nevertheless, we still consider present production indices in farming unsatisfactory. A further increase in agricultural output—necessitated by the high birth rate—depends upon the effects of various factors, such as adequate organization of the settlement system and a well-conceived rural development scheme. This matter is certainly of very great economic importance; moreover, it possesses outstanding significance as a basic social question, since it involves the working and living conditions of many millions of people.

The present situation of the organization of the settlement network and rural development is shown by the following data. Apart from the minor settlement forms, small hamlets, and so on, there are in Poland at present over 40,000 villages organized into 5,250 units called *gromadas,* the smallest administrative units of the country. As a rule there are several settlement units in each gromada. The average population of a gromada is approximately 3,000 persons. Yet the actual figures vary between 1,000 and 4,000 or more persons, depending upon the size of the individual gromada and the population density. The average area of agricultural land of a gromada is approximately 3,900 hectares.

Over several years we have observed a constant extension of rural building programs in Poland. This is exemplified by the approximate number of rooms which have been made available during successive planning periods, or have to be completed in the current five-year plan:

1950–1955	325,000 rooms
1956–1960	662,500 rooms
1961–1965	950,000 rooms

In the present five-year plan special stress is also laid on agricultural buildings and above all on the construction of shelters for livestock. A further considerable expansion in the construction of rural housing and agricultural buildings is forecast for the period 1966–1980.

Parallel to the development of rural housing and farm buildings, there is notable activity in the construction of social and cultural facilities (schools, social clubhouses, health centers) and also communal equipment (water-supply, street systems). The great investment effort required by this must of course be made in the most effective way both in terms of the national economy and in terms of the working and living conditions of the village population.

Above all there is the problem of skillful design of the new development pattern; the modern rural settlement system must be shaped to meet the needs of the contemporary community, and to work toward both rapid progress in agriculture and improvement of the social and living conditions of the rural population. The previous pattern of rural development was far from able to satisfy these requirements.

Characteristics of the Rural Settlement System in Poland

In the past the rural settlement network in Poland was characterized, in general, by a large number of middle-sized and small villages—that is, by a relatively high development density. Among the factors causing this situation we may list the complicated soil structure and the geological structure of the landscape, both results of the movements of the huge Scandinavian glacier. Another factor was the division of feudal property at the time the basic pattern of rural settlements was being shaped.

Calculating roughly from the figures given earlier—over 40,000 rural settlements with about 15.5 million inhabitants, and 20,400,000 hectares of agricultural land—we find that the average rural unit in Poland has 390 inhabitants and an area slightly over 500 hectares. This is of course merely a statistical average; there are rural settlements in Poland much larger than this. A number of such settlements now having the character of agriculture and service centers were small feudal towns in the past. Some of them have retained their municipal rights.

Large rural settlements with a mixed population (peasants and workers) of up to several thousand also developed in industrial regions —for instance, in Silesia and in the voivodship of Kraków—during the rise of capitalism. Nevertheless, the overwhelming majority of rural settlements in Poland are smaller than the statistical mean.

Another typical feature of many rural settlements is the dispersion of farm developments into "colonies" (minor farms). Many of these scattered "colonies" emerged during the last decades as a result of the division of large estates, and were built on the isolated lands of individual proprietors and not as organized and concentrated settlements.

Development in length is also typical of a large part of the existing rural settlements. There exist villages many kilometers long, stretched out along rivers (for instance, in the valleys of mountainous areas) and along important roads.

Moreover, we find in Poland rural settlements in which development pattern shows overdensity, as in the old villages dating from feudal times; in these villages the division of land among family members has led to the creation of plots much too narrow for adequate development. The pattern also reveals excessive thriftlessness—observed in settlement areas where the plots are several tens of meters and more in width. This, in turn, tends to stretch out the development pattern and to increase the costs of roads, electrification, and other technical adjustments and equipment.

Existing Interdependencies between Elements of the Rural Settlement System

The present state of rural development in Poland requires effective correction. First of all, selection must be made among the rural settlements of those which—owing to function, situation, production conditions, traffic connections, and so on—are best suited to become development units. Endowed with the required services as well as the necessary communal and technical facilities, these units will gradually attract the rural population. Concurrently, it is necessary to designate settlements that should be condemned to decay or be transformed into cores of large modern breeding farms.

A theoretical basis for modern rural development in Poland has not so far been established. Yet the necessity for controlling current investment processes requires the formulation of some principles—if only preliminary ones—which take into account both agricultural production and the social and living conditions.

Two starting points for theoretical development have been chosen: (1) the characteristic interdependencies existing between elements of the rural settlement network; and (2) the changes which should be brought about in the present pattern.

For a better understanding of actual conditions in rural Poland, it seems desirable to compare the living conditions of the urban and the rural populations as far as production, housing, and services are concerned.

A town, especially a large one, usually includes all basic functions:

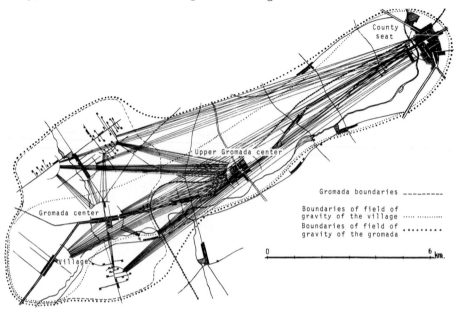

County
seat

Upper Gromada center

Gromada boundaries _ _ _ _ _ _ _

Boundaries of field of
gravity of the village ········ ···········
Boundaries of field of
gravity of the gromada ········

Gromada center

Villages

0   6 km.

Map 60. Existing area of intersettlement gravitations among the group of settlement units of a "gromada," the "gromada" center, and the county seat

not only production and housing but also services and public utilities.
The latter are designed to meet, in part, the needs of the population
living outside the town in the areas dependent on it. On the contrary,
a village, especially a small one (which is most common in Poland), provides housing and agricultural functions. It can fulfill only a few of
the existing service needs. The remaining social, cultural, and economic wants are usually satisfied by public utilities and services situated
outside the small village, mostly in larger settlements—for instance,
central gromada villages, upper gromada villages (small towns), or even
district centers.[1]

We may say that the balance between the basic needs and the public
utilities that serve these needs is maintained, as a general rule, in the
towns, with a surplus in favor of the surrounding population. In
the countryside, achieving such a balance at present requires studies of
the services and facilities distributed over a whole group of rural settlements. It is necessary to observe carefully the mutual gravitations,
relationships, and development patterns of the series of units that form
such a group (illustrated in Maps 60 and 61).

[1] "Powiat" in Polish. There are at present 317 districts (or counties), not including towns
with the administrative functions of a district. The territory of a "powiat" ranges between
several hundred and one thousand square kilometers.

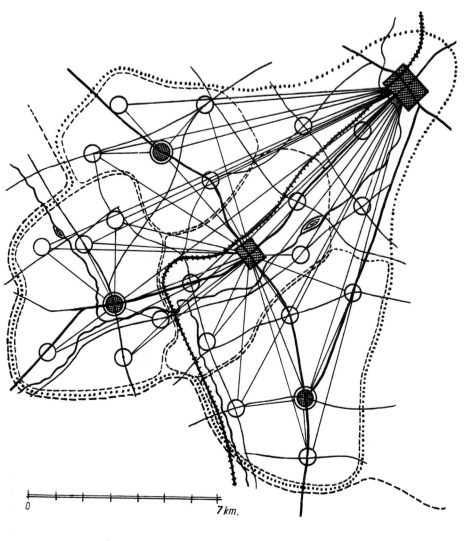

------- County boundaries
------- Gromada boundaries
°°°°°°°°°°°°° Boundaries of field of gravity
——————— Lines of gravitation
⃝ Village ◉ Large gromada village
▨ Center of Upper Gromada
▨ County seat

Map 61. Existing intersettlement gravity field of a "gromada" complex in relation to the county seat

The development program of a city (and also, of course, the socio-economic basis for its spatial organization) is determined by the following functions. Production activities are defined by the national economic plans, which take into account both prospective growth and the distribution of productive forces. Service activities are not limited to the given town and its population only, but extend over the whole region. These functions must be defined in the regional plan; if such a plan is lacking, indices must be established by means of the guiding principles elaborated by the respective organs of economic planning.

In rural settlements, on the contrary, production activities, in terms of agricultural output, are determined above all by the area of land and the geographical environment. Increase in production can take place only within certain limits—by soil improvement as well as by the intensification and rationalization of production. The service activities for a great many villages lie outside their territory. To some degree, a village may be compared to a housing block or (in some cases) to a neighborhood, but never to a self-sufficient settlement unit such as the town.

A large city, considered as the sum of the functions of all its elements and basic balances, corresponds in Poland to a settlement complex of the following pattern: the small village—the gromada village—the upper gromada village (a small town)—the district center. The basic functions of life and work of the village population are limited to this settlement complex. Not included are special situations and needs requiring public services such as schools of university standing, specialized hospitals, sanatoria, organized recreation, theaters, and so on—or the possible commuting of the rural population to jobs outside the district. Internal commuting within the boundaries of the district may modify the theoretical pattern to a lesser or greater degree, depending upon the saturation level of the given area with industrial production or other socioeconomic activities such as organized recreation or touring.

When the organization of rural settlements within a district is considered, it is usually necessary to deal with villages of varying importance; this gradation results both from the size of the villages and from their situation within the settlement network. The mutually superimposed fields of intersettlement gravitation actually cover the territory of the whole district.

The district can be seen as the area within which at the same time (1) the basic activities and the movement of the rural population take place; (2) the fundamental needs of the population are balanced with the public utilities provided to meet them; and (3) the statistical and economic data is gathered. For this reason the powiat (district) is being adopted in Poland (and the counterpart of the powiat in many other countries) as the territorial unit most fit for those rural-development planning schemes that enable the formulation of a program for an adequate evolution of both the over-all rural settlement system and the individual villages.

In this connection it seems necessary to remark that the development schemes for rural settlement groups within districts are being elaborated by planners at the offices of the chief architects of voivodships, while the plans for individual villages are being prepared mainly in the district offices, according to the guiding principles set up by the voivodship planning offices.

Problems of the Transformation of the Rural Settlement System

The characteristics of the rural network in Poland have been presented above as static features in terms of existing conditions. Nevertheless, the profound socioeconomic changes and structural transformations which have been taking place in our country since World War II have been continually penetrating farther into the rural areas.

The large state farms, the state agricultural machinery stations, and the cooperative farms are the basic elements in remodeling the rural economy in Poland. Moreover, the farming circles (kółka rolnicze), organizing farmers in common activities for the purposes of raising the standard of agricultural production and of promoting village culture, are laying the foundation for the modernization of the rural economy and of living conditions in the villages by means of simple cooperation.

Both the present conditions of production and the living conditions of the rural population require important changes in the existing rural settlement system. Planning in this area has made various basic assumptions, some of which should be presented here.

(1) In most countries following either the capitalistic or the socialistic model, the system of small individual farmholdings is, for economic reasons, definitely declining. In our country the change-over to an efficient modern farming system requiring a high standard of mechanization is hardly compatible with a scattered development of little settlements. The question is whether there is any sense in maintaining small villages, minor farmholdings, and "colonies."

(2) Concentration of development leads to territorial economies. Scattered settlements, on the contrary, use more land for buildings,

equipment, and roads. These considerations have essential significance, especially in Poland where the population density is high, the birth rate is very high, and the soil is only of average quality.

(3) Modernization of agricultural production and (in turn) increase of agricultural output can be achieved only by equipping rural settlements with equipment which is difficult or sometimes even impossible to introduce into a scattered development, consisting of small villages, "colonies," or minor farmholdings. First of all there is the question of electric power, water supply, paved roads, and so on. Without modern technical equipment, it will be extremely hard, often quite impossible, to increase present agricultural production. Rural electrification in Poland, which extended to 66 per cent of individual farms, had to bypass a considerable part of the small individual farmholdings scattered in "colonies."

A detailed analysis of the problem of water supply leads to the conclusion that in the majority of cases the construction of reservoirs and water conduits becomes economically effective in conditions in Poland only in a concentrated settlement of approximately 1,000 inhabitants.

(4) The pressure of new social, economic, and cultural requirements in Poland is an important factor in developing existing services rapidly and setting up new ones. The shorter working hours that will accompany progress in agricultural production will certainly speed up the growth of these services. For economic reasons, the adequate distribution of services and equipment must be planned: they should not be located in all small villages. The installation of public services is economically most effective of course when the greatest possible number of persons can make use of them. Thus, for instance, a primary school with a full program is justified—from an economic standpoint—when it serves approximately 2,000 inhabitants. The same is true of the "social house" containing an auditorium for movies and other events, a nursery, a dispensary (health-service station), and various handicraft workshops. When the population is living in "colonies" scattered over extended areas, the use of such facilities is limited by factors such as weather conditions and the time and effort necessary for occasional long journeys.

(5) The migration of the rural population to towns must be seen as generally desirable. Yet, considered in relation to population structure, it raises objections because it is mainly young men and women who migrate to the towns, eager to seek the improved living and cultural conditions that a small rural settlement is hardly able to offer. An increase in this movement may obstruct the modernization and intensification of agricultural production.

(6) In order to improve living, social, and cultural conditions in rural areas, and to equip farms with modern fittings, it may be desirable to concentrate the population in larger settlements; if the distance between the agricultural buildings and the workplaces in the fields is too great it may have a disadvantageous effect on output. Therefore, optimum solutions appropriate to the actual conditions of the given environment must be sought. The terrain of Poland is a complicated mosaic (resulting from the movement of the Scandinavian glacier), making the adoption of uniform agriculture for extended areas difficult. The soils need cow dung as well as mineral fertilizers. The planned intensification of cattle-breeding and swine-breeding for the future will require an increase in pasturage appropriate to climatic and soil conditions. These factors will tend to increase the total amount of local transport—carrying agricultural products to the farm buildings and fertilizer to the fields.

All these factors have to be considered in determining the optimum size of production units (each composed of several farmholdings) for future state and cooperative farms. In most of Poland the optimum sizes will probably fall within several hundred hectares. Nevertheless, because of the available modern means of mechanical transport and a sufficiently developed road pattern, the location of such farms will not necessarily be identical with the dwellings of workers and their families.

(7) The spatial organization of a modern settlement requires intensive use of land area, permitting economical installation and development of systems of power, roads, water supply, and so on. An economical use of land is also recommended for rural housing. It will be of great importance—far more than at present—to plan, for example, for single houses or buildings of more than one story, or at least for buildings with an attic suitable for dwelling purposes. This is particularly recommended for state farms, cooperative farms, and that part of the population employed in services. Next to the cost of grounds equipment, an important argument for the intensified use of building plots is the imperative necessity of economizing grounds for an efficient organization of production in agriculture, horticulture, and pomiculture.

Principles for Rural Development Planning

Based on the assumptions presented above, we can try to outline some major principles for rural development in Poland against the background of the new requirements of social and economic progress. The most important among these principles are discussed below.

(1) The scattered forms of rural settlements (both isolated "colonies"

and small villages or minor hamlets) are to be considered disadvantageous to the continued social and economic progress of our country, and
their gradual decay is to be expected in the years to come within the
period of the plan.

(2) The trend toward clustering housing and service development
within larger settlement units is to be considered correct for the evolution of the Polish rural settlement system. This trend, which appeals to
the village population because it provides favorable conditions for electrification, the building of water conduits, and the construction of roads,
should be methodically guided, according to the plan (Figures 65 and
66).

(3) The transformation of the existing rural settlement layout, adjusted to new socioeconomic needs, will require a long time and great
material effort. It will be necessary here to recognize and deal with
problems such as the amortization of the existing building stock, the
economic practicality of rebuilding, and approval of the changes by the
affected population. These problems should be considered organic components of the whole complex process of transformation.

(4) The recommended concentration of rural development in the
future will require the establishment of optimum sizes for what may be
called the "settlement base units" according to specific conditions in the
country and in individual regions. The optimum sizes should be calculated with respect to the following factors:

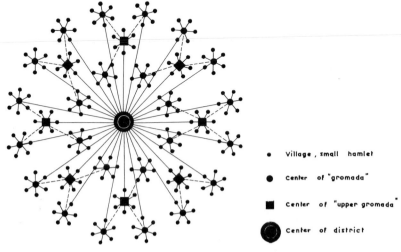

Fig. 65. Settlement network of a district: Scheme of the present system

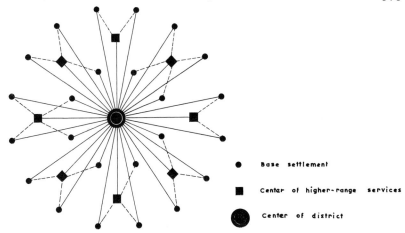

Base settlement

Center of higher-range services

Center of district

Fig. 66. Settlement network of a district: Scheme of the prospective system

(*a*) Main features as well as natural and geographical conditions of the region; type and intensity of agricultural production.

(*b*) Forms of organization of agricultural production adopted for the perspective period, and the proper sizes of farms.

(*c*) Need to guarantee the rural population social utilities and communal services approximating the living conditions of towns.

(*d*) Adoption of the most economical solution for the installation of the network of technical equipment.

(*e*) Need to fix the distances between the home and the workplace (both on the farm and in the fields), within reasonable limits of economical efficiency, by reducing the isochrone home-field to 30 minutes as a general rule, and to 45 minutes in exceptional cases.

(*f*) Existing state and stock of built-up areas, density and efficiency of the existing transport and communications network, etc.

(5) When possible, the perspective solutions should aim at a concentration of the population in base settlements that offer possibilities for acceptable equipment in the chief services and communal utilities—that is, in units of at least 2,000 inhabitants depending on both agricultural and nonagricultural occupations. Such a base settlement could in the future be associated with the administrative-economic unit which would consist of several farms cooperating in agricultural production.

With a view to shaping the "perspective network" of rural base settlements, it seems advisable to develop first of all those of the existing units whose situation, size, state, and the type of investment seem to be most fit for it. In many cases the present centers of gromadas will be among these units (Figure 67).

(6) Planning of the minimal equipment for future base villages should take into account the following utilities:

(*a*) Services: kindergarten, nursery, primary school with full program; dispensary with pharmacy; agricultural service station; social clubhouse with cinema and performance hall; library with reading room; inn (restaurant with coffee house); sports grounds and open pool; public bath and laundry; small department store; storehouse; bakery; workshops for handicrafts; milk reception station; fire station; and, possibly, veterinary service station.

(*b*) Communal equipment: streets and sidewalks, electrical fittings; village water system; possibly gas and sewerage systems.

(7) In order to satisfy the rule of economical and efficient use

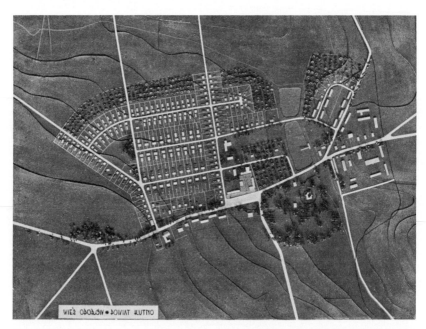

WIEŚ OPORÓW • POWIAT KUTNO

Fig. 67. Example of the spatial organization of a base village (Oporów, District of Kutno, Łódź Voivodship). Model plan of the Praesidium of the Voivodship People's Council in Łódź

In the center of the settlement, a service center is emerging, set in a landscape rich in green space, with ponds and a Gothic castle. Right center, the economic center, with a transportation park, plants, and local industry; left, a large neighborhood unit built on individual lots; top right, a complex of multifamily houses.

Fig. 68. Example of a farmstead in Kraków Voivodship, built according to the "colony" (farm) system (photo: M. Benko)

of building grounds in rural areas, and to take into account the technical equipment of those grounds for the years to come, the following guidelines are recommended:

(*a*) The area to be equipped during the perspective period with power, hard-surface roads, sidewalks and village water-supply systems ought to be limited as a rule to building plots and the land necessary for roads. Such equipment should not be extended over areas where it is not needed: large vegetable and fruit gardens should be located at the edges of the building grounds—in the immediate neighborhood, yet out of the way of equipment lines.

(*b*) Certain solutions are necessary for housing for persons employed by state farms and for the nonagricultural population residing in villages (industrial and service workers, for example): small building plots varying between 300 and 600 square meters per family, with dwelling of at least two stories, if possible, as twin or row-houses, which are more economical than isolated one-story buildings; blocks of multifamily houses of several stories—without individual plots.

(*c*) Cooperative farms should be built most economically in terms of land use.

(*d*) New individual farmholdings ought to be planned so as to reduce the surface (and particularly the width) of plots to the minimum necessary for a rather concentrated development, and to permit the lo-

Fig. 69. Example of an individual farmstead, with buildings under a common roof, in Kraków Voivodship (photo: M. Benko)

cation of the buildings (fireproof constructions) in conformity with existing regulations. This is possible, as a rule, for plots of from 1,500 to 2,000 square meters, the average scale of individual farmholdings in Poland.

(*e*) Extensive use of typical (standard) designs which provide well-conceived solutions for both housing and service buildings is recommended.

Fig. 70. Example of a rural cooperative, compact development, in Kraków Voivodship (photo: M. Benko)

Fig. 71. Rural settlement, compact development, in Kraków Voivodship (photo: M. Benko)

Fig. 72. Rural neighborhood unit composed of two-family houses in the state farm Babsk, Łódź Voivodship (photo: Central Photographic Archives)

Fig. 73. Example of a row-type housing development built on state farms: six-family house in the state farm Pokrzywno (photo: Central Photographic Archives)

(8) The actual transformation of rural building must be divided into stages. Present conditions and equipment taken into account, the first stage should concentrate on the planned guidance of current development, in order to block all processes which, if extended, might prove socially and economically detrimental.

In this connection, it is especially important to:

(*a*) Respect the principles of planned development for villages being built or relocated for reasons of large-scale investment, and for villages being reconstructed after natural calamities—in coordination with the rural-development plans for the given area and in conformity with the principles of the settlement pattern.

(*b*) Select within each district or part of a district those among the existing villages whose size, location, degree of investment, and present functions seem to best entitle them to become service-economic centers (and within the perspective period also housing centers). The gromada villages will certainly appear among those chosen.

(*c*) Reserve land for the future development of these villages and proceed to concentrate the necessary resources and activities now for the large investments to be undertaken in terms of economic, social, and cultural utilities as well as communal equipment. This will avoid the error of too widely dispersed effort and encourage disbanding of unprofitable small settlements.

(*d*) Select among the units those villages in which services of a higher level should be located (such as workshops and technical service stations for the needs of agriculture). Because of the size of the territory served and the size of the population concerned, these and similar services should not be concentrated exclusively in the center of the district.

(*e*) Make skillful and rigorous use of the provisions of the Rural Building Allotment Act of 1961 to counteract scattered development in rural building.

(*f*) Secure sufficiently large land strips along thoroughfares and separate them from local traffic by means of a road system to divert through traffic.

(9) For the time being, until full realization of the postulated transformations in the rural settlement pattern occurs, the existing farms will have to work to raise the agricultural production, irrespective of the type and location of their buildings. In this situation some investments will have to be made in both scattered farmholds and minor hamlets even if they are designated for future decay. These investments should not, however, greatly solidify the defective structure of the rural economy and the scattered settlement forms. Solutions regarding mate-

Fig. 74. Typical grain silo for state farms (photo: Kobus)

Fig. 75. Example of commerce and handicraft service pavilions in a district center (photo: M. Benko)

Fig. 76. Example of a public utilities building assembled from light prefabricated elements suitable for transport (photo: M. Benko)

Fig. 77. Example of a swine-breeding farm in a large agricultural unit

rials and construction should either reduce the building amortization period or designate, where possible, buildings composed of elements which can be reassembled elsewhere.

The theoretic principles briefly exposed above, concerning transformations to be made in the rural settlement system in Poland, can hardly be followed without taking into consideration a series of other essential factors.

I would like to emphasize that Poland, as an industrial-agricultural country, has over a great part of its territory a complex production structure and, consequently, a compound employment pattern. In many rural settlements the nonagricultural inhabitants form a majority of the population. Such a situation is bound to exert substantial influence both in the structure of the rural settlement network and in the structure of individual villages. The first problem finds its solution in the development plans for rural settlement areas and the latter one is being dealt with in local master and detailed plans—spurred by the new Polish planning legislation (Spatial Planning Act and Rural Building Allotment Act, 31 January 1961).

CHAPTER 16

Research Activity of the Committee for Space Economy and Regional Planning

ANTONI R. KUKLIŃSKI

IN the middle fifties an intense and comprehensive discussion began in Poland to deal with all problems of our political, economic, and scientific activities—including a proper evaluation of the spatial dimension of our successes and difficulties. Among many topics considered in this context were the promotion and coordination of research in the field of space economy and regional planning. Substantial agreement was reached on three characteristics of this research. First, it cannot be included within the traditional classification of academic disciplines; it is a typical interdisciplinary field where the methods and concepts of social, natural, and technical sciences are used. Second, in this research the integration of pure and applied studies is especially important. Third, a proper balance should be established in it both between studies on national and on regional scales and between the central and the regional allocation of means and abilities.

In order to create a proper managerial and institutional framework for the development of this type of research, the Executive Board of the Polish Academy of Sciences passed on September 23, 1958, a resolution establishing a Committee for Space Economy and Regional Planning.[1] The sixty members of the Committee were chosen from among eminent scholars and planners who represented a high level of theoretical or practical experience in this field. Stanisław Leszczycki[2] was elected

[1] S. Leszczycki, "The Committee for Space Economy and Regional Planning of the Polish Academy of Sciences," *The Review of the Polish Academy of Sciences*, VII (1962), No. 3/27, 33–39.

[2] Professor of Geography, Warsaw University, and Director of the Institute of Geography, Polish Academy of Sciences.

Chairman, and Kazimierz Secomski,[3] Michał Kaczorowski,[4] and Bohdan Pniewski[5] Vice-chairmen of the Committee. The position of Executive Secretary was allocated to the author.

Types of Research Promoted by the Committee

In a few years the Committee was transformed into a spirited center of research activity promoting differentiated methodological, empirical, and theoretical studies.[6]

METHODOLOGICAL STUDIES

One of its main tasks is to improve the methods applied to regional research and planning in Poland. This can be done in two ways: to adapt to our conditions the international experience in this field and to introduce new methods as our contribution to the development of regional science.

One of the earliest examples of methodological studies in our Committee was the development of a model of current optimization of foreign trade[7] in a planned economy as a rational basis for determining the volume, structure, and directions (that is, the regional allocation among foreign markets) of international trade. The application of this model introduced an important improvement in the economic evaluation of decisions in foreign trade. At the same time the model was

---

[3] Professor of Economics, Higher School of Planning and Statistics, and Vice-chairman of the Planning Commission, Council of Ministers.

[4] Professor of Economics, Warsaw Technological Institute, and Director of the Institute of Housing.

[5] Professor of Architecture, Warsaw Technological Institute, and Chairman of the Committee for Building, City Planning, and Architecture, Polish Academy of Sciences.

[6] The main working units for establishing research projects are the commissions of the Committee. Presently, there are 8 commissions; chairmen are given in parentheses:
The Commission for the Theory of Space Economy and Spatial Planning (K. Secomski)
The Commission for International Division of Labor (S. Rączkowski)
The Commission for Regional Economy (M. Kaczorowski)
The Commission for Urban Development (B. Pniewski)
The Commission for Physiographic Research (F. Barciński)
The Commissions for Spatial Problems of Industry, Agriculture, and Transportation (J. Goryński, J. Kostrowicki, and M. Madeyski)
There is very close cooperation between these commissions and the Department of Space Economy and Regional Planning of the Institute of Geography, Polish Academy of Sciences. The author of this article is the Chairman of this Department.

[7] W. Trzeciakowski, "A Model of Optimization of Foreign Trade in a Planned Economy and Its Application," *Regional Science Association Papers,* VIII (The Hague: European Congress, 1961).

recognized as a contribution to the analyses of external regional economic relations.

In order to improve the analysis of the interregional differentiation of our national economy, the Committee promoted studies on methods of computation of GNP and national income on regional scales.[8]

The next set of studies was designed to improve the methods of analyzing spatial problems in the development of agriculture, industry, and transportation.

In agricultural studies the basic aim is to develop methods of synthetic evaluation and planning of the spatial differentiation of this sector of the national economy.[9] In industrial studies three goals are established: to design an internationally comparable system of indices which could be used for programing activities in development and location of different branches of industry;[10] to develop the application of linear programing techniques for the comprehensive solutions of industrial location problems;[11] to develop methods of synthetic evaluation of the spatial structure of Poland's industry.[12] In transportation studies the most important task is to improve the methods of integrated inventory and analysis of commodity flows, taking into account all basic flows (railway, highway, and river transportation).[13] We know that this field is neglected on the international level and that the development of a comprehensive analysis of commodity flows is very important both theoretically and practically. Another important item is the integrated analysis of the physical volume and value of commodity flows.[14]

Under the supervision of the Committee a new method of urban

[8] M. Kaczorowski, "The Role of Research of National Income in the Studies of Regional Economic Development of the Country," *Bulletin of the Committee,* No. 2, 1960. (In Polish only.) L. Zienkowski, "An Attempt to Estimate the National Income of Poland in the Cross-Section of the Provinces (voivodships) in 1958," *ibid.*

[9] Cf. J. Kostrowicki, "Geographical Typology of Agriculture in Poland," *Geographia Polonica,* No. 1, 1964.

[10] W. Lissowski, "The Indices for Programing the Development and Distribution of Industry," *Bulletin of the Committee,* No. 11, 1962. (In Polish only.)

[11] A. Kukliński, "Some Spatial Problems in the Development of the Cement Industry in Poland 1946–1980," *Geographia Polonica,* No. 2, 1964.

[12] S. Leszczycki and others, "Spatial Structure of Poland's Industry, 1956," *Polish Geographical Review,* 1960, Supplement.

[13] A. Wróbel and others, "Integrated Research of the Spatial Structure of Commodity Flows," *Bulletin of the Committee,* No. 5, 1961.

[14] An attempt to solve this problem is being made in a doctoral study by W. Morawski in the Department of Space Economy and Regional Planning.

analysis was developed: that of threshold analysis, described in some detail elsewhere.[15]

Among the methodological studies of the Committee were also physiographical studies which have introduced a new method of cartographic inventory of all maps concerning elements of natural environment. The first volume of this inventory was printed in 1964; it lists and evaluates all soil maps prepared for different areas in Poland.[16]

We may conclude that the majority of methodological studies have been designed to improve the methods of economic analysis applied to regional research and planning. Another characteristic feature of the studies is the concern for the development of quantitative methods. Continuing the studies outlined above, during the next few years we shall start several research projects to develop analytic and computative techniques that would allow us to design a set of synthetic models. With them we would try to solve the problem of how to include the spatial dimension in the general scheme of the development of the national economy. Within the set three types of models are especially important: the model of regional allocation of investment,[17] that of areal distribution of production in the country,[18] and that of the urban system of the country.[19] A very strong stimulus exists in Poland for such studies, generated by the development of regional and interregional long-range planning.

EMPIRICAL STUDIES

The methodological studies are not an end in themselves. Improved methods are only tools for use in empirical studies or in planning activities that seek optimal solution for the future. The first step in all research and planning is a proper evaluation of past experience—knowledge of the basic facts and the ability to interpret them in an objective and balanced way.

Therefore, the second task of the Committee consists in the promo-

---

[15] See Chapter II, "Urban Planning Theory: Methods and Results," by Bolesław Malisz.

[16] *The Spatial Bibliography of Natural Environment*, Part I. *Studies of the Committee*, V, Warsaw, 1964. (In Polish only.)

[17] Cf. A. Rahman, "Regional Allocation of Investment. An Aggregative Study in the Theory of Development Programing," *The Quarterly Journal of Economics*, No. 1, Harvard University, 1963.

[18] Cf. W. S. Niemczynov, "The Model Economic Region," *Primienienie matiematiki w ekonomiczeskich issledovaniach*, II, Moskva, 1961.

[19] Cf. W. L. Garrison, *Toward a Simulation Model of Urban Growth and Development*, Department of Geography, University of Washington, Discussion Paper No. 39, Seattle, 1960.

tion of numerous research projects to improve our knowledge of spatial differentiations in Poland. The first group of projects will be completed in the next three years, presenting an analysis of the demographic development of Poland. A study composed of several volumes,[20] it will cover classical topics such as the development and distribution of Poland's population in the years 1900–1960, the structure of population according to sex, age, profession and education, and the patterns of migration.

The second group of empirical studies—analysis of urban development—will result in several basic publications. These will present a general evaluation of urbanization processes,[21] an evaluation of the influence of investment processes on urban development, an assessment of the role of planning activities in the transformation of Polish cities, and an evaluation of the sociological problems involved in urban development.

The most advanced is the third group of studies, analyzing the spatial problems in Poland's industrial development.[22] This is not an accident—the industrialization processes are the most important factors in explaining structural and regional changes in our national economy.[23] Several kinds of research are promoted in this field. The first one concerns the long-run spatial differentiation of industrialization processes in Poland for the years 1880–1980. This project is designed to develop a proper historical perspective for the comparative evaluation of present and future industrialization processes. The second kind of research concerns the analysis of the spatial patterns characteristic of different branches of industry; the distinction between spatially concentrated and spatially dispersed industries is recognized as valid here.[24] The third kind concerns the problem of selected areas representing different levels of industrial development.

[20] This research project is directed by Professor E. Strzelecki.

[21] K. Dziewoński, "Urbanization in Contemporary Poland," *Geographia Polonica*, No. 3, 1964. A. Ginsbert, "The Polish Cities and Their Capital Equipment," *Bulletin of the Committee*, No. 29, 1963. (In Polish only.)

[22] K. Secomski, "Analysis of Industrialization Processes and Industry's Spatial Structure in People's Poland," *The Review of the Polish Academy of Sciences*, No. 2, 1962. A. Kukliński, "Report on Polish Industrial Geography," *The Professional Geographer*, No. 5, 1960.

[23] A. Kukliński, "Progress and Changes in the Industrialization of Poland," *Geographia Polonica*, No. 3, 1964.

[24] M. Najgrakowski, "The Spatial Structure of the Brick Industry in Poland," *Bulletin of the Committee*, No. 25, 1964. (In Polish only.) A. Kukliński, "The Spatial Problems in the Development of the Cement Industry in Poland," *Studies of the Committee*, VI, 1964. (In Polish only.)

The fourth group of empirical studies—the most general one—deals with the problem of regional economic development.[25] The following topics are assessed: the changing relations between developed and underdeveloped regions,[26] the spatial differentiation of consumption level,[27] the spatial differentiation of employment, national income, fixed assets and the mutual interrelations of those indices.[28] Recently, a new study was started in cooperation with economic planning commissions of selected voivodships: the influence of investment processes on regional economy and the levels of consumption in a given region.

The promotion of empirical studies almost automatically raises the problem of the improvement of regional statistics. Our Committee has developed very good working relations with the Central Statistical Office. In effect, an introduction of new items into the system of our regional statistics has been possible, especially in the field of regional cross-sections of GNP and national income and, too, in industrial and transportation statistics.

We hope to publish during the next few years a set of volumes presenting a comprehensive and synthetic evaluation of the regional differentiation of Poland's national economy as a whole and of its sectors. These volumes in some way will be similar to the publications of Resources for the Future's analyses of regional economic development in the United States.[29]

THEORETICAL STUDIES

Promoting research in a given field, we have to see the interrelations of methodological, empirical, and theoretical studies. These studies, in fact, constitute a unit of a higher order, where in the long run the general progress of research is dependent on the development of all elements involved. A special role in this context is assigned to theoretical studies, which from time to time create a new big opening for the development of a given field. In most cases a new theoretical generalization will introduce a better explanation of the existing reality and a better

[25] M. Kaczorowski, *op. cit.*

[26] B. Winiarski, "The Factors and Phases of Raising the Intensity of Economic Activity in Less Developed Areas," *Bulletin of the Committee*, No. 31, 1964. (In Polish only.)

[27] Z. Żekoński and others, "The Analysis of the Levels and Structure of Consumption in Selected Voivodships," *Bulletin of the Committee*, No. 27, 1963. (In Polish only.)

[28] B. Prandecka, "The Analysis of the Regional Differentiation of Poland's National Income," *Studies of the Committee*, IX, 1964. (In Polish only.)

[29] Cf., for example, H. S. Perloff and others, *Regions, Resources and Economic Growth* (Baltimore, 1960).

foundation for future planning and programing. Such a situation exists in Poland now in the field of space economy and regional planning. We have arrived at a point where rapid progress throughout the field is dependent on the advance of theoretical studies—especially in the long run.

There are several types of theoretical studies being promoted by our Committee. The first one deals with the problem of integrating the theories of growth and of space economy.[30] Theoretical and dynamic macroeconomic thinking has been an element missing in most regional studies. In our opinion, this deficiency should be compensated. A theoretical reconsideration is necessary, too, in evaluating causes and consequences of the international and the interregional division of labor as an important premise of the growing efficiency of national and regional economy.[31]

Establishing a theory of economic regions is the next logical step in these studies. The changing regional differentiation of national and international economy is creating the demand for new theoretical generalization in this field.[32]

Finally, we need new theoretical approaches in the evaluation of our system of interregional and regional long-term economic planning. One of the most important items concerns the theoretical foundations of the solution to the conflict between sectoral and regional approaches in long-term policies of economic development.[33]

The theoretical studies of our Committee are the most difficult but also the most promising chapter in the Committee's research activities.

This review of our types of studies is neither the fullest nor the best possible account of the Committee's research activity. It is an attempt

---

[30] Cf. paper presented by K. Secomski during a special conference in the Higher School of Planning and Statistics, Warsaw, May 21, 1964: "The Main Problems of the Theory of Distribution of Productive Forces in Relation to the Theory of Economic Growth."

[31] Cf. paper presented by K. Secomski during the Plenary Meeting of the Polish Academy of Sciences, Warsaw, May 14, 1964: "The Problem of the International and Interregional Division of Labor in the Theory of Distribution of Productive Forces."

[32] S. Leszczycki, "The Tasks of Economic Regionalization," *Geographia Polonica*, No. 4, 1964. K. Dziewoński, "Theoretical Problems in the Development of Economic Regions," *Regional Science Association Papers*, VIII (The Hague: European Congress, 1961). A. Wróbel, "Regional Analysis and the Geographic Concept of Region," *ibid.*

[33] Cf. paper presented by W. Lissowski during the meeting of the Commission for the Theory of Space Economy and Spatial Planning, Warsaw, February 12, 1964: "The Relation of the Sectoral and Regional Pattern in Perspective Programing."

to outline some samples of this activity in a way that will give the reader a correct impression of the trends of research.

The Basis of Research—Regional Economic Development

We think that the reader would be better able to evaluate the research activity of our Committee with an introduction to selected items of regional economic development, in other words, to the reality that directly influences the intellectual activity of the Committee.

REGIONAL DIFFERENTIATION OF THE NATIONAL ECONOMY IN 1961

In the evaluation of the regional differentiation of the Polish national economy we find that two synthetic indices are most useful: GNP per capita and GNP per square kilometer. The latter can be called the index of areal density of economic activity. In Map 62, we find the comparison of those two patterns. The areal pattern is much more differentiated than the per capita pattern. The index of areal density of economic activity reflects correctly the special position and the special problems of the province of Katowice, which includes the most important industrial area in Poland, the Upper Silesian Industrial District.

Extending this comparative analysis of the per capita and areal patterns (Tables 29 and 30), let us discuss the materials presented in Maps 63, 64, and 65, comparing the regional differentiation of the two most important sectors of the national economy—industry and agriculture—with respective shares in GNP of 49 per cent and 23.2 per cent in 1961.

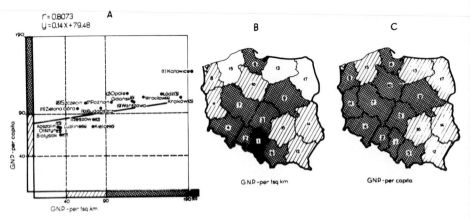

Map 62. G.N.P. per capita and per square kilometer

Table 29. PER CAPITA INDICES OF REGIONAL DIFFERENTIATION OF POLAND'S NATIONAL
ECONOMY IN 1961

Voivodship	GNP	GNP produced in industry	GNP produced in agri- culture	Net output of agri- culture per capita of agri- cultural population	Individual consumption
Katowice	138.0	209.3	28.5	111	119.5
Opole	111.8	108.5	128.8	135	193.4
Łódź	111.3	139.2	82.4	86	96.9
Wrocław	108.5	117.8	95.1	141	105.4
Kraków	107.3	125.8	77.7	75	96.3
Gdańsk	102.9	99.8	73.5	124	111.8
Poznań	102.1	88.0	136.3	141	107.1
Szczecin	101.2	73.5	109.3	130	110.0
Warsaw	101.0	90.8	81.4	86	81.4
Bydgoszcz	95.0	76.6	138.8	140	99.7
Zielona Góra	94.6	77.1	114.8	122	96.7
Rzeszów	81.8	64.4	123.9	81	83.6
Olsztyn	74.7	30.8	129.9	98	86.9
Lublin	74.5	35.8	157.9	91	86.7
Koszalin	74.5	31.2	130.3	110	98.2
Kielce	74.4	61.9	109.1	73	78.7
Białystok	65.5	30.7	130.5	80	80.1
Average for Poland	100.0	100.0	100.0	100	100.0

Several comparisons should be noted:

(1) The difference between the patterns of industry and agriculture, which is the result of different factors explaining the distribution of these two sectors of economic activity.

(2) The similarity of the per capita and areal patterns of industry (see Map 63). The similarity could be explained by the role of concentration in the distribution of industrial activity. The advantages of concentration are expressed both in per capita and in areal relations.

(3) The difference in the per capita and areal patterns of agriculture (see Maps 64 and 65).

(4) The similarity between the general GNP pattern (Map 62) and the pattern of industry (Map 63). The pattern of industrial distribution is the most important factor in regional differentiation of the national economy.

Table 30. AREAL INDICES OF REGIONAL DIFFERENTIATION OF POLAND'S NATIONAL ECONOMY IN 1961*

Voivodship	GNP	GNP produced in industry	GNP produced in agriculture	Net output of agriculture per 1 ha. of utilized land	Population	Urban population	Employment in industry and handicraft
Katowice	502.9	763.0	103.8	116	362.9	568.1	727.3
Kraków	180.3	211.4	130.5	127	167.0	144.7	163.6
Łódź	156.9	196.2	116.2	106	140.2	153.2	181.8
Wrocław	135.2	146.8	118.4	118	123.7	157.4	154.5
Warsaw	124.1	111.6	100.0	92	122.7	138.3	90.9
Gdańsk	122.3	118.5	87.3	92	118.6	163.8	109.1
Opole	116.2	112.8	133.9	131	104.1	83.0	118.2
Poznań	96.6	84.9	128.9	118	93.8	91.5	81.8
Bydgoszcz	82.9	66.9	121.1	116	86.6	87.2	72.7
Rzeszów	73.7	58.0	111.6	112	89.7	44.7	54.5
Kielce	73.4	61.1	107.6	106	97.9	55.3	63.6
Szczecin	64.4	46.8	69.4	73	62.9	80.8	45.5
Lublin	57.2	27.5	121.2	110	76.3	40.4	27.3
Zielona Góra	53.9	43.9	65.4	86	56.7	59.6	45.5
Olsztyn	33.1	13.6	57.6	55	44.3	34.0	18.2
Białystok	32.7	15.3	65.0	63	49.5	31.9	18.2
Koszalin	30.2	12.7	52.8	65	40.2	38.3	18.2
Average for Poland	100.0	100.0	100.0	100	100.0	100.0	100.0

* Data recomputed per sq. km.

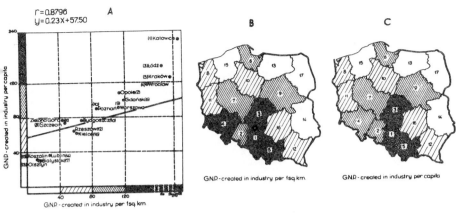

Map 63. G.N.P. created in industry

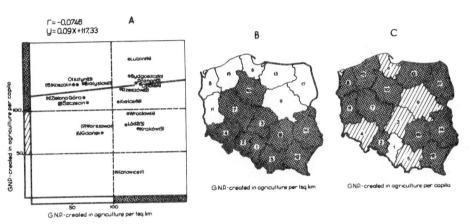

Map 64. G.N.P. created in agriculture

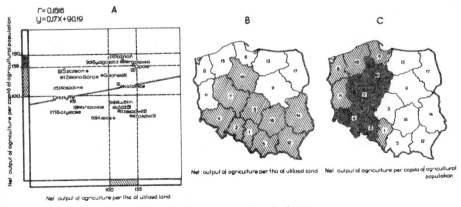

Map 65. Net output of agriculture

399

INTERREGIONAL EQUALIZATION PROCESSES, 1946–1980

The analysis of the regional differentiation of the Polish national economy was limited only to static comparisons for 1961. There exists a basic difficulty in crossing the boundary between static and dynamic analyses in this case. The computation of regional cross-sections of GNP and national income was started in 1956. So it is impossible to use these indices in historical comparisons. In order to overcome this difficulty we will use the well-known assumption which stresses the association between the general level of economic development of a given country or region and the level of its industrial and urban development. This index as applied to Poland is indicated in Figure 78. In this chapter we will analyze the changes in the distribution of urban and industrial population, assuming that they represent the basic factor in the interregional differentiation of the national economy. The empirical materials are presented in Table 31 and in Figures 79 and 80. Data for the years 1946–1960 were taken from the publications of our Central Statistical Office, and data for 1980 from the last version of the regional cross-section of our perspective plan.

Two coefficients were computed in order to determine the basic trends of interregional equalization processes in Poland:

(1) The coefficient of concentration, limited to values from 0 to 1. The value of the coefficient is equal to 0 where the analyzed phenomenon is equally distributed among regions—equally in relation to the

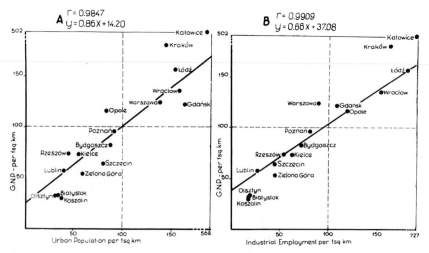

Fig. 78. Relationship of G.N.P. and urban population and industrial employment per square kilometer

Table 31. INTERREGIONAL EQUALIZATION PROCESSES IN POLAND, 1946–1980

Period	Population	Urban population	Employment in industry and handicraft
	Absolute figures in millions of persons		
1946	23.930	8.185	1.444
1960	29.731	14.112	3.182
1980	37.363	22.172	5.650
	Coefficient of areal concentration		
1946	0.282	0.432	0.580
1960	0.266	0.392	0.481
1980	0.259	0.340	0.343
	Coefficient of per capita concentration		
1946	–	0.207	0.383
1960	–	0.180	0.258
1980	–	0.122	0.131
	Coefficient of areal equalization		
1946–1960	1.337	860	461
1960–1980	4.161	819	345
	Coefficient of per capita equalization		
1946–1960	–	520	197
1960–1980	–	247	144
	Absolute growth in millions of persons		
1946–1960	5.801	5.927	1.738
1960–1980	7.632	8.060	2.468

area (coefficient of areal concentration) or equally in relation to the population (coefficient of per capita concentration). The value of this coefficient is equal to 1 where the given phenomenon is concentrated in one point. The diminishing value of the coefficients of concentration, both areal and per capita, reflects the trends of diminishing interregional differences between the levels of industrial and urban development in the years 1946–1980. The same analysis is presented graphically in the form of cumulative Lorentz curves (see Figures 79 and 80).

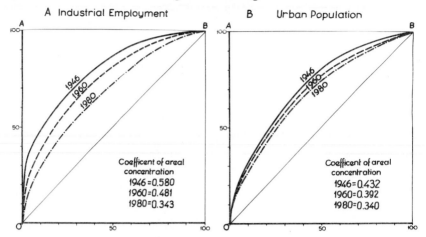

Fig. 79. Derivation of the coefficients of areal concentration for industrial employment and urban population

(2) The coefficient of equalization is an attempt to introduce a
dynamic measure of change. The following example will explain the
methods of the computation of this coefficient. The value of the coefficient of areal concentration of industrial employment for the year 1946
was 0.580 and for the year 1960, 0.481. We can present the following
question: how many years must pass until the value of this coefficient

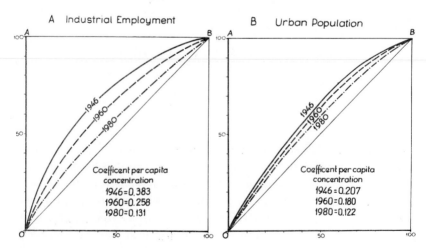

Fig. 80. Derivation of the coefficients of per capita concentration for industrial
employment and urban population

will diminish to o or, let us say, to 0.001, in order to avoid some mathematical problems of infinity. Naturally, in this question the *ceteris paribus* assumption is hidden. We assume that all phenomena influencing the analyzed pattern will exist in the same way as they existed in the years 1946–1960. The answer is presented in the form of the coefficient of the areal equalization of 461 years. In order to stress the conventional character of this value, I propose to drop the word "years" and to keep only the value 461 as a coefficient expressing the relative velocity in the equalization processes or the velocity of the growing inequalities in case we get minus values.

I must stress that these coefficients do not present any projections of the future of 500 or 1,000 years, nor do they express the desire to plan an equal distribution of economic activity. These coefficients are only a tool in analyzing the trends in Polish regional economy in the years 1946–1960, or the results of the assumptions of the regional cross-sections of our perspective plan for the years 1961–1980. The conclusion of this analysis is very clear: the socialist economy in Poland has developed in such a way that there exists a slow but very firm trend to diminish the interregional equalities in our country.

Regional and Superregional Economic Activity

In all discussions of the problems of regional economy and regional planning the valid distinction between regional and superregional economic activities should be recognized. The basic controversy in this field concerns the possibility of optimizing solutions within the framework of a regional plan of a given province. This problem found a clear formulation in the following statement by Kazimierz Secomski:

> The optimal results of the economic development of the country are not equal to the maximization of the rate of growth of different regions. The analysis of the efficiency of national economy and the tendency to optimize the results on the national scale should establish the directions and rate of growth of each region. Not the sum of the maximum growth of all regions, but the sum of effects being the result of the optimal rate of growth for individual regions within the framework of national economic analysis generates the highest rate of economic growth of the country.[34]

One of the main justifications for Secomski's arguments is in the change of proportions between regional and superregional economic

[34] K. Secomski, "Introduction," in W. Kawalec, *Industrialization as a Factor of Regional Economic Development in Poland*, (Warsaw, 1964).

Table 32. REGIONAL AND SUPERREGIONAL ECONOMIC ACTIVITIES IN POLAND: CLASSIFICATION OF REGIONAL AND SUPERREGIONAL ACTIVITIES (ACCORDING TO W. LISSOWSKI)

Activities	Material production	"Unproductive" services
Superregional	Large and medium-scale industrial plants	Science and academic education
	State Agricultural Farms (10% of agriculture)	Specialized hospitals
	Forestry	10% of housing
	Air, maritime, and railway transportation	50% of administration
	Wholesale trade	
Regional	Small-scale industries	Urban utilities
	90% of agriculture	90% of housing
	Roads and cargo traffic	All social and cultural services
	Retail trade	50% of administration

Table 33. REGIONAL AND SUPERREGIONAL ECONOMIC ACTIVITIES IN POLAND: MAIN ECONOMIC PROPORTIONS IN REGIONAL PLANS FOR 1961–1980 (ACCORDING TO W. LISSOWSKI)

Item	Material production			"Unproductive" services		
	Sub-total	Super-reg.	Regional	Sub-total	Super-reg.	Regional
Reproduction Value of Fixed Assets						
1960	59.6	38.9	20.7	40.4	4.0	36.4
1980	65.5	49.0	16.5	34.5	3.3	31.2
Fixed investment in 1961–1980						
New investment	71.4	57.2	14.2	28.6	2.8	25.8
Reinvestment	72.1	43.1	29.0	27.9	2.9	25.0
National income originated at factory prices						
1960	100.0	61.7	38.3	–	–	–
1980	100.0	75.1	24.9	–	–	–
Increase 1961–1980	100.0	81.1	18.9	–	–	–

activities. These proportions were analyzed by W. Lissowski (see Tables 32 and 33), who presented the following conclusion:

There is a marked tendency for the superregional activities to grow more rapidly than the regional ones. This is not due to any centralization policy but to the fact that large and medium-scale industries, research, and higher education grow more rapidly than small-scale economies, agriculture, and primary–secondary education. The regional sphere becomes increasingly less productive, while the super-regional sphere becomes increasingly more productive, originating an increasingly important share of the national income. This is another impact of the industrialization trends.[35]

This partial analysis describes some characteristic features of regional economic development in Poland. The full explanation of causal and functional relations involved in the processes of regional economic development is one of the main tasks of the empirical studies of our Committee.

[35] W. Lissowski, "Comments" to the paper by A. Kukliński, "Regional Economic Planning for the Development of New Towns," United Nations Round Table Conference on the Planning and Development of New Towns (Moscow, 1964).

National Economic Planning

Part Three

Commentary and Orientation

JACK C. FISHER
WOJCIECH MORAWSKI

SPATIAL planning in Poland, in both its theoretical and applied aspects, is closely interwoven with national economic planning. For this reason we feel that a brief review of Polish economic planning is indispensable for comprehending the scope of spatial planning within Polish society. It must be strongly emphasized, however, that this section is complementary to the preceding sections in the volume. The articles in Part Three were written with this relationship in mind and are not to be considered primary source material for the study of Polish economic planning as a whole.

In Part Three the evolution and practice of national economic planning are described; and the impact or effectiveness of investments on regional economic advances, and the basic proportions of the long-range development plan to 1980, are discussed. The concluding chapter presents the thoughts of Professor Oskar Lange, one of Poland's—and indeed one of the world's—most eminent economists, on the role of science in the evolution of socialist society.

The first two sections of the volume have made us aware of the degree to which economic planning inspires the programing of regional and urban development and generalizes from studies that reveal the requirements and possibilities of specific spatial units. The process most vital to economic planning is that of making studies and programs of the general national growth on the basis of trends revealed by particular sectors of production. Hence, demographic problems, distribution of employment, size and structure of consumption, and quality of living standards are keynotes of economic planning. It being understood that synthesis is reached in economic plans by studying economic phenomena through sectoral indications, one can say that economic planning provides a vantage point that dominates both entire economics and development tendencies of the particular sectors. In spatial planning, on the other hand, all economic and social phenomena of a specific region or settlement are analyzed and programed from the point of view of its economy. Whether there is a conflict between the economy of a region or town and the economy of a sector is a subject of lively discussion in Poland. From the point of view of a particular region such a conflict may appear in specific cases when development plans of industrial branches do not coincide with the "regional interests." In many cases such a conflict may arise objectively when the planned general economic growth fails to solve the key problems of the future of the given region, ensuring new jobs in a region of surplus manpower, for example, or making it possible for the surplus population to migrate to other regions. A general planning system creates conditions for eliminating such a conflict by representing both the economy of the entire country and that of a collection of spatial units.

CHAPTER 17

Comments on Economic Planning in Poland

JÓZEF PAJESTKA

Brief Historical Outline

ECONOMIC planning in Poland was started after World War II under conditions that created an institutional basis for a type of planning suitable to the socialist economies. The main economic sectors, primarily large industry, were nationalized, and the most important instruments of economic policy, particularly the banking system and foreign trade, were placed under direct government control. These conditions made it possible to undertake and implement effectively both a reconstruction program to cope with the devastations of war and a bold program of industrialization aimed at the creation of structural conditions favorable to rapid, steady development of the national economy.

The first program to cover the entire national economy was the Three-Year Plan for the years 1947–1949. It was intended primarily for the reconstruction of the economy and restoration of prewar living standards for the majority of the people. Then for the period 1950–1955 the Six-Year Plan was drafted. This program began the accelerated industrialization of the country. It outlined profound structural changes in the economy in order to create conditions favorable to a rapid rate of economic growth over a long run. It also set ambitious objectives for changing the economic geography of the country in order to diminish regional disparities.

Annual plans were in force throughout the period in which the Six-Year Plan was being executed. As conditions changed with the actual performance of the economy, the annual plans were used to reshape the economic development outlined in the Six-Year Plan. Annual plans have since become an important element in the planning system.

The Six-Year Plan had been elaborated by central authorities, but the annual plans were prepared by industrial organizations—including factories and businesses—and by regional agencies. Nevertheless, the planning system was still very much centralized.

Realization of the Six-Year Plan brought spectacular industrial growth but also serious economic strain. Through annual plans certain general rearrangements of the development patterns were introduced during the last two years of the plan, primarily to ease the development drive. This approach was continued in the first Five-Year Plan for the years 1956–1960. The main strategy of this plan consisted in continuing the industrialization policy, but balancing growth better and raising the standard of living more rapidly.

A new phase in development began in about 1958–1959. Most of the large investment projects initiated under the Six-Year Plan were completed by then, and a new "package" of industrial projects had to be designed. At that time the need for a long-term plan was strongly felt, and the planning apparatus had become capable by then of working out such a plan.

Long-term planning, developed after 1957, opened a new chapter in the methodology of planning in many respects. Although it has been rather a kind of analytical exercise, it has influenced seriously the approach to planning for short-term periods, that is, in the five-year plans. The introduction of long-term planning helped to create new conditions for regional planning. Thus, it was only after the capability was developed in economic planning to cope with long-term problems that integrated economic and physical regional planning became possible. Before that development, physical planning tended either toward a system of independent planning, taking the place of economic development planning (in the years 1946–1949), or toward treatment of limited problems of land use within limited areas only.

The second Five-Year Plan, for the period 1961–1965, continued the new development phase. Annual plans again introduced adjustments to actual performance. In 1963–1964 serious adjustments were made as a result of a coincidence of investment strain with a grave drop in agricultural output—the greatest drop in the entire postwar period, it was caused by bad weather in 1962 and consequent low animal production in 1963.

Some general results of national economic development during the postwar periods of industrialization are presented in Table 34.

Table 34. AVERAGE ANNUAL RATES OF GROWTH* (IN PER CENT)

Category	1951–54	1955–58	1959–62
National income†	8.6	8.0	4.9
Industrial output	17.4	10.0	9.7
Agricultural output	0.3	4.2	1.4
Consumption‡ per capita	5.8	6.6	3.1
Capital investment§ (gross)	13.2	6.3	10.2
Employment	6.3	2.9	2.8

* All figures are in real terms.

† The "national income" concept used here resembles the NNP (net national product) used in Western countries, with a main exception: it does not include certain services (defense and government services, various social and cultural services). It is to be observed that the social and similar services were growing much faster than the national income, particularly in more recent years.

‡ "Consumption" covers a part of the national income used for current consumption by the society; it does not cover all expenses for social and similar services.

§ "Capital investment" covers all investment in fixed assets.

Some Features of the Planning System

In Poland planning is institutionally established and is based on the social ownership of capital and the predominant role of the state in directing economic activities. The socialist sector of the economy, as it is called, includes a very great part of the whole. More than 95 per cent of all nonagricultural employment is in this sector. It is only in agriculture that private enterprise plays an important role: about 89 per cent of the total agricultural output and about 85 per cent of the marketable surplus are produced by individual, privately-owned farms. The state, nevertheless, has a great influence on agriculture. The conditions in the agricultural and nonagricultural sectors influence both the character of planning and the methods in its implementation.

One of the most important features of the Polish planning system may be termed *active planning,* that is, the active projection of economic activities as opposed to passive forecasting of the most probable development. Although some elements of active planning appear in private enterprise economies, active planning is a universal characteristic of socialist planning in Poland.

After the war the country needed very active planning. Its economic standards were very low, and the rate of progress reached before the war had been quite unsatisfactory; many historical factors caused the

Polish economy to lag far behind more highly developed European countries. Therefore the country needed a new structure to allow it to move rapidly in social and economic development. Knowledge of possible future economic performance was not expected from planning, but rather the creation of new economic conditions.

Active planning involves serious methodological problems, since it requires the best economic solutions for a future development which is to a great extent determined by the planners themselves. Extrapolation of past development trends (both in simple form and in more refined forms involving the application of economic models) has a rather auxiliary role in such planning. The methods applied in active planning should be appropriate for decision-making; they are actually the methods of programing. In active planning great attention must also be paid to implementation. The change not only has to be designed, it must be put into effect, and for this ways and means must be found.

It may be interesting to note that the second problem proved to be more important and difficult in Poland than the first one. Therefore, in the development of our planning system more attention has been paid to methods of plan implementation than to methods of plan construction.

Planning in Poland was started in macroeconomic forms on the central level. Gradually, however, it has become the system for running the whole economy. Today there exists a system of plans, comprising the central plan (the national economic plan) and plans for various regions, economic organizations, industries, businesses, and so on. All economic units in the socialist sector are engaged in planning.

Construction of the central plan is not the result of self-sufficient and independent action by the central planning body. Planning activities go on throughout the country, out of these arise both the central plan and plans for the various economic organizations, which form a consistent system.

The relation between central planning and planning for separate groups or areas proved to be an extremely important issue in Poland, usually discussed in terms of centralized versus decentralized planning. Polish planning experience has shown that the more active macroeconomic planning becomes (that is, the more that radical changes in existing structures and trends are required and designed), the more centralized planning becomes. Therefore when the country achieved the basic structural conditions for a more balanced steady development, the predominance of central planning began to diminish.

Realization of the objectives adopted in our plans was obviously impossible without strong government intervention. It is particularly interesting, though, that state direction took a highly centralized form of decision-making, mainly using administrative means to realize the plans. These characteristics of planning may show the far-reaching connections between a country's economic conditions, its development targets, and its planning system. The causes of centralization were of course diverse. A particular, important factor was the poor quality of personnel. Here, however, I wish to deal primarily with the economic conditions affecting centralization. It seems that the policy of maximum utilization of economic resources, particularly of manpower, exerted the principal influence upon the character of planning.

The policy of maximum utilization of resources may be explained by the criterion of efficiency (*i.e.,* maximization of output). This criterion, and the economic calculations corresponding to it, are different from the conventional form of analyzing enterprises on criteria of market prices and profitability. It may be stated that perhaps no single enterprise would be able to adopt a policy of full utilization of its technical capacities by maximum expansion of employment, given the normal profitability criterion; whereas on a national scale the policy of full utilization has been the principal factor in the country's economic expansion.

Under different economic circumstances the divergence between central economic criteria and those of business enterprises may be reduced. This has been occurring more recently. The centralization of planning was motivated primarily by the economic situation of the country, characterized by insufficient utilization of the principal factor of productive power, labor, and by the fact that planning was based on the criterion of maximizing the growth of national income. In the course of development, the country's economic situation changed. As a result, the methods of planning and economic management required changing, but serious delays in making the changes were encountered.

Types of Plans and Planning Procedure

In Poland there are three principal types of general economic plans: annual, short-term (five-year), and long-term (perspective) plans. The one-year and the five-year plans operate on a national scale and on a local scale, that is, in all economic units. Recently annual and short-term planning has been supplemented by perspective planning. A perspective plan is elaborated to cover a period of fifteen to twenty years and to cover the entire economy of the country. Perspective plans are also being drafted for the economic regions of the country as well as for certain sectors. There is, however, no one general system of perspective planning to be applied to all economic units.

The perspective plan has become an important instrument in making development policy in Poland. Much current economic policy is derived from the analysis of long-range conditions and requirements formulated in the elaboration of the perspective plan. The perspective plan has somewhat the character of a guide: it is not an operative document. It is assumed that the perspective plan will be re-elaborated from time to time and extended for the next few years.

At present there is a pronounced tendency toward increasing the importance of long-term planning and diminishing that of annual planning. The more smoothly the economy develops, the greater the role of long-term plans becomes and the less necessary detailed intervention of annual plans in economic activities.

To many outside observers the predominance of annual plans, with the drafting of annual objectives for enterprises, has seemed a characteristic feature of our planning system. But it is not an inherent part of Polish planning theory. It was called for by the economic situation of the country and the accepted objectives of economic policy. Planning is by nature a long-term affair.

PLANNING COORDINATION

As indicated, planning of economic development does not consist of plan-studies and economic decisions made by one planning center for the whole economy. The central planning agency makes its own studies, but it also coordinates planning activities throughout the country. Various economic organizations contribute to the preparation of each plan.

Plans are prepared in stages, and in the successive steps of building the plan, participating agencies in the planning process influence one another by exchanging information and comparing views, criteria, and tendencies. All participants have an active part in the procedure, preparing their own proposals, draft plans, opinions, and so on. The successive stages of preparation are actually successive cycles of adapting the planning assumptions made by all participating bodies in the procedure.

The cooperation of various groups participating in the procedure can be presented, in a very simplified way, in the following schematic diagram:

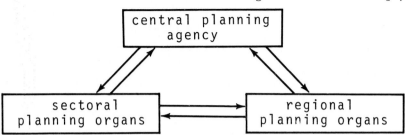

This scheme can be applied as well to annual and short-term planning as to long-term, "perspective" planning. In annual and short-term planning, however, the interrelations between the central planning authorities and the sectoral ones are essential. Regional planning authorities take a limited part in the procedure. They are interested especially in fields that are subject to regional administration (those fields for which they perform the function of sectoral administration), and also in other fields in which regional administration plays a co-ordinating role.

Long-term planning creates better balance between the sectoral and regional participants of the planning procedure; this is true for all problems of economic development. The strategy in organizing the planning procedure for long-term plans requires including the sectoral and the regional points of view as equivalent factors.

The role of participating bodies in the planning procedure is not reduced to "neutral" projections of growth. Individual participants represent not only definite points of view and definite aspects of economic calculation, but also certain trends. That is why the participants in the planning process take part not only as research centers, but also as social and economic units.

Cooperation among the various participants is organized within the general framework of the planning procedure. In the general planning procedure certain successive stages can be distinguished, to which different methods are applied.

STEPS IN THE PREPARATION OF PLANS

Although certain important differences appear in the planning procedure for annual, five-year, and long-term plans, three general stages can be distinguished as more or less applicable for all of them. They are central directives for elaboration of the plan; draft plans of the various economic organizations; and the final central economic plan and plans for various organizations.

The central directives form a preliminary, rather comprehensive draft of the general economic plan. Their main function is to construct a framework for planning in the economic apparatus of the country. At this stage preliminary decisions are taken with regard to the most important, strategic variables (such as volume of capital investment, its distribution among the economic sectors, increase in employment, and output figures for the main sectors). Thus the more detailed work on the plan, which will be carried on later, can develop within the general lines of economic policy.

Elaboration of the directives is the task of the central planning body —the State Planning Commission. Such work is also performed in various stages, or approximations. The first drafts very often resemble more or less complicated forecasts of highly aggregated variables. It is, however, only at the very early stages of work on the directives that the planners apply certain simple forecasting methods. Very soon they resort to concrete analyses and calculations, evidently in preference to reliance on aggregated economic models and extrapolation of past trends.

At this stage the planners make use of numerous economic, technical, and other experts available in various organizations: projections bureaus, scientific institutes, industrial organizations, and even commercial enterprises. Thus, instead of relying on statistical estimates (as of capital coefficients) for the various economic sectors, they resort to calculations presented by experts, assessing the necessary capital requirements for an assumed increase of output, or for labor inputs, raw materials, and so on. They make projections for the separate industries (starting often with the "main" branches), put them together, and attempt to construct a reasonable and internally consistent entity. This process may be repeated several times, producing successive versions of the plan (that is, of the directives), which is continually being improved. Attempts are made to increase the national product by way of better utilization of the human and natural resources, of technical improvements, increased effectiveness of capital investment, and so on. From time to time the proposed changes are put together and made consistent, mainly by "balancing," to produce a new version of the plan.

"Balancing" resembles an input–output analysis. Its main function is to make an internally consistent plan. This is achieved by checking supply against demand for the various factors and commodities and making them consistent.

A commodity balance, which is most typical for application of the "balancing method," resembles a separate row of an input–output table. It takes the following form:

$$P_i = a_{ij}P_i + Y_i + E_i - M_i$$

where P_i = gross output of commodity "i"; Y_i = final domestic demand; E_i = exports; M_i = imports; a_{ij} = technical coefficient.

Certain distinctive features of commodity balances, as compared with an input–output system, may be outlined as follows: (1) Commodity balances are elaborated centrally for the basic commodities only; thus, it is not a full system. In the basic commodities are included, first of all, those which determine the industrial potential of the various sectors; scarce commodities are also included here. (2) The technical coefficients used in the balances (a_{ij}) are not homogeneous; they are set in physical units per value of output of various aggregates, etc. (3) There is no one general accepted rule determining the character of supply-demand relations, *e.g.*, by accepting the final demand as the given and gross output as the dependent variable as in input–output schemes. According to the concrete situation in a given sector, final demand or gross output may be accepted as the independent and the other as the dependent variable. (4) In working with the commodity balances capacity limitations are keenly observed. (5) The procedure of solving the system is iterative. This makes the whole process of plan elaboration rather difficult and laborious and results in certain errors.

It is rather difficult to compare commodity balancing with the input–output method. The former is principally a practical tool, worked out during several years of actual experience, adapted to the existing economic conditions, institutional set-up, and other practical requirements; the latter is a general theoretical scheme. Serious attempts are being made in Poland to make input–output suitable for practical planning.

There is logic to the planning scheme as it appears in practice. Certain restrictions are accepted as more or less exogenous variables. These include the existing economic resources (manpower, existing industrial capacities, etc.), the maximum possibilities for the expansion of certain sectors of the economy, and the limitations on export possibilities. Development projections for the various sectors are made in such a manner as to create an internally consistent program and achieve maximum increase of the national product. It is assumed that the maximum must be attained with the simultaneous realization of certain levels and proportions (such as investment to national income ratio), which are accepted on the basis of social and political principles or as requirements for further economic development.

It can be perceived that these points resemble the general logic of programing techniques: there is a maximization function, including a condition of internal consistency, and various restrictions. It should not be assumed, however, that a mathematical model of, for example, the linear-programing type was elaborated for any of the plans. The problems envisaged in plan construction seem too complicated to be confined within the framework of a manageable model. Practical methods, when compared with the theoretical models, are simpler in some respects but more complicated and elastic in others.[1]

When the planners achieve a version of the plan that is deemed satisfactory, it is presented for approval and eventually becomes a set of formal directives. The directives may be defined as a feasible program, internally consistent with the existing restrictions, and as a program close to the optimum program, which is the final version of the national economic plan. This is an important characteristic, in that the closer the directives are to the final plan, the easier will be the work of making a consistent national plan from the draft plans presented by the various organizations.

Thus, the directives give a framework for elaboration of the draft plans by the various organizations. Work on the draft plans consists mainly in further separating the variables, checking the technical restrictions with regard to existing capacities, calculating coefficients for various inputs, discovering partial optima, and elaborating an internally consistent draft.

All this work is carried on within the directives, which are in a way binding. The directives fix certain limits (minimum output targets, upper limits of capital expenditures, employment limits, and so on), and also indicate optimization criteria (maximum growth of output, minimum costs, minimum capital expenditure, and so on). These optimization criteria, though not necessarily formulated on a systematic basis for individual cases, continue to be applied during the elaboration of the drafts, and particularly in the analysis, appraisal, and corrections of the draft plans, carried on during the various phases of plan elaboration.

The draft plans define both output and input figures—above all for

---

[1] Thus, for example, linear assumption very rarely appears in planning practice.

capital expenditure, but also for employment, with separate calculations for the qualified staff, raw materials, and equipment. Most of the data are formulated to allow for aggregation and coordination of the various draft plans.

Draft plans are elaborated by industrial organizations, various government agencies, regional districts, and commercial enterprises. Thousands of specialists and technicians are engaged in this stage of planning. They can use every kind of initiative and invention in this work and include their proposals in their draft plans. Whether they actually do this and to what extent, recognizing the existing possibilities, is one of the most crucial problems of the planning system.

In the final stage of plan elaboration, the draft plans are thoroughly analyzed, coordinated, and combined, and eventually appear in the form of one aggregated national economic plan. This stage of work is quite laborious; it is often necessary to recalculate the draft plans, change output figures, coefficients, and so on. Hundreds and even thousands of people work on this for several weeks.

A rather common misunderstanding is that the central economic plan is constructed only on the basis of certain central economic calculations. The central planners do not and cannot think out themselves what should be produced in a certain plant and how. They can never have sufficient knowledge to make a proper decision of this character. What they can do, and probably better than anybody else, is: (1) coordinate the activities of the various sectors; (2) check the feasibility of the various proposals, taking into account the availability of capital, manpower, and so on; (3) assure the realization of certain social and political priorities with regard to regional development, income distribution patterns, and so on; (4) assure a high degree of utilization of the country's resources, and so on. Therefore, we say that the main function of the central planning agency is to coordinate the various draft plans in order to keep them consistent and within certain general economic limits, and to discover the development patterns most favorable for general economic development.

The draft plans presented by the various organizations constitute the most important materials on which the central plan is built. The process should not be compared to forecasting or projection-making in private-enterprise economies. There, plans of this sort are not at the disposal of projection-makers, who have to rely mainly on their own statistical and economic analysis.

The method of planning used in Poland explains the great emphasis

put in our country on the organization of the planning work throughout the economy, phases of plan elaboration, unified forms of draft
plans, and so on. It is one of the most important functions of the central
planning body. In this way what I like to call a system of "planistic information" is being organized. It is noteworthy that most of the discussion on improvement of planning methods in our country deals quite
continually with the problems of organizing the planning work.

To sum up the description of the methods applied in constructing
the general economic plan, I would like to point out their following features: (1) The methods applied are mostly analytic, not synthetic.
(2) The synthesis (the aggregated plan) is reached by way of successive
approximations (iterative procedure), and on the basis of aggregation of
the draft plans elaborated by the various economic organizations.
(3) Although consumer demand is not always a starting point for production planning, production plans are confronted with independent
estimates of this demand and adapted to them. (4) The greatest emphasis of coordination methods is put on material balances in physical terms
for basic commodities; for these it is possible to calculate the technical
coefficients. It is worth mentioning that the "basic commodities" happen
to be highly capital-intensive commodities. Thus, the precise determination of the output of these commodities has a great importance for
capital-investment planning.

Major Solutions in Development Planning

The most important strategic solutions in development planning
cannot be explained by methodological premises alone. In order to explain them it seems necessary to describe the main economic alternatives which faced the country in the process of development and the solutions accepted in the plans. Much can also be learned by comparing
planned development with actual performance.

The most crucial problems of economic choice faced the country
after completion of the reconstruction program (the Three-Year Plan).
It was then that the planners had to design new development patterns.

One of the most salient features of the country's economic conditions
before the new development policy was started was found in the structural disequilibrium between labor resources and available capital. This
disequilibrium meant, of course, very low capital endowment per head
of population, and as consequence low level of utilization of manpower,
low labor productivity, and low living standards.

HIGH CAPITAL INVESTMENT POLICY

The first solution to the problem was, of course, the policy of high capital investment. Once the problem was identified, it was an important task for planners to set the volume of capital investment for a few years ahead. The approach to this problem merits attention.

The planners were aiming at the highest possible growth of capital investment in the longer run, observing the factors limiting it or, as we sometimes call them, the barriers to growth of capital investment.

Two factors determine the volume of capital investment: social savings and capacities for investment, or capacities to transform savings into real investment. Western economists focus attention on the first, while in our country (which is rather typical for less highly developed economies) the second factor has proved more important. The capacities to produce capital goods were a kind of technical barrier that limited development possibilities. In considering this problem the planners were faced, of course, with an extremely important decision: to rely mainly on home production of capital equipment, or to rely in great extent on the importation of capital goods. The option in this respect was mainly for long-run development patterns. In the short run the country had to rely on heavy imports of capital equipment. The choice made by planners was in favor of the first solution. The prospective situation in foreign trade was most decisive for the choice.

With over simplification, it can be said that the planners calculated the volume of capital investment by taking into account the feasible expansion of the country's capital goods industry, its import capacities, and the impact of capital expenditure on the level of consumption.

Actual experience has shown that the planners made no greater miscalculation with respect to the volume of capital expenditure. This point, however, needs certain important qualifications.

In planning capital investment not only the volume of capital expenditure and its distribution among the various sectors is determined but also the list of major investment projects. An important miscalculation appeared in appraising the costs of the investment projects. As a consequence, the volume of capital investment, resulting from the list of projects included in the plan and initiated during the first years of the plan, was much above the financial expenditure foreseen and also above the country's technical capacities and the admissible social burden. The situation was still more aggravated while the plan was being executed because another aspect of the investment process had been somewhat neglected in planning. The country became involved in simultaneous construction of a great number of new, closely related large investment projects. The major effects of the great economic effort could have been obtained only after completion of the whole "package" of interrelated projects. This meant a time lapse between expenditure and effects thereof.

Because of these two problems, the investment program foreseen in the plan had to be reappraised. The economy suffered from the unfavorable consequences—including extension of the construction period of many plants and various partial disproportions.

Practical planning experience has shown that the weakest aspects were not so much the over-all planning methods as the concrete calculations of investment projects. Lack of experience in evaluating the real investment costs was the prime cause of the weakness.

A most interesting aspect of the development policy designed in Poland can be found in ways and means used to raise the investment ratio. Domestic savings are generally considered a most important source for capital investment. Polish planners rely principally on domestic savings as a source of investment expenditure. Since this choice is rather obvious in an economy oriented to long-run planning, I will rather concentrate on the measures designed for increasing the investment ratio by internal means.

Interesting in the approach to this problem was the planners' emphasis not so much on calculating the financial sources as on analyzing the real factors determining investment possibilities, and particularly using latent economic resources. In order to increase capital investment a scheme was devised to utilize surplus labor from urban and particularly from rural resources.

POLICY OF EMPLOYMENT EXPANSION

Rapid increase in output of capital goods, particularly in the period from 1948 to 1954, was achieved mainly through increased employment in heavy industry and in building activities. During this period capital investment increased about three times; at the same time employment in the building-materials industry and in building activities more than tripled. A great increase in employment appeared also in the steel and machine industries. Increasing the output of heavy industry (and also of export and other industries) by way of employment expansion was achieved in part by increased number of workshifts and utilization of obsolete equipment. In construction there was a great increase of employment without much capital equipment.

The policy of expanding employment had a great impact on the nation's economic situation and its development. It seems, therefore, worthwhile to indicate certain implications of this policy.

In Poland's economic situation great expansion of employment was the only way to increase capital investment on the basis of internal sources. This kind of strategy for beginning an accelerated growth proved to be the correct economic choice.

The policy of employment expansion contributed also to the growth of output of consumer goods, though to a lesser extent. It also had a serious positive impact on the development of skills. Millions of people moved from agriculture and other technically rather primitive sectors to industry and other modern sectors, and many people obtained their first industrial training.

The employment policy also had a far-reaching impact on agriculture. As manpower was drawn from agriculture the rural population was obliged to change productivity patterns, which was a most important factor in bringing about profound changes in rural social and economic attitudes. Agriculture emerged from its traditional, stagnant conditions and acquired the spirit of change and progress.

The employment policy had certain negative features and effects, which were rather overlooked in planning. First, the policy was an important cause of a temporary decline in the real wages of urban employees, during the most difficult period, 1950–1953, and of severe changes in the income distribution patterns. Though average consumption per capita increased throughout the development period, and even during its most difficult years, this increase was uneven for the various social strata. The highest increase was gained by peasants, and particularly by the new social group, the worker-peasants. Much smaller gains appeared for urban employees and particularly for white-collar workers. Though those changes must be regarded as socially justified, they resulted in social dissatisfaction. More equal growth in consumption of the various social groups appeared after 1955, together with a smaller increase in nonagricultural employment and a decreased saving ratio.

ALLOCATION OF RESOURCES

Allocation of resources, and particularly of capital investment, among the various sectors was another important problem to be solved in planning. The planners designed the main approaches for structural change, aiming to create basic conditions for a long-run high rate of economic growth. To that end the capital-goods industries were chosen as the means of development and resources were concentrated in that field. This proved in general to be the best possible choice for development under the country's economic conditions. It can be clearly seen in retrospect that Poland would have been unable to continue the growing rate of capital investment had domestic capital-goods industries not been developed. While the traditional items of export from Poland —coal, agricultural products, and textiles—find fewer markets, export of capital goods has increased to a point where it almost balances imports. Poland is thus able to assure increasing capital investment on the basis of domestic output of capital goods.

In developing the capital-goods industry, the country first concentrated efforts and resources on semifinished products, that is on the steel industry, on certain exportable products such as rolling stock and ships, and on machine tools, trucks, and so on for domestic demand. Later, the field of expansion was much greater, although it was still mainly oriented to the domestic market. Recently, great efforts have been made to expand production of capital equipment for export.

The process of national development would have been much easier had the capital-goods industry been developed with less investment in raw materials and semifinished products and more in the final, manufacturing stage. Foreign trade possibilities were mainly responsible for the chosen development sequence of the capital-goods sector. The actual development experience has shown, however, that the planners did concentrate sufficiently on foreign trade. The change in orientation occurred chiefly after 1958, when it became evident that lack of foreign trade might hamper the rate of development of the country. Since that time foreign trade has been growing more rapidly than national income. It is being developed through cooperation with the other socialist countries (within COMECON) and through expansion of exports in other markets.

Chemicals were another important field of industrial expansion chosen in the development plans. Certain delays in the development of this sector in earlier years were caused by long hesitation about the choice of a raw material base, which particularly delayed development of petrochemicals. In recent years this industry has had the highest rate of growth, which will continue for the near future.

These two fields of industrial expansion (capital goods and chemistry) are well supported by the studies of comparative advantages of the country in the export markets. One may safely assume that they will not experience adverse changes in the terms of trade, a prospect that is less certain for Poland's traditional exports.

ECONOMIC ACHIEVEMENT

The designed development policy, with the readjustments necessary during the execution of the development plans, brought about substantial economic achievement. The economic and social structure of the country has been radically altered. The percentage of agricultural population has declined from about 60 per cent before the war to 38 per cent in 1960 and still continues to decline. The investment capacities of the country were increased so that now five times more per capita may be invested than during the early postwar period.

The greatest success was achieved in industrial development. In comparison with the prewar period, output in 1962 increased as follows: in electric power from 4 million to 35.4 million kw-hr; in crude steel from 1.4 million to 7.7 million tons; in cement from 1.7 million to 7.5 million tons; in cotton textiles from 288 million to 693 million meters; in sugar from 491,000 to 1.2 million tons. The population of the nation declined from 35 million to 30.5 million; industrial employment increased from 859,000 to 3,274,000.

Important gains were also achieved in raising the living standards of the nation. The average consumption of certain staple commodities increased from prewar levels as follows: in meat and animal fats from about 20 kilograms per capita to about 53 kilograms; in sugar from about 10 kilograms to about 30 kilograms; in cotton textiles from about 10 meters to about 19 meters.

By means of these and other transformations the nation achieved the most important objectives of the take-off period—it created the basic structural conditions for rapid, steady social and economic development.

Regional Development within the General Strategy of Economic Growth

Among postwar economic development policies in Poland national economic growth had first priority, while the development of separate geographical regions was subordinate to the general strategy of economic development. Actual development experience has shown, however, that rapid development, industrialization in particular, is the best way of solving regional problems as well as national ones.

The employment policy discussed above was particularly influential

Table 35. Nonagricultural population

Distribution	Per cent of total population, 1950	Increase 1950–1960
Total	52.9	139.4
Group I	63.8	133.6
Voivodships above the national average*		
Group II	35.4	156.6
Voivodships below the national average		

* With respect to the share of nonagricultural population in the total population.

in diminishing regional disproportions. Increasing nonagricultural employment was especially rapid in economically underdeveloped regions, which had relatively greater labor resources. The more rapid increase in employment, as well as in rural income, stimulated more rapid growth of income in general in those underdeveloped regions. The prime influence of the changes in income distribution created by the employment policy was particularly noticeable in the first period of extensive employment increase, which ended in 1954–1955. Later, regional change was shaped more by the impact of new capital investment.

The policy of structural change may have an essential influence on regional development within a country. This is especially possible when structural change is related to the difference between industries with a "determined" location and those with an "optional" location. This situation was clearly defined in Poland's economic development.

During the first stage of development, 1951–1954, while the economy was entering the period of intensive industrialization, investment policy tended to concentrate resources on industry, and especially on production of capital goods, fuels and power (based on coal), and the basis for a chemical industry. Concentration of investment outlays on these industries did not help to liquidate regional disproportions, especially during that first stage of development. Investment in those industries, consisting in extension of existing plants or construction of new ones, was determined by the need for location near known sources of raw materials. Efforts to deconglomerate the steel industry were made within economically permissible limits. This led to the creation of three new steel centers, two of the largest ones (Nowa Huta near Kraków and Częstochowa), however, were located at a relatively short distance from the old Silesian district. Still fewer alternatives were possible for the location of basic fuel and power plants, based on bituminous coal.

In the first period, insufficient knowledge of the geological resources of the country hindered better displacement of basic industrial outlays. In the course of development, however, improving geological research was one of the factors to determine the location of new industrial areas, for fuel and power (brown coal and natural gas) as well as for other minerals (sulphur and copper). Eventually new mining and industrial areas were created, especially two important centers for fuel and power based on brown coal in Turów near Wrocław and in Konin near Poznań; a new center based on sulphur mines in Tarnobrzeg and Piaseczno, on the boundary between the Kielce and Rzeszów districts; and a new copper-mining center in the Wrocław district.

All these new centers developed outside the old industrial region of Upper Silesia, because geological discoveries pointed to new sites.

Introducing natural gas and oil on a larger scale as raw materials for the chemical industry also had an important influence on the location of new industries. The greatest chemical plants built recently—oil refineries in Płock (Warsaw district), fertilizer factories in Puławy (Lublin district) and Tarnów (Kraków district)—are being constructed far from old industrial centers, in fairly underindustrialized regions, whereas in the first period basic investment for the chemical industry was located in Silesia.

During Poland's industrialization the importance of geological research for the development of backward areas was obvious. It appeared that mineral raw materials are distributed throughout the country on a much broader scale than was initially supposed. Historical industrial concentration in Upper Silesia can be explained not only by the abundance of raw materials (especially of coal) in that region, but also by insufficient knowledge of mineral resources in other regions of the country. Future research in this field will also be of vital importance for the industrial geography of the country, especially the anticipated discoveries of oil and natural gas.

The growth of the processing industries created still greater possibilities for transforming Poland's economic geography. During the process of development, investment was shifted from the basic raw materials to final products, which gave more freedom in the location of new plants. Most new construction for the processing industries (machine-building, chemical, light industry) occurred outside traditional industrial centers throughout the country. This kind of investment was aimed at filling the "gaps" in regional development of basic industry.

Nevertheless, the leveling of regional disproportions through the processing industry was hindered by the relatively little investment of this type compared to the scale of the problem itself, and also by deficiencies of the infrastructure in the most backward regions. This latter factor led to concentration of outlays in chosen areas, in order to obtain "external economies." Thus, the liquidation of regional disproportions did not take place simultaneously and proportionately in all regions, but rather in successive steps, with the creation of major industrial centers. Economies in outlay on infrastructure led also to the tendency to locate new plants in bigger cities. To the extent to which this was feasible and economically expedient, the development outlined above was supplemented by investment in small-scale industry.

On the whole, it should be said that the investment policy chiefly followed the lines of the general structural change of the economy. With progress it was also eliminating regional disproportions. Because of economic conditions resulting from historical development of various regions, and also the tendency for maximum effectiveness of investment, there was still relatively high concentration of investment in the more industrialized regions. Usually, underdeveloped regions are still behind the highly developed ones, as far as capital endowment per capita is concerned. This can be seen from the following table for 1960.

It is obvious that equal capital endowment and equal output per capita among regions are not the premises for rational development of various regions. With a relatively low national economic level, connected in particular with low efficiency in agriculture, however, the pattern of industrial investment is a factor of income distribution. In Poland, investment in underdeveloped areas still has the function of substantially improving the situation of the inhabitants. It is worth indicating, however, that the process of equalizing the per capita incomes in various regions has gone much farther than one might judge from

Table 36. PROPORTION OF POPULATION AND CAPITAL INVESTMENT IN 1960

Type of region	Per cent of population	Per cent of fixed capital
I. Most highly developed regions*	47.9	55.5
II. Regions with average development	26.7	26.3
III. Regions least developed	24.1	18.2

* Group I comprises the voivodships of Katowice, Szczecin, Gdańsk, Poznań, Warsaw, Wrocław, and Opole; Group II the voivodships of Bydgoszcz, Koszalin, Łódź, Kraków, Zielona Góra; Group III, the voivodships of Olsztyn, Lublin, Rzeszów, Białystok, and Kielce. Voivodships have been divided into the three groups on the basis of per capita consumption.

observing only the diminishing differences in capital endowment of those regions.

Polish postwar economic development led to substantial leveling of previous regional disproportions. Although various regions differ greatly from one another in capital endowment and level of output per capita, differences in the level of consumption are much slighter. This is a result of the general lines of development policies, particularly of those of income distribution. Special roles in the process of leveling regional disproportions were played by a significant increase in nonagricultural employment and by the rise in consumption levels of the rural population. The differences in per capita consumption now range from 20 per cent above the national average in the richest district among the seventeen regional districts to not more than 20 per cent below the national average in the poorest district.

CHAPTER 18

Location Policy and the Regional Efficiency of Investments

ANDRZEJ WRÓBEL

STANISŁAW M. ZAWADZKI

THIS article deals with the question of the relation between investment policy and the influence of investments on the economic development of different regions of the country. Because of Poland's considerable regional variation in economic development, this question is closely connected to the problem of the economic progress of underdeveloped areas.

The Importance of Industrial Investment

Bearing in mind the thesis that industrialization is the chief factor in economic progress and in the transformation of a country's regional structure, we are limiting our analysis to the problem of industrial investment and development. It is in accordance with this thesis that 42 per cent of Poland's investments[1] from 1946 to 1960 were assigned to industry.

We may begin with the statement that policy on the location of industrial investments is an integral part of the general policy of industrialization—especially in a planned economy. The state, which makes decisions of investment and fixes programs of future production, has broad opportunities for influencing location. Every investment decision is, to a certain measure, a decision about location. Therefore, in realizing its industrialization policy, the state is also taking over the task of locating industries. It is a difficult task, especially when the means are limited and the aims complicated (and sometimes even contradictory). We shall probably be right to state that changes in the location of industry in Poland in the last fifteen years have resulted from two basic aims: to reach the highest attainable yield from investment, and to

[1] Including housing investments.

stimulate the economic growth of neglected areas. These two aims do not always harmonize. Locating new plants in nonindustrial areas often requires higher initial outlay than if the same plants were placed in industrial areas. On the other hand it sometimes happens that both profits and efficiency decline when industries are concentrated in one area. Both situations have appeared in Poland and have had to be taken into account in decisions on location.

National Investment Policies

The location of industry has been one of the most important problems to be solved since the introduction of planned economy in Poland. It has been expressed in legislative acts defining the general lines of successive long-range economic plans. These acts in turn have determined the investment policy of the state in given periods.

The first long-range plan was The Three-Year Plan of Economic Reconstruction (1947–1949). Capital investment policy naturally concentrated on two basic problems: the reconstruction of production facilities and the integration of Recovered Territories with the rest of the country. The act promulgated by the National Home Council on September 21, 1946, reads:

During the planned period the reintegration of the Old Territories and the Recovered Territories should be accomplished. The reintegration should consist in the equal disposition of the population in towns and villages of the Old and of the Recovered Territories; in the amalgamation of industry; in the creation of uniform conditions of agricultural production; and in the connection of the whole of the country by a uniform network of communication.[2]

Investment policy was defined in part by the need to concentrate outlays in regions which had been most devastated and which were the most vital to the national economy. The Act says: "Industrial investments should be undertaken according to the promptness of productive effect and the importance of these investments to production, and in view of preserving the national property from destruction."[3] The same act states, however, that one of the factors behind investment decisions should be "the regional point of view" and that "in the absence of a decisive factor of location, further extension of industry in the region of Silesia should be avoided."[4]

[2] The Plan of Economic Reconstruction, Warsaw, 1946, p. 6.

[3] *Ibid.*, p. 10.

[4] *Ibid.*, pp. 20–21.

The realization of the Plan of Reconstruction did not bring any substantial changes in the locating of industry in Poland. Nearly half of the industrial investment outlay was directed to Upper Silesia, the most industrialized region of Poland, with the intention of obtaining the highest production effects in the shortest time. The greater part of the remaining investments was directed to the Recovered Territories,[5] which had a decisive influence on the repopulation and economic recovery of these areas.

Willful shaping of changes in the location of production and in the industrialization of different regions of the country was given full expression in the Six-Year Plan (1950–1955). The Act of Parliament introducing this plan stated that in order to obtain basic economic objectives one should "raise the economic and cultural activity of the backward eastern and central parts of the country, and of several districts, not yet economically recovered, in the western and northern voivodships, by an adequate policy of locating productive forces."[6]

The Plan also considered regional problems (chapter IV of the Act), by defining the basic indices of economic development of the particular voivodships. In the introduction to this chapter we read: "In the operation of the plan a long-range process will be initiated pointing toward a more uniform placement in the whole country of both productive forces and social and cultural facilities. The disparities in the economic and cultural development of the country, resulting from Poland's economic conditions in the era of capitalism, will be diminished."

The Six-Year Plan provided for the building of more than one thousand industrial establishments. The parliamentary act concerning the Plan—voted in July, 1950—fixed the location of the greater part of the projected industrial investments. Plants built outside the old industrial regions were to employ two-thirds of the increase of the working force resulting from the new investments. With these decisions as a base, a planned index of the growth of industrial employment was calculated for each voivodship; the indices for the less industrialized voivodships proved the highest.

During the realization of the Six-Year Plan, however, an essential divergence from the primary objectives of the plan occurred. The changes appeared not only in the quantity and structure of industrial

---

[5] The first figure, concerning investments in Upper Silesia, contains also a part of investments in the Recovered Territories.

[6] The Six-Year Plan, Warsaw, 1950, p. 96.

investments but also in the location of such investments. The general economic situation of the country compelled the government to give up the building of 470 new industrial plants. Of them, the location of 278 had already been fixed; 203 of them were to be built in nonindustrialized voivodships.[7]

Nevertheless, efforts to reach a more rational location policy were begun during the period of the Six-Year Plan. The degree of economic development in the different areas cannot yet be properly estimated. Furthermore, problems of industrial investment must be studied jointly for the Six-Year Plan and the first Five-Year Plan. In the majority of cases we can speak about the unity of industrial investments for the years 1950–1960 both from economic and locational points of view. The results of planned location of industrial investments in the years 1950–1955 have become fully evident only in the territorial changes of production between 1956 and 1960. Our statement is based on the fact that one of the basic objectives of the Five-Year Plan (1956–1960) was the concentration of investment outlays on plants already existing or started in the period of the Six-Year Plan. This decision meant that the liberty of choice in location of investments had been seriously limited.

With this in mind, we can compare the actual results of both long-range plans (from the point of view of location) with the general lines of economic policy presented at the beginning of this chapter.

Regional Differences

The historical development of Polish territories and the location of mineral resources, greatest in the western and southern areas of the country, caused an important disproportion in the economic situation of the different regions.

As illustration of this, it is sufficient to say that in 1950 the voivodship of Katowice, covering only 3.1 per cent of the nation's area, contained 11 per cent of the inhabitants, 17 per cent of the urban population and 29.4 per cent of the industrial employment.[8] In the same year five eastern and northern voivodships (Lublin, Białystok, Olsztyn, Koszalin, and Szczecin), covering 40 per cent of the country's area, totaled only 17 per cent of the population and 5.5 per cent of the industrial employment.

Between 1950 and 1960 this situation changed. A very high rate of development appeared in the underdeveloped voivodships, and a much

[7] Mrzygłód, *The Policy of Location of Industry in Poland 1946–1980* (Warsaw, 1962), p. 62.

[8] All figures about employment in industry include employment in industrial handicraft.

lower rate in industrialized voivodships. For instance, the index of growth of industrial employment, which was 45 per cent for the entire country, rose to 90 per cent and as high as 159 per cent in the underdeveloped voivodships. In the same period this index for the industrialized voivodships was lower than the country's average, reaching only 17 per cent in the voivodship of Katowice. These figures indicate the results of pursuing that aspect of location policy which aims at activating the underdeveloped areas.

The second goal (that of achieving the highest yield from investments) can be represented by figures showing the increase of employment in different voivodships. The increase of industrial employment in the voivodship of Katowice was 11 per cent, and in the voivodships of Wrocław, Łódź, Opole, and Kraków, 26 per cent of the country's total increase. The same figure for the underdeveloped voivodships amounted only to 14.5 per cent. Thus their share in the country's industrial employment rose slightly from 5.5 per cent in 1950 to 8.4 per cent in 1960 while the share of the voivodship of Katowice dropped from 29.4 per cent to 23.7 per cent.

Even more illuminating than these are the figures representing the division of the investment quotas in the analyzed period: the underdeveloped voivodships obtained a little less than 8 per cent of the general outlay, while the voivodship of Katowice had 26 per cent, and the voivodship of Opole 16 per cent. All told, over 60 per cent of the country's investments were concentrated in the industrialized zone of four voivodships in southern and western Poland (Wrocław, Opole, Katowice, Kraków)[9] and in the metropolitan area of Warsaw.

Comparing data on the absolute growth of employment with that on the territorial location of investments, we see that, generally speaking, the investments in the group of industrialized voivodships were more capital-intensive. On the other hand, the labor-intensive nature of the investments made in the underdeveloped areas suggests that the most important goal of the policy of location was the economic improvement of those territories by creating new places of work.

The general results of the location policy pursued in the period 1950–1960 which aimed at raising the economy of underdeveloped areas appear, in spite of some achievements, to be relatively insignificant. Furthermore, analysis of the economic effectiveness of investments

[9] Moreover, the majority of investment in the voivodship of Kraków was situated in its western part, which territorially and economically is connected with the voivodship of Katowice.

in those regions shows their relatively high costs. This was sometimes caused by faulty choices of site for the construction of new plants, because of insufficient exploration of all possible locations; consequently, while investment outlay grew, these plants did not offer proper conditions for further development.

But the heart of the matter lies elsewhere; it concerns the main problem of the regional effectiveness of investments, which is a socially and economically based compromise between the objective of rapidly obtaining the highest yield from investment and that of straightening out regional disproportions of development. This second objective is the basis of the complicated problem of the industrialization of the backward areas. Of course there are certain other aims, but they are less important.

Having this aim in mind, we want to point out that the proper solution of this problem depends on the method of realizing the superior objective, that is, the objective of industrialization. The opinion that industrialization is an instrument of economic progress may be of great influence here. A mechanical application of this principle in order to raise up the backward areas (where reserve of manpower is the principal premise for industrial investment) produces growth in the social costs of industrialization and consequently, when means are limited, can intensify economic difficulties. This opinion can also influence the theoretical grounds of location policy; the thesis of "uniform" location of industry, stressed particularly in the first period of accelerated industrialization, in due course gives preference to activating backward regions. On the other hand, acceptance of economic calculation of the current efficiency of investment as the sole basis of decisions gives a privileged position to regions already industrially developed.

Polish economists interested in problems of location have for several years discussed this specific discrepancy. The difference in their opinions amounts to the difference between calculating effectiveness from the national viewpoint and from the regional viewpoint. This is true even in a country which is not very large, such as Poland. Excluding capital investments placed near recently discovered mineral resources or agricultural and forest stocks in underdeveloped areas, industrial investment in developed areas nearly always proves to be more economical.

The validity of this thesis is not affected by the possibility of the inconveniences caused by excessive agglomeration. Only in the Upper Silesian region and in the metropolitan areas of Warsaw and Łódź do conditions approach the point where economic benefits from new investments may diminish. Nowadays, these inconveniences appear more clearly as social, housing, and urban planning problems than as problems in the economic soundness of new investments and of plants already existing.

The principal motive for locating industrial investments in backward areas, the one that would compensate for increased investment outlay and operating expenses, was undoubtedly that of giving employment to the inhabitants of these regions. The principal advantage to these regions from investment was the increase of employment in industry (mostly obtained by reducing the employment in agriculture) and consequently the growth of the consumer's per capita income. In reality, when the existing agricultural overpopulation with its latent threat of unemployment was considered, local manpower, brought into production and not being a "scarce resource," was not a cost in the social meaning. On the other hand, if the new plants—as happened in several cases—were not connected either presently or potentially to the regions by the bonds of supply and outlet, they could not have any "multiplier effects" on the economic development of these regions.

The location of industrial plants in underdeveloped areas in practice necessitated additional, sometimes very important, investments in infrastructure. Because these investments were adapted to industrial investments already being exploited or developed and therefore not a part of a well-studied plan of the development of the settlement network, their effectiveness and consequently the effectiveness of the whole regional plan of investments was diminished.

The New Location Policy

The growing understanding of the complexity of policy on location, based on practical experience (presented here only in summary), exerted an influence on the evolution of investment policy. We find evidence of this evolution in the propositions for the economic development of Poland for the Five-Year Plan of 1961–1965, which were introduced to the XII Plenum of PZPR. Three principles of location policy were presented in these propositions. The first is the principle of taking fullest advantage of natural resources of the different regions. Second is the principle of limiting excessive migrations of the population by locating new plants in order to make possible the employment of local resources of manpower. Third is the principle of diminishing—within economically reasonable limits—the excessive difference in the economic development of different regions and in the living standards of their inhabitants. The principle includes diminishing those differences by the development of settlements, communication networks, and service trades.

In this approach, the objective of removing the differences in regional economic development, given third place in the hierarchy of objectives of location policy, was subordinated to the distinctly expressed principle of economic calculation. Means indicated to realize this aim were investments in communications, housing, and service trades, which have—according to previous experience—a fundamental value in the efficient realization of industrial investment of many kinds, and simultaneously help to equalize the standard of life of the population.

These new general formulae of location policy do not mean necessarily that proper methods of calculating the efficiency of investments in different regions have been found. Nevertheless, this problem has been placed in the working program of the Committee for Space Economy and Regional Planning attached to the Polish Academy of Sciences. Several aspects of the problem are being studied: theoretical models of planned economic development in different regions; questions of economy of scale, both for industrial plants and factories and settlement centers; the process of industrialization; and the process of urbanization.

Great efforts has been made to obtain statistical data for the various regions necessary to analysis of this kind; in recent years figures have been collected concerning among other things national income in regional section, amount of investment for every year since 1949, and amount of real property.

CHAPTER 19

The Long-term Plan for Polish Expansion, 1961–1980

KAZIMIERZ SECOMSKI

Introduction

THE postwar period in which the Polish national economy was reconstructed and developed was characterized by an intensely dynamic economic growth. After the first years spent overcoming the great difficulties of rebuilding the country from its wartime devastation, the possibility emerged of making plans to cover many future years. The plans for the years from 1950 to 1960 greatly accelerated the rate of economic growth and effected essential transformations in the social and economic structure of the country.

Two objectives were thus attained in Poland from 1947 to 1960: rapid *reconstruction of the country* (from 1944 to 1949) and the execution of an important phase of the *fundamental industrialization* of the country. Important transformations took place during that period in the socio-economic structure of the population, expressed mainly in the transfer of great numbers of people from agricultural work to industrial and construction work, thus from the farms to the cities. Methods were devised and perfected for more efficient management and direction of the national economy as a whole. These methods stressed centralized control of the key problems of economic growth, plus decentralized control by regional agencies of local needs and possibilities.

The long-term plan elaborated for the development of Poland from 1961 to 1980 formulated the problem of economic growth differently. Since a relatively high level of economic growth had been attained in the previous period, and a relatively high degree of maturity has been reached in methods of management and economic planning, new possibilities were opened for solving the more complex problems of accelerated economic growth. The formulation of the rate of such growth, its trends, and estimates were, however, based on totally different premises.

Immediately after the war quantitative indices played the decisive role in economic planning. Primary efforts were directed toward increasing goods and services per capita in the shortest time possible. Actual social and economic needs had to be met immediately. As basic needs were being satisfied during that period by the increasing output of goods and services, two further needs arose: to diversify the output and to improve the quality of the goods and services. Satisfaction of these needs is set under the perspective plan to be accomplished within twenty years. Until basic needs were fulfilled, a new long-term twenty-year plan had to rely initially on considerations of both increased quantity and quality; subsequent priority was given to quality indices. It was not sufficient to plan the expansion, for instance, of metallurgical production only on quantitative indices per capita. Qualitative indices also had to be established by taking estimates of essential changes in the structure of the metal-products industry and adapting them to the needs of the second phase of the development of the national economy. Similarly, it was not enough to make a general formulation of quantitative indices (for instance, a threefold increase in consumption for the population); essential transformations in the structure of consumption had also to be defined. These transformations were linked to a new, higher level in personal income and the resultant increased demand for better goods and services. Such a transformation and transition had to be taken into account in all fields of the national economy.

The long-term plan must, by its very nature, be general and flexible. Estimates of the growth of the national economy and the way in which it might develop must be set within a framework. It is neither possible nor relevant to plan in great detail the numerous problems that might arise in a twenty-year period of economic growth. A long-term plan should primarily indicate general lines of national economic growth, predicting an estimated rate of expansion and defining the principal structural changes, especially social and economic changes.

The infinite number of problems involved in long-term economic growth requires many elaborations and revisions. Work on the Polish long-term plan lasted for about five years. Unlike five-year and one-year plans, long-term plans must include regular updating, and the target year must remain flexible. The initial long-term plan was scheduled to run from 1957 to 1975; but now the target limit is established for 1980. The plan is to be revised every five years. At each revision consideration will be given to the changes which have taken place in the economic situation of the country as well as to the experience acquired and results attained during the previous five years. At the same time the target date of the long-term plan will be shifted forward five years.

In the first stage of plan development an extended study should be the starting point for formulating an appropriate guideline for the expansion of the entire national economy. As the work advances, an internal methodic verification can be made of the long-term plan, and coordinated as fully as possible by the balance method. In addition to internal coordination of directives in the long-term plan, external coordination must also be carried through. This is based on policies of international cooperation, division of work, and specialization. It assumes particularly that economic cooperation with socialist countries will be extended.

The Need for Research and Analysis

The first steps in preparing a long-term plan should always be thorough analysis of actual conditions and their possibilities for the country's economic expansion as well as a characterization of the requirements for expansion and of the existing possibilities for meeting such needs. This many-sided analysis of basic data permits a more realistic appraisal to be made of the potential for national economic expansion in the perspective of twenty-years. The substance and value of a long-term plan is decided by a correct approach to the data and by a realistic estimate of the rate of economic growth. The following are primary factors in the first conception of a long-term plan:

(1) *Demographic phenomena;* the analysis of vital statistics for the present and the future, as well as inferences based on their application to the country's economic expansion. Specific demographic conditions are basic to the perspective plan. From 1946 to 1960 Poland experienced an unusually high rate of natural population increase. It rose from 18 per mil to 19.5 per mil between 1946 and 1958, but slowly decreased thereafter. The high birth rate of those years will provide great numbers of young people for the labor market during the period 1964–1980. One of the main objectives of the Polish perspective plan—along with improvement of living standards and development of the productive potential—is full employment of this large labor force.

(2) *Predictions for the economic and social development of the country* for the twenty-year period, as well as for the five-year periods within it. In ad-

dition to a synthetic index of the increase in the national income, such predictions embrace a definite program for raising the national living standard and directives for the development of particular branches of the national economy, especially industry and agriculture.

(3) *International cooperation,* based on an appraisal of the advantages acquired from commercial exchange; among these would be the international division of work and specialization among socialist countries, making possible an expanded coordination of decisions among particular long-term plans.

(4) *Technical progress,* considering problems related to the universal introduction of new techniques in particular branches of the national economy, especially emphasizing modernization. Trends of technical development in each country must issue from its own potential. They should also be based on premises in specialization of production. By means of international cooperation achievements in modern techniques by individual nations should be rendered accessible to others in order to accelerate the development of a material base.

When the principal components of a long-term plan are thus formulated, preparations can be made for a more expanded study and for a prognosis of social and economic development. It is natural that the problems of demographic phenomena or directives for technical progress should develop in various ways, depending on the specific conditions prevailing in a country. Hence, certain concepts of economic expansion may be demographic in character; or they may issue from appropriately expanded international cooperation; or they may arise in the field of technical progress. On the whole, however, demographic problems, the assumptions for economic and social advance (including living standards), the assumptions for international cooperation, and the problem of technical advancement must jointly constitute the principal elements of a long-term plan. Conceptions based on all these factors should ultimately lead to a complex and many-sided approach to the expansion of the national economy, utilizing entire aggregates of objectives, assumptions, and directives for economic and social expansion.

Demographic Phenomena

Demographic phenomena constitute a natural starting point for shaping the principal conceptions of a Polish long-term plan. Poland had, in the early postwar-period, large unexploited resources of manpower, and even now, against the background of a high birth rate, the demographic problem continues to play a prime role in planning eco-

Table 37. BIRTH RATE, 1938–1960 (PER THOUSAND)

1938	1950	1955	1960
10.7	19.1	19.5	15.0

nomic growth. Table 37 illustrates the scale of the birth rate in postwar years compared to that of prewar years. The high birth rate was maintained until 1959. In the perspective of the long-term plan with its directives for new places of work the drop has been negligible. Starting at the age of eighteen, large groups of young people, born between 1945 and 1960, will be successively entering the labor market beginning in 1963. This makes a particularly large investment effort necessary, first to expand the school system and subsequently to erect new factories and places of employment.

Thus, demographic phenomena indicate important transformations in Poland. The severe losses in population during the years of the war and of the Nazi occupation resulted in a demographic deficit until 1962. Increment of working-age population was insignificant, and there was a labor shortage. The population loss nevertheless facilitated the shift from the countryside to the town, and provided employment other than farming. Within the perspective of twenty years such a situation can undergo a radical change, as illustrated by the figures in Table 38. These figures reveal that the total increase of population is almost stabilized in specific five-year periods. Profound changes, however, take place in the age structure of the population. Not until 1963 is there a marked increase in working-age population, from the entrance into the labor market of those people born in the late forties.

Along with the changes in the age structure of the population an exceptionally rapid urbanization took place in Poland after the war. Such a process meant an actual revolution in Polish cities. This is seen in Table 39. In the fourteen years of the postwar period the urban

Table 38. PROJECTED FUTURE POPULATION (IN THOUSANDS)

Population	1956–60	1961–65	1966–70	1971–75	1976–80
General increase	2,238	1,856	1,781	2,056	2,142
Increase in working-age population	373	1,024	1,646	1,944	1,042

Table 39. POSTWAR POPULATION INCREASE (IN MILLIONS)

Population	1946	1950	1955	1960
Total	23.9	25.0	27.6	29.9
Urban	7.5	9.2	12.1	14.2

population almost doubled partially at the expense of the rural population. A similar intensification of the urbanization process is expected for the planned twenty-year period, as the data in Table 40 indicate. The continued revolution in the cities marked a radical transformation in the professional structure of Poland and a rapid growth of the country's economic potential. The new industrial stage has had a decided influence on the acceleration of the rate of economic growth.

From the study of demographic phenomena, successive working hypotheses were elaborated concerning labor power and ways of using it. Among other problems these dealt with the employment of women, youth, and elderly people who were needed because of their qualifications or because there was a local shortage of manpower. The estimates had also to include possible further migrations from countryside to town. An appraisal had to be made of the influence of modern techniques on a drop in the demand for manpower; and an evaluation of how low intensification in agriculture would affect employment was required.

An employment balance sheet on a nationwide scale, and in regional cross-sections, called for expansion of schooling and lengthening of the educational period. It also sought increasing labor productivity in various branches of the national economy and a program for the gradual shortening of working hours in successive five-year periods. Preliminary estimates are illustrated in Table 41. This theory of the balance of manpower was based on a slow rate of shortening the work week, which would average 35 hours in the 1976–1980 period, but would be shortened sooner in difficult or onerous professions.

The demographic problem was taken into account in an expanded

Table 40. PROJECTED POPULATION INCREASE (IN MILLIONS)

Population	1965	1970	1975	1980
Total	31.6	33.4	35.5	37.6
Urban	15.7	17.3	19.3	21.6

Table 41. PROJECTED AVERAGE WORK WEEK

Period	Work Week
1966–1970	46 hours
1971–1975	40 hours
1976–1980	35 hours

form in the decisions of the long-term plan. The goal was universal use of manpower in all regions of the country, taking into account migrations from farms to cities and essential transformations in the professional structure.

Defining the Rate of Economic Expansion

The key problem of a long-term plan lies in an appropriate definition of the rate of economic expansion. Such growth cannot be hastily determined. A complete analysis of the problems and possibilities of economic development, decisions regarding expansion of productive power, and many other elements make up the definition of the actual rate of economic growth.

The necessity of analyzing a number of factors of economic growth often leads to inferences regarding the acceleration or reduction of the initially determined rate of economic growth. In this case, a group of factors *accelerating* a planned economic growth is often differentiated from a group of factors *restraining* it.

A preliminary analysis of the possibilities of economic growth, based on an examination of the material-technical base and anticipated changes in the final objectives, leads to a preliminary determination of the rate of economic growth. The dynamics of the rate of the expansion of national economy depends, of course, on many premises and on developmental trends in subsequent years. Studies concerning manpower and its utilization; progress in organization and techniques of increased labor productivity; knowledge of natural resources; geological discoveries and an appraisal of their usefulness; the reserves inherent in the national economy—these are the most essential accelerating factors with a positive influence on economic expansion.

In a long-term plan one must also reckon with the negative influence of many factors which would restrain the rate of economic expansion. There are, for example, the difficulties arising from building up foreign commerce in cooperation with capitalist countries, especially in dealing with the Common Market countries. There are also difficulties connected with expanding the raw-material base of the country. Expansion of a raw-material base is often "by leaps and bounds." The construction of big mines or mines of newly discovered raw materials often requires much time. A sudden marked increase of extracted raw materials will be noticed in a given year, but until such a time the national economy must undergo many difficulties in adjusting its balance of raw materials; this transitory period may adversely influence foreign commerce. In Poland this constitutes a vital problem in a long-term plan, when considered against a background of extensive investments in raw materials (bituminous and brown coal, sulphur, copper and other nonferrous metal ores, as well as iron ore).

All the deliberations concerning factors that accelerate or restrain the planned rate of economic expansion constitute a general maximizing of the rate of economic growth. The scale of material outlays and organizational efforts indispensable for increasing the rate of economic growth by, for example, 1 per cent, must be examined in detail by various methods of economic analysis. Maximizing the rate of expansion always leads to an increased tension in foreign commerce, as well as to the danger of disturbing the internal economic balance. The Polish long-term plan was based on the assumption of an *optimal* rate of economic growth, in opposition to a *maximal* rate. The excessively high material outlays connected with an especially great effort on the part of the entire community find no proper economic substantiation. Calculations indicate that the price paid by the national economy is excessively high for a relatively slight acceleration of the rate of economic expansion.

At the same time, the premises point to the necessity for a relatively flexible long-term plan. The plan necessarily contains a sizable number of approximate decisions. In addition to comparatively accurate and precise decisions with regard to industrial expansion, many estimates, evaluations, and previsions must be adopted for the planning period. The dynamics of change and economic expansion are also based on hypotheses relative to foreign commerce, international economic cooperation, expansion of modern techniques, and so on. Hence, verifying the decisions in the long-term plan becomes indispensable; as does constant checking of estimates to utilize possibilities for expansion.

Growth of National Income

The index of increase of the national income generally constitutes the most synthetic approach to the *dynamics of economic growth*. The shaping of the national income, especially the rate of its increase and the principles of its distribution, both reflects the scale of the social effort and indicates the fulfillment of the needs of the people (consumption) and the objectives for expanding productive power (investments).

At the same time the dynamics of an increased national income are linked to a number of fundamental political and economic decisions and to the rate of change in the social and economic structure of the country. In addition to capital investment, the growth scale of national income involves the estimates of the long-term plan regarding increase in labor output through technical and organizational progress; increased employment and utilization of manpower (especially skilled manpower); and the lowering of material costs, especially by improving consumption indices per production unit and reducing spoilage. Therefore, growth of the national income, its structure and distribution, is justly ranked as the central ideal of the long-term plan in relation to the general target of the whole plan. The target formulated by the Polish long-term plan is *an uninterrupted and maximum expansion of productive power with marked improvement in living conditions.*

With such an approach the goals of planned expansion and an integrated whole are distinctly outlined as are social and economic policies on a twenty-year scale. A marked rise in living standards requires unceasing pressure for a rapid, universal growth of productive power. Such growth is simultaneously linked to the solution of the difficult demographic problems, previously analyzed.

Increased national income and the principles governing its distribution are, as a matter of fact, a reflection of the ultimate effect of a number of specific decisions undertaken in individual branches and sectors of the national economy. The synthesis emerging from this background of data illustrates most clearly, however, the substance of the concept of the long-term plan. Hence, it will be relevant to present the fundamental indices relating to the increase in national income and the consumption and accumulation of funds (Table 42). A more than fourfold increase in the national income within twenty years indicates a very high rate of economic expansion. In order to attain such a marked elevation of the level of the national income by the target year 1980, a number of large-scale capital investments are necessary. These would assure—in addition to an increased labor output and improvement of other indices —a mean yearly rate of 7.5 per cent of the growth of the national economy. The fact must be stressed that every 1 per cent of growth in the national income, in each subsequent year and in each subsequent five-year period, represents an increasing absolute value.

The necessity of developing large investment capital means that the

Table 42. ESTIMATED GROWTH INDEX AND AVERAGE ANNUAL RATE OF GROWTH (1960 = 100)

Category	Growth index 1980 ————— 1960	Average annual rate of growth (%)
National income produced (in retail prices)	336	6.2
National income allocated for distribution (in retail prices)	319	6.0
Consumption fund	289	5.5
Accumulation fund	409	7.3
Consumption per capita	231	4.3

accumulation fund, which was destined chiefly for investment purposes, must indicate a correspondingly increased rate of growth in comparison with the general index of increase in national income, especially in the consumption fund. The rate of realizing investment capital, with a direct increase in the national income, must be very high, especially in the first ten years of the planning period.

Consumption per capita should increase threefold during the twenty-year interval. By reaching such a level of consumption, the population of Poland would be assured of better living conditions than those now existing in the most highly developed European countries.

A rapid increase in the national income and the possibilities for a marked improvement of consumption are linked to fundamental structural changes in the national income. Such changes are also a reflection of the social and economic transformation planned throughout the entire country. The share taken by industry in the creation of the national income is becoming considerably greater, being linked to a simultaneous reshaping of the professional structure of the population. The result will be a markedly greater share of skilled labor in the total balance of manpower.

The figures in Table 43 illustrate the substance of the structural transformation occurring in the national income. While the share of industry in the formation of the national income is becoming predominant because of the rapid rate of industrialization, agricultural production is markedly diminishing, and will be reduced within twenty years to one-half of its initial percentage share in 1960. Although agricultural production will be doubled during the twenty-year period, a relatively rapid reduction becomes evident in the proportion of agricultural produce in the national income, especially when compared to the very

Table 43. PERCENTAGE DISTRIBUTION OF NET NATIONAL INCOME (IN PER CENT)
(1961 FACTORY PRICES)

Sources	1955	1960	1970	1980
Industry and building	48	53	63	69
Agriculture	34	28	19	13
Other	18	19	18	18
Total	100	100	100	100

high rate of growth of other sectors of the national economy. The new structure of the national income envisaged for 1975–1980 corresponds to the economic structure of a country with an outstandingly high level of industrialization.

In terms of an essential transformation of the national income, the entire period of the long-term plan can be divided into two ten-year intervals. The prime necessity during the first ten years is acceleration of the rate of increase in investments, especially those connected with the expansion of industry. This also includes the preparation of new places of employment for the young people finishing their education. Thus, the first ten-year period (from 1961 to 1970) can be called the period of large investments and fundamental reshaping of the structure of employment, the tendency being to utilize fully the manpower already available. In consequence, the first ten-year period will produce a slow rise in living standards.

An essential shift in favor of increased consumption is anticipated for the second ten-year period. When the extent of consumption is markedly increased, a significant structural change also takes place (Table 44). The outlook is that the level of consumption defined at

Table 44. CHANGES IN THE STRUCTURE OF CONSUMPTION

Goods	Percentage of total consumption		
	1960	1970	1980
Food	52.7	46.6	39.2
Stimulants	9.9	7.7	5.4
Clothing and footwear	17.0	18.0	18.0
Durable metal goods	5.1	8.8	12.7
Furniture and household furnishings	2.2	2.9	4.0
Other goods	8.2	9.2	12.5
Services	4.9	6.8	8.2
Total consumption	100	100	100

present by physiologists as optimal (class D), will be attained in the period 1971–1975. Worth stressing is the fact than an increase in consumption is linked above all to an increase in the total expenditure on food. Thus, the percentage of food consumption in the total consumption in the first ten years indicates a comparatively slight change. A radical reshaping of the structure of consumption will not become apparent until the second ten years. This is also connected with the changing demands of the population; as people's needs for food are met in full and as their individual incomes become notably larger, they will desire other goods.

Stress must also be laid on the fact that collective consumption will likewise be increased during the planning period. Emphasis in the first ten-year period is put primarily on an appropriate increase in wages and the formation of a basis (by a system of individual economic incentives and a higher labor productivity) for increasing individual earnings, thus making it possible to raise the individual consumption level. The significance of the collective consumption fund will become increasingly greater, along with an improvement in living conditions of the working population. The entire twenty-year period will see continuous improvement of housing conditions. This includes the building of flats at an increasing rate in the cities, as well as the construction of schools, which are needed to prepare cadres and to provide universal education.

An analysis of the formation of the volume of consumption and the changes in its structure is one of the most interesting social problems— theoretically, as well as in devising a long-term plan. It involves, among other things, a profound study of the flexibility of market demand and variability in the shaping of demand for a number of goods (especially durable goods). The rising level of wages and actual incomes in various social groups and families requires that postulates be made for different stages of increased individual and collective consumption. The general social and economic policy must be able to influence the consumption structure of the population and strengthen trends of consumption by adjusting wage and price levels.

Thus, it is indicated that the organization of the structure and distribution of income is one of the most essential problems of long-term planning.

Changes in Economic Structure

Postulates regarding the increase in national income and amelioration of living standards are based on the development of an intensive *industrialization program* and the *modernization of agriculture*. The main driving force here is industry, which produces rapid development and modernization of other branches of the national economy.

The first phase of the fundamental industrialization of the country was realized during the postwar period up to 1960. Consequently, Poland substantially transformed its social and economic structure, and simultaneously attained a much expanded material base, which at present constitutes the starting point for greater development in the long-term plan for 1961–1980. The rapid progress in the industrialization of the country was connected with numerous internal developmental disparities. Such disparities appeared also within industry itself, especially between the development of the raw-material and the processing branches of industry.

The second period of universal industrialization (from 1961 to 1980) not only ought to assure complete elimination of internal disparities in industry and in the entire national economy, but by means of *specialization of work distribution* should also result in a higher technical level and a more correct industrial structure. Cooperation was examined on two levels. International division of labor, production specialization, and a division of tasks among the socialist countries was considered, as well as the task of implanting and making more efficient cooperation within the industry of each country.

In addition to specialization, division of labor, and cooperation, the *development of a national raw-material base* was given first place among the tasks of the long-term plan. Recently Poland recorded several valuable geological discoveries, which are now partially exploited or in the preliminary stage of exploitation or being prepared for future exploitation. It may be expected that the results of further intensive geological work as well as the exploitation of raw-material deposits already discovered (or those which will be discovered) will allow the creation of a particularly strong base for our own industry.

In the future an important role should be played by the joint efforts of the socialist countries to make feasible the exploitation of natural resources. Many joint investments have already been undertaken for such raw materials as bituminous and brown coal, copper ore, and potassium salts. Undoubtedly cooperation in this field will speed the process and facilitate industrialization of the interested countries.

Technical progress as a whole must also be reckoned as one of the prime problems of industrialization. The second stage of the universal industrialization of Poland emphasizes extensive introduction of modern techniques into all domains of the national economy, especially industry. The mutual-aid policies of the socialist countries, particularly that of the Soviet Union, will facilitate technical progress in the entire national economy. Not only already known and mastered forms of modern techniques will be affected, but also specialization and distribution of tasks within the scope of the entire scientific research program. Joint utilization of the results is foreseen, primarily in the great scientific achievements in several branches of the chemical and machine industries.

The Polish long-term plan postulates that within the twenty-year period industrial production ought to increase about 5.5 times. Differentiation of the rate of development in individual industrial branches is also considered within this total index of growth, as presented in Table 45. As seen in the table, the concentration of investment and organizational effort is primarily concerned with the development of heavy industry, especially its extractive, raw-material branches. The development of the fuel–electric-power base usually constitutes the starting point for the general shaping of the rate of industrial expansion.

The chemical industry shows the highest growth index. Its increase is 2.5 as high as the average increase of the entire industrial production, as a result of its present important role.

Similar is the remarkable rate of the expansion of particular branches of the machine industry and its primary base—ferrous and nonferrous

Table 45. INDEX OF NET INDUSTRIAL PRODUCTION GROWTH
FOR 1980 IN FIXED PRICES (1960 = 100)

	Industry	Growth
Total		435
I.	Basic industry and raw material	
	Electric and thermal power production	677
	Fuel and coke-chemicals	252
	Iron metallurgy	409
	Nonferrous metallurgy	531
II.	Group A: means of production	
	Chemicals	1.071
	Machines	660
	Building-materials	392
III.	Group B: consumer goods	
	Timber	235
	Paper	410
	Textiles	316
	Leather and footwear	298
	Food	245
	Remaining branches	462

metallurgy. The machine industry is the foundation for modernization of the entire economy, developing modern techniques, and gaining, in the balance of foreign commerce, a predominant position in exporting machinery, equipment, and needed units. Such exports play a fundamental role in overcoming the difficulties of establishing a balance of trade.

The increase in production in the consumer industries is directly connected with the task of the long-term plan to improve consumer goods and raise living standards. Because of the marked development of agriculture, the increasing possibilities of a Polish base for agricultural raw materials creates a strong foundation for expanded production in the agricultural and food industries.

Finally, special emphasis must be put on the particular significance of *production for export*. Effort must be made to export goods in order to assure that a number of needs in the country will be met. This especially concerns the importation of raw materials for industry, grain, and other consumer goods, as well as modern machinery and equipment for new industrial plants. For that reason the main tasks are industrial, and preference must be given to the expansion of this export branch. One must take into account the fact that exporting agricultural products, increasing within a very limited scale because of market difficulties, cannot achieve a balance of trade. Hence, export production has been taken under special care. It is also necessary to consider the varied character of the demand for industrial goods by socialist countries and capitalist countries. Production tasks for meeting commercial demands of economically underdeveloped countries constitute a further problem.

Industrially, the long-term plan faces particularly difficult problems. The decisive role played by technical and organizational progress and the level of technical knowledge required of the increasingly numerous engineering and technical staff (both managerial and executive) deserve special attention. For that reason, industrial expansion cannot be measured merely by a total production index of a 5.5 increase. The technical revolution taking place in Poland, and the fundamental progress in technical knowledge and organizational and managerial patterns are essentially more important. Furthermore, such a quantitative and qualitative expansion of industrial production—including many modern goods not previously manufactured—constitutes a decisive link in the entire long-term plan, and simultaneously conditions the expansion of other sectors of the national economy.

The *intensification of agricultural production* constitutes—next to industrialization of the country—the second decisive link in long-term expansion. The importance of raising the level of agricultural production to improve living standards must be especially stressed.

Agricultural production should double during the twenty-year period from 1961 to 1980. Such an increase in production requires concentration on improvements in agricultural methods, primarily involving the necessity of a large program of agricultural mechanization and full electrification. The long-term plan also allows for a marked increase in the supply of artificial fertilizers and plant-protecting agents.

To assure farm managements of adequate means, goals have been established for the expansion of plant and animal production. In particular, an increase in crop yield per hectare has been planned. This will solve the problem of crop deficits in Poland and basically expand a fodder base for the breeding of animals. Thus, rapid increase in agricultural produce should ensure raised living standards. This is linked to a corresponding improvement in the consumption structure.

In addition to raising living standards, agricultural expansion is of great significance in the creation of strong raw-material bases for the food industry and for the further increase in the exportation of agricultural goods (high quality goods primarily), which is connected with the modernization of agriculture.

The entire agricultural program is closely bound to the modernization of state farm management, productive cooperatives, and the development of various other forms of cooperation. At present emphasis is being put on the mechanization of agriculture, based on a special fund for agricultural development. A universal socialization of farms is envisaged within the twenty-year period.

Finally, the necessity of linking the agricultural aid program to a higher level of agrotechnics merits special stress. Only by raising the level of skill in farm management can the complex diverse forms of aid for agriculture be effectively used.

Tasks concerning the industrialization of the country and the modernization of agriculture as a whole should be treated as integral parts of the decisions of the long-term plan. For example, rapid modernization and mechanization of agriculture will make it possible to release thousands of farm hands, for whom new jobs must be prepared, mainly in industry. In addition to the demographic changes taking place in the countryside and the city as a consequence of intensified agricultural production and industrialization, a new distribution of agricultural productive power over the long-term planning period should be emphasized. In view of geological discoveries and other developments, an intensive program is anticipated. Production will be distributed differently, with special emphasis on increased efficiency in the farm management of underdeveloped regions. Along with the creation of new industrial districts, favorable changes in farm structure will become apparent in different regions. Regionalization of agriculture and the elimination of differences in the efficiency of agricultural production in individual provinces will produce these changes. Needless to say, the requirements of regionalization and the specialization of cultivation (making best use of natural soil and climatic conditions) were fully considered in the decisions of the long-term plan.

The tasks of industrializing Poland and of modernizing agriculture, as principal programs in the policies of the long-term plan, are linked to all the tasks of the plan, to the increased rate of the national income and its distribution, and particularly to increasing investments and raising living standards.

Foreign Trade

The extensive theme of the long-term plan and the complex, interrelated problems involved require a detailed elaboration and an over-all coordination of dates and hypotheses. Initial hypotheses concerning foreign commerce and international cooperation are perhaps the most difficult problems of this type.

Concomitant with the relatively intense dynamics of increase in the national income, a correspondingly greater increase in foreign commerce is assumed. A dominant transformation of the trade structure itself will take place. For example, the exportation of machinery and equipment, which in 1960 constituted about 27.6 per cent of total exports, should increase to about 51 per cent by 1980. A similar shift will be seen in the geographical structure of trade, with a marked increase in trade with socialist and economically underdeveloped countries. An essential transformation in the scale of foreign commerce and its structure is evident from the data in Table 46. The long-term plan anticipates similarly difficult tasks, with quantitative and qualitative changes in many key sectors and branches of the national economy. This primarily involves technical and organizational progress, increased labor productivity, and reduction of production costs. From 1975 to 1980 Poland should reach the average level of development of the four leading west European countries.

Table 46. FOREIGN TRADE PER CAPITA (IN ZŁOTYS)

Nation	Year	Total trade (per capita)	Machinery and means of communication (per capita)
Poland			
	1960	380	105
	1970*	676	236
	1980*	1,144	456
Socialist countries:	1960		
USSR		208	52.8
GDR†		1,008	306.4
CSSR‡		1,096	369.2
Capitalist countries:	1960		
Italy		675	135
France		1,150	228
GFR§		1,617	449
Great Britain		1,697	399
Average for 4 capitalist countries:	1960	1,299	308
USA	1960	784	187

* Working hypothesis.

† German Democratic Republic.

‡ Czechoslovakia.

§ German Federalist Republic.

Conclusion

Thus to solve its problems the Polish long-term plan requires a number of profound theoretical analyses and defined practical decisions. Many studies deal with the diversity of the economic and social problems of the country. Especially important are such problems as correct definition of the proportion between consumption and accumulation; determination of the rate of growth of collective and individual consumption; formation of the size of investments and reserves; analysis of wage dispersion; and primarily the rate of improvement of rural and urban living conditions, with emphasis on solving the difficult housing, education, and welfare questions.

Interesting research is being done on the economic regionalization of the country and the complex development of particular regions. Especially emphasized is the specialization of production, as well as the correlation and cooperation of neighboring regions within the framework of a new distribution of productive manpower. Utilization of existing raw-material bases and development and coordination of the electric-power and communication systems require that regional plans for development should be dealt with as components of a fully coordinated national plan.

For these reasons work on the long-term plan must be continuous. To define the optimal rate of development and its correct proportions, the plan must be constantly worked out in detail and perfected, as progress is made in internal and external coordination for its greatest possible economic and social effectiveness.

CHAPTER 20

The Role of Science in the Development of Socialist Society

with Special Regard to the Science of Economics

OSKAR LANGE

SCIENCE plays a role in shaping three elements of socialist society: the productive forces, the economic basis, and the political and cultural superstructure.

The role of science is immediately apparent in the shaping of productive forces, which we usually call the material and technical foundation of socialist society. This role falls primarily to the natural and technical sciences, but also to the social sciences in so far as they deal with problems of efficient organization and management of production processes. Important contributions are made by medicine and pedagogy, which raise the efficiency and skill of human labor and extend the range of human potentialities. The role of those sciences as a factor that shapes the development of productive forces dates back to capitalism, since it was under capitalism that modern technology, based on a scientific understanding of the laws of nature, was born; it was also under capitalism that modern methods of organizing productive enterprises and of rational calculation of production outlays and results were evolved. Under capitalism, however, all this was subordinated to the private objectives of individual capitalist enterprises, to the aim of private profit.

The absence of an all-embracing social objective makes planned development of productive forces impossible in a capitalist economy. Recently some efforts have been made to plan the development of science and technology—partly under the impact of the planned development of productive forces in the socialist countries and as a consequence of the need to compete with the socialist system. Under capitalism, however, this generally means planning within the framework of individual enterprises or business concerns only. Such elements of planning on a national scale as exist are rather restricted to the development of the theoretical foundations. Introduction into practice is left to the private initiative of business concerns and enterprises. As a result, the development of productive forces continues to be spontaneous.

It is only socialism that enables a truly planned development of productive forces. Such development does not begin at once; it is a gradually ripening fruit of, on the one hand, the formation of socialist relations of production and the organization of socialist production and, on the other, of the experience gained in planning the development of science and technology and their practical applications. It is a process beset by many difficulties. The main source of such difficulties lies in the historical fact that the first socialist societies were established in nations less developed economically, nations where the process of industrialization took place only under socialism. Under such circumstances, in the course of planning the development of productive forces, these nations have had gradually to acquire the experiences of the old capitalist industrial nations, while at the same time they developed new methods peculiar to the socialist system. The difficulties disappear, however, as the socialist nations reach the level of highly industrialized nations; the superiority of socialist planned direction of the development of productive forces then becomes increasingly apparent.

The more effectively we plan the development of productive forces, the more important becomes the role of science in this respect. As a result, to quote from the program adopted by the Twenty-Second Congress of the Communist Party of the Soviet Union, "science will fully become a direct productive force." This implies a profound change in the social role of those branches of science which are linked to the development of productive forces. In earlier times, science was chiefly a questioning, while partly (in such fields as most of the natural sciences and mathematics) an element of social culture not necessarily directly linked to the superstructure of the social system in question. It certainly was never an integral part of society's productive applications. Now, as some branches of science participate in the conscious, planned shaping of productive forces, they are becoming an integral component of the development of society's productive forces.

The economic and sociological sciences are an instrument for shaping the economic basis of socialist society, that is, socialist production relations, their organization, and proper functioning. Under capitalism those sciences were limited to the role of passive observers of spontaneous social processes, frequently—and, in some periods, as a rule—becoming nothing more than apologists for capitalist production relations, with consequent abandonment of their scientific and cognitive functions. Only Marxist social science, connected with the working-class movement, achieved a true understanding of the objective laws of development of capitalist society, and will influence the course of that development through the revolutionary actions of the working class, based on the theoretical analysis provided by that science. The triumph of socialism involves new tasks for social science—tasks consisting of the conscious shaping of production relations and of the conditions for their efficient functioning.

A new branch of political economy has been developed: *the political economy of socialism*. Its task is the investigation of the characteristics and regularities of socialist relations of production. On this basis, relations of production are deliberately shaped, the purpose being an arrangement of them (such organizational forms of socialist production) that will make the resulting incentives fully conducive to the development of productive forces. Just as in the case of planned development of productive forces, we do not reach this objective immediately. We reach it only gradually, as we overcome diverse elements of relations of production together with the stimuli and modes of reaction they engender, inherited from the capitalist past, and as our knowledge and skill in managing the economy grow. The study of such problems is the subject of the political economy of socialism, which is assisted in it by various branches of applied sociology, especially by the science of organization of labor. The political economy of socialism and the branches of sociology which I have mentioned are still young sciences; they are maturing gradually, along with the socialist production relations in the study of which they are engaged, sometimes lagging behind the practical needs of shaping such relations.

Parallel to shaping the socialist relations of production and the related question of stimuli and incentives for development of productive forces is the problem of directing the development of the socialist economy. This problem derives from the fact that socialist social development is *consciously* shaped. It is the subject matter of the science of national economic planning and also of various applied economic sciences dealing with the direction of different sectors or branches of the national economy. All such sciences are intimately linked with the political economy of socialism, making concrete the basic results of the latter and putting them into practice.

The science of planning the national economy deserves special attention. It is a result of the socialist mode of production, as is the planning of the national economy itself. Interest in planning the national economy has also been displayed recently in capitalist nations, and particularly in economically underdeveloped nations. Such interest is an outgrowth of the rapid rate of growth of the socialist economy, and also of the fact that the present development of productive forces to an increasing extent bursts the framework of private capitalist ownership and requires planned social direction. The need for planning economic development is especially apparent in underdeveloped nations which want to overcome their economic and social backwardness.

In this connection, some contribution to the science of economic planning has been made also in nations that are not socialist, including the developed capitalist nations. The fragmentary character of planning under capitalism, however, and especially the difficulty of implementing national economic plans in practice in countries where the means of production are privately owned, is the reason why a major part of this scientific contribution cannot find application in such nations. Its full application is possible only within a socialist economy.

The development of the science of planning the national economy in the socialist countries has had two distinct stages. In the first stage, the main—and almost exclusive—interest was centered on the question of the internal consistency of plans. An increase in steel production requires a proper increase in the output of coal, iron ore, and electric power, as well as the training of a suitable labor force. An increase in the wage fund requires an appropriate increase in the market supply of consumer goods, while an increase in financial investment outlays calls for an appropriate increase in the amount of physical means of production. The lack of internal coordination of various sections of the plan leads to disturbances in the development of the national economy.

Balance accounting is the instrument for coordinating plans. Balance sheets of the national economy and of its parts are also used today in capitalist countries. They were first applied in the Soviet Union when the first five-year plan was being drawn up. Balance accounting as applied to the national economy is increasingly being formulated mathematically in the form of sets of equations solved with the help of electronic computers. This makes the calculations increasingly accurate, and at the same time enables them to embrace an expanding range of phenomena.

The second stage has begun rather recently. The *optimization of plans* has now become the key problem. The internal consistency of a plan is a prerequisite for its practical feasibility, since without it disturbances are caused in the economic process. But the number of plans internally consistent is very great (in theory, infinite). From among them must be chosen an optimal plan—one ensuring the highest degree of realization of the objective that is set. In the national economy taken as a whole, this objective is an increase in national income. In the specific sectors of the economy, the objectives are much more detailed—for example, the minimization of the cost of production or transport, or the maximization of the output of an enterprise or an industry. The problem of optimization has become the subject matter of a separate science, the theory of programing and operations research—a science, incidentally, which finds applications not only in economic research. This science, too, first emerged in the Soviet Union, and later was developed in the West. Only under socialism can it be applied in the planning of the national economy as a whole.

The possibility of applying the theory of programing in the planning of the national economy did not arise until the introduction of electronic computers. The computers created a technological revolution which has deeply affected the science and practice of planning the national economy. This revolution has enable the development of balance accounting and the wide application of the calculus of program optimization, which would be impossible to apply without computers. We see here how the development of technology not only influences productive forces, but also makes it possible to perfect the planning and management of the national economy.

Efficient planning and direction of the national economy require knowledge of the numerical value of various parameters, such as the norms of outlays of various means of production and of labor per unit of output, the norms of investment outlays per unit of growth of output, the elasticity of demand for various consumer goods, and so on. These parameters—called econometric parameters—are determined by means of statistical observation, or directly by way of research in the laboratory or in the workshop. Mathematical statistics plays an important role in their calculation. The methods of determinating such parameters constitute the subject matter of econometrics. The term *planometrics* has recently been proposed in connection with the application of econometrics to national economic planning.

Finally, a few words on the role of science in shaping the superstructure of socialist society. In this aspect, the direct role of science has hitherto been the weakest. We have subjected the relations of production and the development of the national economy to a decisive extent to conscious planned direction. We are beginning with increasing effectiveness to direct the development of productive forces in a planned manner. The development of the superstructure of socialist society continues to proceed to a large extent empirically only, in a spontaneous *ad hoc* manner. The sociological and legal sciences and the humanities have a particular role to play in shaping this superstructure.

The contribution of the legal and sociological sciences is made in shaping the organizational forms and the norms regulating the activities of the state and of individuals in society, in shaping the whole complex of interhuman relations.

The humanities exert a profound influence on social consciousness. Historical knowledge—in the widest meaning of the term, embracing social, economic, and political history, the history of all the expressions of human culture—produces understanding of the road traversed by human society in general and by the nation in particular, of the origins of existing social relations; it facilitates the formulation of the objectives which society sets itself. Psychology reveals the secrets of human mental processes and helps to mold the personality of socialist man.

Finally, the philosophical sciences—logic, the methodology of science, praxiology, and philosophy itself as a generalizing summing-up of the whole of scientific knowledge—develop the abilities of rational thought, of correct analysis of situations, and of clear perception of the structure of means and ends; they equip human minds with a scientific world outlook. This is indispensable for a society which wants to liberate itself wholly from the blind and elemental forces that dominated it in the past, and to become the master of nature and the conscious builder of its own historical fate.

The influence of science on the shaping of the superstructure of socialist society, however, proceeds not only by way of the direct impact of the various specialized sciences. No less strong—and indeed even stronger in the present stage—is the general influence on social consciousness of scientific thought, of the scientific way of interpreting phenomena. Science becomes an increasingly powerful culture-forming agent. Science creates a definite cultural and psychological climate, which becomes a part of the superstructure of socialist society. The main role is played here by the humanities, but an increasing influence on this climate is also exerted by the natural sciences, and above all by technological achievements.

Of special importance to the shaping of a socialist society—of both its economic basis and its superstructure—is Marxist political, social, and philosophical thought. Marxist thought has not as a rule been born and developed in the workshops and laboratories of professional scholars. It has been brought to life and shaped by the vast laboratory of the historical experiences of the revolutionary working-class movement and of the construction of socialism. Nevertheless, it is scientific thought in the truest meaning of the term. Born out of a practice of transforming reality, it generalizes the experiences of that practice for whole nations and on an international scale; it determines general regularities; it analyzes concrete situations and draws conclusions for effective action. In the process of shaping socialist society, Marxist thought acquires great importance for the various specialized sciences, not only for the social sciences and the humanities. Generalizing on a national and international scale the experiences of the construction of socialism—and in an extended perspective those of the construction of communism, it sets the tasks and roles of the individual sciences in the process of the conscious and purposeful guidance of social development. It becomes the organizer of this historical process.

I have presented successively the role of science in shaping the productive forces, the economic basis, and the superstructure of socialist society. Various sciences have a particular role to play in those different realms. The latter, however, are interrelated, and that is why the influences of the various sciences intermingle. I have recalled how technological developments in electronic computers have affected the planning and management of the national economy. The mutual links between the various aspects of life—between the process of mastering nature and that of shaping social relations—are reflected in the emergence and development of sciences the scope of which extends to both natural phenomena and those of social life. One such science is *mathematics,* which at first found its principal application in investigations of nature, but which today makes its presence felt increasingly in the economic sciences and the practice of planning and managing the national economy, in sociology and psychology, and recently also in linguistics. The calculus of probability and mathematical statistics are branches of mathematics which have an especially wide range of applications. This range embraces both natural and socioeconomic phenomena and finds applications wherever the regularities under study are statistical or stochastic in nature. The expanding range of applications of mathematics brings to life ever more new branches of it—for example, the theory of games and the theory of rational decision-making.

One science, relatively recent but now developing very rapidly, is of special importance to the shaping of socialist society. This is *cybernetics:* the science of controlling complex systems of cause-and-effect relationships. Like mathematics, with which it is closely connected, it has an extensive range of applications: in technology, biology, economic science and sociology, linguistics, and more and more new fields. Like the calculus of probability and mathematical statistics, it studies natural and social processes distinguished by specific kinds of regularity. These are regularities in which the decisive role is played by what is called feedback of cause and effect and by the automatic regulation and control of the course of processes. It is a further development, in concrete and mathematized form, of the basic ideas of the materialist dialectics of Marx and Engels. Hence, the particularly close relation between cybernetics and Marxist philosophy.

Cybernetics is interested in automatically functioning machines and industrial equipment, in self-regulating biological processes, and in problems of directing and regulating economic and social processes.

Cybernetics constitutes the scientific foundation for the automation of production processes. Automation is proceeding rapidly in industry, transport, and communications, and is beginning to invade even agriculture. Automatic self-controlled devices made possible the conquest of outer space. Automatically operating electronic computers make possible the solution of problems which hitherto exceeded the capabilities of man. Mechanization, along with automation, today invades the processing of statistical data, economic information and accounting, the management of production, trade and finances. It has reached even to medical diagnosis, to the deciphering of texts (for instance the deciphering of Maya writings was done with the help of an electronic computer), and to translations from one language into another. Now, construction of a machine which would serve for legal classifications and inference is contemplated.

Deserving special attention are studies in what is usually called the *general science of organization.* This science uses the conceptual apparatus of cybernetics and praxiology to deal with material supplied by economic science and sociology, such application aiming at the establishment of methods to direct social processes efficiently. Application to problems of planning and management of national economy, to the organization of labor in production and distribution (called economic cybernetics), to administration of the state and of other organizations, and to many other fields is obvious.

The roles of mathematics, mathematical statistics, and especially cybernetics, as here referred to, are indications that the boundaries between the various sciences are being blurred. The methodological instruments of the various sciences are becoming increasingly similar, and at the same time the distinctions between their social functions are disappearing. All the sciences have an increasing influence on the productive forces, the economic basis, and the superstructure of socialist society, even though the influence of one specific science on various fields may be more or less indirect.

Hence arises the practical need for more complex scientific research. Research must embrace increasingly extensive ranges of interconnected problems and make use of the instruments of increasingly numerous branches of science—including the technical sciences. Of growing importance are research programs requiring the cooperation of the natural and the social sciences. Cooperation cannot be limited to particular natural and social sciences. Cooperation between the natural and the social sciences, between technology and the humanities, becomes indispensable; at the same time all the sciences—even though to varying degrees—require the assistance of mathematics, cybernetics, and philosophy. Such cooperation is possible only on condition that research work is collective and planned and that material complexes of problems are of key importance to social development.

From this outlook flow far-reaching consequences for the organization of scientific research, and also for the training needed by the modern scientist. The sharp division between education in the humanities and in the natural sciences is an anachronism, and the frequent discussions in the press, in which the humanities are opposed to the natural sciences or vice versa, are simply irrelevant. In the socialist society the natural sciences and technology are subordinated to the humanistic goals of shaping social relations and shaping social consciousness, while at the same time they serve to create the material and technical basis indispensable to the realization of those humanistic goals.

Another anachronism is the link between education in mathematics and the natural sciences on the one hand, and between education in philosphy, history, and the humanities on the other. Now that mathematics and technology are invading the humanities, that the natural sciences and technology pose novel philosophical problems, that technology directly leads to far-reaching social consequences, and that the methods of cybernetics are acquiring an increasingly extensive range of applications in technology and in the direction of social processes, the unity of science becomes fully apparent. The need arises for a novel type of scientific training, as for novel programs of education, very different from the traditional.

As a result, novel links among the various sciences will be shaped, novel instruments of research, novel forms of research organization, and novel ways of influencing natural and social processes will be evolved. And this will contribute to the increasingly complete realization of the vision of scientific socialism of which I have spoken: the vision of a world in which man will increasingly approach perfect mastery over nature, and over the development of his own social life—one in which he will be more and more effectively the conscious creator of his own fate. This is the role to which science is called under socialism.

After these general deliberations, I will discuss more closely the special role and importance of economic sciences. I will document this with the development of the economic sciences in Poland.

In the years 1948–1950 the socialist tasks of socioeconomic reconstruction and expansion of Poland began to crystallize. The nature of the economists' knowledge proved inadequate; in fact, it often became an impediment to their active participation in the processes of social transformation than in progress. This was because bourgeois economics concentrated on market and monetary and credit processes and, furthermore, approached those processes in a manner which idealized the rationality and efficiency of the automatic functioning of capitalist economy. Problems of economic growth and of transformations in the social system were basically alien to bourgeois economics, or at best were seen by it in a distorted way. Thus, the necessity to remodel the economic sciences arose and such a remodeling could be effected only if they were based on the heritage of Marxist thought, in which the problems to be handled predominated.

As a consequence, there followed a period which might be termed a Marxist turning point in Polish economics. This period covered 1950 and the following years. Of special importance in this respect was the first Congress of Polish Science and the work preparatory to it.

The turning point occurred particularly when large numbers of scientific workers and of students became acquainted with the foundations of Marxist economic theory and Marxist social theory. At the same time, rising out of the beginnings of the country's intensive industrialization (this was the early stage of the great Six-Year Plan) was a quantitative growth in instruction in the economic sciences. New colleges of economics were founded, the old colleges were reconstructed and expanded, a department of political economy was established at Warsaw University, and research institutes were set up. Thus, there was a large-scale development of economic studies, designed to prepare a new body of workers for the needs of expanding industry. Instruction in economics during this period was further tied to the extensive work concerned with shaping a socialist consciousness in the community, and above all among the intelligentsia. As a result, knowledge of the foundations of Marxism became widely disseminated.

This diffusion of knowledge of Marxist economics, however, was not followed by a development of independent, creative scientific research. Several factors accounted for this.

One was the dogmatism inherent in the system then prevailing, a system usually referred to as "the cult of personality." Attempts were made to contain Marxist thought within rigid limits which were regarded as a criterion of political orthodoxy. This was hardly conducive to the development of independent, creative scientific thought; it found expressions in, among other things, disregard for the rich tradition of Polish Marxist thought (to mention only such great names embodying that tradition as those of Krzywicki, Rosa Luxemburg, Marchlewski, Kelles-Krauz, and many writer-members of the Communist Party of Poland); this tradition was rejected because the prescribed limits were incapable of accommodating it.

That, however, was only one of the factors involved. Another went much deeper, and consisted in the nature of Marxist economics as then practiced. Marxist economics had evolved as a critique of capitalism. This critique had disclosed the broad features of the social content of the capitalist system, its laws of development and internal contradictions. It had not, however, been concerned with any of the detailed issues involved in management of the economy. This was understandable. Management of the economy had been in the hands of the bourgeoisie: the working class, whose aspirations were expressed by Marxist theory, have had no influence on managing the capitalist economy. Consequently, interest in those problems did not develop within the limits of Marxist theory. Nevertheless, those were precisely the problems which came to the fore in the course of socialist construction. Marxist economics—unprepared by earlier tradition—had now to enter new territory.

Immediately after the October Revolution in the Soviet Union wide theoretical discussions had been pursued. But they had proceeded along a line concordant with traditional Marxist science. Just like the earlier critique of capitalism, the discussions had revolved around the principal directions of social transformation and economic progress—around such problems as the rate of economic growth, the rate of accumulation, the structure of investments, the proportions among the various branches of national economy, the transformation of the agrarian system, and so on. In spite of the dogmatism and schematism of later years, there emerged from those discussions a new science, a new branch of political economy: the political economy of socialism.

The new science created a foundation for what might be called great "macrodecisions" of economic policy in the fields which I have just mentioned. This was a science which by its very subject—the great outlines of social transformation and socioeconomic growth—addressed itself to the decision-makers. I would describe it as "economics for members of the Political Bureau and the Government." Moreover, this political economy of socialism helped the broad masses of society, and especially the working class and the intelligentsia involved in the economic apparatus, to realize the significance of the social and economic changes taking place. In this way, it became an instrument of ideological and psychological mobilization of the masses to active and conscious participation in socialist construction.

The outlines of the political economy of socialism as then evolved were, however, too rough and too blurred to serve as a basis for decisions in the lower ranks of economic management and administration. It might be said that the "political economy for members of the Political Bureau and the Government" was not complemented by a "political economy for the industrial associations and enterprises, for farms, transportation, banking, and so on." And there were certainly practical needs for one. These were met by the various branches of so-called applied economics. The level of the political economy of socialism at the time, however, did not provide a sufficient theoretical basis. Thus, applied economics developed as collections of practical rules of thumb, learned from experience—to a large extent, from the experience, earlier than ours, of socialist economic construction in the U.S.S.R., and also from the experience of management of industry and other branches of the economy in capitalist countries.

That period of socialist industrialization was marked by a highly centralized system of management. Such a system was indispensable in a period of revolutionary reconstruction of the social order, and of mobilization of all economic resources for intensive and rapid industrialization. Under these conditions, administrative measures primarily were used in the management of the national economy. This did not create any need to make the political economy of socialism more concrete, to adapt it, for the lower ranks of management. People in the lower ranks had only very restricted decision-making power; on the whole, they received very detailed directives from above.

The situation began to change as the socialist economy matured. Productive forces and production grew, and socialist economic relations became, accordingly, more complex. The need arose for new methods of economic management and of planning and administration, as well as for new knowledge required to use such methods. Also, the difficulties which emerged in the final stage of the Six-Year Plan increased the awareness of those new needs. A strong feeling then developed concerning the necessity both to renovate the methods of economic management, and to forge a deeper understanding of management and a better scientific instrument to serve it. In 1956 the system of the cult of personality, as well as the dogmatism and schematism that it involved in the social sciences, was subjected to criticism. In this way were created both the needs and the conditions for throwing the door wide open to new, creative economic thought.

A tendency to renovate Marxist economic thought also became apparent. The renovation was directed primarily toward making economic science more concrete, toward research on concrete issues relating to the functioning of a socialist economy. To the fore came problems such as centralization and decentralization of decision-making in the management of a socialist economy; democratization of management, and especially workers' self-government in industry; the role in economic management of economic measures and administrative measures; the role of economic incentives; the principles of price formation; and balancing the market. In Poland such problems used to be described as those of the economic model. The discussion that developed was called a discussion of the model.

Along with such problems, the earlier, by then more traditional, problems of the political economy of socialism were pursued. The approach to these, however, was novel—affected as it was by the more concrete knowledge acquired—and free from dogmatism. Within this range of problems, there now came to the fore, in turn, questions of the rate of growth and of proportions in socialist economy. These development problems, seen in a new light, attracted attention—just as did the model problems—to the question of the efficiency of the socialist econcmy, the efficiency of its functioning and the efficiency of its development mechanism. In the development field the issue boils down primarily to that of the effectiveness of investments and the economic effectiveness of the various directions and forms of technological progress, such as labor-saving, capital-saving, materials-saving progress and so on. Problems affecting employment had also to be considered.

In these circumstances, interest in the development of economic research in capitalist countries revived, especially in the possibility of using some of its elements in order to streamline the management of the socialist economy. This interest concentrated on new directions of economic research, on the new technical methods developed by certain of the specialized sciences (which I should call the auxiliary sciences of political economy), such as the programing theory of econometrics, the mathematical theory of rational decision-making, and, quite recently, cybernetics.

In an understandable reaction against the dogmatism of the preceding period, many economists attributed too great a significance to these new research techniques. They believed that the new techniques could somehow replace the fundamental Marxist problematic propositions of socialist political economy. Then also, some—especially those reared in the old school of bourgeois economics—looked to bourgeois political economy for devices to manage and administer a socialist economy. Confronted with the needs of the socialist economy, however, their enthusiasm soon faded. Practical needs turned out to be the best school of Marxist thought. And so, in the course of the discussions and controversies, the conviction gradually spread that none of the achievements in the technique of economic analysis in capitalist countries could acquire any practical importance until properly incorporated into the solid framework of Marxist political economy.

Closer study, incidentally, showed that in the capitalist countries the importance of the new research techniques was limited by the private economic framework of the particular company or corporation: such techniques could not be applied beyond that framework under the conditions of capitalism. The possibilities of those modern techniques under capitalism are limited: they can find full application only in a planned socialist economy. This, by the way, is a fact of which many scholars in capitalist countries are to a considerable extent aware; they feel that their technical knowledge and research capabilities begin to transcend the possibilities of application within the capitalist system.

Thus, we have come to the present situation in the economic sciences and the tasks they face. Let me restrict myself here to the political economy of socialism and its auxiliary sciences. This is not to say that I attach no importance to our economists studying the problems of contemporary capitalism as well. An understanding of economic changes, of the development trends in progress under contemporary capitalism, is of more than purely academic importance. In our circumstances, it is of importance for the management of the socialist economy. Problems of foreign trade are the most obviously affected, as are wider issues involved in coexistence. Suffice it to bear in mind the importance for the planning of our own economic development of a correct assessment of the integration tendencies, and of other phenomena, now developing in western European countries, such as the Common Market. Of even greater significance to us, also from the point of view of planning our own future economic development, is knowledge of the structural transformations and development trends in the countries of what has come to be called the Third World. These are matters of importance to our own national economy as well.

The overwhelming majority of Polish economists now accept Marxist political economy as their basis, and try creatively to develop Marxist theory. Evidence of this is the voluminous literature of recent years. Numerous monographs have been written about various branches and problems of socialist political economy, and about the problems of economic growth under socialism and in the conditions prevailing in the countries of the Third World. Further, our economic literature has dealt with problems of contemporary capitalism, the history of economic thought, and other subjects. The first broader synthetic outlines of different topics have now appeared, and, most important, an increasing number of them are being written by young scholars. In earlier years we invested, so to speak, in training a body of young scientific workers. The investment is now bearing fruit, and what it has yielded so far has been most interesting and a good augury for the future.

The greatest interest is displayed in—and relatively the greatest amount has been written on—the problems of planning and management of a socialist economy, and the problems of growth in a socialist economy. These have been approached from the angle of increasing the efficiency of the socialist economy. Particular attention, especially on the part of junior scholars, has been devoted to mathematical-economic and econometric methods as instruments for deepening economic analysis and making economic calculation more accurate. Recently, Polish economists have also taken an interest in cybernetics and its possible role as an instrument for streamlining economic planning and management. This interest has been considerably assisted by the general atmosphere now prevailing in science, especially by the development and increasing practical role of electronic computers. These phenomena are a harbinger of a revolution in the methods of economic planning and management, because they open up new possibilities in the co-ordination and optimization of economic planning and in making management more efficient.

All this more detailed economic knowledge to which I have referred has created a basis for the development of applied economics: the economics of industry and of enterprise; the economics of agriculture, of transport, finances, and so on. Conditions already exist today for the development of applied economics on the basis of the general achievements of socialist political economy.

As a result, Polish economic research is now evoking considerable interest in the world at large, not in the socialist countries alone. In the socialist countries, however, interest is increasing because the development of the problems in which our economists engage coincides with topics of interest to scholars in other socialist countries, particularly in the U.S.S.R. The subjects of scientific discussions raised in Poland are also dealt with in the U.S.S.R., and increasingly frequent references are made there to the work of Polish economists. Outside the socialist camp interest in Polish economic thought has been increasing. Suffice it to recall that more than twenty books by Polish economists have been translated into foreign languages and that further translations are planned. In the exportation of Polish scientific thought, the economic sciences take second place, after mathematics.

Special interest in Polish economic science is displayed in the countries of the Third World—in Asia, Africa, and Latin America. The interest is reflected in the frequent visits to Poland by economists from those countries to study the theory and practice of economic planning. The very fact that Poland has developed rapidly from a country with an underdeveloped economy into one with growing industry and one that plays an increasingly important role in world economy explains why economists from those countries come here in search of knowledge and of methods for accelerating social and economic progress. Contacts are facilitated by the ability of a great number of Polish economists to write in languages accessible to their colleagues from those countries. Another expression of their interest has been the participation by many economists from the countries of the Third World in the special course on planning opened for them two years ago at the School of Planning and Statistics in Warsaw. Numbers of Polish economists have been invited to those countries as advisers on economic planning and development. The example of the Republic of Ghana might well be cited here: the entire faculty of political economy at the university there has been manned, reorganized, and in fact set up by Polish scholars.

Nevertheless, all these major achievements must not hide from us our shortcomings. The development of economic studies in Poland, as indeed in other socialist countries, tends to concentrate on problems of planning and management. These are problems of rational activity—praxiological problems. On the other hand, economists both in Poland and in other socialist countries pay less attention to what in fact has been the traditional—and basic—subject matter of the political economy of socialism: problems of shaping socialist relations of production, problems pertaining to the social relations evolving in a socialist economy. Included here must also be the problems of the driving forces of development of a socialist economy, of the contradictions present in such an economy, of the dialectics of its development mechanism. In this group of problems only one—that of economic incentives—has been attracting much interest. But this particular matter is linked to the question of the efficiency of functioning and development of the socialist economy; hence, the close interest in it. Still lacking, though, is a broader scientific analysis of the fundamental historical experience gained during the various periods of socialist industrialization, of both the successes attained and the failures suffered, of the transformation of the agrarian system, and—above all—a comparative analysis of the experiences of the different socialist countries.

The political economy of socialism took as its point of departure the problems involved in the general outlines of the transformation of the social system and the basic social conditions for economic growth. At a certain stage in the development of the socialist economy, this proved to be insufficient. The need arose for an economic science dealing with the more detailed questions involved in planning and management, in rational economic activity under socialism. Now, however, the time has come to close the circle. Armed with the concrete knowledge acquired, with the new and precise research methods and techniques, we can and, indeed, must return to a synthesizing treatment of the great problems, of the main lines of construction and development of the socialist economy; we must return to the fundamental social issues of the socialist system. These are the true responsibilities of the political economy of socialism in its traditional Marxist sense. I have no doubt that we shall return to those problems soon, and that we shall study them fruitfully, approaching them from a new historical perspective and in the light shed by the new research methods now at our disposal.

Polish economic science becomes increasingly mature, able to cope with the basic responsibility with which it is charged by scientific socialism—the role of an effective tool in shaping the socialist economy, a tool to ensure the efficient functioning and development of the socialist economy. This ambition of economic science has found considerable coverage in its achievement during the last twenty years. And with this ambition Polish economic science approaches the next twenty years of the history of the Polish People's Republic.

Notes on the Authors

ADAM ANDRZEJEWSKI, professor of economics at the Central School of Planning and Statistics in Warsaw, is Vice-President of the Housing Research Institute, a member of the Committee for Space Economy and Regional Planning of the Academy of Sciences, and a delegate to the UN Committee on Housing, Building, and Planning of the Economic Commission for Europe. He is also a member of the International Federation for Housing and Planning.

MARIAN BENKO, architect, is Director of the Department of City Planning, Ministry of Building.

KAZIMIERZ DZIEWOŃSKI, professor, architect and economist, is Associate Director of the Institute of Geography, Academy of Sciences, and a member of the Praesidium of the Committee for Space Economy and Regional Planning.

STANISŁAW DZIEWULSKI, architect, is a research associate at the Institute for Town Planning and Architecture and Vice-President of the Polish City Planners' Association. He was co-author of the general plan of Warsaw.

WIESŁAW GRUSZKOWSKI, architect, is head of the Department of City Planning, Praesidium of Gdańsk Voivodship People's Council.

CZESŁAW KOTELA, architect, was formerly Director of the Group of Experts for City Planning, Ministry of Building. He is now Chief Architect of Warsaw and Vice-President of the Association of Polish Architects.

JERZY KRUCZAŁA, economist, is chief of the Regional Plan Workshop for the Voivodship and City of Kraków. He is a member of the Committee for Space Economy and Regional Planning of the Academy of Sciences, of the Committee for Economics (Kraków branch) of the Academy, and of the International Federation for Housing and Planning.

ANTONI R. KUKLIŃSKI, associate professor, economist and geographer, is head of the Department of Space Economy and Regional Planning, Institute of Geography, Executive Secretary of the Committee for Space Economy and Regional Planning, both the Academy of Sciences, and managing editor of the *Polish Geographical Review.*

OSKAR LANGE died in London October 2, 1965. He had been professor of political economy and member of the Academy of Sciences, and was Deputy Chairman of the Council of State of the People's Republic of Poland and member of parliament. He was also chairman of the Commission for Mathematical Methods and Machines Application of Planning and Management and Vice-President of the Polish Economic Society. He was Fellow of the Econometric Society and Honorary Fellow of the Royal Statistical Society.

STANISŁAW LESZCZYCKI, professor of economic geography, member of the Academy of Sciences, is Director of the Institute of Geography and chairman of the Committee for Space Economy and Regional Planning, Academy of Sciences. He is also chairman of the Polish National Committee for the International Geographical Union.

BOLESŁAW MALISZ, associate professor of physical planning at the Warsaw Polytechnic, is Director of the Institute for Town Planning and Architecture. He is also a member of the Praesidium of the Committee for Space Economy and Regional Planning of the Academy of Sciences.

WOJCIECH MORAWSKI, economist, is chief of the Division, Department of Transport, Planning Commission of the Council of Ministers, member of the Committee for Space Economy and Regional Planning, and member of the Advisory Board for Economics and Technology of the Ministry of Communications.

WACŁAW OSTROWSKI, architect and professor of city planning at the Warsaw Polytechnic, is a member of the Praesidium of the Committee of Architecture, City Planning, and Building, Academy of Sciences, and chairman of the Standing Committee for the Study of Historic Urban Areas, International Federation for Housing and Planning.

JÓZEF PAJESTKA, economist and associate professor at the University of Warsaw, is Director of the Institute for Economic Research of the Planning Commission of the Council of Ministers.

BOHDAN PNIEWSKI, architect and professor at the Warsaw Polytechnic, was a member of the Academy of Sciences, Chairman of the Committee for Architecture, City Planning, and Building, and Vice-President of the Committee for Space Economy and Regional Planning, both of the Academy of Sciences. He was also Director of the Institute for Research on Architecture, City Planning, and Building of the Ministry of University and Polytechnic Education. Professor Pniewski died September 5, 1965.

KAZIMIERZ SECOMSKI, member of the Academy of Sciences, professor of planning and economic policy at the Central School of Planning and Statistics in Warsaw, is Deputy Chairman of the Planning Commission of the Council of Ministers. He is also Vice-Chairman of the Committee for Space Economy and Regional Planning, member of the Scientific Council of the State Committee of Sciences and Technology, and of the Praesidium of the Committee for Economic Sciences of the Academy of Sciences, and Vice-President of the Polish Economic Society.

RYSZARD SZMITKE, economist, is an associate of the Regional Plan Workshop attached to the Praesidium of Katowice Voivodship People's Council.

ALEKSANDER TUSZKO, professor of hydrogeology at the University of Warsaw, is a member of the Praesidium of the Committee of Water Engineering and Economy of the Academy of Sciences. He is also scientific secretary of the Commission for Planning and Coordination of Scientific Research of the Academy.

BOGUSŁAW WEŁPA, economist, is demographer and regional planner in the Department of Perspective and Regional Planning, Planning Commission of the Council of Ministers.

ANDRZEJ WRÓBEL, associate professor, economist and geographer, is research associate of the Institute of Geography and member of the Committee for Space Economy and Regional Planning, Academy of Sciences.

JÓZEF ZAREMBA, economist, is Associate Director of the Department of Perspective and Regional Planning, Planning Commission of the Council of Ministers, a member of the Committee for Space Economy and Regional Planning, and President of the Polish City Planners' Association.

STANISŁAW M. ZAWADZKI, associate professor of economic regional planning at the Central School of Planning and Statistics in Warsaw, is a member of the Committee for Space Economy and Regional Planning of the Academy of Sciences.

TADEUSZ ZIELIŃSKI, economist, is chief of the Regional Plan Workshop attached to the Praesidium of Katowice Voivodship People's Council.

JANUSZ ZIOŁKOWSKI, associate professor of sociology at the Mickiewicz University in Poznań and at the Polytechnic in Warsaw, is a member of the governing board of the Polish Sociological Society and of the Committee for Space Economy and Regional Planning. He is an associate member of the American Sociological Association.

Index

Alberti, Leon Battista, 211
Architecture: Gothic, 21, 115; Romanesque, 21, 115; Renaissance, 25, 35, 115; baroque town (Góra Kolwaria), 35, 36; individualistic, 203; research institutions formed, 203; trends in other countries, 204, 205; effect of industry on, 205; effect of technology on, 205, 206; proportion in, 206; composition in, 206, 207, 208, 209; perfect or powerful, 207; expressiveness in, 210; problem of apogee, 210; Institute for Research on Architecture, City Planning, and Building, 211; qualities of architects, 211; proposed solutions to problems in, 211, 212
August, Stanislaw, King of Poland, 29, 30, 36
August II, King of Poland, 29, 30
Austria, 25, 36

Bialystok voivodship: description of, 327; effect of World War II on, 327, 328; improved economic standards (1950–1960), 328; basically underdeveloped, 328, 329; past planning studies, 329, 330
—Regional plan: structure of, 330; problems and premises of, 331; for population, 331, 332, 333; for industry, 333, 334; for agriculture, 334, 335, 336; for forestry, 336; for transportation, 336; for services, 336; for settlement network, 337; subregion development, 337, 338, 339
Bielinski, Marshal, 33
Brukalska, B., 189, 189n
BWS (Board of Worker Settlements), 189
Bydgoszcz, 84, 253, 260, 264, 267

Calvary Way, 29
Central Economic Planning Office, 61
Central Physical Planning Office, 61

Chmielewski, J., 59, 62, 187, 272
City planning: as component of spatial and regional planning, 3 (*see also* Regional planning *and* Spatial planning); dependence on national economic planning, 4, 5, 6 (*see also* National economic planning)
—History: origin of Poland, 9; early settlements, 9, 10, 11; German colonization and influence, 11; medieval towns, 11, 12, 13, 14, 15; medieval physical planning, 13, 14, 15, 16, 21; first rational plan, 14; Polish expansion, 21, 24; economic and political decline, 24, 25; first partition of Poland, 25; urban building, 25, 26; Swedish invasion, 27; Warsaw rebuilt, 27, 28, 29, 30, 33; economic growth, 33, 35; effect of religion on towns, 35, 36; second partition of Poland, 36; early industrial centers, 36–40; Polish independence regained, after World War I, 40, 41; planning progress in interwar years, 40–44; Gdynia built, 41, 42, 43; "wishful" planning, 43, 44; Central Industrial Region Plan, 44; effect of World War II, 44, 45; postwar planning, 45–55; administration of, 57; prewar developments, 58, 59, 60; effect of new government on, 61, 62, 63; improved methods of, 64, 65, 66; stage planning, 66, 67, 68, 69, 70 (*see also* Stage planning); perspective planning, 70, 71, 72, 73 (*see also* Perspective planning); threshold theory, 73, 74, 75, 76 (*see also* Threshold planning); scientific research in, 77, 78, 79; changing shape of cities, 79; spatial and structural changes, 80, 81, 82; transportation network changes, 82, 83; central cities redevelopment, 83, 84; development of Warsaw plan, 85–109 (*see also* Warsaw); problems in Silesian-Kráków Industrial Region, 111–132 (*see also* Silesian-Kráków Industrial Region); planning in the Gdańsk-Gdynia Conurbation, 133–152 (*see also* Gdańsk-

487

M/